The Foundations
of Social Work
Knowledge

The Foundations of Social Work Knowledge

Frederic G. Reamer

Columbia University Press

New York

Columbia University Press
New York   Chichester, West Sussex

Copyright © 1994 Columbia University Press
All rights reserved

Library of Congress Cataloging-in-Publication Data

The Foundations of social work knowledge /
Frederic G. Reamer, editor.
p.   cm.
Includes bibliographical references and index.
ISBN 0–231–08034–4
1. Social service.   I. Reamer, Frederic G., 1953–   .
HV40.F68   1994
361—dc20   94–7273
                                                       CIP

Casebound Editions of Columbia University Press books
are printed on permanent and durable acid free paper.

Printed in the United States of America

c 10 9 8 7 6 5 4 3 2

For Deborah, Emma, and Leah

Contents

Preface

Knowledge comes, but wisdom lingers.
—Alfred Lord Tennyson

The knowledge base that social workers use has matured considerably since the profession's formal inauguration in the late nineteenth century. We have expanded our understanding about the magnitude and determinants of problems in living that stem from poverty, mental illness, substance abuse, crime, aging, domestic violence, child abuse and neglect, and so on. We have a keener grasp of various ways of helping and of their effectiveness. We do not know enough, of course; we are constantly struggling to insert additional pieces of knowledge into a very large puzzle.

While acknowledging the limits of the breadth and depth of the profession's knowledge, social workers have a compelling obligation to impart what they *do* know to the profession's practitioners and students. After all, the profession's corpus of knowledge—which entails its principal ideas, values, and skills—ultimately shapes social work's approaches and contribution.

There has always been legitimate and constructive debate about what social workers actually know and should convey to the profession's practitioners and students. Social workers have engaged in intellectual discourse about the merits and demerits of particular schools of thought and practice, ranging from theories of human behavior and intervention techniques to the political aims and agenda of the profession. Such intellectual winds shift over time, and debate about the validity of various ideas and approaches is healthy and essential.

The principal purpose of *The Foundations of Social Work Knowledge* is to explore leading social work educators' views about what social workers need to know at the foundation level. In the following pages, prominent educators with impressive expertise in their respective areas offer their views about the foundations of social work knowledge. The various chapters are organized around substantive areas that are widely held to be key components in the profession's foundation: social work practice, social welfare policy and services, human behavior and the social environment, research and evaluation, field education, values and ethics, oppression and social injustice, and diversity and populations at risk (ethnic minorities and people of color, women, lesbians and gays, and people with disabilities). Following my introductory chapter on the evolution of social work knowledge, these scholars present their essays on the various foundation areas. In each chapter the authors explore the nature of foundation-level knowledge and the ideas, values, and skills that, from their perspective, all social workers must be exposed to and cultivate.

Taken together, these essays explore in more depth than we have seen to date in social work's literature what practitioners must know, at a minimum, about the profession's foundation. Clearly, to be competent, social workers must know more than is presented between these covers. Practitioners in public welfare, mental health, substance abuse treatment, child welfare, or correctional settings, for example, need specialized knowledge and skills that are not always included in foundation-level education. What we offer here is an attempt to locate a common denominator for the profession, a way to understand and define social work's essential components, from which more specialized training and education, adapted to specific settings and aims, should emanate. We also offer a sense of vision about foundation-level knowledge for the profession.

Such an intellectual foundation is vitally important to social work's integrity and effectiveness. After all, it is from the foundation that the rest of the profession's apparatus is built. What we place at the foundation has everything to do with what will be taught, in the long run, about how to practice social work. As the late A. Bartlett Giamatti (1990) observed in one of his presidential addresses at Yale University: "The teacher chooses. The teacher chooses how to structure choice. The teacher's power and responsibility lie in choosing where everyone will begin and how, from that beginning, the end will be shaped. The choice of that final form lies in the teacher's initial act" (p. 193).

There have, of course, been various attempts over the years to explore the nature of social work's knowledge base, to draw out the boundaries of essential knowledge in the profession. Tufts's (1923)

Educating and Training for Social Work, Haggerty's (1931) *Training of Social Workers*, Hollis and Taylor's (1951) *Social Work Education in the United States*, and Boehm's (1959) *Social Work Curriculum Study*, for example, are clear landmarks in the profession's effort to clarify and convey its intellectual foundation.

My hope is that *The Foundations of Social Work Knowledge* will add to this important and impressive legacy. In addition to reinforcing the importance of age-old ideas in social work, many of which have endured since the turn of the century, the essays in this book offer the authors' contemporary assessments of prevailing ideas and approaches. Although some of what we now consider essential foundation-level knowledge has persisted for decades, some of this content is of more recent origin. This is due, in part, to the maturation of social workers' thinking about professional practice, reflecting the sort of insight and understanding that develop over time. In addition, some foundation-level content of more recent origin has been stimulated by the onset of various individual and social problems that could not possibly have been imagined by the profession's founders and earliest scholars.

What appears in these pages will, I suspect, generate considerable discussion and debate. Readers are likely to explore and critique the various merits and demerits of the authors' views, particularly with respect to their perspectives on what every social worker ought to know. This is as it should be. Nothing here is written in stone or intended to constitute the final word, and all the authors clearly write from their own unique vantage points. Competing views exist. Instead, these essays constitute compelling *points of departure*, to encourage social work educators and practitioners to engage in the sort of serious, and difficult, intellectual work required to define a profession's theoretical base. Such discourse and debate are essential to a profession's growth.

I would hope that whatever debate this book triggers will be conducted in a civil fashion. As in many other domains, social work has had its share of impolite, vitriolic exchanges among those who disagree with one another. This serves no useful purpose. Far more constructive is the spirited, open-minded exchange of ideas and the sustained and constructive critique of opposing ideas that help sort out what is right. As Giamatti (1990) says in his *Free and Ordered Space* about the virtues of civil intellectual debate in university settings,

Its essence is that give-and-take, that civil conversation in its innumer-able forms. When that conversation, the to-and-fro of ideas is stymied or foreclosed or frozen, when the questing for truth is told that it must cease because there is only one Truth and it is Complete, then the insti-tution in its essence is chilled and its life threatened. (p. 25)

In the end, of course, some disagreement is bound to endure. Some questions are so difficult that it would truly be surprising, and perhaps even distressing, to achieve unanimous consensus.

It is hard to express what a rich opportunity it has been for me to work with the authors of these chapters. These essays reflect the prod-uct of remarkable minds at work. The authors are among the intellec-tual leaders in social work and in their respective areas of expertise. Their imaginative work over the years has left lasting impressions on the profession, impressions which have changed the nature of what social work is and aims to be. I firmly believe that the collective wis-dom expressed in these pages will provide a critically important and much-needed compass for the profession, one that should lead to vig-orous discussion and debate about the contours of the profession's knowledge base.

Social work's ultimate purpose, of course, is to convert this knowl-edge into meaningful, effective efforts to help people with their prob-lems in living. As Confucius said, "The essence of knowledge is, hav-ing it, to apply it."

The Foundations
of Social Work
Knowledge

1

The Evolution of Social Work Knowledge

FREDERIC G. REAMER

From its roots in the charity organization society and settlement house movements, social work has evolved into a full-fledged profession with a distinctive value base, body of knowledge, and method of training. Although debate may continue as to social work's standing among the so-called major and minor professions (Glazer 1974), there is, by now, relatively little question about its status *as* a profession. It is generally conceded that social work now satisfies the principal criteria of a profession cited by Flexner in his oft-cited 1915 speech before the National Conference on Charities and Correction.

Especially during the late nineteenth and early twentieth centuries, social work depended to a great extent on knowledge adapted from allied disciplines, principally psychology, sociology, economics, and political science (Kahn 1954; Kadushin 1959; Khinduka 1987; Rothman 1985). Since then, however, social work's indigenously developed knowledge base has matured considerably. Particularly since the 1970s, social work scholarship has broadened and deepened. Although there may be some debate about the quality and value of a portion of this scholarship, there is little doubt that the knowledge base of the profession has been strengthened by the advent of new social work journals, enhanced doctoral education, and more ambitious research agendas (Thomas 1978, 1985).

Over time, as social work has cultivated its own cadre of scholars and researchers, the profession's self-generated fund of knowledge has expanded substantially. From the early contributions of such luminaries as Edith and Grace Abbott, Sophinisba Breckinridge, Grace Coyle,

Porter Lee, Kenneth Pray, Bertha Reynolds, Mary Richmond, and Charlotte Towle, social work has generated a wide array of carefully conceptualized, albeit widely debated, models of helping. Social work can now lay claim to unique practice and policy perspectives on problems such as child abuse, mental illness, aging, substance abuse, poverty, domestic violence, and delinquency. Although the boundaries distinguishing social workers' and social scientists' views on these problem areas may, at times, be blurred, there is certainly a distinctive lens through which well-trained social workers view these matters (Bartlett 1958; Compton and Galaway 1989; Gordon 1962; National Association of Social Workers 1977, 1981). Home-grown conceptual perspectives such as the "ecological model," "person-in-situation," "the problem-solving model," and the "life model" have given shape and meaning to social workers' understanding of and approach to complex social problems (Germain and Gitterman 1987; Hollis 1965; Perlman 1957; Sheafor and Landon 1987).

The emergence of social work's knowledge base has clearly strengthened its identity as a profession. Social work's growing corpus of theoretical knowledge has enabled it to evince one of the essential ingredients of professional status: the existence of an identifiable and specialized body of knowledge that is transmitted systematically through formal education (Barber 1965; Becker 1962; Carr-Saunders and Wilson 1933; Greenwood 1957; Hughes 1965; Khinduka 1987; Larson 1977; Moore 1970; Toren 1969).

The common denominator that characterizes the diverse elements of social work's knowledge base is keen sensitivity to the complex intersection of individually based concerns and environmental forces that affect them. Social work's unique contribution to the human services is its persistent, simultaneous concern about the private troubles of individuals—especially those who are oppressed and vulnerable—and the public issues that surround them.

For quite some time there has been at least a rough consensus among social work's intellectual leaders about the *foundation* knowledge every social worker should have in order to practice competently. Ultimately, of course, this foundation content finds expression in the education of social workers. It is here, in social work's educational programs, that the profession's intellectual leaders implement their understanding of the fundamental core of social work knowledge that must be imparted to practitioners. In the final analysis, the product of debates about the content of foundation knowledge defines what it means to be a social worker, think like a social worker, and act like a social worker. In this sense, there is a direct and essential relationship between foundation content conveyed in social work education and the ultimate impact of the profession. As Blackey (1968) noted in her 1966 address to those attending the Thirteenth International Congress of Schools of Social Work:

> To say that the development of the purposes and objectives of the overall curriculum, as well as those of each of its component parts, is the cardinal principle and first step in curriculum building may seem obvious, even trite. Yet this is the major guiding task to all others. It lays the foundation for the school's relationship to the society in which it exists, for the characteristics of the student body to be admitted, for the nature of the curriculum to be developed and for the type of graduate to be produced. (p. 25)

The evolution of social workers' thinking about foundation knowledge for professional practice—that is, what every practitioner must know, at a minimum, in order to take on the distinctive purposes and identity of a social worker—is reflected most clearly in the way the profession has trained and educated subsequent generations of its students. Close examination of these developments, beginning with the six-week summer training program offered in 1898 by the New York School of Philanthropy under the auspices of that city's charity organization society, reveals a remarkable persistence of what social workers now call an ecological perspective (Germain and Gitterman 1987), where individuals' problems are addressed within the framework of their environmental circumstances—including their community, cultural, ethnic, religious, political, economic, and organizational context. Although the contours of what has been considered foundation content in the profession have changed over time, there has been an unmistakably consistent embrace of the person-in-situation perspective.

Trends in Foundation Content

Views about essential knowledge for social work have, not surprisingly, been a function of the profession's unique history. Social workers' intense involvement with the charity organization society and settlement house movements had direct bearing on training content related to casework, community organization, and social reform (Hollis and Taylor 1951; Richmond 1917). So too did such significant developments as the introduction of medical social work in 1905, the creation of the U.S. Children's Bureau in 1912, the founding of the Child Welfare League of America in 1920, the formation of an independent psychiatric social work organization in 1926, and the passage of legislation in 1933 creating the Federal Emergency Relief Administration. Each of these red-letter events, along with many others, introduced new challenges and goals for social work education.

Throughout social work education's history there have been various attempts to identify a core body of knowledge that should, at minimum, be incorporated into every educational program. Tufts, in his compelling 1923 report, *Educating and Training for Social Work*, argued that social work training needed to be broadened, that its content had been conceived too narrowly, focusing primarily on "relief, aid, and administration or oversight" (p. xi). Tufts ultimately went on to suggest that at least some members of the profession need to be educated to pursue "tasks which may be conceived under the analogy of social engineering or social statesmanship" (p. xii). This was followed in 1923 by the influential Milford Conference, which focused on construction of a comprehensive definition of the generic base of casework as practiced in all specialized settings (Boehm 1959a; Dinerman 1984).

In 1924 the Association of Training Schools for Professional Social Work, formed in 1919 with seventeen charter members (most located outside of universities), suggested standards for an organized social work curriculum. In 1928, in an address delivered at the National Conference of Social Work, Edith Abbott (1931) outlined and advocated a basic curriculum and foundation content for the profession. And in 1931 Haggerty published *The Training of Social Workers*, in which he examined a variety of controversial issues related to the content of professional education.

Until 1932, however, there was no basic curriculum of any kind that was generally followed by schools of social work. In that year the American Association of Schools of Social Work (AASSW) adopted a minimum one-year curriculum that included prescribed courses in subject areas such as medical and psychiatric "information," research, social legislation, and legal aspects of social work (Dinerman 1984).

These first three decades of social work education's history constituted an important stage in the profession's development. During this
period, social work began to formulate its own unique practice and
intellectual identity, one that foreshadowed subsequent developments.
As Hollis and Taylor (1951) observed in their landmark report to the
National Council on Social Work Education:

> A considerable professional literature developed out of three decades
> of concentrated attention to defining the field of social casework and
> developing practice and educational programs. Through these efforts
> there emerged the central core of social work—its basic philosophy
> and ethics, its fundamental principles and conceptual values, its
> knowledge and processes. Social casework moved from altruistic and
> moralistic motivations exercised through a managing way of rehabili-
> tating the less fortunate to a focus on social and psychiatric under-
> standing, on self-determination of the individual, and on the dignity of
> the human personality. While these concepts were first seen in relation
> to individuals, they are now recognized as valid in the group process
> and in community organization and planning. The service of the pro-
> fessional social worker is recognized as an enabling process by which
> the person, the group, or the community is helped to identify needs, to
> clarify goals, and to resolve personal and social problems.   (p. 47)

In subsequent years there were a number of ambitious attempts to
further identify core knowledge for the profession. In 1944 the AASSW
promoted the "basic eight" curriculum to be taught in accredited programs, focusing on the areas of public welfare, social casework, social
group work, community organization, medical information, social
research (statistics and research methods), psychiatry (human behavior and psychopathology), and social welfare administration. In 1946
the National Council on Social Work Education was established in an
effort to resolve differences among the standards that had been developed by AASSW and the National Association of Schools of Social
Administration, the latter having been formed in 1942 by a group of
training programs that were not eligible for AASSW membership. As
its first major project, the council sponsored a study of the objectives
and content of social work education, which culminated in Hollis and
Taylor's (1951) influential publication, *Social Work Education in the United
States.*

In 1955, under the direction of Werner Boehm, the recently formed

Council on Social Work Education (CSWE) sponsored what has turned out to be the profession's most comprehensive, and perhaps controversial, examination of essential knowledge for professional practice. Boehm's *Social Work Curriculum Study*, published in 1959, was launched in an effort to define the content and boundaries of social work knowledge necessary for sound preparation of practitioners. Boehm's project focused on knowledge related to human growth and behavior, casework, group work, community organization, administration, social welfare policy and services, values and ethics, and research, particularly as it pertained to the fields of corrections, rehabilitation, and public social services. The effort resulted in a thirteen-volume study that set forth prevailing views about the nature of social work knowledge and education. Boehm also proposed a controversial continuum model of social work education that would include undergraduate and graduate education.

The Development of Curriculum Content

Since the creation of CSWE in 1952, there have been a number of attempts to develop curriculum policy guidelines that broadly define core social work knowledge. Soon after its creation, for example, CSWE issued a policy statement suggesting that content should be organized under just three broad headings: social services, human growth and behavior, and social work practice.

The first formal curriculum policy statement appeared in 1962, shortly after the publication of Boehm's study. As Dinerman (1984) suggests, it draws rather directly from Boehm's work, with its clear emphasis on the "restoration, maintenance and enhancement" functions of social work, directed toward the "prevention, treatment and control of problems in social functioning of individuals, groups, and communities." This curriculum policy statement also identified only three major knowledge areas: social welfare policy and services, human behavior and the social environment, and methods of social work practice.

The next revision of the curriculum policy statement was issued in 1969. This version, like its predecessors, concerned only graduate education. It organized social work knowledge in the same three categories included in the 1962 statement. Changes in the 1969 statement provided greater latitude to programs in the design of their curricula, a broader definition of social work practice, acknowledgment that undergraduate social work education can prepare students for professional, as opposed to preprofessional, practice, and less emphasis on research content (Dinerman 1984).

The subsequent revision of the curriculum policy statement, issued in 1982, was far more ambitious and comprehensive. In addition to spelling out in greater detail the nature of social work knowledge to be transmitted to graduate students, the document also included the first statement of curriculum policy for undergraduate (BSW) programs. The 1982 policy statement also clarified the role of the liberal arts perspective in social work education and acknowledged in greater detail the importance of professional values and ethics, cultural, ethnic, and social diversity, oppression, and discrimination. The statement also indicated that social work students must be acquainted with foundation content in *five* major areas: human behavior and the social environment, social welfare policy and services, social work practice, research, and field practicum. Thus, the 1982 policy statement was the most detailed and broad-based of the various versions developed up to that point.

A decade later, in 1992, a new curriculum policy statement was adopted. Separate statements were issued for undergraduate and graduate programs, each addressing nine knowledge areas to be incorporated into social work education: social work values and ethics, cultural and ethnic diversity, social and economic justice, populations at risk, human behavior and the social environment, social welfare policy and services, social work practice, research, and field practicum (the master's degree guidelines also addressed advanced social work practice in various concentration areas).

It is clear that the various curriculum policy statements have, over time, become increasingly detailed and comprehensive. The boundaries of what has been considered essential social work knowledge have expanded considerably. The first modest statements of curriculum content appearing in the late 1950s and early 1960s have evolved into much broader, more prescriptive guidelines.

By now there is rather substantial consensus about the essential content of foundation-level social work education, at least in the form of broad topics to be addressed. Virtually no one questions the need for contemporary practitioners to have a firm grasp of knowledge related to professional values and ethics, cultural and ethnic diversity, social and economic justice, populations at risk, human behavior and the social environment, social welfare policy and services, social work practice, research, and field practicum. As Siporin (1984) concludes, "a significant feature of practice and education today is the recognition that there is a basic core of purposes, values, knowledge, and skills that is generic for professional social work practice. Although this core has not been formulated in any systematized, doctrinal form, there is a consensus in the profession about its essential elements" (p. 240).

What is necessary, however, is for social workers to have a greater appreciation of the range of conceptual viewpoints and theoretical perspectives that are germane to each of these content areas. This is not to say that uniformity in social workers' beliefs is necessary. To the contrary, diversity in understanding and perspective can enliven and enrich social work practice. Moreover, no one perspective can claim hegemony. As Reynolds (1965 [1942]) wisely noted in her classic *Learning and Teaching in the Practice of Social Work*, "We have competing schools of thought, extremely valuable in the intensive study they give to one phase or another of the whole, but wasteful and destructive in their assumption that no one but themselves has the truth" (p. 8). Our ultimate aim as a profession must be for social workers to have a firm command of what the profession's intellectual leaders believe constitutes its foundation, and to apply this knowledge in practice skillfully. We should not be encouraging random or undisciplined eclecticism but, rather, the purposeful integration of conceptual viewpoints that define and serve as pillars for each social worker's understanding of and approach to practice.

The essays that follow provide in-depth discussions of the nature of social work knowledge in the areas now considered constitutive of the profession's foundation: social work practice, social welfare policy and services, human behavior and the social environment, research and evaluation, field education, values and ethics, oppression and social injustice, and diversity and populations at risk (ethnic minorities and people of color, women, lesbians and gays, and people with disabilities). Their primary purpose is to provide, from the authors' respective and unique vantage points, analysis of intellectual content that makes up the foundation of the profession's knowledge base. The principal goal here is to present arguments about what contemporary practitioners need to know in order to be effective social workers, in light of the maturation of the profession and of the growth of knowledge within social work and in allied disciplines and professions.

These are not trivial issues. Throughout social work's history, there has been diverse and fruitful exploration of a wide range of intellectual paths. Some of this exploration has led to a dead end. Some of it has brought the profession to new levels of insight and understanding about the nature of human beings' problems and effective responses to them. And some of this exploration has triggered intense, protracted, and both constructive and destructive controversy about the very purpose of social work.

To some, social work practice, for example, consists primarily of various clinical strategies designed to ameliorate the problems encountered by individual clients and their families. Moreover, these services do not necessarily need to be provided primarily to low-income or oppressed individuals. To others, this is an unacceptably narrow construction of practice. Instead, the borders must be expanded to include social action and advocacy, and focus on issues of social justice and oppression that affect the most vulnerable and least advantaged. Anything less, some argue, is to strip from social work its soul and raison d'être.

There is comparably intense debate about the place of science and empiricism in social work. On one side we find passionate pleas for social workers to get down to the business of empirically evaluating their interventions at all levels—whether clinical, social action, or administrative—in a disciplined effort to assess more systematically the effectiveness of social work practice. On the other side we find ardent critics of this sort of positivism, those who decry the move toward counting, measuring, documenting, and evaluating. For them, social work embraces empiricism at its peril.

As the various chapters in this book amply demonstrate, similar controversy exists with respect to other foundation content as well, including social welfare policy, human behavior, cultural and ethnic diversity, and field education. These various essays may actually serve to enhance this much-needed controversy.

Our collective goal, then, is to provide social workers with a sense of vision—though one certainly open to debate—concerning its intellectual core. What we offer is a diverse set of views about essential knowledge for the profession, knowledge that, in the end, binds together the diverse and noble aims of all social work practitioners.

REFERENCES

Abbott, E. 1931. *Social Welfare and Professional Education*. Chicago: University of Chicago Press.

Barber, B. 1965. "Some Problems in the Sociology of the Professions." In K. S. Lynn and the Editors of *Daedalus*, eds., *The Professions in America*, pp. 15–34. Boston: Houghton Mifflin.

Bartlett, H. M. 1958. "Toward Clarification and Improvement of Social Work Practice." *Social Work* 3(2):3–9.

Becker, H. S. 1962. "The Nature of a Profession." In N. B. Henry, ed., *The Sixty-First Yearbook of the National Society for the Study of Education*. Chicago: University of Chicago Press.

Blackey, E. 1968. "Building the Curriculum: The Foundation for Professional Competence." In E. Younghusband, ed., *Education for Social Work*, pp. 11–27. New York: Council on Social Work Education.

Boehm, W. W. 1959a. *Objectives of the Social Work Curriculum of the Future*. Vol. 1. New York: Council on Social Work Education.

——. 1959b. *Social Work Curriculum Study*. 13 vols. New York: Council on Social Work Education.

Carr-Saunders, A. M. and P. A. Wilson. 1933. *The Professions*. Oxford: Clarendon Press.

Compton, B. R. and B. Galaway. 1989. *Social Work Processes*. 4th ed. Belmont, Calif.: Wadsworth.

Council on Social Work Education. 1971. "Curriculum Policy for the Master's Degree Program in Graduate Schools of Social Work." In *Manual of Accrediting Standards for Graduate Professional Schools of Social Work*, Appendix I, pp. 55–60. New York: Council on Social Work Education.

——. 1984. "Curriculum Policy for the Master's Degree and Baccalaureate Degree Programs in Social Work Education." In *Handbook of Accreditation Standards and Procedures*. New York: Council on Social Work Education.

——. 1992a. "Curriculum Policy Statement for Baccalaureate Degree Programs in Social Work Education." Alexandria, Va.: Council on Social Work Education.

——. 1992b. "Curriculum Policy Statement for Master's Degree Programs in Social Work Education." Alexandria, Va.: Council on Social Work Education.

Dinerman, M. 1984. "The 1959 Curriculum Study: Contributions of Werner W. Boehm." In Dinerman and Geismar, eds., *A Quarter-Century of Social Work Education*, pp. 3–24.

Dinerman, M. and L. L. Geismar, eds. 1984. *A Quarter-Century of Social Work Education*. Silver Spring, Md.: National Association of Social Workers.

Flexner, A. 1915. "Is Social Work a Profession?" In *Proceedings of the National Conference of Charities and Correction*, pp. 576–590. Chicago: Hilman.

Germain, C. B. and A. Gitterman. 1987. "Ecological Perspective." In A. Minahan et al., eds., *Encyclopedia of Social Work*, 18th ed., 1:488–499. Silver Spring, Md.: National Association of Social Workers.

Glazer, N. 1974. "The Schools of the Minor Professions." *Minerva* 12(3):346–364.

Gordon, W. E. 1962. "A Critique of the Working Definition." *Social Work* 7(5):3–13.

Greenwood, E. 1957. "Attributes of a Profession." *Social Work* 2(3):45–55.

Haggerty, J. E. 1931. *The Training of Social Workers*. New York: McGraw-Hill.

Hollis, E. V. and A. L. Taylor. 1951. *Social Work Education in the United States*. Westport, Conn.: Greenwood Press.

Hollis, F. M. 1965. *Casework: A Psychosocial Therapy*. New York: Random House.

Hughes, E. C. 1965. "Professions." In K. S. Lynn and the Editors of *Daedalus*, eds., *The Professions in America*, pp. 1–14. Boston: Houghton Mifflin.

Kadushin, A. 1959. "The Knowledge Base of Social Work." In A. J. Kahn, ed., *Issues in American Social Work*, pp. 39–79. New York: Columbia University Press.

Kahn, A. J. 1954. "The Nature of Social Work Knowledge." In C. Kasius, ed., *New Directions in Social Work*, pp. 194–214. New York: Harper.

Khinduka, S. K. 1987. "Social Work and the Human Services." In A. Minahan et al., eds., *Encyclopedia of Social Work*, 18th ed., vol. 2, pp. 681–695. Silver Spring, Md.: National Association of Social Workers.

Larson, M. S. 1977. *The Rise of Professionalism*. Berkeley: University of California Press.

Lloyd, G. A. 1987. "Social Work Education." In A. Minahan et al., eds., *Encyclopedia of Social Work*, 18th ed., vol. 2, pp. 695–705. Silver Spring, Md.: National Association of Social Workers.

Moore, W. E. 1970. *The Professions: Roles and Rules*. New York: Russell Sage Foundation.

National Association of Social Workers. 1977. "Conceptual Frameworks I" [Special Issue]. *Social Work* 22(4).

——. 1981. "Conceptual Frameworks II" [Special Issue]. *Social Work* 26(1).

Perlman, H. H. 1957. *Casework: A Problem-Solving Process*. Chicago: University of Chicago Press.

Reynolds, B. C. 1965. *Learning and Teaching in the Practice of Social Work*. New York: Russell and Russell.

Richmond, M. 1917. *Social Diagnosis*. New York: Russell Sage Foundation.

Rothman, G. C. 1985. *Philanthropists, Therapists, and Activists*. Cambridge, Mass.: Schenkman.

Sheafor, B. W. and P. S. Landon. 1987. "Generalist Perspective." In A. Minahan et al., eds., *Encyclopedia of Social Work*, 18th ed., 1:660–669. Silver Spring, Md.: National Association of Social Workers.

Siporin, M. 1984. "A Future for Social Work Education." In Dinerman and Geismar, eds., *A Quarter-Century of Social Work Education*, pp. 237–251.

Social Work: Generic and Specific: A Report of the Milford Conference. 1974 [1919]. Reprint; Washington, D.C.: National Association of Social Workers.

Thomas, E. J. 1978. "Generating Innovations in Social Work: The Paradigm of Developmental Research." *Journal of Social Service Research* 2(1):95–115.

——. 1985. "The Validity of Design and Development and Related Concepts in Developmental Research." *Social Work Research and Abstracts* 21(2):50–55.

Toren, N. 1969. "Semi-Professionalism and Social Work: A Theoretical Perspective." In A. Etzioni, ed., *The Semi-Professions and Their Organization*, pp. 141–195. New York: Free Press.

Tufts, J. H. 1923. *Educating and Training for Social Work.* New York: Russell Sage Foundation.

2

Social Work Practice

ANN HARTMAN

Social work includes a broad and varied array of activities and is practiced with different size systems and in a variety of arenas. There is scant agreement in the field on the worldview, epistemology, or even on the principles or shape of practice. Volumes have been published on the different models (Turner 1986; Dorfman 1988) and some have concluded that the only common thread that runs through all of social work is a shared value stance (National Association of Social Workers [NASW] 1981).

In the face of such diversity, it is not a simple task to define and describe the foundation of social work practice. Although the accreditation standards of the Council on Social Work Education (CSWE) require that each program include the body of knowledge, skills, and values comprising that foundation, it is likely that each institution, and within institutions even each practice instructor, would present a different vision of such a foundation. Approaches to the foundation are shaped by the practice perspective embraced by the instructor and the institution, including among others, the ecological (Germain and Gitterman 1980), ego-psychological or psychosocial model (Woods and Hollis 1990; Goldstein 1984), task-centered (Reid and Epstein 1977), family-centered (Hartman and Laird 1983), cognitive-behavioral (Gambrill 1977; Rose 1980), and the structural (Middleman and Goldberg 1974). Some of these approaches are defined by method, others by the unit of attention (i.e., client populations, organizations, communities). Some easily encompass work with groups and communities, whereas others are more difficult to stretch to include larger systems. Most are transferable to the various arenas or fields of practice where social workers do their work.

Because of the diversity of their practice and the breadth of their domain, social workers have had difficulty defining their profession, although we seem to never tire of the attempt (Bartlett 1970; Gordon 1965; NASW 1977, 1981). It is the difficulty in definition and description that complicates any effort to present the foundation of social work practice. But even with these difficulties, each instructor, each curriculum, and each practitioner must come to terms with the challenge and in action express some view of the essential components of practice.

Professions are constructions growing out of social, political, economic, and knowledge development contexts. On an individual level, a professional's practice is an expression of his or her participation in these contexts and experience in the profession. This essay will inevitably be my vision, my construction. It will be influenced by my worldview, experience, training, and interests. Postmodern thinkers have taught us that we cannot separate the observer from the observed, the report from the reporter. It is therefore necessary to identify this observer that the reader may place the presentation in a context and identify and critique the biases and assumptions.

My professional background includes practice in public child welfare, family agencies, community mental health, a family therapy center, and with individuals, families, groups, and communities, as well as a long career in social work education. My education in social work began with a psychodynamic perspective and my own intellectual interests—or perhaps I should say passion—has been to attempt to integrate the psychological and social. This interest in context led to the study of the social sciences, the exploration of general systems theory, an ecological perspective, family-centered practice, and more recently to the adoption of a constructivist view. Each of these perspectives implies different metaphors and shapes practice differently, and threads of them will probably appear in the following discussion.

I will begin with some general principles and a vision of the social work practitioner in action. This will be followed by an attempt to define the core of practice and to explicate that common core.

Finally, the practice will be illustrated with examples.

Values in Practice

We must begin with the value base of social work, as there seems to be general agreement that it has been shared values that have held the profession together in the face of diversity. Social work is based on a valuing of and respect for each individual. This includes a belief in each person's potential for growth and ability and right, within certain limits imposed by social good, to determine his or her own destiny, to choose his or her own goals (Weick and Pope 1988). These values get translated into such practice principles as client self-determination, the prescription to "start where the client is," and the empowerment of clients. In some respects these principles have been embraced as ideals yet not fully translated into practice. Such a translation radically alters our practice. "The moss-grown aphorism `start where the client is' is not, after all, a piece of hollow rhetoric, but a sound and instructive principle. Ethically and practically, it advises us that effective practice begins and continues within the ground of the client's own interpreted reality" (Goldstein 1990:38).

Social workers are also concerned about social values, about nurturing and preserving relatedness, integration, social commitments, and the general social welfare. Our profession's first name is, after all, "social." These multiple value commitments shape our practice but also lead us into value dilemmas, to tensions between individual and social good, to conflicts around social change and social control, which provide ongoing challenges to all social workers. The exploration and clarification of the values implicit or the potential value conflicts existing in any practice situation is part of all social work practice and an essential component of the foundation of social work knowledge (Dean and Rhodes 1992; Holland and Kilpatrick 1991; Reamer 1990).

An Epistemological Position

Social work practice is shaped by knowledge as well as values, as both are translated into action. An essential element in that practice is, therefore, the nature of knowledge. What are the sources of our knowledge? How do we know what we know? What should be our stance in relation to theory and knowledge? Differences around the definition of knowledge and alternate visions of the "truth" have divided the profession (Heineman 1981; Hudson 1982; Imre 1984; Witkin 1991; Tyson 1994). This is neither a trivial matter nor one solely for academics to argue about in erudite journals (Hartman 1990). Epistemological positions define practice and education for practice.

The epistemological position I take in this chapter is postmodern in that it is assumed that we can only know the world through our construction or interpretation of it. Further, it is believed that these constructions and interpretations grow out of social, political, cultural, and economic contexts (Gergen 1991; Geertz 1983). It is also assumed that those in power tend to control the social discourse and the definition of knowledge, subjugating the knowledge and the truths of oppressed people (Foucault 1980; Hartman 1992; Collins 1990; White and Epston 1990).

This position is translated into a critical stance for all students of practice and practitioners. That is, as we draw on our theory and our knowledge, we do so knowing that they are shaped by context. We make use of knowledge and theory but always examine the value assumptions and the sociopolitical and cultural processes that gave birth to and sustained them. We are ready to attend when our experiences or our clients' experiences challenge our theories and our truths. We reach for subjugated knowledge as we are aware that the voices of many of the people social workers traditionally serve have long been silenced (Hooks 1989; Collins 1990; Hartman 1992).

Defining the Unit of Attention

Finally, different approaches to social work practice vary a great deal in the way they draw boundaries around the unit of attention. Not only is there variation in the extension of the boundaries in space, but also through time. Models differ in terms of the inclusion of history, the extent to which the inner life of the client is a focus, the extent to which the extended social, political, and economic environment are considered a part of the "case." How these boundaries are drawn shapes the nature of every phase of the practice. In this presentation, I will draw the boundaries widely, both through time and space. As Goldstein has written, "The unique ethos of our profession is expressed in our concern not only with the whole person and his or her social and physical context, but more important, the transactional and symbiotic bond that unites the two" (Goldstein 1990:41).

In recent years, an ecological metaphor has been widely adopted as a way of capturing this complex focus. This metaphor may be useful if one is careful to remember that mind is a part of nature in the Batesonian sense (Bateson 1979). "An ecological perspective must include meaning and value, memory and imagination, spirituality and aesthetics" (Hartman 1986).

Thinking in Action

In turning now to an application of these principles in the practice foundation, I will start with an elaboration of the thinking-in-action skills required of all practitioners of any profession, and particularly in a profession that is so complex, one in which the territory is so broad, the context so ambiguous, and the options so numerous. The goals of such a profession cannot be adequately served by exclusive reliance on the rational application of technical knowledge.

We start with Erikson's conviction that every individual is a universe of one who must be understood in terms of the unique experiences of his or her own life. As social workers, we can add that every family, group, organization, or community is also a universe of one. We must prepare as social workers for a "reflective conversation with a unique and uncertain situation" (Schon 1983:140).

We may adopt a particular body of practice theory but always with the recognition that it is but one lens. And we must always be ready to amend it or discard it if the theory is found to be incongruent with our clients' or our own lived experience. Schon (1983) describes the thinking-in-action process of the reflective practitioner: "When the phenomenon at hand eludes the ordinary category of knowledge-in-practice, presenting itself as unique or unstable, the practitioner may surface and criticize his initial understanding of the phenomenon, construct a new description of it, and test the new description with an on the spot experiment" (63).Further, "reflection-in-action in a unique case may be generalized to other cases, not by giving rise to general principles but by contributing to the practitioner's repertoire of exemplary themes from which, in subsequent cases of his practice, he may compose new variations" (140).

The intellectual demands on the practitioner are great in that he or she must simultaneously apply and critique the application of knowledge, while concurrently constructing and deconstructing interpretations. Social workers must not only learn to live with but embrace uncertainty and ambiguity (Amundson, Stewart, and Valentine 1993). That is the nature of our profession and our practice. "Reflection in action is the art by which practitioners deal with situations of uncertainty, instability, uniqueness, and value conflicts" (Schon 1983:50).

In social work there is so much complexity, ambiguity, and uncertainty and so many competing explanatory and practice theories, the critical reflective stance cannot be reserved as the exclusive position of the wise and seasoned practitioner but must be a basic part of the foundation, no matter what particular practice perspective may be adopted.

Framework for the Foundation of Practice

Having established certain assumptions upon which this foundation is built, the next task is to translate this into practice principles and prescriptions. In order to do this, a commonly used framework for defining the processes of social work practice will be used. These processes include identification and engagement of the client(s), definition of the problem, assessment, intervention, termination, and ongoing evaluation. These familiar phases of social work practice are not discrete, nor are they necessarily sequenced, but they seem to occur, at least to some extent, in every practice situation with individuals, families, groups, or communities, no matter what the perspective or model of practice. The framework is fleshed out differently in different approaches to practice but all social workers must have a body of knowledge and skills that enable them to understand, participate in, or enact these processes.

Identification of the Client Systems

The worker and client(s) must meet and be engaged in the work. The first phase of the engagement is completed when the client(s) and the practitioner have agreed that they have a common purpose and that they will work together toward that purpose. This seems like a fairly simple and straightforward process but an important part of the practice knowledge base is an understanding of and the ability to analyze the complex variables that make it possible for worker and client(s) to meet and that shape the nature and direction of that meeting. Some of these crucial variables are as follows.

The accessibility and availability of the service influences the nature of the contact and whether the contact will ever take place. How comfortable, sophisticated, and assertive do the clients have to be to find their way to the service? Is the service visible? Is it both physically and psychologically accessible? In an effort to reach disempowered and oppressed populations, social workers must be aware of the psychological, cultural, social, and physical barriers that often exist between these populations and services. If the obstacles are not attended to and removed, social workers become estranged from their historical mission. Bertha Reynolds (1934) explored these issues and suggested that services should be located on the highways of life where ordinary traffic passes by. We must ask how close is our service to those highways.

Second, it is important to understand the nature of the "gate-keeping" processes of the agency or other service delivery system. Is the intake process enabling and facilitating or does it present a series of obstacles that must be overcome to obtain services, obstacles that alienate and therefore exclude certain client populations? It is useful to ask students and practitioners to trace the process of becoming a client in their agencies, to think about everything a person must do and be to become a client, and to consider who might be excluded. An analysis of these variables in any practice situation introduces important aspects of organizational theory and analysis and opens up the possibility of change in situations in which barriers exist.

Third, a social worker must be able to reflect on the variables that define or identify the nature of the client system. Who is to be seen and how? The agency function, theoretical base, and ideology, rather than the client's need, are frequently the major determinants of client definition and the nature of the service. In this sense, rather than starting where the client is, we tend to start where the worker or the agency is. If a family is referred to a traditional child-guidance clinic, it is likely that the child will be seen in individual treatment and the mother or both parents in parent counseling. If they happen to find their way to a family-oriented agency, they will probably end up in conjoint family therapy. Sometimes the variables that determine the nature of the client system can be serendipitous. For example, one family-service agency had very few family cases. It was discovered that the receptionist, a long-time employee of the agency, routinely set up individual appointments for the caller unless the applicant specifically requested a conjoint couple or family appointment.

Individual workers' convictions can also shape the nature of the client system. For example, one student, convinced about the helpfulness of groups, converted her caseload of four chronically ill clients in a hospital setting who had been assigned to her as individual cases into a group. Anderson and Goolishian (1988) have suggested that we work with language-determined systems, that is, with all those that are concerned and in conversation about a problem, including clients, workers, and neighborhood residents.

In practice with groups, the identification and development of the client system has added dimensions. Groups may be formed in a variety of ways. People may voluntarily come together in open-ended or short-term groups, organized around a specific shared life issue or challenge. For example, a hospital may offer a group for parents of children with chronic illness or families of patients hospitalized with acute mental illness. Support and psychoeducational groups may be organized around a variety of shared stresses or problems.

In other situations, treatment groups may be formed by an agency to help people deal with a variety of personal and relationship problems. In these situations attention is paid to the planned composition of the group to be sure that the group members share enough to encourage cohesion. Furthermore, care is taken that, although there will always be and should be diversity in the group, no one member of the group should feel isolated, for example, one male in an all-female group or one person of color in an all-white group. The adaptation of principles that guide the identification of the client system and the group formation is a part of the foundation of social work practice.

Community organization also makes special demands in the formation of the client system. In community organization practice, community groups may be discovered or formed. Organizational efforts may be devoted to the discovery and engagement of preexisting groups or organizations and to building coalitions. New community groups generally form around a common problem in order to bring about change. Frequently, a major part of community organization practice involves the formation of a network that can identify people who have a shared concern, reach out to them, and bring them together. Often, social workers reaching out to communities find alienation and a sense of hopelessness and powerlessness. The process of organizing includes communicating hope and the conviction that people joined together in common cause can make a difference. Alienation and hopelessness are frequently the major barriers to successful organization, while the development of community, connection, and competence is a major goal of the work.

In summary, the foundation of practice includes an understanding of the processes of identification and development of the client system as they are adapted to work with individuals, families, groups and communities. Further, it is also essential that all social workers be able to reflect on and to critique the definitions of the client system and identify the variables that construct those definitions. The worker and agency's biases and theoretical perspectives have an enormous impact on the direction of the contact and should not be assumed as a given.

In organizational change, the task is to locate those within an organization who share the change objectives and build a working coalition with them. As in community work, an organizational change group is brought together through a shared purpose or concern (Patti and Resnick 1972). In discussing the identification of the client system, I have focused primarily on voluntary or semi-voluntary clients. Work with involuntary clients raises different issues as, in a sense, a person brought into contact with a social worker involuntarily and through external authority is not truly a client and the social worker in such a situation must understand that she or he is acting as an agent of social control. The phrase "involuntary client" is perhaps an oxymoron as the term "client" implies that a person has *engaged* the services of another. Whether a person involuntarily seeing a social worker assumes the role of "client" awaits a successful process of engagement and the establishment of a working agreement or contract. The foundation of practice includes the understanding of the profession's social control role, the dilemmas inherent in our profession's ideal of self-determination and our use of authority, as well as an appreciation of the limitations and challenges when people are in the relationship under duress.

Engagement of the Client System

Engagement of the client grows out of several things. First and most crucial is the concept of purpose. Everyone in the helping system (which includes the worker) must to some extent share the purpose for being together. That is the glue that begins to build and hold relationships together. The initial questions, "What brought you here today?" and "What do you hope to achieve by coming?" are questions that evoke the client's purpose and a discussion and negotiation about whether there is congruence between the client's purpose and the agency/worker's purpose as expressed in the agency's values, policy, and function. This must be clarified in all practice situations as nothing is more frustrating and self-defeating than working at cross-purposes.

Finding common purpose is particularly delicate and important in multiple-client systems as there must be shared purpose among all the actors. For example, in marital counseling, if one member wants help in terminating the marriage and the other wants to save the marriage, the purpose of the contact is not shared and a working agreement cannot be established. Sometimes the conflicting purposes are hidden and the work can be totally undermined. However, a shared purpose does not imply absence of conflict or agreement on everything. On the contrary, it is the shared purpose that enables members of a multi-client system to tolerate and manage conflict. For example, a bitter and angry divorced couple can work together around sharing child custody and dealing with other issues related to their children if they are able to join in a shared concern for the welfare of the children. In a group of unrelated individuals, it is the common purpose that helps the group deal with issues of difference. The stronger the sense of common purpose, the more diversity and conflict a group is able to handle. In community organization practice, there will be many conflicting interests in a community group and it is the strength of the shared purpose that enables members of the community to put aside their differences and work together. The shared purpose becomes a part of the contract in working with any size client system. A major role of the practitioner in work with individuals, families, groups, or communities is to keep the process related to the purpose and to initiate a discussion of the possibility of revising the purpose should the client(s) begin to move in another direction.

A second major ingredient in the engagement process is the establishment of trust, both in the worker and in the integrity of the process. The worker can only earn the client's trust through his or her competence, humanity, and integrity through action, in other words, through the demonstration of such trustworthiness. Practice principles include an understanding of the actions in a practice situation that develop trust, such as establishing a true collaboration, being on time, listening and remembering, being open and genuine, responding respectfully and with interest to clients' narratives. It is also important in all situations, and particularly in multiple-client systems, that the worker demonstrate the ability and the strength required to keep the helping situation safe for everyone, to help clients deal with conflict where it emerges in a helpful and productive way. In order to establish trust, the worker does not have to be the expert and have all the answers. On the contrary, a reflective and trustworthy practitioner knows that clients are the experts on their own situations and the worker should allow herself to experience, recognize, and express puzzlement, wonder, confusion, or surprise in a unique and uncertain situation (Schon 1983; Amundson, Stewart, and Valentine 1993; Anderson and Goolishian 1992).

The social workers' stance in relation to their expertise also has significance in terms of the power dynamics of the worker-client relationship. To be the expert is to adopt a position of power. This is in direct conflict with social work's avowed interest in the empowerment of clients. In developing a trustful and collaborative relationship, often across barriers of considerable social distance, it is necessary to traverse that distance and find ways to join, to share commonality. When clients and workers are of different sexes, races, social class, or age grouping, the distance can be considerable and it is the worker's task to find the common ground (Davis and Proctor 1989). Whatever the differences may be, worker and client both bring attitudes shaped by their life experiences in the social, cultural, and political context. These differences may be ignored but at the risk of undermining the developing relationship. The issues of trust are particularly crucial and sensitive in situations where clients and workers are of different races, as eloquently explored in Pinderhughes (1989). An essential component of the foundation of social work is the knowledge and skill required in the recognition and exploration of differences so that these differences will not be an obstacle to the work.

A third component of the engagement process is the collaborative establishment of norms and agreed-upon plans for the contact. Some of these agreements will be negotiated early in the work, whereas others will emerge or be negotiated as a part of that process. The practical features of the working agreement, such as the details of when and where meetings shall take place, how long they shall be, whether it is to be a planned short-term contract or open-ended, fees to be charged, if any, must be settled early in the contact.

Issues of confidentiality should also be explored early (Schwartz 1989). This is not a simple matter and all practitioners must be clear about the limits placed on confidentiality by law, for example, the requirement that suspected abuse of children be reported as well as the growing concern about the "duty to warn" should a client's planned action be dangerous to others (Reamer 1991). Obviously, blanket statements such as "everything you tell me will be held in strictest confidence" are not necessarily accurate and the client and worker must both be aware of the limits.

Further, most family-oriented practitioners, although carefully observing the requirements of confidentiality outside the family, will not be bound to keep secrets within the family. Such secrets bring the family worker into collusion with one member of the family and generally serve to induct the worker into the family system (Imber-Black 1993). Secrets thus learned cannot be used in the work or they will constrain the process. An honest and thoughtful discussion of issues around confidentiality will develop more trust in the relationship than would a blanket statement that the client knows could not be maintained in all circumstances.

The issue of confidentiality in groups is particularly complicated and can only be resolved by a thorough discussion among all the group members and the establishment of mutual understanding and agreement concerning the nature and limits of confidentiality. For example, a common question in groups is "Can I talk with my wife about what goes on in group as long as I don't identify anybody?" Such an issue must be settled by the group and the actual process of doing this is useful for the development of the group and of interpersonal skills.

Expectations and norms around behavior during the contact generally emerge as work goes on. Is it all right to cry? To express anger? To criticize the worker or other members of the client system? How is anger or conflict to be expressed? Is it all right to talk about anything? Are there limits and, if so, what are they? It is important that family and group members work out the norms together and that they are active in enforcing, challenging, or changing those norms. Through this they have the opportunity to practice observing and reflecting on interpersonal processes and to learn to shape and change them. Norms must also be developed in community groups. There must be an understanding of the various roles to be carried, norms about the nature and responsibility of leadership, and agreement concerning change strategies to be utilized. Norms must be developed that define decision-making processes and the process through which it is determined to embark on new strategies or escalate the level of conflict. Community groups must be involved when a decision is made to move from collaboration to confrontation. Norms about communication must also be established to ensure that all members of the community group or organization are appropriately informed and able to participate. Information is power and therefore sharing information shares power.

When a small cadre within an organizing or an organizational change effort withholds important information, a hierarchical structure of "insiders and outsiders" quickly develops that undermines cohesion and results in anger and competition.

Definition and Exploration of the Problem

As we approach the issue of the definition of the problem to be addressed, we encounter increasing diversity among various approaches to practice. Ideological, epistemological, and value positions shape the definition of what is "wrong" that needs to be put "right." First, what is defined as "wrong" is a social construction, shaped by cultural, social, political, and economic forces. One need only review the differing views of what is considered problematic across cultures or through history to be aware that problem definitions are varied and changing. Many examples come to mind. One of the problems frequently defined in our profession is the inability to adequately perform social roles. But role definitions are cultural artifacts and changing. For example, not long ago women involved in marital counseling were often considered problematic if they did not accept or adequately perform the "feminine" role in the marriage. The treatment prescription was to help her embrace and accept her female role as, until recently, very narrowly defined. The women's movement has created new definitions of women's roles and thus has redefined the definition of what is "wrong."

Until less than two decades ago, homosexuality was defined as a psychiatric disorder in the APA's *Diagnostic and Statistical Manual (DSM)*, an illness in need of cure. Social workers have been deeply involved in child welfare and child protection and there have been few areas where problem definition has been more contentious and complex (Giovannoni and Becerra 1979). Problematic conditions and behavior are defined through social processes and generally, as Foucault (1980) points out, by those in power. Those defined as problematic by society tend to internalize those definitions, which then become a part of the person's construction of the self. These self-constructions then shape the person's behavior and experience. Social workers are frequently called upon to act as instruments of social control, to deal with behaviors or situations that have been defined by someone in authority as problematic. In such situations, it is important not to take "problems" as a given but to learn to deconstruct these definitions.

A key question to ask in understanding problem definition is "Who defined the problem?" Parents and school personnel tend to define children's problems and spouses will define the behavior of their partners as the problem. Judges, principals, physicians, and others in authority define problems and refer. This principle is also demonstrated by problem definition within larger systems. For example, the administration of a large inner-city hospital defined a group of hospitalized paraplegics as a problem because of their constant complaints and uncooperative behavior. A social worker was asked to organize a group as a vehicle for dealing with the behavior. The worker, guided by the clients' concerns and his own values, converted the group into an active coalition for social change that focused on the very real problems in the organization and attendant neglect of the patients.

In truly voluntary situations, problems are self-defined when people seek services for an already identified concern. Even in these cases, social and cultural factors have influenced the person's definition of the problem. People take on the definitions formulated by others and make them their own.

Not only do larger social processes define problems but different practice perspectives tend to disagree on what is "wrong." Some focus on a specific and limited behavior to be changed (Gambrill 1977) or a specific and limited problem to be solved (de Shazer 1985; Reid and Epstein 1977), some more globally on an "absence of fit" or conflict between the client system and the social environment (Germain and Gitterman 1980), and others on individual or family dysfunction (Goldstein 1984; Hartman and Laird 1983) or the inability to productively enact social roles. Most practice models tend to redefine the client's vision of "what is wrong" through their theoretical, practice, or value lenses and produce a problem definition that is an expansion, elaboration, alteration, or focusing of the client's presenting problem. Although we may "start where the client is," it is quite clear that in most models of practice we quickly begin a process that moves beyond "where the client is" with a redefinition of the problem.

Recently, the focus on "the problem" has been challenged as too focused on pathology and insufficiently emphasizing the potential and the strengths in the situation (Weick et al. 1989; Saleebey 1992b). Some theorists feel that attending to available strengths and resources that might be mobilized to achieve client goals will better help people move toward desired outcomes.

Michael White (1989) has pointed out that generally when people seek help and are seen by the community or themselves as being in trouble, they are burdened with a problem-saturated story and are unable to see any other options in their view of themselves or their world. This dominant-problem-saturated narrative is highly selective and excludes much of the client's lived experience. It is White's conviction that much of our work with individuals and families entails the co-construction of a different nonproblematic narrative that is congruent with more of the client's lived experience and offers expanded and varied options. Such "restorying" (Laird 1989) opens up new ways of conceiving the past and therefore shaping the future.

In summary, different practice perspectives approach problem definition quite differently. Some focus on discovering "what is wrong," while others support a strengths perspective, focusing on goals to be achieved and strengths and resources available. Others take the position that individuals and families, groups and communities are caught in problem-saturated narratives and need help in co-constructing an alternative narrative with more possibilities and options.

The foundation of social work practice includes listening with great care and appreciation to the client's definition of the problem and developing collaboratively with the clients a workable definition of the problem that is congruent with the client's lived experience and also points to possibilities for solution or change. At the same time, the foundation includes the ability to critique a problem definition, to examine the assumptions, cultural biases, practice procedures, values, and administrative constraints that shape that definition.

Assessment

Closely related to definition and exploration is the assessment process that begins at the first visit and continues throughout the contact. This process includes the definition of the unit of attention, or the drawing of boundaries around the relevant areas for inquiry. It also includes the gathering of information relevant to the situation and the thinking process through which the worker and client attempt to make sense out of the information gathered.

Assessment is a central part of all social work practice with individuals, families, groups, or communities. However, as with problem definition, the nature of the process varies a great deal in relation to the particular approach to practice and the size of the client system. Approaches to assessment differ in terms of what is to be assessed, how the information gathered is to be understood, and who is to do the assessment. First, in terms of the "what" of assessment, in work with individuals and families, some approaches to practice support a broad and holistic vision of the person or family-in-situation and gather extensive biopsychosocial information (Boyd-Franklin 1989; Hartman and Laird 1983; Germain and Gitterman 1980; Meyer 1993).

Other assessments may be very focused, limited to an inventory of problematic behaviors and an examination of the antecedents and consequences of those behaviors. Baseline data are established to indicate the frequency of the behaviors that have been selected as a target for change (Gambrill 1977). The approach presented in this chapter defines the unit of attention broadly in part because of a conviction that the foundation should include the knowledge and skill to do a broad-based ecological and historical assessment even though such an assessment will be neither required nor appropriate in all situations. Further, no matter how focused the definition of the unit of attention is, a social work perspective demands that an understanding of the situation must include the sociocultural context.

There are also differing epistemological positions, different views of the truth and of how data are evaluated. Many professionals see assessment as a search for the objective truth, a search primarily conducted by the professional as expert. Although the clients are sources of information, their views are evaluated with care. This position is stated in a widely used social work practice text: "Though it is the primary source of information, verbal report is highly vulnerable to error because of possible faulty recall, distorted perceptions, biases, and limited self-awareness on the part of clients. It is vital to keep this limitation in mind and to avoid the tendency to accept clients' views, descriptions, and reports as valid representation of reality" (Hepworth and Larson 1982:158).

This view, which privileges the professional's knowledge and subjugates the experience and knowledge of the client, is incongruent with an empowerment model of practice (Hartman 1993). Knowledge is power and privileging the professional's knowledge "furnishes the client with a lesson in inferiority"(Gergen and Kaye 1992:171).

An alternate view is that the clients' narratives are the clients' reality and provide the ground upon which our understanding and our work should be built (Goldstein 1990; Pray 1991; Borden 1992; Laird 1989). According to this perspective, "human action takes place in a reality of understanding that is created through social construction and dialogue. From this position, people live, and understand their living, through socially constructed narrative realities that give meaning and organization to their experience" (Anderson and Goolishian 1992:26). Narratives, as shared with us by our clients, are their efforts to make sense out of their lives, to create and preserve a sense of coherence and continuity in identity and self (Borden 1992:126). In this exploration, the client, not the worker, is the expert on his or her own unique reality (Pray 1991; Amundson, Stewart, and Valentine 1993). The worker "asks questions from a position of not knowing rather than asking questions that are informed by method and demand specific answers" (Anderson and Goolishian 1992:28).

Our professional heritage includes this position, as expressed by Bertha Reynolds, who wrote that the client is "the ultimate source of authority in his (or her) affairs"(1934:35). This perspective is particularly important in a profession that embraces the vision of working with oppressed populations. It is the voices of just those populations that have been subjugated, the voices of people of color, of women, of people in poverty, of gays and lesbians. The dominant discourse about these oppressed groups is rooted in the sociopolitical context, often developed without reference to their own lived experience, and is frequently a part of their oppression (Collins 1990; Hooks 1989; Foucault 1980).

In our attempt to become more skilled and more sensitive in our work with people of color, we have sought to gather information about cultures, to learn about "difference," to become "experts." Unfortunately such an approach tends to lead to stereotypes, to present various groups as if their members were alike, and to a perspective that separates and objectifies. If we abandon our expert role and really listen to our clients and believe and trust their experience, we will learn from them. The foundation should include not a potpourri of descriptive information about ethnic and racial groups but rather an understanding of the dynamics and impact of oppression and the knowledge and skill required in identifying and listening to meanings, to values, to culture, to ritual, to racial and ethnic narratives.

Further, it is essential that each practitioner understand that they, too, belong to a race, a class, a gender, one or more ethnic groups, and have a sexual orientation. As Rabinow and Sullivan (1987) remind us, "Our capacity to understand is rooted in our own self-definitions, hence in what we are. We are fundamentally self-interpreting and self-defining, living always in a culture environment, inside a web of signification that we ourselves have spun. There is no outside, detached standpoint from which we gather and present brute data"(7). To be able to identify one's own biases, one's values, one's own standpoint is the heart of professional self-awareness.

Finally, and very much related to epistemological positions, approaches to practice differ in terms of who carries major responsibility for the assessment. In models that privilege the expertise of the professional, the worker gathers the data and makes the assessment and the client is usually informed, at least in part, of the findings. In practice shaped by a social constructivist epistemology, the worker and the clients share the assessment process, which is one of collaborative exploration and discovery in which they are fellow seekers.

A number of assessment tools have been developed that may be used in the collaborative assessment process. Particularly useful to social workers with their focus on person-in-situation is the eco-map (Hartman 1978; Hartman and Laird 1983), a paper-and-pencil simulation that provides a graphic representation of the client's relationship with the social world. The map depicts available resources and those resources that are needed yet not available, stresses, conflicts, supports, and opportunities. The particular advantage of the map is not only its ability to capture in a visual metaphor a complex ecology but also the fact that the map is co-constructed by worker and clients, who can create a joint understanding and assessment of the situation.

The genogram (Hartman 1978; Hartman and Laird 1983; McGoldrick and Gerson 1985) is another useful tool that is widely used to capture a family's history. The clients carry major responsibility for developing the genogram and are clearly in the position of expert as worker and client together explore the intergenerational family story. The assessment or interpretation is shared and in a strengths perspective can be focused on resources and on new ways of enriching the individual's or family's narrative.

In the same vein, Weick et al. (1989) write, "By placing an emphasis on the already realized positive capacities of an individual, the individual is more likely to develop along the lines of these strengths"(353). White, in his effort to alter the client's problem-saturated narratives, externalizes the problem. He takes the unique but commonsense position that the family is not the problem, the individual is not the problem, the problem is the problem. His effort is to objectify the problem and separate it from the family. Instead of assuming that dysfunctional aspects of the family or of people in the family have created the problem, in the assessment process he focuses on the influence of the problem on the family or the individual and on how the influence of the problem has, at times, been subverted or avoided.

In the course of joint exploration in the assessment process, the client's concerns, social functioning, adaptive capacities, needs, hopes, and goals begin to emerge and together worker and clients begin to chart new options, new ways of thinking about and dealing with mutually identified concerns.

The assessment process in work with groups, organizations, and communities can also be expert-driven or collaborative but also requires particular knowledge and skills related to these larger systems. The foundation should include an understanding of and an ability to recognize various views of group development over time (Shulman 1992). Information on group assessment should also include other processes, such as the development of mutual aid, the changing nature of the relationship between the leader and the group, the group members' issues in dealing with difference, coalition building, and scapegoating (Davis and Proctor 1989). Again, in the process of group assessment, the professional may take major responsibility for the assessment or the members and worker may collaborate in examining the group process (Berman-Rossi 1992).

The reflective practitioner in the assessment process calls upon a wide range of theory and knowledge in thinking about and interpreting the data gathered (Germain 1991). The theory and knowledge available to social workers may enhance our understanding but also must be used with care. As discussed earlier in this chapter, the social worker must not adhere dogmatically to theory and must always be ready to alter or discard a theory when it does not reflect the experience reported by the client. Further, it is important for the social worker to share his or her reflections with the client in understandable, jargon-free language. The notion that the assessment is an expert professional judgment, developed by the worker and withheld from the client, disempowers the client and puts the worker in the position of power, which is contrary to the spirit of an empowering and egalitarian model of practice. Clearly, the worker's reflections should not be shared with the client as a matter of fact but as tentative interpretations that are no more privileged than the client's interpretations. The client and the worker participate in a cointerpretive process that in itself has the potential to change both worker and client. Quite naturally, a plan of action flows from such a co-construction.

Intervention

To describe the foundation content on intervention is to tackle the question so often asked of social workers, "What do social workers do?" The activities engaged in by social workers are so varied that the profession itself has struggled to define what it does. Students often complain that in learning about social work processes there is more attention to "beginnings" and to "ends" than to the "middle." Social work theorists have attempted to develop categorizations of social work interventions, starting with Mary Richmond's famous typology in *What is Social Casework* (1922): action of mind upon mind and environmental manipulation. Florence Hollis pursued this conceptualization, developing specific interventions under the psychological and the environmental rubrics (1965). Although it was Hollis's effort to conceptualize "psychosocial" intervention, the dichotomy between psychological and social intervention built into Richmond's conceptualization continued to characterize the profession.

Efforts to resolve this dichotomy have also been a part of social work's heritage. Lucille Austin, for example, added a third category to Mary Richmond's, which she called "experiential" intervention. In this approach, experiences in the client's social world are consciously developed and used as change strategies. This "experiential" tradition in casework has been elaborated by Germain and Gitterman (1980) in the life model and by Maluccio in his work on client competency (1981). The experiential view of interventions also has linkages with behavioral and task-centered work in which the focus is on behavioral change that affords client new experiences in their social worlds, leads to altered feedback, and potentially to psychological change. Saleebey (1992b) and others build on the experiential tradition in the strengths perspective. In other words, although dichotomization and primary reliance on "talking therapy" have characterized work with individual clients, many practitioners and theorists have elaborated on Austin's third type of intervention.

The tradition in group work has been strongly experiential, beginning with Grace Coyle's (1948) emphasis on the achievement of social goals and social skills through group participation. Conjoint family work is also highly life-experience-focused as the interpersonal processes within the family are both the context and the resources for change.

Although these many efforts toward psychosocial integration in practice have made important contributions, the dichotomization enunciated by Richmond continues to haunt the field. This can be seen in the language about practice that has developed over the past two decades. The term *casework*, which, as Mary Richmond said, traditionally included both psychological and social interventions began to disappear from our professional discourse and before long a new name emerged, "clinical social work," which carried with it a medical or psychological treatment (action of mind upon mind) vision. Although there were efforts by some (myself included) to define clinical social work as a synonym for "direct practice" (Hartman 1980), in the ongoing discussions that shaped the meaning of the term, clinical social work was increasingly defined as psychotherapy. Words do create worlds. The reasons for this language and meaning change are complex and beyond the purpose of this chapter but would provide a fascinating study in the sociology of knowledge.

When a profession moves away from a crucial and needed function, or at least when it ceases to name it, it will be reinvented and renamed and before long "case management" emerged, a practice that focuses on the client's relationship with his or her environment. There is now considerable uncertainty about the relationship between case management and the profession of social work (Rose 1992). Many non-social workers are practicing case management, which, if practiced sensitively, skillfully, thoughtfully, and based on a careful individualized assessment, sounds very much like our old friend casework. In the meantime, many social workers are taking the position that case management is not "real" social work. Mary Richmond's dichotomy seems to have spawned either two professions or a hierarchical bifurcation of social work.

At the same time, the profession has increasingly embraced the goal of client empowerment as one of the primary desired outcomes of our work. Clearly, power is related to the possession and effective use of both psychological and socioeconomic resources. Practice focused on empowerment must include the possibility of psychological, experiential, and environmental interventions. Social workers must not lose sight of the relationship between private trouble and public issues. The definition of our practice is unclear and there is confusion and disagreement about the nature and location of our interventions. A thoughtful examination of this confusion, of these unresolved issues must be a part of the foundation of social work practice.

From my perspective, social work interventions include those defined as "clinical social work" and as "case management." Thus, the foundation should include an introduction to all of the interventive roles that may be carried by a social worker, including therapist, counselor, educator, mediator, organizer, network builder, broker, social change agent, with and in behalf of individuals, families, groups, organizations, and communities, as appropriate.

These interventive roles involve a number of skills that are described in detail in a variety of practice texts (Shulman 1992; Reid and Epstein 1977; Germain and Gitterman 1980; Hartman and Laird 1983; Boyd-Franklin 1989; Middleman and Wood 1980; Rose 1980; Saleebey 1992b; Davis and Proctor 1989; Garvin and Seabury 1984; Fortune 1985; Hepworth and Larsen 1982; Gambrill 1977; Goldstein 1984; Woods and Hollis 1990).

Two major challenges face social work as we define and develop professional practice and interventive methods. First, we must continue in our quest for integration. A primarily environmental intervention may be the best avenue to an intrapersonal change, intervention in the psychological may achieve major environmental change, and experiential intervention consistently works with the individual's inner and outer world simultaneously. We must contextualize our practice and continue to explore the person-in-situation, the psychosocial meeting point, for that is our territory, that is what makes us social workers. The second challenge is to find ways to call upon and enact our professional skills in such a way that clients are empowered (Hartman 1993). In working with individuals, families, groups, organizations, and communities, such empowerment takes place through the creative expansion of options and the opening up of multiple alternatives, through the collaborative construction of new ways of thinking, feeling, acting, problem solving, interrelating, and through the discovery or mobilization of new opportunities and resources in the environment.

Termination

All social work-client contacts come to an end and the foundation includes an understanding of the components of planned and unplanned termination. Planned termination is worked out collaboratively between the individual, family, group, or community and the worker, and includes a joint review and evaluation of both the process and the outcomes of the contact, planning for the future, and saying goodbye. Each of these steps will evolve in different ways, depending on the nature of the contact, but they must be a part of the ending process or worker and clients will be left with a sense of incompletion. It is often around the termination process that questions come up about the relationship, for example, around the possibility of continued contact. It is important for all social workers to have the skill to discover the meaning of such questions and to work with the client to make a joint decision about how things should be left between them. Of course, in some approaches to practice, particularly in short-term episodic work with individuals and families, it is assumed that there may or will be another opportunity to work together.

An unplanned termination, occasioned by the worker's departure from the agency or some other external constraint, includes the same steps but can only begin after clients have had an opportunity to express their reaction to the interruption in the work, which may include feelings of anger, disappointment, or of having been let down or abandoned. After these feelings are expressed and accepted, and clients are clear about why the contact must be interrupted, it is usually possible to go on with productive work around ending.

Although social work practitioners are usually aware of the meaning of termination to individual clients, they have often been less sensitive to the impact of termination on the members of different kinds of groups, communities, or organizations. Perhaps the focus with larger groups on instrumental activities and goals leads workers to forget the emotional and relational components to the work. Furthermore, not only are the members of organizations and groups saying goodbye to the worker, they may also be saying goodbye to the group and to the valued connections made through the social change effort. Termination in such groups is often best experienced through the use of a ritual as rituals tend to be a natural communal mode for the management

of transitions. A farewell get-together with a review of accomplishments and an opportunity for saying goodbye helps a group consoli-
date endings.

Evaluation

Finally, evaluation, the ongoing monitoring of the process and outcomes of the work, is an essential part of the practice foundation and,
indeed, the hallmark of any professional (Schon 1983). Evaluation, however, is variously defined and performed in different models of practice
shaped by the epistemological assumptions upon which that practice is
based. Obviously, assumptions about *how* we know will determine
views on how we know change is taking place or how we know goals
are achieved. No matter what particular form the evaluation process
takes, it is important for every professional to have some method to the
ongoing assessment of the actions and outcomes in work with an individual, family, group, or community (Bloom and Fischer 1982; Barlow,
Hayes, and Nelson 1984; Videka-Sherman and Reid 1990).

Different approaches to practice promote different kinds of evaluative procedures. If the model is focused on the alteration, development,
or extinction of specific behaviors, then the evaluation is focused on the
monitoring of the frequency or intensity of those behaviors and the
course of the intervention. A variety of tools and procedures have been
developed to aid in this monitoring process (Grinnell 1988; Blythe and
Tripodi 1989).

In the approach to practice described in this chapter, evaluation is
defined as an ongoing process, built on clarity of goals and hoped-for
outcomes of the contact. It is a shared process and if clients and worker identify together the problem or situation to be the focus of attention
and share the assessment and intervention process, the evaluation will
be a natural and continuous part of the contact. In work with individuals, families, groups, and communities, the question, "how are we
doing?" should be explored frequently and initiated by either worker
or clients. This question can be directed at movement toward desired
goals or outcomes or toward the nature of the process itself. It is important for both worker and clients to reflect not only on where they are
going but also on how they are getting there. This includes attention to
the interpersonal processes between worker and clients and among all
of the participants in a multiple-client system. Any kind of work can

founder if process issues are ignored and the skill and comfort required in opening up a reflective discussion on the process and the relationship is an essential part of the foundation of practice. Some sort of record must be kept to aid the evaluation process. This may be done in a variety of ways. An eco-map can be used as an evaluative tool so that together the worker and clients can compare an eco-map drawn early in the contact with one drawn close to termination and together evaluate changes. Notes and audio and video recordings can also provide materials that aid in evaluation.

Perhaps the most important part of evaluation is self-evaluation, the professionals' ability to look at themselves, to evaluate their actions, to critique, to examine their thinking, their attitudes and biases, and to assess their strengths and areas where they need to learn.

Reflection on or evaluation of the process in their cases is a major way practitioners enhance their knowledge and perfect their skills. Schon (1983) points out, as we deal with a universe of one, unlike any other situation we have experienced, we must apply our knowledge and skill in small experiments, always evaluating the impact of our actions on the situation and taking next steps based on the findings of the experiments. This open, experiential, evaluative, reflective, and self-reflective stance characterizes the creative practitioner.

Integration Through Example

The case method of teaching and learning is as old as the profession. We can analyze and describe the knowledge, skills and values upon which our practice is based but it is only through the case situation that the complexity of the universe of one and the integration of all the elements of practice emerge.

The following case situations will be presented to demonstrate the thinking and action in social work practice. The first will offer an opportunity to reflect on the story of one elderly women and to consider her relationship with her community, her neighbors, and the social and mental health service systems.

The second is briefly presented to illustrate a generalist model of practice in which the worker follows the problem wherever it leads, "moving across the boundaries of different size systems, demonstrating what I have called an extended action system model of practice" (Hartman 1974).

The Story of Mrs. Carson

Several years ago, in a rural western state, Faye Carson, seventy-nine years old, was admitted to the state hospital many miles from her community. It was her first hospitalization and her first contact with mental health services. She had fired a shotgun through the ceiling of her home at an imaginary intruder and her physician and a local judge arranged for her commitment. The admitting psychiatrist diagnosed her as suffering from senile psychosis, paranoid type, although there was no evidence of organic deterioration. Mrs. Carson was sad, angry about her hospitalization and, except for the fixed "delusion" that she was being persecuted by a neighbor boy and his family, she was appropriate and in good contact. She made a good adjustment in the hospital, busied herself in the kitchen, and was very helpful to the other patients. However, she longed to return to her beloved home and couldn't understand why she was being punished for a neighbor boy's behavior. She asked, "Why do scientists get people to live longer if their twilight years are to be spent in a mental hospital like rusty locomotives in some terminal?"

Fortunately, Mrs. Carson captured the interest and concern of a young social worker in this severely understaffed facility and, in time, her story began to unfold.

Mrs. Carson, a widow, had lived for over thirty years in a small and modest home that had been built by hand by her husband. The home was located in a rural area outside of a mid-sized town, but over the years, as the community expanded, her home was surrounded by a typical middle-class suburban development.

Mrs. Carson, although she tried to be friendly to her new neighbors, felt somewhat alienated from the families that surrounded her. She contented herself with her passion for her gardening and needlework, her contact with old friends, and her contact at church. One day, three years before her hospitalization, the boy next door, playing ball with his friends, broke one of her prize plants. She berated the boys and they retaliated by calling her an old witch.

This began a period of harassment by the neighbor boy. He would throw the ball against her house and hide when she looked out. He climbed on her roof and threw dirt down her chimney. She made many complaints to the police but no real action was taken. Sometimes when the wind blew branches against the house, or the old building creaked, she would think it was the boys and call the authorities.

Two years before her hospitalization she fell and sustained a serious leg injury. This limited her mobility and, although friends and her minister visited when they could, she became increasingly isolated. Calls to the police escalated until finally they told her she had the right to defend her own home. In response to this, she oiled her husband's old shotgun, bought some shells, and the next time she heard a noise on the roof, she fired, awakening the neighbors and creating considerable alarm. The neighbor boy had been away at college for some time.

Mrs. Carson's history revealed a series of losses and considerable strength. She had been raised on a small farm in the east, second child but oldest girl of a large family. Her mother died in childbirth when Mrs. Carson was sixteen. She took over the household, caring for her younger siblings and then her father until his eventual death. At that time, she married Mr. Carson, a miner and old friend of her family and the couple moved west. Her only child, a son, died of measles encephalitis at the age of five. Twenty years before her hospitalization, Mr. Carson was killed in a mining accident. Mrs. Carson supported herself through domestic work and sewing and for the past ten years had received old-age-assistance.

A reflection on this story can describe and define much that is central in the foundation of social work practice. First, the case of Faye Carson dramatically illustrates the value of social work's basic perspective—a focus on the person-in-situation. We are sensitive to Mrs. Carson's growing alienation from her surroundings to hostility and rejection in the middle-class family neighborhood directed toward an aging poor woman who lived in a home described by some as a "shack." And we may ask, why didn't the parents intervene when their sons harassed Mrs. Carson? Could it be that the boys, on some level, were acting for the community, that the community wanted her gone? We must listen to Mrs. Carson's story of harassment and attend to her perception of the hostility in her environment.

Also illustrated is the growing isolation and the impact of limited mobility and a shrinking social world so common in the lives of the aging. When there was noise on the roof, there was no one with whom to check her perceptions. She had no one to ask, "Did you hear that? What do you think it was?" We also see either a lack of resources in the community or a lack of outreach and accessibility which would connect Mrs. Carson to needed resources. As she is cut off, she increasingly conforms to her neighbors' definitions.

It is clear that Mrs. Carson's hospitalization was related to the growing deterioration of her relationship with the world. Drawing an eco-map of Mrs. Carson in her life space quickly pictures the nature of the person-in-situation configuration and leads to a discussion of all the ways that a social worker could have intervened or social services could have been made available to make possible another outcome. Such reflection illustrates primary, secondary, and tertiary prevention, as well as the multiple roles that can be a part of social work and the many levels upon which a social worker may intervene.

When the conflict first started and Mrs. Carson complained to the police, mediation between Mrs. Carson and the boy and his family may well have obviated the harassment. Linkages also could have been forged between Mrs. Carson and her community. Her interests in gardening, quilting, and needlework are undoubtedly shared by others in the community and help in networking, in finding resources, and with

Figure 2.1 Genogram: Faye Carson, 6–27–94

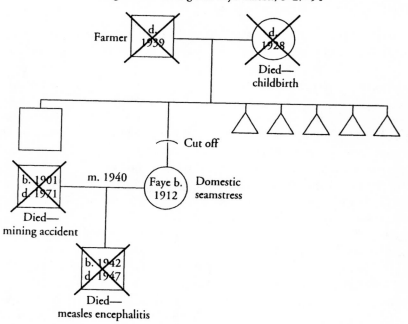

transportation and building connections would have kept her involved in a social world.

Empowerment in this case is also crucial. Mrs. Carson was evidently feeling increasingly helpless in her situation. The advice from the police—to take matters into her own hands—was empowering but inappropriate and ultimately destructive. Mrs. Carson needed an advocate who listened to her story, who understood her feelings of vulnerability, and who could find ways of helping her take constructive control of her situation.

In exploring what might have been and what should have been available to Mrs. Carson, the whole range of services that should be available to all of our Mrs. Carsons are defined and described, thus making clear the direct importance of social policy and services and illustrating how policy shapes practice and defines options. Further, the problems of access, of service delivery are made obvious. How can services be structured in a community so that the private troubles of such people may come to the attention of those who can provide the help needed?

It is also important to reflect on the assessment of Mrs. Carson that is constructed by those in authority, an assessment that both led to and was a result of her hospitalization. An important part of the foundation of social work practice is a critical deflective stance that examines assumptions, listens to the client's narrative, and recognizes that the narrative is the client's effort to make sense out of lived experience. A social worker, rather than assuming that Mrs. Carson is suffering from an intrinsic disease process, raises the possibility of other understandings of Mrs. Carson's story.

Mrs. Carson's "delusion" was an effort to make sense out of her experience. The boy's harassment became a metaphor for her experience of hostility and isolation. The story she constructed of the boy's continuing harassment was a problem-saturated story but it was preferable to the other limited number of stories that were available to her in her narrowing world: that she was a witch, that she was crazy, that she did not belong in her neighborhood, that people did not want her there. This reframing and contextualizing of Mrs. Carson's "illness" respects Mrs. Carson's experience and opens up the possibility of helping Mrs. Carson consider other less problem-saturated stories of her situation.

In the Faye Carson story, we see how knowledge, values, social welfare policy, and the structure of services are all contained in the case situation, illuminate our understanding, and shape our practice. In the hospital, over time, as Mrs. Carson developed a strong and trusting relationship with the hospital social worker, and as the worker listened to and accepted Mrs. Carson's construction of reality, Mrs. Carson began to consider other less problem-saturated stories of her experience. She began to consider other ways to make sense of her experience. She suggested that perhaps sometimes it was the wind in the trees that she heard. She began to talk about her loneliness and even speculated that if her son had lived, he might

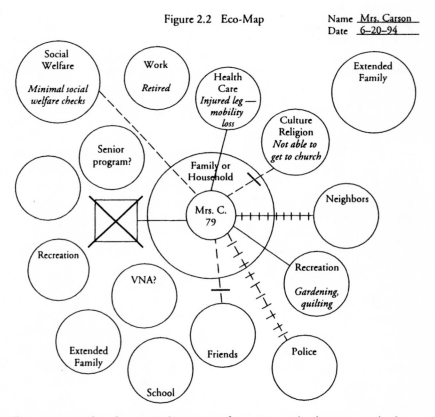

Figure 2.2 Eco-Map

Name Mrs. Carson
Date 6–20–94

Fill in connections where they exist. Indicate nature of connections with a descriptive word or by drawing different kinds of lines: ———— for strong, – – – – for tenuous, ++++++ for stressful. Draw arrows along lines to signify flow of energy, resources, etc. ➔ ➔ ➔ ➔
Identify significant people and fill in empty circles as needed.

have been as mischievous as the boy next door. In the context of a supportive relationship with a sensitive social worker who was able to listen to her story, Mrs. Carson co-constructed a new story and the diagnosis of senile psychosis with paranoia that was considered to be based on organic brain disease was no longer considered. Before long it was clear that Mrs. Carson was ready to leave the hospital and the social worker began to plan for the future with Mrs. Carson. The worker contacted Mrs. Carson's home community and, despite her advocacy efforts, it was clear that the community was closed to her and there was insufficient support available to her for her to return to her home.

In the meantime, Mrs. Carson had developed a friendship with a sister of one of the patients. This woman lived alone and shared many of Mrs. Carson's interests. She also had a garden plot where Mrs. Carson could raise her flowers. After several visits, the patient's sister asked if Mrs. Carson could come and live with her. After considerable advocacy by the worker with the hospital administration, permission was given and Mrs. Carson moved to the home of her new friend. The worker, at Mrs. Carson's request, arranged with an attorney in Mrs. Carson's home town for the sale of her property and the transfer of her personal belongings to her new home.

The social worker acted as counselor, broker, mediator, manager, and advocate in behalf of Mrs. Carson. The value of social work practice is clearly demonstrated when one considers what may well have happened to Mrs. Carson in this large, understaffed, primarily custodial institution, which confirmed her worst fears had the social worker not been there for her.

Generalist Models of Practice

The foundation of social work is defined as everything any social worker should know and be able to do. As has been discussed throughout this chapter, it should include some understanding of and ability to work with individuals, family, groups, and communities. No matter how specialized a social worker becomes, he or she should have the ability to follow the problem wherever it might lead, to move across different size systems, and intervene as appropriate. Without this general foundation knowledge, a practitioner may well be constrained to rely on one level of attention and intervention. The ability to work with different size systems and to move across boundaries, following the problem wherever it may lead, is a characteristic of social workers and may well differentiate them from the other helping professions. This extended model of practice is briefly exemplified in the following story.

A second-year social work student was placed in an outpatient mental health clinic in an impoverished neighborhood in a large urban area. Early in her placement, she was assigned a three-year-old child who was exhibiting uncontrollable hyperactivity and some slowness in development.

Subsequent tests revealed that the child was suffering from lead poisoning. In working with the family and in visiting the home it became apparent that the child was eating chips of lead paint that were available to him in this deteriorating tenement building. Although the mother had tried to control this, he had found corners, for example, in the back of a closet where he could hide himself and eat the paint.

The student worked with the family around how to prevent this. Clearly, the only long-range answer was to cover the exposed lead paint with wallboard and another heavy covering.

At the same time it became apparent that the incidence of children with lead poisoning was high in the clinic and that many old buildings in the area were dangerous to children because their walls were covered with thick layers of peeling lead paint.

The student and the family began pressuring the landlord, to no avail, for repairs. The family began to share their concerns with other families in the building and the student was asked to speak with some of the other parents.

The tenants began to meet as a group and together with the student began to strategize on how they might get the landlord to move. The student acted as adviser and fellow strategist and, finally, after several contacts with various regulatory agencies, the landlord agreed to supply materials if the tenants would provide the labor.

The tenants' group organized themselves and with the student's help identified and distributed various tasks and, over a period of months, apartment by apartment was repaired. Obviously the success and collaborative activity of the group served many social integrative functions as well as the practical function of making the building safer. The project became known as a model of self-help and the student had the opportunity to consult with health department and housing officials about the tenants' activities.

Before the end of her placement, a U.S. congressional committee was holding hearings on new legislation on the use and removal of lead paint and the student was asked to testify.

In this sample of a generalist practitioner at work, the practitioner entered the situation via one troubled child but, following the problem, she moved across different size systems and made use of a range of skills with the family, groups, the community, and even the nation in testifying and bearing witness in the creation of social policy.

The same kind of opportunities for generalist practice can be made available when social workers work in institutions, depending on how the practice is conceptualized. For example, school social work can be defined as working one by one with children in trouble, or in a very different way. The potential client system can be extended to include the whole school community—the students, teachers, parents, and the neighborhood within which the school is located. Extending the client system in this way broadens the role of the social worker to include counselor, educator, mediator, broker, and advocate, and also opens up the door to working with groups, families, the school as a community, and the larger community. It also suggests preventive intervention at both the primary and secondary levels.

Many social work positions, if broadly conceptualized, include the opportunity to practice in a variety of modes and with different size systems. The foundation of social work not only lays the groundwork for specialization but introduces social workers to the breadth of roles available to them.

REFERENCES

Amundson, J., K. Stewart, and L. Valentine. 1993. "Temptations of Power and Certainty." *Journal of Marriage and Family Therapy* 19(2):111–123.

Anderson, H. and H. A. Goolishian. 1988. "Human Systems as Linguistic Systems." *Family Process* 27(4):371–393.

——. 1992. "The Client as Expert: A Not-Knowing Approach to Therapy." In S. McNamee and K. Gergen, eds., *Therapy as Social Construction*, pp. 25–39. Newbury Park, Calif.: Sage.

Austin, L. N. 1948. "Trends in Differential Treatment in Social Casework." *Journal of Social Casework* 29 (March):203–211.

Barlow, D. H., S. C. Hayes, and R. O. Nelson. 1984. *The Scientist Practitioner: Research and Accountability in Clinical Educational Settings*. New York: Pergamon.

Bartlett, H. M. 1970. *The Common Base of Social Work Practice*. New York: National Association of Social Workers.

Bateson, G. 1979. *Mind and Nature: A Necessary Unity*. New York: Dutton.

Berman-Rossi, T. 1992. "Empowering Groups Through Understanding Stages of Group Development." *Social Work with Groups* 15(2/3):239–255.

Bloom, M. and J. Fischer. 1982. *Evaluating Practice: Guidelines for the Accountable Professional*. Englewood Cliffs, N.J.: Prentice-Hall.

Blythe, B. and T. Tripodi. 1989. *Measurement in Direct Practice*. Newbury Park, Calif.: Sage.

Borden, W. 1992. "Narrative Perspectives in Psychosocial Intervention: Following Adverse Life Events." *Social Work* 37:135–143.

Boyd-Franklin, N. 1989. *Black Families in Therapy: A Multi-Systems Approach*. New York: Guilford.

Collins, P. H. 1990. *Black Feminist Thought*. New York: Routledge.

Coyle, G. 1948. *Group Work with American Youth*. New York: Harper and Row.

Davis, L. E. and E. K. Proctor. 1989. *Race, Gender and Class: Guidelines for Practice with Individuals, Families, and Groups*. Englewood Cliffs, N.J.: Prentice-Hall.

Dean, R. G. and M. L. Rhodes. 1992. "Ethical-Clinical Tensions in Clinical Practice." *Social Work* 37:128–134.

de Shazer, S. 1985. *Keys to Solution in Brief Therapy*. New York: Norton.

Dorfman, R. A., ed. 1988. *Paradigms of Clinical Social Work*. New York: Brunner and Mazel.

Ewalt, P. L., ed. 1980. *Toward a Definition of Clinical Social Work*. Washington, D.C.: National Association of Social Workers.

Fortune, A. 1985. *Task Centered Practice with Families and Groups*. New York: Springer.

Foucault, M. 1980. In C. Gordon, ed., *Power/Knowledge: Selected Interviews and Writings, 1972–1977*. New York: Pantheon.

Gambrill, E. D. 1977. *Behavior Modification: Handbook of Assessment, Intervention, and Evaluation Methods*. San Francisco: Jossey-Bass.

Garvin, C. and B. Seabury. 1984. *Interpersonal Practice*. Englewood Cliffs, N.J.: Prentice-Hall.

Geertz, C. 1983. *Local Knowledge: Further Essays in Interpretive Anthropology*. New York: Basic Books.

Gergen, K. J. 1991. *The Saturated Self: Dilemmas of Identity in Modern Life*. New York: Basic Books.

—— and J. Kaye. 1992. "Beyond Narrative in the Negotiation of Therapeutic Meaning." In A. McNamee and K. Gergen, eds., *Therapy as Social Construction*, pp. 166–185. London: Sage.

Germain, C. B. 1978. "Space: An Ecological Variable in Social Work Practice." *Social Casework* 59:515–522.

——. 1991. *Human Behavior and the Social Environment: An Ecological View.* New York: Columbia University Press.

—— and A. Gitterman. 1980. *The Life Model of Social Work Practice.* New York: Columbia University Press.

Giovannoni, J. M. and R. M. Becerra. 1979. *Defining Child Abuse.* New York: Free Press.

Goldstein, E. G. 1984. *Ego Psychology and Social Work Practice.* New York: Free Press.

Goldstein, H. 1990. "The Knowledge Base of Social Work Practice: Theory, Wisdom, Analogue or Art." *Social Casework* 71:32–43.

Gordon, W. 1965. "Knowledge and Value: Their Distinction and Relationship in Clarifying Social Work Practice." *Social Work* 10(3):32–39.

Grinnell, R. M., ed. 1988. *Social Work Research and Evaluation.* 3d ed. Itasca, Ill.: F. E. Peacock.

Gutheil, I. A. 1992. "Considering the Physical Environment: An Essential Component of Good Practice." *Social Work* 37:391–396.

Hartman, A. 1974. "The Generic Stance in the Family Agency." *Social Casework* 55(4):199–208.

——. 1978. "Diagrammatic Assessment of Family Relationships." *Social Casework* 59:465–476.

——. 1980. "Competencies in Clinical Social Work." In P. Ewalt, ed., *Toward a Definition of Clinical Social Work*, pp. 33–41. Washington, D.C.: National Association of Social Workers.

——. 1986. "The Life and Work of Bertha Reynolds: Implications for Education and Practice Today." *Smith College Studies in Social Work* 56(2):79–94.

——. 1990. "Many Ways of Knowing." *Social Work* 35(1):3–4.

——. 1992. "In Search of Subjugated Knowledge." *Social Work* 37(6):483–484.

——. 1993. "The Professional is Political." *Social Work* 38(4):365–366, 504.

—— and J. Laird. 1983. *Family Centered Social Work Practice.* New York: Free Press.

Hasenfeld, Y. 1987. "Power in Social Work Practice." *Social Service Review* 61(3):469–483.

Heineman, M. 1981. "The Obsolete Scientific Imperative in Social Work Research." *Social Service Review* 55:371–396.

Hepworth, D. and J. A. Larsen. 1982. *Direct Social Work Practice.* Homewood, Ill.: Dorsey Press.

Hess, H. and P. Hess. 1984. "Termination in Context." In B. Compton and B. Galaway, eds., *Social Work Processes*, pp. 559–570. 3d ed. Homewood, Ill.: Dorsey Press.

Holland, T. P. and A. C. Kilpatrick. 1991. "Ethical Issues in Social Work: Toward a Grounded Theory of Professional Ethics." *Social Work* 36: 138–145.

Hollis, F. M. 1965. *Casework: A Psychosocial Therapy.* New York: Random House.

Hooks, B. 1989. *Talking Back: Thinking Feminist: Thinking Black*. Boston: South End Press.

Hudson, W. H. 1982. "Scientific Imperatives in Social Work Research and Practice." *Social Service Review* 56(2):246–258.

Imber-Black, E. 1993. *Secrets in Families and Family Therapy*. New York: Norton.

Imre, R. W. 1984. "The Nature of Knowledge." *Social Work* 29:41–45.

———. 1985. "Tacit Knowledge in Social Work Research and Practice." *Smith College Studies in Social Work* 55(2):137–149.

Kramer, R. M. and H. Specht, eds. 1983. *Readings in Community Organization Practice*. Englewood Cliffs, N.J.: Prentice-Hall.

Laird, J. 1989. "Women and Stories: Restorying Women's Self-Constructions." In M. McGoldrick, D. Anderson, and F. Walsh, eds., *Women in Families*, pp. 426–450. New York: Norton.

Lee, J., ed. 1988. "Group Work with the Poor and Oppressed." (Special Issue) *Social Work with Groups* 11(4):1–139.

Levy, C. S. 1976. *Social Work Ethics*. New York: Human Science Press.

McGoldrick, M. and R. Gerson. 1985. *Genograms in Family Assessment*. New York: Norton.

Maluccio, A. N. 1981. *Promoting Competence in Clients: A New/Old Approach to Social Work Practice*. New York: Free Press.

Meyer, C. 1993. *Assessment in Social Work Practice*. New York: Columbia University Press.

Middleman, R. and G. Goldberg. 1974. *Social Service Delivery: A Structural Approach to Social Work Practice*. New York: Columbia University Press.

Middleman, R. R. and G. G. Wood. 1980. *Skills for Direct Practice in Social Work*. New York: Columbia University Press.

National Association of Social Workers. 1977. "Conceptual Frameworks I." (Special Issue) *Social Work* 22(5).

———. 1981. "Conceptual Frameworks II." (Special Issue) *Social Work* 26(5).

———. 1990. *Code of Ethics*. Silver Spring, Md.: National Association of Social Workers.

Nelson, M. 1991. "Empowerment of Incest Survivors: Speaking Out." *Families in Society* 72(10):618–624.

Patti, R. and R. Resnick. 1972. "Changing the Agency from Within." *Social Work* 17(4):48–57.

Pinderhughes, E. 1989. *Understanding Race, Ethnicity and Power*. New York: Free Press.

Pinkston, E. M., J. L. Levitt, and G. R. Green. 1982. *Effective Social Work Practice: Advanced Techniques for Behavioral Intervention with Individuals, Families, and Institutional Staff*. San Francisco: Jossey-Bass.

Pray, J. E. 1991. "Respecting the Uniqueness of the Individual: Social Work Practice within a Reflective Model." *Social Work* 36:80–85.

Rabinow, P. and W. M. Sullivan. 1987. "Introduction," in P. Rabinow and W.

M. Sullivan, eds., *Interpretive Social Science*, pp. 1–21. Berkeley: University of California Press.

Reamer, F. G. 1991. "AIDS, Social Work and the `Duty to Protect.' " *Social Work* 36:56–60.

———. 1990. *Ethical Dilemmas in Social Service*. 2d ed. New York: Columbia University Press.

Reid, W. J. and Epstein. 1977. *Task Centered Practice*. New York: Columbia University Press.

Reisch, M. and S. Vinocur. 1986. "The Future of Community Organization in Social Work: Social Activism and the Politics of Profession Building." *Social Service Review* 60(1):70–93.

Reynolds, B. 1934. "Between Client and Community." *Smith College Studies in Social Work* 5:5–128.

Richmond, M. 1922. *What is Social Casework?* New York: Russell Sage.

Rodwell, M. 1987. "Naturalistic Inquiry: An Alternative Model for Social Work Assessment." *Social Service Review* 61:232–246.

Rose, S. D. 1980. *A Casebook in Group Therapy: A Behavioral Cognitive Approach*. Englewood Cliffs, N.J.: Prentice-Hall.

Rose, S. M. 1992. *Case Management and Social Work Practice*. White Plains, N.Y.: Longman.

Saleebey, D. 1989. "Professions in Crisis: The Estrangement of Knowing and Doing." *Social Casework* 70:556–563.

———. 1992a. "Biology's Challenge to Social Work: Embodying the Person-In-Environment Perspective." *Social Work* 37:112–119.

———, ed. 1992b. *The Strengths Perspective in Social Work Practice*. White Plains, N.Y.: Longman.

Schon, D.A. 1983. *The Reflective Practitioner: How Professionals Think in Action*. New York: Basic Books.

———. 1987. *Educating the Reflective Practitioner*. San Francisco: Jossey-Bass.

Schwartz, G. 1989. "Confidentiality Revisited." *Social Work* 34:223–226.

Scott, D. 1990. "Practice Wisdom: The Neglected Source of Practice Research." *Social Work* 35(6):564–568.

Seabury, B. A. 1971. "Arrangement of Physical Space in Social Work Settings." *Social Work* 16:43–49.

Shulman, L. 1992. *The Skills of Helping Individuals, Families, and Groups*. 3d ed. Itasca, Ill.: F. E. Peacock.

Solomon, B. 1976. *Black Empowerment: Social Work in Oppressed Communities*. New York: Columbia University Press.

Staples, L. 1984. *Roots to Power*. New York: Praeger.

———. 1990. "Powerful Ideas about Empowerment." *Administration in Social Work* 14(2):29–42.

Swigonski, M. E. 1993. "Feminist Standpoint Theory and the Questions of Social Work Research." *Affilia* 8(2):171–183.

Tobias, M. 1990. "Validator: A Key Role in Empowering the Chronically Mentally Ill." *Social Work* 35(4):357–359.

Turner, F. J. 1986. *Social Work Treatment: Interlocking Theoretical Approaches.* 3d ed. New York: Free Press.

Tyson, K. 1994. *New Foundations for Scientific Social and Behavioral Research: The Heuristic Paradigm.* Newbury Park, Calif.: Sage.

Videka-Sherman, L., and W. Reid, eds. 1990. *Advances in Clinical Social Work Research.* Silver Spring, Md: National Association of Social Workers.

Walz, T. and V. Groze. 1991. "The Mission of Social Work Revisited: An Agenda for the 1990's." *Social Work* 36(6):500–505.

Weick, A. 1983. "Issues in Overturning a Medical Model of Social Work Practice." *Social Work* 28:467–471.

——. 1986. "The Philosophical Context of a Health Model of Social Work." *Social Casework* 67:551–559.

——. 1987. "Reconceptualizing the Philosophical Perspective of Social Work." *Social Service Review* 61(2):218–230.

—— and L. Pope. 1988. "Knowing What's Best: A New Look at Self-Determination." *Social Casework* 69:10–16.

Weick, A., C. Rapp, W. P. Sullivan, and W. Kisthardt. 1989. "A Strengths Perspective in Social Work Practice." *Social Work* 34(4):350–354.

White, M. 1989. *Selected Papers.* Adelaide, Australia: Dulwich Center Publications.

—— and D. Epston. 1990. *Narrative Means to Therapeutic Ends.* New York: Norton.

Witkin, S. L. 1991. "Empirical Clinical Practice: A Critical Analysis." *Social Work* 36(2):158–163.

Wood, K. M. 1990. "Epistemological Issues in the Development of Social Work Practice Knowledge." In L. Videka-Sherman and W. J. Reid, eds., *Advances in Clinical Social Work Research*, pp. 373–390. Silver Spring, Md.: National Association of Social Workers.

Woods, M. E. and F. Hollis. 1990. *Casework: A Psychosocial Therapy.* 4th ed. New York: McGraw-Hill.

3
Social Welfare Policy

BRUCE S. JANSSON

The inclusion of social welfare policy in the literature, education, and practice of social work has been a distinguishing and unique characteristic of the profession since its inception. Social welfare policy possesses a pivotal role in social work in furthering a mission for social work that distinguishes it from other, competing professions such as psychology, counseling professions, and macro fields like business and public administration that increasingly prepare administrators in the human services. But this pivotal role of social welfare policy in shaping the direction of the profession is in considerable jeopardy for reasons that I will discuss in this chapter. Before discussing these reasons and possible antidotes, I will analyze the contributions social welfare policy can make to the profession, its evolution, widely used theoretical approaches, and important issues that confront it today.

Twin Functions of Social Welfare Policy

Social welfare policy serves two broad functions in social work. First, it provides perspectives, values, and sensitivities that enrich and shape the social work practice of direct service, administrative, and community-based social workers (which I will call adjunctive functions since they buttress the practice of social workers). Second, social welfare policy provides its own form or kind of social work practice when it provides social workers with knowledge and skills to participate in the policy-changing process in agencies, communities, and legislatures (which I will here call policy-practice functions).

Policy as An Adjunctive Discipline

Social welfare policy enhances the professional work of direct-service and indirect-service social workers in numerous ways. It provides the need for sensitivities toward oppressed populations, helps practitioners question prevailing values in the broader society, provides critical understanding of the social work profession, helps students apply materials from the social sciences to social work practice, provides knowledge about the programs and policies of the American welfare state, and reinforces ecological approaches to social work practice.

Knowledge of the Programs and Policies of the American Welfare State

Whether they are employed by government or nongovernmental agencies, or work as independent practitioners, social workers require some knowledge of major programs and policies of the American welfare state. They need to refer clients, patients, employees, and others to these programs, to know about basic structural features of programs (such as means-tested versus universal eligibility), and to know about different policy sectors such as child welfare and mental health programs. Since social workers uniquely occupy the interstices of the complex welfare state in their work, they have to possess sufficient knowledge of it so that they can intelligently work within it.

Social workers also need to be aware of the limitations of social welfare policies so they do not become mere apologists or rigid enforcers. Their clients are likely to experience frustrations in their dealings with the welfare bureaucracy due to its gaps, omissions, punitiveness, or failed strategies. Social workers need to obtain critical perspectives about the welfare apparatus and specific programs within it to anticipate likely problems that their clients will encounter so as to be advocates for them.

Oppressed Populations

Despite the recent growth of a cadre of social workers who work with white, affluent clients in private practices, most social workers help populations that are relatively stigmatized in American society, such as women, racial minorities, or those with substance abuse, mental illness,

poverty, and AIDS. Were social workers to respond to these populations with the stereotyping, racist, or prejudiced views of much of mainstream society, they would not only provide insensitive and misdirected services, but they would lose the credibility and trust of their clients.

A social welfare policy curriculum is uniquely able to provide perspectives about oppressed populations because of its societal vantage
point. Racism, prejudice, and inequality have arisen in societal contexts
and cannot be understood from individualistic or even community
perspectives. While prejudice is sometimes expressed in interpersonal
transactions, it is often embedded in the policies and operations of government and the private sector, including social welfare agencies and
institutions. The genesis of policies that are unresponsive to the needs
of oppressed populations cannot be understood without examining
political, economic, and social factors that cause and sustain them.

Critical Perspectives About Widely Held Values

As intermediaries between American social welfare institutions and
persons who often come from stigmatized populations, social workers
encounter difficult value dilemmas. Should they enforce specific rules
and policies or seek to evade, circumvent, or even disobey them?
Should they accept policies that they find to be inadequate or should
they engage in case or class advocacy? When their clients express dis-
content with specific policies, should they merely listen or actively side
with them? What positions should the profession or a specific agency
take with regard to existing policies? When should social workers
engage in civil disobedience by joining groups like ACT UP that mili-
tantly protest social policies, in this case with respect to victims of AIDS
(Campbell 1991)?

These kinds of choices, which are often encountered by social workers, cannot be made intelligently unless social workers have grappled
with their personal and professional values. What do people in need
"deserve?" To what extent should society redress inequalities? When
should society attach conditions to the receipt of social benefits, such as
requiring people to take part in training programs?

Social workers need to be able to engage in ethical reasoning about
myriad policy issues that they confront in their work, such as
euthanasia, abortion, parental notification, involuntary commitments, and confidentiality. They not only need to make ethical choic-

es in specific case-based situations, but to participate in policy making with respect to these issues, whether in agency, community, or legislative settings.

Critical Knowledge About the Social Work Profession

Like all professions, social work evolved in a broader political and economic context. It depends on social agencies, legislatures, government programs, public and private insurance, and philanthropy to provide jobs or resources for its members. Licensing and the classification of jobs for persons with social work training provide members of the profession with jobs, titles, and special access to third-party payments. Social work competes as a profession with other human-service professions for jobs in the public and nonpublic sector; both licensure and classification, not to mention policies about insurance payments, sometimes give the profession equal—or special—access to resources and jobs when compared with competing professions.

In this political and economic context, the social work profession has developed its own policy positions through such organizations as the National Association of Social Workers (NASW), the Council on Social Work Education (CSWE), numerous specialty organizations, and political-action groups like Political Action for Candidate Election (PACE). The profession has also developed its own ethical standards, embodied in the NASW *Code of Ethics*—and is constrained by myriad court rulings, legislation, and administrative regulations.

As professionals, social workers need critical knowledge of its structure and directions (Ehrenreich 1985; Richan 1988; Wenocur and Reisch 1989). They need to understand how the profession began and evolved during the twentieth century. They need to understand the *Code of Ethics* since they are bound by it professionally and can be censured or ejected if they violate it. Social workers need to view the profession as an arena where values, views about oppressed groups, and positions about the American welfare state developed. What positions do they think the profession should take in its official policy statements and through its election of leaders with respect to a range of controversial positions regarding abortion, national health insurance, civil rights, and national budget priorities? Do economic and political realities influence the profession to be too accommodationist to government agencies and policies both in earlier times and today?

Linking Social Work to the Social Sciences

Social workers need familiarity with social science research because they work with clients, employees, and patients who experience social problems like homelessness, AIDS, child abuse, and substance abuse. Because social welfare policy provides an overview of societal responses to social problems, social work is an ideal vehicle for using social science research to explore alternative policy and service-delivery strategies. When discussing mental health services, for example, social workers should examine research on the effects of deinstitutionalization on their clients, the effects of inadequate living and social-service supports for persons with mental conditions, the effects of poverty on mental illness, and the effectiveness of alternative service strategies with homeless persons (Rochefort 1989).

Broadening the Practice Perspectives of Social Workers

Social welfare policy reinforces the use of an ecological framework of social work practice. Choices available to low-income people are constrained, for example, by economic realities, the nature of training programs, job markets, eligibility criteria for entitlement and welfare programs, and available health care. Social workers who work with clients as if they did not confront these kinds of external realities would be unable to provide intelligent assistance, would fail to empower clients to cope with these realities, and would fail to be advocates for them when they were unfairly denied assistance (Wyers 1991). By focusing on these external realities, policy promotes practice that is sensitive to environmental factors and buttresses the use of policy-related activities like case-based advocacy, case-management work, and liaison or coordinating work (Weissman and Savage 1983).

Policy as a Practice Discipline

Social work literature is filled with adulatory references to the founders of the profession, such as Jane Addams, who provided examples of policy advocacy in city, county, state, and federal arenas. Many social workers are unlikely to participate in policy advocacy, however, unless they receive knowledge and skills that enable them to engage in policy interventions. To engage in policy interventions, social workers need to be familiar with decision-making processes in agencies, communities, and legislatures. They need to discuss the nature and uses of power, assertiveness, persuasion, networking, coalitions, political strategy, proposal development, budgets, troubleshooting, and policy design.

The Evolution of Social Welfare Policy

Social welfare policy has evolved by accretion as older forms, such as an emphasis on social welfare history, have remained but become supplemented by newer forms, such as various kinds of policy analysis, sectoral analysis, and policy practice. As a result, there is now an array of alternative approaches and models.

Phase 1: The Use of History as the Primary Vehicle, 1920–1970

As an outgrowth of the Progressive movement in the early twentieth century, social work was embroiled in social welfare activism from its inception. It was axiomatic to many of the founders of the discipline that its curriculum would contain social welfare policy courses, but there was also ambiguity about social welfare policy. As Wenocur and Reisch (1989) suggest, the settlement-house wing of the social work profession was not viewed kindly by the social-casework wing, epitomized by Mary Richmond, who wanted social workers to focus on casework in agencies funded by private philanthropy and federated fundraising. The supremacy of the social-casework faction, as well as the reliance of the profession on social agencies and universities that were dependent on philanthropic elites for their survival, meant that the profession retained only a mildly reformist mission, but hardly one that emphasized radical change. While social reform was decidedly secondary to social casework in the 1920s in most social work schools, it obtained additional support during the ferment of the 1930s when many social work leaders emerged as public bureaucrats of the New Deal.

Social welfare history offered a vehicle to provide a policy curriculum in a way that was acceptable to a profession strongly wedded to social casework as its organizing theme yet retaining a reformist tradition. Students could be taught about the emergence of the American welfare state, but in a manner that did not emphasize activism in contemporary society (Abbott 1938, 1940; Breckinridge 1938). Even as late as the 1960s, social welfare history was the prevailing method of teaching social welfare policy in many schools of social work. In one major school, for example, two semesters of social welfare history were required of all students in 1972, with the material reaching only the New Deal by the end of the two-course curriculum.

An innovative book by Eviline Burns (1956) suggested new directions. Instead of describing current policies and programs or focusing on their historical evolution, she analyzed a range of policy options with particular reference to social security and income maintenance, such as universal versus means-tested eligibility. She suggested that difficult policy choices must be made between competing options that each possess advantages and disadvantages. If Burns presaged the development of policy analysis in the next phase of policy development, a book by Wilensky and Lebeaux (1958), which discussed social welfare policies in the context of societal economic factors, was a harbinger of the emphasis on political economy in the 1980s and 1990s.

Phase 2: The Growing Complexity of Policy Curriculum: 1968–1980

The monopoly enjoyed by social welfare history was challenged in the late 1960s by new kinds of social policy literature for a variety of reasons. Because the explosion of federal programs during the Great Society enlarged the scope of federal policies beyond the narrower programs of the New Deal, the policy environment of social work became far more complex and involved a range of programs and policies that required attention in social work curriculum. Older historical literature had tended to idealize social work and other reform leaders who had obtained specific social reforms, such as the ending of child labor in the Progressive Era, the Social Security Act in the New Deal, or the Full Employment legislation of 1946. In the tumult of the 1960s, however, some activists and academics became radicalized and took a far dimmer view of the accomplishments of prior reformers. Piven and Cloward (1971) suggested, for example, that many of the older social welfare programs, including Aid to Families with Dependent Children (AFDC), were punitive, ill-conceived programs that reflected the interests of large agricultural and corporate interests.

A new set of people, often with training in economics and public affairs, became prominent participants in deliberations about social welfare policy, whether in government, in academe, or in think tanks like the Brookings Institution (Aaron 1981). These policymakers used quantitative information to evaluate policies, to "cost out" specific policy options, and to use census and other social indicators to gauge the seriousness of specific social problems. Their methodology quickly took hold and gave them prominence in policy deliberations, particularly as their work was subsidized by increases in government funding of policy research. Their work fostered the development of analytic treatments of social welfare policy.

The politicizing of the American welfare state in the 1960s led some theorists to suggest that political realities and interests shaped policies more potently than rational considerations. We have already noted that writers like Piven and Cloward (1971), drawing on the theory of C. Wright Mills (1959), believed that many policies resulted from the power of corporate and economic elites.

Social welfare policy curriculum became more complex and diverse in the 1970s under the combined influence of these various changes. The older tradition of social welfare history remained firmly in place in many schools, though its role became truncated in many schools to a single semester (or even less). But it was supplemented by value-based literature, several varieties of analytic literature, and literature that variously described and analyzed the American welfare state.

When discussing the value premises of social welfare policy, American educators made extensive use of the work of Richard Titmuss (1968), the English socialist, who favored redistributive functions of the welfare state. Drawing on the distinction made by Wilensky and Lebeaux (1958), Romanyshyn (1971) contrasted "residual" versus "institutional" views of the American welfare state in a text that was officially sanctioned by the Council of Social Work Education. His book provided a strongly normative case that the American welfare state should extend universal services and rights in areas of economic security, education, and health care. (Programs targeted specifically to the poor were viewed as stigmatizing.) A text by Gil (1973) was widely used in the 1970s and emphasized an analytic process to be guided by values of redistribution, social justice, and equity.

Analytic literature that placed values in a secondary position also emerged in the 1970s. In contrast to the aforementioned texts by

Romanyshyn and Gil, which were undergirded by a normative point of view, two widely used texts (Gilbert and Specht 1974; Kahn 1973) suggested that many policy options have legitimacy and that numerous considerations, including cost, administrative feasibility, and political considerations, must be considered when making choices. Nor were these authors alone in their emphasis on a rational, deliberative process when selecting policies; some theorists within and outside of social work developed analytic approaches that are akin to a research process where data are gathered in a systematic effort to identify the best policy options (Kahn 1969; Mayer and Greenwood 1980; Quade 1982). Rein (see 1970, 1983a) contributed numerous articles and edited books to social policy literature in the late 1960s and 1970s that are difficult to characterize because he wrote on a range of topics. Like Gilbert and Specht (1974), he emphasized program design options, planning, and processes of choice, as well as the uses of social science research in policy making. Following work by Kahn (1973), Kamerman and Kahn (1976) explored an array of program design issues when examining children's programs in various cities and regions.

Several works in the 1970s inaugurated an array of books that examined the structure of the American welfare state, usually by focusing on the content of policies in specific sectors, such as child and family, mental health, and health. This tradition, which began with Friedlander's text (1955), was carried forth by Schorr (1968), who combined description with analysis that represented a combination of empirical information and his own redistributionist values.

Phase 3: Elaborations on Prior Models and the Development of Policy-Practice Models in the 1980s and early 1990s

By the end of the 1970s, then, most of the subdisciplines of social policy had emerged and were further elaborated upon in the 1980s and early 1990s, either in revised editions by authors of earlier works or by new books. But several new emphases emerged in this phase that are worth noting here.

Some theorists placed greater emphasis upon political economy of social welfare policies. While it will be recalled that many theorists had previously emphasized rational deliberations, they paid scant attention to political and economic realities that often powerfully shaped the kinds of policies that were selected by legislators or other decision makers. Thus, Kamerman and Kahn (1976:6) noted that they did not "take account, except in passing, of the economic, interest group, social class, professional, and political power struggles which provide the context in which . . . programs are launched and developed" though they noted that policy analysts "must be prepared to cope" with these realities. Writing in the context of a profoundly conservative era that frustrated liberal policymakers at every turn, many writers in the 1980s and 1990s gave these political and economic factors a primary position in their work. I (Jansson 1988, 1993) emphasized political, cultural, and economic factors that led to the historical evolution of a "reluctant" American welfare state. Wenocur and Reisch (1989) discussed how economic dependencies by the social work profession on philanthropic and university elites shaped the social work profession; DiNitto and Dye (1983) and Morris (1985) emphasized political factors that conditioned policy choices in various policy sectors; Dobelstein (1980) discussed interest group and bureaucratic factors that shape welfare policy; Karger and Stoesz (1990:58), as well as Bell (1987), emphasized the influence of ideology on policy choices, including the effects of ideology on the conduct, interpretations, and recommendations of research by various think tanks that can be classified as promoting relatively conservative, centrist, liberal, or radical positions.

At the same time, many policy theorists of the early 1990s, when compared with theorists like Romanyshyn (1971) and Titmuss (1968), did not champion liberal or radical perspectives; indeed, portions of their work suggested a relativistic posture that emphasized the presentation of an array of perspectives. While Bell (1987) asserted a liberal vision of the American welfare state when attacking the premises of conservatives, her book and a book by Schorr (1986) contrast markedly with texts by DiNitto and Dye (1983) and Karger and Stoesz (1990), who are quite ambiguous in their ideological stance. While they present data to show that economic inequalities and many social problems fester, they do not present a strongly reformist position. Karger and Stoesz (1990) suggest, for example, that the traditional liberal vision is outmoded; they argue that if the proponents of social justice are to reassert their role in welfare reform, they must begin to rethink social welfare.

A major innovation of the 1980s and early 1990s was the development of books that suggested that social workers might themselves participate in the making of policies in agency, community, or legislative arenas. Several reasons may account for why social welfare theorists took so long to develop materials to help social workers develop policy-practice competencies. Social welfare policy had been widely perceived to be a conceptual, philosophical, and descriptive discipline in the decades prior to 1990. In its exhaustive discussion of social work curriculum in 1959, for example, CSWE defined professional practice as casework and group work on the direct service side and as community organization and administration on the macro side, thus relegating social welfare policy to only an adjunctive status. In a multi-volume study that was devoted to social welfare policy, Weissman (1959) devoted only one page— and at the end of the volume—to a social reform function for social welfare policy. It was widely assumed in the social agitation of the 1960s that social change fell under the purview of community organization rather than social welfare policies. Moreover, the analytic emphasis of many policy theorists in the 1970s, which downplayed the importance of politics, contributed to a disinclination to develop a practice of policy. To policy analysts, the framing of a position is the endpoint of policy work, so other skills and tasks, such as enacting or implementing a proposal, fall outside their purview. Unlike schools of public affairs that prepare students for jobs in public service, moreover, it was not obvious how most social workers, who occupy direct-service and supervising positions, can participate in policy reform. As the implementers of policy, what curriculum materials would usefully prepare them to make policy change a part of their professional practice? Since most policy literature emphasized high-level policies, such as federal legislation, policy theorists in social work could not easily develop a policy-practice methodology that was attuned to the work of most social workers.

Prompted by the sense that social workers had to try to influence policy in the conservative era of the 1980s, a number of books and articles emerged that took related, if divergent, approaches. Some concentrated on skills needed to participate in the legislative process (Mahaffey and Hanks 1982; Haynes and Mickelson 1991; Richan 1991; Tropman et al. 1981). I (Jansson 1984, 1990b) coined the term "policy practice" and suggested that it required values clarification, conceptual, interactional, political, and position-taking skills that could be used not only in legislative settings, but agencies and communities to engage in policy reforms. Tropman (1987) argued that policy practitioners should use an array of planning skills. Pierce (1984), Flynn (1992), and Resnick and

Patti (1980) emphasized policy change in agency or community settings. While not specifically a book on policy practice, Brager and Holloway (1978) discussed numerous skills and case examples of policy change within social agencies.

Some theorists suggest that policy practice might even be conceptualized as a part of direct-service practice. Since social workers are the implementers of agency (and legislative) policy, their personal orientations toward established policies, as well as their professional activities with clients and colleagues, can be viewed as expressions of policy (Schorr 1985; Wyers 1991).

Different Theoretical Models

Distinctive approaches of the leading writers in the field during the past several decades provide a means of developing a typology of policy literature and theory. I discuss historical, ethical, position-taking, program design and implementation, policy sector, and policy practice areas, while noting that theorists often possess different perspectives within each of these broad areas. As I discuss existing theory in these areas, I will ask how various theorists contribute to the adjunctive and policy-practice goals that were presented at the outset of this chapter. I will also examine some limits of theory in each of the areas to lay the groundwork for my contention, in the concluding portion, that no single model, area, or perspective should dominate social welfare policy, which should instead be conceptualized as a multifaceted, multi-branched discipline.

Social Welfare History

Theorists variously analyze the evolution of the profession, actions of professional leaders, and policies in traditional fields like child welfare (Trattner 1989); policy enactments such as seminal pieces of legislation (Axinn and Levin 1992); relationships between political, cultural, and economic factors and the content of policy (Jansson 1993); or patterns of oppression of specific groups such as women (Abramovitz 1988; Jansson 1993). They can emphasize historical periods such as the Progressive Era (Trattner 1989) or place greater emphasis on policy developments during and after the New Deal (Jansson 1993). They can present a relatively sympathetic discussion of the emergence of social programs in American society (Leiby 1978, 1983) or view the policy developments as largely representing the interests of corporate and class interests (Piven and Cloward 1983; Trattner 1983).

In light of this shift in policy study, it can be fairly asked: Is social welfare history outmoded? If the focus is placed (merely) on description of historical policies, social welfare history would seem to fulfill neither the adjunctive or policy-practice functions of social welfare policy. Nor is it likely to be viewed as relevant to social work education if it focuses excessively on developments predating the twentieth century since the bulk of the social policy enactments occurred during and after the New Deal.

While each of the widely used surveys of social welfare history approaches the subject in different ways, they nonetheless suggest that social welfare history can powerfully contribute to the adjunctive goals of social welfare policy. It can sensitize social workers to the needs of specific oppressed groups in the population when it examines the historical evolution of policy with respect to African Americans, Latinos, Native Americans, women, gays and lesbians, the physically challenged, and other groups. Considerable historical research now exists with respect to each of these groups in various historical eras where they confronted an array of obstacles to equality such as racist laws, discriminatory practices of many kinds, and punitive policies (e.g., Abramovitz 1988; D'Emilio 1983; Quinones 1990; Takaki 1989; Williams 1987). A study of history promotes the analysis of the structural causes of inequality in a nation that has systematically limited opportunities for specific populations through a combination of policies and practices that promote segregation, inferior services and job-related discrimination (Smith 1987).

Social welfare history sensitizes social workers to the need for policy practice when it discusses barriers to the enactment of social reforms and the tactics of reformers in different historical eras. Dorothea Dix, Jane Addams, and Harry Hopkins were activists, after all, and skilled tacticians in eras when federal social policies hardly existed.

Social welfare history helps social workers understand the contours of the American social welfare system since its policies have developed through the successive additions of policies and programs. An examination of policies of the New Deal, the Great Society, and the early 1970s, for example, yields understanding of the underpinnings of the contemporary policies, even though many of the original policies have been altered. Historical analyses of the evolution of policy in specific sectors, such as mental health, health care, or child welfare, provide social workers who work in those areas with critical understandings of dominant policies, key interest groups and their characteristic positions, and the division of labor between different levels of government and between the public and private sectors (see Costin 1991; Starr 1982).

Social welfare history yields useful insights and critical perspectives about the social work profession, including its distinctive mission, various factions within it, and whether it has acted in specific periods as an agent of the status quo or sought reforms in existing policies (Ehrenreich 1985; Leighninger 1987; Wenocur and Reisch 1989). Social welfare history provides exemplars or models that inform or shape the actions of contemporary social workers, such as Bertha Reynolds, who coupled direct service with radical criticisms of social policies in the 1940s and 1950s (Hart 1989).

Ethics and Values

Social workers need to be able to think in ethical terms about a range of issues, including the extent government should intercede to reduce economic and social disparities between different ethnic groups and social classes (Reamer 1990, 1993). Ethical issues associated with abortion, mandatory reporting of persons who are HIV-positive, euthanasia, use of government data, involuntary commitments, and the taking of children from their parents in cases of alleged abuse need to be discussed in foundation courses in social welfare policy since social workers confront these issues in their direct-service or administrative practice or in policy enactments.

Moroney (1981, 1991) asserts that some policy theorists have deemphasized ethical issues because of a widespread belief that policy should be scientific in its approach. Indeed, the works of economists, who have dominated the analytic approach to policy, often take value premises as given, i.e., they develop quantitative studies to evaluate policies with respect to specific cost, efficiency, and other criteria without necessarily asking whether the criteria are meritorious or sufficiently reflect a range of program outcomes that should be considered. Policy theorists need to discuss moral or value-based goals—such as the merits of reducing inequality—and *then* use research and theory to examine alternative means of reaching these value-based goals. Moreover, they need to vigorously question interpretations of research data that are simplistic or (even) morally flawed. Specific policy analysts may suggest that a program should be terminated because it fails to achieve specific outcomes, but they may fail to consider the effects of economic realities, excessive caseloads, or other factors that could suggest that the program "failure" stems from exogenous factors rather than inherent defects. Or they may fail to ask whether a program achieves other, alternative outcomes that indeed have merit.

There is a dilemma when discussing ethics in social work: to what extent should policy theorists develop relatively liberal (or radical) positions on issues or to what extent should they define alternative positions without themselves taking a position? This dilemma is illustrated in the policy literature. On the one hand, some theorists (Gil 1973; Bell 1987; Schorr 1986; Moroney 1991) insist that values favored by liberals or radicals should assume a central role in shaping the policy positions of social workers. While Gil's analysis includes the collection of data, his discussion centers on methods of developing policy options that equalize resources and rights in society. Other theorists subscribe to relativism, i.e., to the presentation of alternative policy positions while refraining from developing a specific position of their own. DiNitto and Dye (1983) and Heffernan (1992) take relatively neutral positions on many issues, often presenting both conservative and liberal alternatives. Other theorists (Atherton 1989; Gilbert 1986; Karger and Stoesz 1990) search for some middle point between contending alternatives; these theorists suggest that older, liberal positions are outmoded in contemporary society and that new positions are needed in a society that has devolved many programs to the states and when global, economic realities require government to cooperate with the private sector. While they sometimes imply that the expenditure of more resources is not a solution, however, they risk failing to note that a considerable portion of urban and social problems stem from chronic underinvestment in infrastructure, housing, and services when American society is compared with many other developed nations.

Perhaps social workers need exposure to a variety of ethical discussions in policy literature. In light of the traditional mission of the profession, as well as the extent of inequalities in the United States, they should read radical and liberal critiques, but they should also be familiar with centrist and conservative positions so that they can develop their own by comparing and contrasting alternatives.

In addition to exposure to a range of positions, social workers also need to develop their own styles or approaches to ethical reasoning so that they are not reduced to merely accepting the conclusions of other people. It is difficult for many social workers to develop their style, however, because few policy theorists have presented alternative modes of ethical reasoning, such as consequentialist approaches (which derive ethical conclusions by comparing the consequences of ethical options), deontological approaches (which derive ethical conclusions by comparing ethical options with respect to "first principles" such as not lying, not killing, and not violating confidentiality), or subjectivist approaches (which emphasize the effects of interests and culture on the development of ethical positions). Social workers can be exposed to a diversity of approaches (Jansson 1990b; Mackie 1977), to eclectic approaches that are used to shape specific positions (Rawls 1971), or to an approach that a single ethicist has developed that is extended to an array of moral issues (Reamer 1990). Whatever approach is used, social workers need to be able to engage in moral reasoning about a range of ethical topics, i.e., to develop positions, to understand that ethical issues rarely submit to single positions but to an array of solutions, and to be able to debate persons who take divergent positions.

While ethical reasoning should be integral to all disciplines in social work, it should be particularly prominent in policy literature because ethical choices are often embedded in those collective and binding rules, laws, and regulations that constitute social welfare policies in agency, community, and legislative settings. Ethical choices involve not only high-level policies, but many issues that social workers directly experience in their work (Goodin 1988; Reamer 1990, 1993).

Ethical considerations do not, of course, provide solutions to many problems since they are often supplemented (or supplanted) by political, cost, effectiveness, and administrative considerations. Nor is ethical reasoning a certain path to the selection of "right" solutions since competing values, as well as alternative modes of moral reasoning, make alternative positions on complex issues likely. A policy that makes euthanasia available on demand maximizes the rights of people to determine their destiny, for example, conflicts with the ethical principle of not killing—and can be used inequitably against low-income and older persons if safeguards are not fully established. Even ethicists who use the same approach to ethical reasoning often take divergent positions on controversial issues like euthanasia.

Position-Taking Models

Social workers need to be able to develop policy positions on specific issues that they confront in their work, whether they take the form of proposed legislation, administrative regulations, agency policies, program proposals, funding proposals, or budget recommendations. Policy theorists have developed different models of position taking that rely on different kinds of information and criteria.

Traditional Analytic Models

These models emphasize the use of quantitative data and research to locate the policy option that best addresses a problem or issue. They use a research methodology; a data-gathering stage about the causes of a problem or issue is followed by a systematic search for policy options and the selection of a preferred policy. Research is used to rank policy options with respect to specific criteria such as cost, effectiveness in addressing problems of clients, savings to society from increasing tax revenues, or some combination of criteria such as costs *and* benefits.

Traditional analytic models have the merit of exposing students to social science and research literature, structured investigation, and methods of framing positions. But analytic models risk conveying the misleading impression that policymakers are (essentially) rational. Political and bureaucratic considerations often override evaluative or rational considerations (Dunn 1983; Rein 1983b; Wolf 1981). Moreover, analytic models risk overstating the scientific characteristics of policy research since values intrude at many points, such as shaping the selection of a research paradigm that guides the research process, the selection of criteria to be used in determining the relative ratings of policy options, and the interpretation of data (Jansson 1990b; Rein 1983a, 1983b).

Composite Position-Taking Models

There has been a recent and salutary movement in social work literature toward position-taking models that combine value, quantitative, program design, and political considerations in the shaping of positions (Heffernan 1992; Jansson 1990b; Dobelstein 1990; Flynn

1992). If position taking *is* a central feature of the policy-making process, why not portray it as it really occurs, i.e., as a process where multiple analytic, political, and moral considerations shape choices? Skilled policy practitioners *vary* their position-taking approach, moreover, according to the realities that they confront. When an issue is sufficiently politicized that rational considerations have little impact, for example, policy practitioners need to emphasize political considerations, whereas they can emphasize analytic considerations in those situations where technical information can shape ultimate policy choices (Hudson 1979). The discussion of alternative styles of position taking represents a significant change from older models, such as Kahn (1969) and Gil (1973), who presented relatively fixed approaches.

Program Design and Implementation Models

Other theorists examine an array of eligibility, administrative, resource, staffing, and program options that are used to develop programs and regulations. Drawing on the work of Eviline Burns (1956), Gilbert and Specht (1974) identify a range of programmatic and policy options, such as policies that govern eligibility, the content of the services, patterns of governance, funding levels, routes or patterns of transferring funds between levels of government, and staffing. Kamerman and Kahn (1976) applied a program design approach to policy sectors when they examined the structure of programs and policies in various regions in the child-and-family sector. If Gilbert and Specht aim to familiarize readers with an array of policy options, Kettner (1990) and Hall (1988) discuss program design from a planning and evaluation perspective.

Familiarity with recurring policy options that are used to design programs and policies helps social workers to understand the features of programs that employ them, to develop the ability to critically analyze them, and to frame proposals to reform them. The work of Kamerman and Kahn (1976) provides a particularly interesting approach that links high-level policy with program design in specific localities—an approach that is particularly relevant to social workers since they work in agencies and communities where high-level policies and operating programs meet. Despite this promising lead, few policy theorists have followed in the succeeding years. Of course, social workers who design programs in local areas need to realize that bureaucratic, turf, political, and other "nonrational" factors often frustrate their work, particularly when they develop innovative projects that conflict with established procedures.

Beginning with the classic book by Pressman and Wildavsky (1974), an array of theorists have examined the implementation of existing policies. Some of them have emphasized factors that shape the work of direct service or line staff (Lipsky 1978); political and bureaucratic factors that have diverted implementers from the policy intentions of legislators (Chu and Trotter 1974; Hasenfeld 1991); factors that predict whether specific policies will be implemented (Montjoy and O'Toole 1979); technical or planning techniques that improve the implementation process (Spiegel and Hyman 1978); or intergovernmental or bureaucratic factors (Bardach 1977). The burgeoning literature on implementation is directly relevant to social workers. When coupled with policy-practice literature, implementation theories should stimulate social workers to be creative agents for change within their programs (Hasenfeld 1980). It must be acknowledged, however, that implementation processes are often complex, multiple barriers to the effective implementation of specific policies often exist, and it is often difficult to know where to initiate changes in systems with strong hierarchical patterns of control.

Policy Sectors

Many policy theorists analyze the policies of specific sectors. By sensitizing social workers to relations between the different sectors such as between health care, mental health, and child welfare sectors where a single family may need concurrent services from each of them, sectoral analysis promotes discussion of case management and an array of policy strategies for decreasing fragmentation in the human services.

Sectoral analysis contributes to other adjunctive goals of policy. Much like social welfare history, discussion of policy sectors sensitizes social workers to the problems of oppressed minorities who often receive inadequate or misdirected services as illustrated by the classic analysis by Billingsley (1974) of mistreatment of African-American children in child welfare services, as well as numerous research monographs of the Children's Defense Fund (e.g., 1990).

Sectoral analysis helps social workers develop analytic skills by drawing on social science research to analyze the effectiveness of services, since large bodies of research examine mental health, child welfare, health care, and other sectoral policies (Dobelstein 1990). For example, considerable research suggests that the failure of Medicaid, Medicare, and private health insurance providers to fund a range of preventive services has contributed to the escalating costs of health care (Callahan 1987).

Sectoral analysis provides social workers with information to enable them to participate in the shaping of policies in specific sectors. Advocates in mental health, for example, need to understand the array of interest groups that assume prominent roles in shaping policy choices around issues of involuntary commitments, such as unions, not-for-profit providers, public agencies, the American Psychiatric Association, the American Civil Liberties Union, the National Institute of Mental Health, associations of board-and-care providers, homeless shelters, private insurance companies, client advocacy groups composed of clients or former clients and their families, and specific legislative committees in state and federal governments (Mechanic 1989).

Many overviews of policies in an array of sectors have emerged in the past several decades. Theorists use somewhat different frameworks and take different ideological positions; they variously place greater emphasis on analytic (Dobelstein 1990), political (DiNitto and Dye 1983; Karger and Stoesz 1990; Morris 1985), or ideological factors (Bell 1987; Schorr 1986; Moroney 1991). Because these theorists seek to cover an array of sectors in a single volume, however, they necessarily devote most of their discussion to description of many policies.

Political Economy of Policy

Radical theorists, such as Galper (1975) and Piven and Cloward (1971), suggest that political considerations often dominate policy making, whether corporate interests, interest groups, class interests, or powerful individuals. In the introduction to her history of women, Abramovitz (1988) provides an interesting discussion of the confluence of class, gender-based prejudice, and corporate influence in shaping policy toward women. Some political scientists implicate a milder process of politics when they analyze the role of myriad interest groups and public opinion in the shaping of policies (Dahl 1989; Lindblom 1968).

Various theorists outside of social work examine the political economy of policies. Some theorists examine the way conservatives have shaped the political agenda during the past three decades to place social reformers on the defensive and to incite white, ethnic voters against the Democratic Party (Edsall and Edsall, 1991). Reich (1991) and Barlett and Steele (1992) discuss economic and social factors that are related to the global economy that have exacerbated economic inequality in American society during the 1980s and 1990s. Writings on the political economy of contemporary policies represent a vital part of social welfare policy because they discuss those contextual factors that must be considered by policy advocates when they engage in social reform projects.

Comparative Policies

An extensive literature on comparative social welfare policies provides insights into those factors that prompt Americans to take divergent approaches to a range of social welfare issues (e.g., Flora and Heidenheimer 1981; Friedmann, Gilbert, and Sherer 1987; Kahn and Kamerman 1975; Pinker 1979; Rimlinger 1971).

Comparative studies serve a number of useful functions. By contrasting American policies with policies of other nations, they point to innovations that should be considered in the United States. While quantitative comparisons must be treated with caution because many societal factors intrude, cross-national comparisons of health care, economic, and other measures of well-being yield information that can be used to promote changes in American policies. By comparing political, cultural, and economic factors that shape policy choices in different nations, comparative studies clarify distinctive attributes of the political economy of American social welfare policies (Katznelson 1985). Comparative studies also sensitize social workers to their international responsibilities in a world where inequalities between Third World and industrialized nations are extraordinary.

Policy Practice

I noted at the outset of this chapter that social welfare policy serves many adjunctive goals in the social work curriculum, but that it can also be viewed as a practice discipline in its own right, much like direct-service practice or macro practice. Professional and ethical rationales exist for developing a policy-as-practice. The profession has a vested interest in developing policy competencies among its members since its jobs, its definitions of "the good society," and its preferred strategies for helping its clients are shaped in decision-making arenas in agency, community, and legislative settings. If social workers adhere to moral values, such as social justice, they cannot expect them to be reflected in official policy unless they participate in political arenas. Policy-practice models also have the promise of making policy seem more relevant to social workers since they make policy an integral part of professional practice.

Policy Formulation Models

Many theorists inside and outside of social work have discussed "phases" or "stages" or "steps" of the policy formulation process (e.g., Prigmore and Atherton 1979; Morris 1985; Chambers 1986; Jansson, 1984, 1990b) that typically include the defining of problems, proposal making, political enactments, implementation, and assessment. A policy formulation model discusses characteristic questions, data gathering, and processes that occur during each of these stages.

Policy formulation models usefully introduce students to policy processes, but they often fail to discuss how specific social workers, in specific situations, can actively participate in the shaping of policies by making effective presentations, establishing coalitions, developing and using power resources, and developing positions. By disaggregating the policy formulation process in a way that allows description and analysis of the activities of policy participants within it, however, policy formulation models can be viewed as transitions to policy-practice models.

Like other models, policy formulation models have their limits. As even cursory examination of the legislative process suggests, for example, decision makers often do not progress from one phase to another in an orderly way; they may backtrack, skip ahead, delete entire phases, and or engage in several phases simultaneously.

Policy Practice Models that Build on Policy Formulation

As a vehicle for making policy more relevant to students, I (Jansson 1984) used the terminology "policy practice," "policy roles," and "policy skills" to connote actions of participants. I defined a policy-practice role for each of the phases to make them less abstract; thus, policy practitioners are engaged in a "change agent role" when they participate in the political or legitimation phase. I argued, as well, that policy practitioners used specific skills when they filled the various roles, such as value clar-ification, political, conceptual, and interactional skills. I developed a nomenclature, then, that was conducive to describing policy activities of participants in policy formulation. In two succeeding books (1990b, 1994), I greatly expanded discussion of these policy-practice skills.

Argumentation or Policy Persuasion

Many theorists in psychology and communications have analyzed processes of argumentation, debate, and persuasion (e.g., Simons 1986). While the shaping of a formal position by recourse to research is important, social workers must also be able to defend their positions in the give-and-take of debates and to persuade other persons that a specific position is meritorious in the first instance.

Richan (1972) discussed the need for social workers to obtain skills in argumentation and debate; he argued that social workers need to be trained in these skills, much like attorneys. In a succeeding book (1991), he likened policy positions to "briefs," discussed the substantive content of such briefs, and then analyzed how these briefs can be present-ed to decision makers. Richan's lead has not been followed extensively in other policy literature, even though policy advocates cannot be effec-tive if they are not skilled in communication, interpersonally, when tes-tifying before legislative committees, and when making presentations to larger groups.

Political Models

A range of theorists analyze techniques of lobbying, coalition building, and testifying in legislative settings (Dear and Patti 1987; Haynes and Mickelson 1991; Mahaffey and Hanks 1982; Richan 1991). Social work-ers need to be grounded in legislative policy making since it is rela-tively complex and requires specialized knowledge. Social workers also need to learn to use the mass media to sensitize the public to spe-cific social issues and to mobilize support for legislation.

Policy literature often implies that social workers engage in legisla-tive advocacy in freestanding projects, but policy advocacy is increas-ingly conducted by myriad advocacy groups that have emerged in the last three decades around specific social problems (such as AIDS and homelessness), populations (such as children and the elderly), or specific neighborhoods. (These groups exist on the local, state, and national levels.) Policy theorists need to discuss these advocacy groups in more detail—and provide social workers with tools for linking their concerns to the ongoing work of these groups, which often have relatively sophisticated legislative and lobbying programs. Social workers can also work through the lobbying activities of NASW, as well as other professional groups. Social workers also need literature that helps them participate in political campaigns at all levels of government, whether as individuals or in liaison with NASW's political action committee (PACE) so that they can obtain the political power that groups like the National Education Association have obtained by mobilizing their members for those candidates who are relatively liberal.

Social workers need to realize, of course, that political interventions are time-consuming and do not necessarily yield immediate results because most important issues are heavily contested by an array of interests, including conservatives. Social workers must often be willing to engage in compromises since politicians often insist upon changes in legislation during the give-and-take of the political process (Dear and Patti 1987). At the same time, however, they risk their integrity if they are too willing to accommodate the policy preferences of opposing interests.

A number of theorists conjecture that social workers have been relatively remiss in participating in advocacy because of the belief that the development and use of power is unethical (Hasenfeld 1987; Jansson 1990b:436–437). Or they may be excessively fatalistic, i.e., believe that they cannot influence political outcomes in any event (Amidei 1982). While also noting ethical misuses of power, social welfare policy provides a useful place to discuss the positive uses of power to secure policies that serve the interests of clients and the profession.

Models That Focus on Direct Service Staff

Wyers (1991) raises the interesting question: can (or will) policy practice that involves legislative advocacy be performed by direct-service social work staff? Can a generic framework, that discusses policy-changing skills and tasks, prepare students *both* to engage in agency-based and legislative advocacy—or are separate models of curriculum required?

There are arguments on both sides of this issue. Amidei (1992) suggests that efforts to limit policy practice to agency settings will bring a self-fulfilling prophecy, i.e., make social workers disinclined to seek broader social change in the society. Moreover, the use of power, the development of coalitions, and the use of analytic skills apply to social-change projects in any setting, so discussion of power in a legislative setting can easily be enlarged to include power relationships within agencies. Yet it is doubtless true that many direct-service social workers will not engage in legislative advocacy. And change projects within agencies *are* different in many respects than change projects in legislative settings since they do not generally use the mass media or lobbying. Indeed, social workers in agency settings have to think about implications for their careers if they engage in extensive criticisms of existing policies, unlike lobbyists and advocates who do not face these kinds of reprisals (Bok 1981).

Flynn (1992) and Pierce (1984) concentrate on policy making in or from community or agency sites. Flynn suggests that existing policy literature concentrates excessively on national policy rather than at the community or agency level where most social workers are employed. His discussion seems to provide support, however, for the assertion that certain skills, such as policy analysis and the mobilizing of power, do not significantly vary as one moves, say, from policy making at the community level to policy making at the legislative level since he discusses many of the same skills as Richan (1991) and others who discuss legislative strategies.

In a more controversial approach, Pierce (1984) argues that social workers are themselves policy. Workers, he says, possess personal policies that determine which clients they see and how they interact with them. He emphasizes informal networks in agencies that importantly influence whether and how direct-service workers implement specific policies. Pierce is correct in asserting that personal preferences of staff, as well as informal networks, influence whether they implement specific policies. In similar fashion, Schorr (1985) suggests that professional practice "may be an expression of policy" since it reflects higher-level policies.

Comments by Pierce and Schorr suggest linkages between direct-service and policy-practice components of social work practice. The practice models that social workers employ, such as psychosocial ones, have or imply policies within them. Social workers who were guided by the older psychotherapeutic models, for example, were trained *not* to engage in outreach or advocacy since their approach emphasized office-based services; were such persons employed in a community mental health center, they would likely ignore policies that emphasized these activities or would implement them with indifference. In this perspective, social workers themselves, not defective policies, may sometimes sabotage meritorious policies, so they should be exposed to literature and theory that enable them to examine the intersection of policy and practice in specific settings.

Conversely, social workers often find their work to be frustrated by defective policies and by organizational factors. Social workers may want to engage in outreach, for example, or to provide preventive services, but find that existing procedures, work loads, union rules, or the culture of their colleagues intervene. Policy theorists should devote more effort to analyzing techniques for changing organizational mission, specific policies, or organizational factors that sabotage the implementation of meritorious policies.

Discussion of personal orientations of staff should not imply, of course, that policy practice can or should limit itself to this narrow sphere. It is important to understand what factors sabotage or shape the implementation of policies, but personal orientations of staff are often not as important as shortage of resources, poor leadership, and fragmentation among providers.

Challenges Confronting Theorists

During the 1940s and 1950s, the profession was close enough to its origins and to the Great Depression that the traditions of the settlement wing of the profession gave social welfare policy a visible role as illustrated by the fact that most schools required several semesters of policy courses. The role of policy in social work lessened during the 1970s and 1980s, however, when many schools reduced their policy courses in their foundation content to a single course. This marginalizing of policy in academic settings occurred, paradoxically, when policy has become more integral to NASW, which vastly increased its lobbying and public policy activities during the past two decades (Alexander 1992). And it has occurred when major social problems, such as homelessness, AIDS, and economic inequality, have emerged or become more serious.

When seeking to retain (or regain) a significant role in social work, social policy theorists confront several barriers. Their discipline lacks the coherence of practice, behavior, and research, so they need to develop a method of structuring and explaining it to a range of practitioners and academicians. It is difficult to craft an overview of theory and research because the discipline lacks an internal logic like practice, behavior, or research. Theory in behavior uses, for example, a life cycle perspective that examines human development from birth to death. Or it employs a systems perspective to examine societal, community, group, familial, and personal factors that shape human behavior. Practice theory can be characterized by phases of the helping process, by alternative schools, such as Freudian, psychosocial, behavioral, and cognitive, or by practice methodologies that are used with individuals, groups, and communities. Discussion of research can be organized around various research tasks such as design, sampling, and data analysis. No comparable methods exist for discussing or classifying the base of knowledge in social welfare policy, which includes historical, analytic, political, policy-practice, program design, and sectoral materials.

Connections or the relevance of social welfare policy to the direct-service (or indirect-service) functions of the profession are not clearly articulated in existing literature. Many social workers view social welfare policy as a relatively abstract set of materials or as providing lists of programs, events, and dates rather than shaping the course of professional work in important ways.

New Directions

Social welfare policy theorists need to explicate new directions in their field to make it relevant to the profession in approaching decades. I suggest five innovations.

First, social welfare policy theorists need to conceptualize their discipline as a set of subdisciplines that are linked to overarching goals or perspectives. These subdisciplines should include six areas: social welfare history, political economy and policy practice, position taking, program design and implementation, ethics, and comparative policies. Social welfare history uniquely allows social workers to examine their profession, the causes of oppression, alternative sets of values, and the structure of the American welfare state. Political economy focuses on the context of policy in contemporary society and provides information that is useful to policy practice, which endeavors to help social workers obtain skills to change existing policies. Position taking that draws on analytic, political, and value-based perspectives allows social workers to develop and defend positions to reform existing policies. Program design and implementation allows social workers to understand how formal policies are (or are not) translated into operating programs and how these operating programs can be changed to reflect specific policies or values. While ethical choices are often made by individual practitioners (such as decisions by social workers in their clinical work to protect confidentiality of information), they are often codified in legislation, court rulings, codes of ethics and administrative regulations that require them, for example, to protect confidentiality of information *or* to breach confidentiality in cases of suspected child abuse. Comparative studies provide stimulus for policy innovations at home and to underscore responsibilities of the profession to Third World nations.

Were social welfare policy to articulate these six subdisciplines, its theorists could present a more coherent portrait of their discipline to other social workers. Social welfare history is useful to understanding the political economy of American policies and to clarifying value choices. Position taking is needed by those social workers who engage in policy practice. Ethical reasoning often prompts social workers to engage in policy practice since it identifies policies that are ethically flawed. Program design and implementation allows social workers to improve operating programs so that they are more consonant with their values.

Second, the six subdisciplines of policy need to be linked to overarching adjunctive and policy-practice goals that were presented at the outset of this chapter. Rather than constituting (merely) a compendium of dates and events, for example, social welfare history can shed light on patterns of oppression in American society, help social workers examine and shape their values, understand the profession, and sensitize social workers to environmental and policy realities that intrude upon their clients. Position taking, ethics, program design and implementation, and policy practice can similarly be explicitly linked to these various adjunctive and policy-practice goals.

Third, we suggest that theorists in each of the six subdisciplines use nomenclature, such as skills, tasks, styles, and sensitivities, to make clear that policy involves practice competencies like direct service, administration, and community organization. Even social welfare history can be used to inform *skills* of value clarification, *sensitivities* to oppressed populations, and *skills* in policy practice (e.g., by examining reform activities of social reformers in prior eras). Policy practice should receive, moreover, greater attention in social policy writing, theory building, and curriculum. This subdiscipline provides the most concrete method of making social welfare policy part of professional practice in more than a rhetorical way. It allows concepts of practice competencies, practice interventions, styles of practice, and policy skills to become fully incorporated into the discipline of social welfare policy.

Fourth, social welfare policy theorists need to develop a sense of "partnerships" with other disciplines in social work, including practice, behavior, research, and other macro disciplines. They need to examine the ways direct service is shaped by policies and how direct-service practitioners can, in turn, influence policies. The effects of policies on behaviors of clients, as well as theories of human behavior that are embedded in policies, need to be examined. Researchers who examine the implementation of policies need to use concepts drawn from organizational theory. To establish linkages with community organization, policy theorists who examine policy practice need to discuss in more detail how social workers collaborate with existing advocacy organizations and coalitions.

When thinking of partnerships, social welfare policy theorists should envision their discipline as lying at the center of a wheel that is connected to outlying and related disciplines of social work in research, curriculum, and theory. Policy theorists can raise the visibility of their field and make it more relevant to a range of professional concerns by forging these partnerships.

Finally, social welfare policy theorists need to enlarge their scope in a world with a global economy. Comparative studies in social welfare policy have the potential of informing domestic policies—or at least indicating that alternative strategies should be considered (Flora and Heidenheimer 1981; Friedmann, Gilbert, and Sherer 1987; Kahn and Kamerman 1975; Pinker 1979; Rimlinger 1971). American social workers need to be concerned about nations in the Third World. Issues of international trade need to be analyzed by social workers, since an erosion of the job base in the United States and the deterioration of wages have deprived millions of Americans of resources, work, and fringe benefits (Barlett and Steele 1992).

Social Welfare Policy and the Mission of Social Work

There is a broader rationale for social welfare policy in social work, one that is admittedly value-based and that draws on distant traditions of the Progressive Era settlement-house movement. Social work will be at a crossroads in coming decades as its leaders and theorists decide whether to emulate other counseling professions or to retain an ecological framework, service to oppressed groups (including the poor), and social reform. Social welfare policy emphasizes this traditional mission. Many counseling professions have incorporated ecological frameworks into their theory, but social work uniquely possesses a body of knowledge that gives primacy to the environment rather than discussing it as an afterthought. Policy theorists concentrate on policy, economic, social, and institutional factors that are social stressors, limit access to services, deprive people of basic needs, and discriminate against certain populations. Minus social welfare policy, social work would likely continue to subscribe to ecological frameworks, but they could emphasize a narrower range of environmental factors such as family networks. Social workers who believe that they can confine themselves to fixing people and returning them to harmful environments, or who believe that they can conduct their work in isolation from a range of societal and policy constraints, place artificial boundaries on their work.

Social problems are not randomly distributed in the broader population; African Americans, women, gays and lesbians, Latinos, Native Americans, the physically challenged, the elderly, children, and poor people (among others) confront formidable obstacles, stressors, and deprivations. Absent social welfare policy, social work would likely emphasize these groups, as emerging literature on multicultural diversity suggests, but the profession would be more likely to limit its interest to consideration of cultural factors that impinge on the work of direct-practice staff. While these cultural factors are important, they do not provide directions for far-reaching societal and institutional reforms that can fundamentally equalize conditions and opportunities for oppressed populations.

And social policy can further the reformist traditions of the profession by giving practitioners skills in policy practice. Without social welfare policy, a reformist tradition would remain, but it could be limited to rhetorical pleas to continue the traditions of Jane Addams rather than efforts to place practitioners at the cutting edge of political and policy change.

The role of social welfare policy in social work ultimately depends on value preferences of the profession, i.e., whether its members, leaders, theorists, and researchers prize social reform, ecological frameworks, and service to oppressed populations. Value preferences need to be rediscovered and reaffirmed as new cadres of leadership replace older leaders at successive points in the history of the profession. The profession will be at a critical juncture during the next two decades when new leaders come forward who have had no personal experience with reform periods such as the New Deal and the Great Society—and when preoccupation with obtaining insurance and vendor payments in private practice could divert many practitioners to practice with relatively affluent clients. When we celebrate the centennial anniversary of the birth of the social work profession early in the twenty-first century, we must enliven and reprioritize social welfare policy if we want a profession that Jane Addams would recognize and value, yet that is also relevant to the political economy of contemporary society.

REFERENCES

Aaron, Henry. 1981. *Politics and Professors*. Washington, D.C.: Brookings Institution.

Abbott, Edith. 1940. *Public Assistance*. Chicago: University of Chicago Press.

Abbott, Grace. 1938. *The Child and the State*. Volumes 1 and 2. Chicago: University of Chicago Press.

Abramovitz, Mimi. 1988. *Regulating the Lives of Women: Social Welfare from Colonial Times to the Present*. Boston: South End Press.

Alexander, Chauncey. 1992. Personal communication.

Allison, Graham. 1971. *Essence of Decision*. Boston: Little, Brown.

Amidei, Nancy. 1982. "How to Be An Advocate in Hard Times," *Public Welfare* 40 (Summer):37–42.

———. 1992. Personal communication.

Atherton, Charles. 1989. "The Welfare State: Still on Solid Ground." *Social Service Review* 63:167–179.

Axinn, June and Herman Levin. 1992. *Social Welfare: A History of the American Response to Need*. New York: Longman.

Bardach, Eugene. 1977. *The Implementation Game*. Cambridge, Mass.: Massachusetts Institute of Technology Press.

Barlett, Donald and James Steele. 1992. *America: What Went Wrong?* Kansas City: Andrews and McMeel.

Bell, Winifred. 1987. *Contemporary Social Welfare*. New York: Macmillan.

Billingsley, Andrew. 1974. *Black Families and the Struggle for Survival*. New York: Friendship Press.

Bok, Sissela. "Blowing the Whistle." 1981. In Joel Fleischman, Lance Liebman, and John Hanks, eds., *Public Duties: The Moral Obligations of Government Officials*, pp. 204–220. Cambridge, Mass.: Harvard University Press.

Brager, George and Stephen Holloway. 1978. *Changing Human Service Organizations: Politics and Practice*. New York: Free Press.

Breckinridge, Sophinisba. 1938. *Public Welfare Administration in the United States*. Chicago: University of Chicago Press.

Burns, Eviline. 1956. *Social Security and Public Policy*. New York: McGraw-Hill.

Callahan, Daniel. 1987. *Setting Limits: Medical Goals in an Aging Society*. New York: Simon and Schuster.

Campbell, Courtney. 1991. "Ethics and Militant AIDS Activism." In Frederic G. Reamer, ed., *AIDS and Ethics*, pp. 155–187. New York: Columbia University Press.

Chambers, Donald. 1986. *Social Policy and Social Programs: A Method for the Practical Public Policy Analyst*. New York: Macmillan.

Children's Defense Fund. 1990. *Children, 1990: A Report Card, Briefing Book, and Action Primer*. Washington, D.C.: Children's Defense Fund.

Chu, Franklin and Sharland Trotter. 1974. *The Madness Establishment*. New York: Grossman.

Costin, Lela. 1991. *Child Welfare: Policies and Practice*. New York: Longman.

Dahl, Robert. 1989. *Democracy and its Critics*. New Haven: Yale University Press.

Dear, Ron and Rino Patti. 1987. "Legislative Advocacy." In *Encyclopedia of Social Work*, volume 2, pp. 34–42. Silver Spring, Md.: National Association of Social Workers.

D'Emilio, John. 1983. *Sexual Politics, Sexual Communities*. Chicago: University of Chicago Press.

DiNitto, Diana and Thomas Dye. 1983. *Social Welfare: Politics and Public Policy*. Englewood Cliffs, N.J.: Prentice-Hall.

Dobelstein, Andrew. 1980. *Politics, Economics, and Public Welfare*. Englewood Cliffs, N.J.: Prentice-Hall.

——. 1990. *Social Welfare: Policy and Analysis*. Englewood Cliffs, N.J.: Prentice-Hall.

Dunn, William. 1983. *Values, Ethics, and the Practice of Policy Analysis*. Lexington, Mass.: Lexington Books.

Edsall, Thomas and Mary Edsall. 1991. *Chain Reaction: The Impact of Race, Rights, and Taxes on American Politics*. New York: W. W. Norton.

Ehrenreich, John. 1985. *The Altruistic Imagination*. Ithaca: Cornell University Press.

Flora, Peter and Arnold Heidenheimer, eds. 1981. *Development of Welfare States in Europe and America*. New Brunswick, N.J.: Transaction Books.

Flynn, John. 1992. *Social Agency Policy: Analysis and Presentation for Community Practice*. Chicago: Nelson-Hall.

Friedlander, Walter. 1955. *Introduction to Social Welfare*. New York: Prentice-Hall

Friedmann, Robert, Neil Gilbert, and Moshe Sherer. 1987. *Modern Welfare States: A Comparative View of Trends and Prospect*. New York: New York University Press.

Galper, Jeffrey. 1975. *The Politics of Social Services*. Englewood Cliffs, N.J.: Prentice-Hall.

Gil, David. 1973. *Unravelling Social Policy: Theory, Analysis, and Political Action Towards Social Equality*. Cambridge, Mass.: Schenkman Books.

——. 1990. *Unravelling Social Policy: Theory, Analysis, and Political Action Towards Social Equality*. 4th ed. Rochester, Vt.: Schenkman Books.

Gilbert, Neil. 1986. "The Welfare State Adrift," *Social Work* 31:251–256.

—— and Harry Specht. 1974. *Dimensions of Social Welfare Policy*. Englewood Cliffs, N.J.: Prentice-Hall.

Goodin, Robert. 1988. *Reasons for Welfare: the Political Theory of the Welfare State*. Princeton: Princeton University Press.

Hall, Mary. 1988. *Getting Funded: A Complete Guide to Proposal Writing*. Portland, Ore.: Continuing Education Publications of Portland State University.

Hart, Aileen. 1989. "Teaching Policy to the Clinical Master's Student: An Historical Approach." *Journal of Teaching in Social Work* 3:35–45.

Hasenfeld, Yeheskel. 1980. "The Implementation of Change in Human Service Organizations." *Social Service Review* 54:508–520.

——. 1987. "Power in Social Work Practice." *Social Service Review* 6:475–482.

——. 1991. "Implementation of Social Policy Revisited." *Administration and Society* 22:451–479.

Haynes, Karen and James Mickelson. 1991. *Affecting Change: Social Workers in the Political Arena*. New York: Longman.

Heffernan, W. Joseph. 1979. *Introduction to Social Welfare Policy: Power, Scarcity, and Common Human Needs*. Itasca, Ill.: F. E. Peacock.

——. 1992. *Social Welfare Policy: a Research and Action Strategy*. New York: Longman.

Hudson, Barclay. 1979. "Comparison of Current Planning Theories: Counterparts and Contradictions," *Journal of the American Institute of Planners* 45:387–398.

Jansson, Bruce. 1984. *Theory and Practice of Social Welfare Policy: Analysis, Processes, and Current Issues*. Belmont, Calif.: Wadsworth.

——. 1988. *The Reluctant Welfare State: A History of American Social Welfare Policies from Colonial Times to the Present*. Belmont, Calif.: Wadsworth.

——. 1990a. "Blending Social Change and Technology in Macro Practice:

Developing Structural Dialogue in Technical Deliberations." *Administration in Social Work* 14:13–28.

———. 1990b. *Social Welfare Policy: From Theory to Practice*. Belmont, Calif.: Wadsworth.

———. 1993. *The Reluctant Welfare State: A History of American Social Welfare Policies from Colonial Times to the Present*. Pacific Grove, Calif.: Brooks/Cole.

———. 1994. *Social Policy: From Theory to Policy Practice*. Pacific Grove, Calif.: Brooks/Cole.

Kahn, Alfred. 1969. *Theory and Practice of Social Planning*. New York: Russell Sage.

———. 1973. *Social Policy and Social Services*. New York: Random House.

——— and Sheila Kamerman. 1975. *Not for the Poor Alone: European Social Services*. Philadelphia: Temple University Press.

Kamerman, Sheila and Alfred Kahn. 1976. *Social Services in the United States: Policies and Programs*. Philadelphia: Temple University Press.

Karger, Howard and David Stoesz. 1990. *American Social Welfare Policy: A Structural Approach*. New York: Longman.

Katz, Michael. 1986. *In the Shadow of the Poorhouse*. New York: Basic Books.

Katznelson, Ira. 1985. "Working-Class Formation and the State: Nineteenth-Century England in American Perspective." In Peter Evans, Dietrich Rueschemeyer, and Theda Skocpol, eds. *Bringing the State Back In*, pp. 56–72. Cambridge: Cambridge University Press.

Kettner, Peter. 1990. *Designing and Managing Program: An Effectiveness-Based Approach*. Newbury Park, Calif.: Sage.

Leiby, James. 1978. *A History of Social Welfare and Social Work in the United States*. New York: Columbia University Press.

———. 1983. "Social Control in Historical Explanation." In Walter Trattner, ed., *Social Welfare or Social Control?*, pp. 90–113. Knoxville: University of Tennessee Press.

Leighninger, Leslie. 1987. *Social Work: Search for Identity*. New York: Greenwood Press.

Levitan, Sar. 1985. *Programs in Aid of the Poor*. Baltimore: Johns Hopkins University Press.

Lindblom, Charles. 1968. *The Policy Making Process*. Englewood Cliffs, N.J.: Prentice-Hall.

Lipsky, Michael. 1978. "Standing Implementation on Its Head." In Walter Burnham and Martha Wagner, eds., *American Politics and Public Policy*, pp. 391–402. Cambridge, Mass.: Massachusetts Institute of Technology Press.

Mackie, J. L. 1977. *Ethics: Inventing Right and Wrong*. London: Penguin.

Mahaffey, Maryann and John Hanks. 1982. *Practical Politics: Social Work and Political Response*. Silver Spring, Md.: National Association of Social Workers.

Mayer, Robert R. and Ernest Greenwood. 1980. *The Design of Social Policy Research*. Englewood Cliffs, N.J.: Prentice-Hall.

Mechanic, David. 1989. *Mental Health and Social Policy*. Englewood Cliffs, N.J.: Prentice-Hall.

Mills, C. Wright. 1959. *The Power Elite*. New York: Oxford University Press.

Montjoy, Robert and Laurence O'Toole. 1979. "The Implementation of Change in Human Service Organizations." *Public Administration Review* 39:465–477.

Moroney, Robert. 1981. "Policy Analysis Within a Value Theoretical Framework." In Ron Haskins and James Gallagher, eds., *Models for Analysis of Social Policy: An Introduction*, pp. 78–102. Norwood, N.J.: Ablex Press.

——. 1991. *Social Policy and Social Work: Critical Essays on the Welfare State*. New York: Aldine De Gruyter.

Morris, Robert. 1985. *Social Policy of the American Welfare State: An Introduction to Policy Analysis*. New York: Longman.

Nathan, Richard. 1988. *Social Science in Government*. New York: Basic Books.

Pierce, Dean. 1984. *Policy for the Social Work Practitioner*. New York: Longman.

Pinker, Robert. 1979. *The Idea of Welfare*. London: Heinemann Educational Press.

Piven, Frances Fox and Richard Cloward. 1971. *Regulating the Poor: The Functions of Public Welfare*. New York: Pantheon.

——. 1983. "Humanitarianism in History: A Response to Critics." In Walter Trattner, ed., *Social Welfare or Social Control?*, pp. 114–148. Knoxville: University of Tennessee Press.

Pressman, Jeffrey and Aaron Wildavsky. 1974. *Implementation*. Berkeley: University of California Press.

Prigmore, Charles and Charles Atherton. 1979. *Social Welfare Policy: Analysis and Formulation*. Lexington, Mass.: D. C. Heath.

Quade, Edward. 1982. *Analysis for Public Decisions*. New York: Elsevier North Holland.

Quinones, Juan Gomez. 1990. *Chicano Politics*. Albuquerque: University of New Mexico Press.

Rawls, John. 1971. *A Theory of Justice*. Cambridge, Mass.: Harvard University Press.

Reamer, Frederic. 1990. *Ethical Dilemmas in Social Service, 2d ed.* New York: Columbia University Press.

——. 1993. *The Philosophical Foundations of Social Work*. New York: Columbia University Press.

Reich, Robert. 1991. *The Work of Nations: Preparing Ourselves for the Twenty-First Century Capitalism*. New York: Knopf.

Rein, Martin. 1970. *Social Policy: Issues of Choice and Change*. New York: Random House.

——. 1983a. *From Policy to Practice*. Armonk, N.Y.: M. E. Sharpe.

——. 1983b. "Value-Critical Policy Analysis." In Daniel Callahan and Bruce Jennings, eds., *Ethics, the Social Sciences, and Policy Analysis*. New York: Plenum Press.

Resnick, Herman and Rino Patti. 1980. *Change from Within: Humanizing Social Welfare Organizations*. Philadelphia: Temple University Press.

Richan, Willard. 1972. "A Common Language for Social Work." *Social Work* 17:14–22.

——. 1988. *Beyond Altruism: Social Welfare Policy in American Society*. New York: Haworth Press.

——. 1991. *Lobbying for Social Change*. New York: Haworth Press.

Rimlinger, Gaston. 1971. *Welfare Policy and Industrialization in Europe*. New York: Wiley.

Rochefort, David, ed. 1989. *Handbook on Mental Health Policy in the United States*. New York: Greenwood Press.

Romanyshyn, John. 1971. *Social Welfare: Charity to Justice*. New York: Random House.

Rothman, Jack. 1979. "Three Models of Community Organization Practice." In Fred Cox, ed., *Strategies of Community Organization*, pp. 25–45. Itasca, Ill.: F. E. Peacock.

Schorr, Alvin. 1968. *Explorations in Social Policy*. New York: Basic Books.

——. 1985. "Professional Policy as Practice." *Social Service Review* 59:178–196.

——. 1986. *Common Decency: Domestic Policies After Reagan*. New Haven: Yale University Press.

Simons, Herbert. 1986. *Persuasion*. New York: Random House.

Smith, J. Owens. 1987. *The Politics of Racial Inequality: A Systematic Comparative Macro-Analysis from the Colonial Period to 1970*. Westport, Conn.: Greenwood Press.

Spiegel, Allen and H. Hyman. 1978. *Basic Health Planning Methods*. Germantown, Md.: Aspen Systems.

Starr, Paul. 1982. *Social Transformation of American Medicine*. New York: Basic Books.

Takaki, R. 1989. *Strangers from a Different Shore: A History of Asian Americans*. Boston: Little, Brown.

Titmuss, Richard. 1968. *Commitment to Welfare*. London: George Allen and Unwin.

Trattner, Walter, ed. 1983. *Social Welfare or Social Control? Some Historical Reflections on Regulating the Poor*. Knoxville: University of Tennessee Press.

——. 1989. *From Poor Law to Welfare State: A History of Social Welfare in America*. New York: Free Press.

Tropman, John, et al. 1981. *New Strategic Perspectives on Social Policy*. New York: Pergamon.

——. 1987. "Policy Analysis: Methods and Techniques." In *Encyclopedia of Social Work*, vol. 2, pp. 268–283. Silver Spring, Md.: National Association of Social Workers.

Weissman, Harold and Andrea Savage. 1983. *Agency-Based Social Work: Neglected Aspects of Clinical Practice*. Philadelphia: Temple University Press.

Weissman, Irving. 1959. *Social Welfare Policy and Services in Social Work Education*. Volume 12. New York: Council on Social Work Education.

Wenocur, Stanley and Michael Reisch. 1989. *From Charity to Enterprise: the Development of American Social Work in a Market Economy*. Urbana: University of Illinois Press.

Wildavsky, Aaron. 1988. *The New Politics of the Budgetary Process*. Glenview, Ill.: Scott, Foresman.

Wilensky, Harold, and Charles Lebeaux. 1958. *Industrial Society and Social Welfare: The Impact of Industrialization*. New York: Russell Sage.

Williams, Juan. 1987. *Eyes on the Prize: America's Civil Rights Years, 1954–1965*. New York: Viking.

Wolf, Charles. 1981. "Ethics and Policy Analysis." In Joel Fleischman, Lance Liebman, and Mark Moore, eds., *Public Duties: the Moral Obligations of Government*, pp. 131–141. Cambridge, Mass.: Harvard University Press.

Wyers, Norman. 1991. "Policy-Practice in Social Work: Models and Issues." *Journal of Social Work Education* 27:241–250.

4
Human Behavior and the Social Environment

CAREL B. GERMAIN

The search for understanding of human development and behavior has been characteristic of social work since its beginnings in the 1890s. Even then, practitioners had felt a pressing need for more knowledge as they struggled to help people who faced baffling life situations. Initially, social work training courses sought to meet the need by providing sociological "information." Gradually, however, content that later was to be known as the "Human Growth and Behavior" course moved uneasily from the emphasis on social conditions to an emphasis on personality factors in development and behavior, with diminished attention given to social factors.

A look back over social work's first century, however, reveals a slow but steady development of the profession's integrative focus on person-in-environment, and its growing influence on what became the "Human Behavior and the Social Environment" curriculum, or HBSE. The Council on Social Work Education (CSWE) now requires that HBSE foundation courses select, arrange, and present theory, research findings, and knowledge that bear on the complex interplay between personal and environmental factors in human development and functioning throughout life.

A look ahead to the twenty-first century, and social work's second century, the profession's dual, yet one-dimensional, focus appears to be in the process of transformation to a multi-dimensional focus on "diverse person(s) in diverse environments." In HBSE courses, the transformational process is strengthened by new concepts and research findings on human and environmental diversity that are derived from the biological, social, and behavioral sciences and from social work itself. The concepts reflect a clearer vision of the profession's mission in society, and they are to be woven together in a way that supports the profession's values and ethics (Germain 1984, 1992).

This chapter begins with a brief look back on the history of the HBSE curriculum, a longer look at its present composition, followed by a brief look ahead at anticipated developments and issues pertaining to the HBSE foundation.

Historical Overview

Among the early graduate programs established in the first two decades of the twentieth century, knowledge-for-practice was limited to sociological information about such social problems as crime, mental and physical disease, and poverty. By the 1920s, however, medical and psychiatric casework had become established specialties in practice and graduate education for practice. In response, the growing number of graduate programs minimized their sociological emphasis in favor of required courses in "medical information" and "psychiatric information" taught by physicians and psychiatrists, respectively. As interest in psychoanalysis spread during the next decades, many "psychiatric information" courses began to include Freudian concepts.

In 1932 the American Association of Schools of Social Work mandated medical and psychiatric "information" courses for all students in member schools. Throughout the 1930s and 1940s, these courses were strongly influenced by psychoanalytic drive theory and the psychosexual stages of libidinal development. This was especially the case within the East Coast establishment of schools and private agencies, where the major emphasis in the psychiatric information course was either on Freud's drive theory within the so-called diagnostic school of social work thought, centered in New York and Boston, or on Rank's neopsychoanalytic theory of the human will within the smaller, so-called functional school of social work thought, centered in Philadelphia.

In 1952 the newly formed Council on Social Work Education (CSWE) issued a Curriculum Policy Statement (CPS) that became part of the accreditation standard for graduate schools of social work (Dinerman 1984:5). It adopted a way of structuring the newly named

"Human Growth and Behavior" (HGB) content of the curriculum into a sequence of courses over two years of graduate work. Although the standards also required that equal weight be given to the biological, social, intellectual, spiritual, and emotional realms of the personality, a disproportionate emphasis on the emotional realm continued.

During the late 1950s new factors came into play that helped bring about a beginning shift in the HGB curriculum from a focus on the drives to a focus on the ego and environmental influences. First, there was the impact on practice courses of Hartmann's ideas of reality, adaptation, and ego autonomy (1958, 1964); Anna Freud's further development of the ego's defenses against anxiety aroused by the drives (1966 [1946]), and Erikson's framework of ego development (1950, 1959). The latter was probably the most widely taught personality theory in the graduate HBSE curricula from the 1960s to the present.

Second, demands for supplementary courses on the social environment were sparked by practice teachers in the group work and community organization sequences (Coyle 1958). However, such courses tended to be descriptive, which may have reflected the state of the art in the social sciences themselves. Few attempts were made to integrate such courses with the HGB course. It was as though the environment were merely a static backdrop against which "real" life was played out.

Third, during the 1950s and 1960s psychiatrists developed 1) crisis theory and crisis treatment (borrowed in part from the public health and prevention movements), and 2) family theory and family therapy.* From these developments, in part, environmental content that was more dynamic entered practice and then casework courses in the 1960s. As it had many times before, HBSE later followed the casework lead and incorporated concepts of maturational and situational crises, family structure and functions, and social networks as part of the social environment.

Fourth, the force of the War on Poverty and the civil rights and welfare rights movements of the 1960s bolstered the efforts to integrate the person-in-environment focus as a unitary system of theory/knowledge through the gradual addition of group and community

*Although social work had been involved with families from its beginnings in the charity organization and settlement movements, the profession had to wait for initial concepts of family dynamics, functioning, and structure to be developed by psychiatry and sociology.

concepts and theories of power and social conflict into practice and eventually into some HBSE courses. The 1962 CPS renamed the sequence HBSE, which was now to include social and cultural influences on behavior. Later, the 1969 CPS called for 1) a shift from the psychiatric model of HBSE to an interdisciplinary approach that would present human development and behavior in families, groups, and communities instead of the heretofore single emphasis on the individual alone; and 2) a shift from providing foundation knowledge for "micro" practice alone to foundation knowledge for "macro" practice as well.

As a consequence of these factors, some HBSE instructors (by then nearly all were social workers) followed the lead of practice and seized upon social systems theory (Parsons 1951) as a potential avenue to the desired integration of the person-in-environment. Others were drawn to general systems theory. Throughout the 1970s and 1980s, it was clear that the chief competitive perspectives in the selection and organization of HBSE content were the psychoanalytic and systems approaches. Several other perspectives took minor roles in the contest, such as behavioral and cognitive approaches.

Before taking up the competing theory bases and 1992 curriculum policy, HB courses at the undergraduate level in the decades prior to 1980 are examined.

HBSE in Undergraduate Programs

At the undergraduate level, growing numbers of early social work programs that prepared students for the public services either required or merely advised students to take courses in sociology, psychology, and sometimes biology during the first two years of their liberal arts education, whatever the actual content of such courses and however they were taught. Undergraduate psychology courses, for example, often consisted of experimental studies of animal behavior.

By the 1950s and beyond, many undergraduate programs still relied mainly on biological/maturational and non-Freudian psychological theories of human development to supplement their traditional sociological emphasis. In most instances these courses continued to be taught by faculty in the biology, psychology, and sociology departments of the college or university. Their application to social work, however, was left to social work faculty, who also were responsible for connecting social work content to the liberal arts base of the students.

In 1969 the National Association of Social Workers (NASW) reversed an earlier stand and granted professional status and full membership to graduates of BSW programs that are approved by CSWE. By 1971, CSWE standards for approval were in place, and in 1974 approval became accreditation. A continuum of professional education for social work was now a reality, and the number of BSW programs grew rapidly. The 1984 CSWE Accreditation Standard on HBSE content referred to both BSW and MSW programs, but decisions on content and focus of HBSE were left to the individual BSW program.

Interested in securing data on the current state of HBSE in the baccalaureate curriculum, Gibbs (1986) conducted a survey by mail (date not given) of all 303 BSW programs accredited as of 1981, and received 191 responses (63 percent). Of the programs responding, 171 (89.5 percent) reported that the HBSE course(s) were taught within the social work department. This is a strong trend (in contrast, only 21.8 percent of the programs in a 1971 study taught a required HBSE course). Conceptual frameworks used by the 171 programs included the following: ecosystems, 46 programs (26.9 percent); systems, 38 (22.2 percent). However, 53 additional programs (31 percent) used systems combined with other approaches (developmental, psychosocial). The remaining 24 of the 171 programs taught varied approaches or their combinations. Alone or in combination, systems clearly was the dominant approach in 90 percent of the reporting programs. Prerequisites to social-work-taught HBSE courses that were most frequently mentioned included psychology (83 times) and sociology (77 times). Notably, biology was mentioned only 33 times. Hence, a serious gap in required content exists, and this is probably the case in MSW programs as well.

Competing Theoretical Perspectives

This section summarizes psychoanalytic and systems theories as the dominant approaches to the selection and organization of HBSE foundation content. Psychoanalytic theory is the oldest continuing approach to HBSE at the graduate level, while systems theory entered HBSE courses at both levels more recently. Both perspectives are given primary attention in this section because they have influenced the substance and direction of the profession's development more than any other systems of thought. Behavioral, cognitive, and social learning approaches have adherents in social work but in smaller numbers. Hence, as potential or actual HBSE content they are touched on also, but briefly.

Psychoanalytic theories, as they shifted and were altered over the years, shaped large sectors of social casework and group therapy from the late 1920s to the present. Their influence derived in part from 1) casework's striving for professional status through adopting an established (medical) model of practice; 2) the need for knowledge to explain difficult phenomena with which practice was involved; 3) the entrance into the general culture of psychoanalytic ideas; and 4) political and economic contexts that, from time to time, emphasized individual culpability over social justice and societal responsibility (Reamer 1983).

Many social workers came to view people's problems as intrapsychic in origin and appropriate treatment as a verbal and transference therapy. Therefore, clients needed to be highly motivated, introspective, and articulate. They also needed adequate time and energy to pursue treatment aims. Those who were inarticulate, who faced severe environmental problems that required immediate action rather than talk, or who held cultural values and norms different from those of agencies and their casework staffs were referred to other types of agencies. This led to the claim in the 1960s that casework had abandoned the poor and social work's historic commitments, thus helping to pave the way to the adoption of systems theory. Nevertheless, psychoanalytic concepts and especially ego psychology and object relations theory continue to be a major emphasis in some graduate HBSE curricula and a significant supplement in others.

Many instructors who present a different approach nonetheless believe that all students should be taught about defense mechanisms at the very least since they are encountered so frequently in practice and in oneself. Theories of defense also offer an opportunity for students to engage in a comparative analysis of theories—in this instance, a) the psychodynamic theory of defenses as unconscious, stereotyped, unrealistic efforts to manage internally generated anxiety. As such, defenses are tied to early experiences and unrelated to the present demand (Kroeber 1963); b) stress theories that view defenses as adaptive coping efforts over the short term when used to manage disabling emotions aroused by a severe external stressor (Hamburg et al. 1953); and c) the view of defenses as learned or conditioned behaviors in behavioral and cognitive theories (Schwartz 1983; Werner 1986).

Ego Psychology*

Classical psychoanalytic theory is not presented here since most readers are probably familiar with the main concepts and the varied critiques of its biological and psychic determinism; the Oedipus complex, penis envy, and female inferiority and subordination; and inattention in treatment to cultural and societal influences (e.g., Mitchell 1974; Miller 1976; Chodorow 1978, 1989).

The psychoanalyst Heinz Hartmann sought a base for the ego independent of the id that would solve the "problem of adaptation" without departing from the drive-oriented, pleasure-seeking, tension-reducing model of Freud. His solution was to suggest that both id and a primary autonomous sphere of functioning within the ego exist at birth or shortly after. The primary sphere includes innate, unconflicted ego functions that confer on the newborn a state of preadaptedness to an average, expectable environment. These are crying, sucking, and the clinging and rooting reflexes; sensory-perceptual and cognitive structures; physical structures for learning and speaking a language; skeletal and muscular structures for posture and movement; and memory and judgment. Hartmann believed that these abilities were built into the species' genetic structure over evolutionary time according to Darwinian principles.

Acquired ego functions, on the other hand, arise out of conflict between the child's id wishes and the environment (parents); hence, these functions are dominated initially by the drives and by the pleasure principle and primary-process thinking. Normally, they gradually achieve autonomy from the drives through 1) the child's identification with loved and loving parents and later with other admired adults, followed by 2) "neutralization" of their drive elements, which lead to 3) a change in function from serving the id to serving the ego. They then constitute the secondary sphere of ego autonomy and include reality testing, object relations, impulse control, coping skills, and the self-concept. They are characterized by the reality principle and secondary-process thinking.

However, any one of the acquired functions may not achieve autonomy because of developmental obstacles that block positive identifications, the neutralization of drive elements, and changes in function.

*Parts of this section are adapted from Germain (1991:445–449).

Such conflicted functions remain in the conflict sphere of the ego and continue to be dominated by the drives, the pleasure principle, and primary-process thinking. Through later identifications, neutralization, and change of function, however, they may leave the conflict sphere and enter the sphere of secondary autonomy, but they are vulnerable to stress and may again regress. The conflict sphere also includes the ego function of anxiety and defenses against it. Social workers have made use of these ideas in practice (e.g., Bandler 1963).

The psychoanalyst Erik Erikson built on Hartmann's concepts to create an eight-stage model of the ego's development (1950, 1959). It parallels Freud's libidinal stages and, contrary to popular belief, is rooted in Freud's ideas as well as Hartmann's. Erikson carried his ideas of ego development beyond childhood with a stage in adolescence and three stages in adulthood. Each stage is a period of marked physical, social, and psychological change, and all are conceived of in terms of the embryological principle of epigenesis. That is, each organ of an embryo has its critical period in which certain aspects of its development must occur or the full development of the organ will never take place, or will be severely damaged or missing. So too with psychosocial development, according to Erikson. The completion of one stage depends upon the successful completion of the prior stage. Each stage successfully completed becomes the foundation for the next.

Erikson maintains that these stages and their associated crises are experienced by all human beings. While each stage has its time of ascendance and specific ego task, each persists to some degree throughout life. The assumption of persistence seems to imply, despite the emphasis on the rigidity of epigenesis, that later opportunities may appear for the improved resolution of poorly resolved earlier stages. Erikson's works do not clarify this ambiguity.

Outcomes are formulated in terms of more-or-less polar, though not necessarily opposite, positions. A successful outcome is reflected in the dominance of the positive polar position as a quality of the autonomous ego (trust, autonomy, industry, identity, intimacy, generativity, and integrity) together with corresponding "virtues" of hope, will, purpose, competence, fidelity, love, care, and wisdom (Erikson 1964). An unsuccessful outcome is the dominance of the negative polar position as a quality of the ego within its conflict sphere, and the corresponding "virtue" is missing or weak.

As the centerpiece of Erikson's model, ego identity is rooted in the earlier achievement of trust, autonomy, initiative, and industry but has its ascendance in adolescence. After adolescence, ego identity incorporates elements derived from the later achievements of intimacy, generativity, and integrity. Each of the first three stages has a corresponding "organismic mode" that, through identifications, neutralization, and change of function becomes a behavioral modality, presumably in the ego's secondary sphere of autonomy. For example, psychosexual orality becomes the psychosocial ability to take in and to receive and, reciprocally, to give, and it leads to trust in the self and others. Anality becomes the ability to hold on or to let go as appropriate in the struggle for self-regulation. The intrusiveness of the phallic mode becomes the capacity for curiosity. It is not clear how the intrusive phallus can be a universal mode for females as well as males. The behavioral modality of the latency period is learning, which leads to the ego quality of industry.

The notion that identity is followed by intimacy presents several difficulties. In Erikson's scheme, for example, after completing the task of identity, the ego task for young adults is to develop the capacity for intimacy with a loved person of the opposite sex. This heterosexual bias overlooks the different task of the lesbian or gay young adult, whose need for intimacy is fulfilled by a person of the same sex. From a male bias, Erikson asserted that women had no identity of their own but derived their identity first from their fathers and later from their husbands. Following criticism by feminists, he is said to have withdrawn this assumption (source unknown). And the assumption that intimacy follows identity achievement does not hold for women for whom close social relations are paramount in adolescence and before.

Since Erikson's model continues to be the prevailing theory of personality development in HBSE curricula, most social workers are familiar with his ideas, although not necessarily with their derivation from classical psychoanalytic theory. The model was first welcomed in social work education and practice as replacement for the earlier emphasis on the id and its drives. Its emphasis on age-specific tasks and the reciprocal provision of resources by the environment for their completion ensured its continuance in HBSE for it seems to fit the aims of social work.

Currently, however, Erikson—like Freud—is faulted for not taking

account of human, cultural, and environmental diversity, and historical contexts, in his developmental framework. Like his gender assumptions, sequential stages and the epigenetic principle are also in question. Epigenesis is a biological process in embryos and does not really
apply to psychological or social processes, even metaphorically. These
and other troublesome issues in all stage models are discussed in the
next section.

Other stage models constructed by Vaillant, Levinson, Gould,
Piaget, and Kohlberg are probably used in some HBSE courses. Vaillant (1977) and Levinson (1978) constructed universal stage models for
adulthood that are gender- and class-biased. Both models use male
samples, reflect middle-class values, and ignore cultural differences,
the effects of social change, and the impact of oppression. Levinson
used a very small sample of forty men, from which he drew sweeping
generalizations. Vaillant's model seems to suggest that life is an illness,
since ego defenses appear to be the centerpiece of life, health, and
growth. Gould's (1980) five-stage model of adulthood focuses on work
and love, and on transformations that are generated mainly by internal
processes, but also by environments of work and significant others. In
those respects it is superior to the other two models. However, it is
based on observations of therapy groups. And universality of internal
processes and predictable sequences are implied.

Despite the usefulness of many of Piaget's (1952) constructs on cognitive development in childhood, his idea of invariant stages casts
some doubt on his model. Bruner (1983), for example, pointed out that
both culture and brain plasticity give human beings a wider range of
possibilities than Piaget allowed for. Cross-cultural studies show that
not all children pass through Piaget's universal invariant stages. Different cultures have different ways of knowing—and some assert that
the two sexes also differ in their ways of knowing (Belenky et al. 1986).
Further, certain cognitive abilities that Piaget viewed as developing in
later childhood are now known to be present at birth or shortly there-
after (Lichtenberg 1981; Stern 1985).

Kohlberg's (1969) model of sequential stages of moral reasoning has
been criticized on several grounds. Controversial issues include the
research instruments (said to reflect hypothetical resolutions to hypothetical dilemmas without testing actual moral behaviors) and the
model's view of women as being deficient in moral judgment when
compared to men (e.g., Gilligan 1982).

The Life Course Conception

All stage models have been under attack in segments of the social and behavioral sciences because they are believed to rest on faulty assumptions about human development and behavior. For example, stage models assume universal, sequential pathways to development that lead to fixed, predictable endpoints, without regard either to human or environmental diversity (Germain 1990). They do not and cannot absorb the effects of new family forms, tremendous shifts in community, group, and family values and norms, changes in gendered roles, AIDS, homelessness, addictions, crime, and poverty on individual and collectivity development and functioning, and the critical significance of the global environment and world peace to continued life on earth. Stage models also fail to take account of the self-regulating, self-determining nature of human beings and the indeterminate nature of nonuniform pathways to biopsychosocial development and social functioning within varied environments and cultures. Indeed, nonuniform pathways are actually essential to social organization in complex societies such as ours (Freeman 1984).

Concerned about these and other problems with stage models, collaborative and individual work by biological, social, and behavioral scientists (e.g., Hareven 1982; Neugarten 1979; Riley 1985; Myerhoff and Simic 1978; Chess, Fernandez, and Korn 1980; Thomas 1981; Dubos 1981; Murphy 1974; Rutter 1979) have produced a "life-course" conception of individual and collective development and functioning. Space permits only a brief description of its elements here (for details, see Germain 1990).

The conception incorporates the multiplicity of biological, social, psychological/emotional, and cultural factors, and fits neatly with social work's historic commitments and with the 1992 CPS on foundation HBSE. It incorporates the structure, functions, and development of families, groups, and communities, relying in part on cohort theory, gender and age crossovers, and analysis of the sources and effects of developmental phenomena in historical, social, and individual time. The life-course concept also suggests that family members develop simultaneously in continual processes that involve both generations in which parents and offspring are active agents in their own and one another's development over the life course and within varied environments and cultures.

The life-course concept demonstrates how individual biological, emotional, cognitive, sensory-perceptual, motivations and emotions, spirituality, resilience, relatedness and caring, self-concept, self-direction, and so on, merge into collective processes (e.g., communication and relationship patterns, roles, values, norms, beliefs, myths, rituals, worldviews, and so on) within families, groups, and, on occasion, within communities. All developmental processes over the life course are regarded as outcomes of transactions between person(s) and environment(s) rather than as separable segments of life confined to predetermined ages and stages of experience. Hence, the conception also can incorporate issues of power abuses, conflict, and oppression as obstacles to optimal development and adaptive functioning. The merging of individual, collective, and environmental processes is an important conceptual advantage for, as Ewalt (1983) states,

> The mandatory focus on person-in-environment will be carried out in HBSE content by conveying not only knowledge about the discrete entities of individuals, families, groups, cultural systems, organizations, and communities, but also knowledge about how all of these are interrelated . . . [and] have an impact on one another.   (p. 39)

The life-course conception appears to hold promise for social work in general and for the HBSE foundation curriculum in particular.

Object Relations Theories

The British and American object relations theorists moved from the centrality of drive satisfaction to the centrality of object relations and thus shifted the critical issue in development back from the Oedipus complex to the beginning object relations of infancy.

The psychoanalyst Margaret Mahler conceived of pre-oedipal development as consisting of three universal stages: normal autism, normal symbiosis, and separation-individuation (e.g., Mahler, Pine, and Bergman 1975). The latter has three subphases: differentiation, practicing, and rapprochement. When all stages have been traversed successfully, they culminate in identity formation and object constancy in the third year of life.

Mahler's assumptions of normal autism and normal symbiosis are under attack on the basis of findings of a large body of neonate and infant research. The findings reveal that newborn and very young infants are remarkably capable human beings (e.g., Bower 1976; Lichtenberg 1981; Sander 1980). The respected psychoanalyst and infant researcher Stern (1985) reviewed extensive findings that bear directly on Mahler's "normal autistic" and "normal symbiotic" stages. He concluded that the concept of a normal autistic stage is no longer tenable because from the beginning "infants are deeply engaged in and related to social stimuli" (p. 234). Stern notes that at about two to three months the infant becomes more social, but that is not the same as becoming less autistic. He also reports that recent research on primary autism, an actual but rare disorder, shows the presence of brain abnormalities that occur early in brain development and not through deterioration after development. Such a biological base of autism is likely to shift treatment from emphasizing parental causation to helping parents cope with the difficult behaviors.

Infant research also reveals an innate ability to transfer knowledge from one sensory modality to another. For example, a newborn moves her eyes to the right when a sound is on the right, and to the left when the sound is on the left, demonstrating an expectation that there will be something to look at, a source for the sound. This is a simple form of intersensory coordination already present at birth. This and other experiments led Stern to conclude that the presence of innate cross-modal capacities makes it highly improbable that the infant consistently confuses self and other through a long stage of undifferentiation or so-called normal symbiosis. Rather than having to individuate from an initial symbiotic position, it appears to Stern that the infant simultaneously forms various mental representations of self and self-fused-with-other from nondifferentiated (as distinguished from undifferentiated) experiences. He adds:

> Many of the phenomena thought by psychoanalytic theory to play a crucial role in very early development, such as delusions of merger or fusion, splitting, and defensive or paranoid fantasies, are not applicable to the infancy period—that is, before the age of roughly eighteen to twenty-four months—but are conceivable only after the capacity for symbolization as evidenced by language is emerging, when infancy ends. (1985:11)

For Stern, the evidence from infant studies suggests the need to reconsider the concept of normal symbiosis and the extent of its explanatory power in childhood psychosis, borderline states, and other regressive phenomena. In his opinion, continued research may reveal that some of the earliest deviations in social and cognitive functioning are traceable to deficits in cross-modal and other innate infant capacities rather than to supposed distortions in the mother-infant relationship.

The work of such British analysts as Klein (1950), Guntrip (1969), Fairbairn (1952), Kohut (1977), and Winnicott (1965) are probably drawn upon in HBSE courses that emphasize object relations theory. The British work constitutes a large and influential body of thought most of which was influenced by Klein. However, space permits a few observations on only the work of Winnicott. In the United States his ideas appear to be used more than those of the other British theorists.

Winnicott's work appeals to many practitioners and HBSE instructors largely because of his concepts of the "holding environment" (1965) and "transitional phenomena" (1958). Practitioners, for example, apply them to client-worker relationships and to work with case management clients and others in need of environmental provisions (e.g., Chescheir 1985). In the holding environment of infancy, the "nursing pair" is the "center of being." It represents the state of "primary maternal preoccupation" within which the "unintegrated" infant is contained and which facilitates the anticipatory and immediate empathic responses of a "good enough mother" to the infant's needs. The hungry infant hallucinates the breast, and it magically appears. This gives the infant the illusion of omnipotence that is necessary for development. The mother's empathic anticipation of the infant's needs is crucial in the process of illusion, and for a brief period she provides a necessary "perfect environment" for the child. Once omnipotence is firmly in place, however, the mother must begin a gradual decrease in responsiveness so that the infant learns about reality. At about the same time, his other ego functions are also developing.

Omnipotence and the spontaneous emergence of the sense of self can be jeopardized by any continued demands from the caregiver that conflict with the infant's needs. Eventually the infant may give up and yield to the greater power (the "impinging environment"). He forfeits his "true self" and takes on a fractured, complying, nonautonomous "false self," with negative impact on later development.

Somewhere between hallucinatory omnipotence and awareness of external reality lies a transitional realm of experience. It is a "retreat" to pleasurable solitude where the baby creates and has control over her "subjective objects." It is essential for development that adults accept the cherished teddy bear, blanket, or other transitional object as the child's own creation over which she has complete control. That acceptance enables the baby to make the shift from seeing herself as her own world to seeing herself as one among separate others. This realm is also a valued experience of healthy adults. It consists of playful fantasies, ideas, and imagery that are pleasurable, give relief, and may even lead to creativity.

Attachment Theory

Object relations theorists attempted to fit object relations into drive theory by viewing them as derived from the vicissitudes of the drives. This sets them off entirely from attachment theorists. Bowlby (1958, 1973), for example, proposed that attachment to others is part of the genetic equipment of the human species. It is already there and does not simply emerge as the consequence of anaclitic dependence on the mother, as posited by object relations theory. It developed in the evolutionary environment because of its survival value. That is, attachment behaviors such as crying, sucking, clinging, and following kept mother and infant in proximity as protection against predators in that evolutionary environment. Adult attachment behaviors are different from those of infants and children, and they may or may not include a sexual relationship. Attachments are few at any age, and separation from or loss of an attachment figure is excruciating and a burden of prolonged grief for babies, children, and adults alike (see also Ainsworth 1969; Sroufe 1978; Weiss 1982).

Systems Theories

Systems theories entered practice in the 1960s and were welcomed as a unified approach to understanding personal and environmental factors and their interplay in human development and functioning. Social systems theory (SST) and general systems theory (GST) have a common interest in living systems, and both view the individual as a system. However, SST was derived from sociology, social psychology, and symbolic interactionism, while GST was derived from biological organismic theory, the physical sciences, and cybernetics. Their different derivations account for some different emphases. On the other hand, one might say that GST includes SST, insofar as the former is concerned with all living systems, including social systems.

Systems ideas began to enter some HBSE courses during the 1970s and 1980s, either as the major emphasis or as an important supplement to other emphases. While systems theories have little to say about human growth and development per se, they do clarify connections between individuals and collectivities on one hand, and their physical and social environments, and culture on the other.

Social Systems Theory (SST)

As Polsky put it (1969:12), SST "seeks to overcome the vagueness of social context in the interpersonal perspective by emphasizing the impact of environment upon individuals via social systems in which they are actors." The social system carries out its function through a structure of roles that fall into two classes: instrumental or task-oriented and expressive or socially and emotionally oriented. Both are found in any social system, including families, groups, communities, professions, networks, and organizations. Many types of role behaviors are represented by concepts such as role complementarity, conflict, and so on. Hence, *social role* is an important construct in SST. In social work, SST and the role construct held promise for the integration of the person-in-environment focus. It embraces external expectations for role performance and the internal responses, perceptions, cognitions, and emotions of the actor.

Each social system develops *values and norms* out of the shared experiences of its members and the influence of larger systems. Values and norms, like roles, are shaped in part by the person's membership in *reference groups*—ethnic, racial, religious, gender, work, social networks, and so on. In these and other ways, social systems are linked to the personality, biological organism, cultural, economic, and political systems—as each carries out its specific functions (Parsons 1951).

Social reality is the environment that consists of all systems interacting with the focal system. Hence,

> behavior is considered to be a consequence of the total social situation in which an individual subsystem, group subsystem, or other social unit finds itself. . . . The systems themselves persist in time while the position of social units within them may change. The person in the family or group, the group in the community, and the community in society are illustrations of this construct.   (Shafer 1969:31–32)

General Systems Theory (GST)

GST entered social work practice and HBSE courses a little later than SST, but seemed to attract greater support. This was because its dynamic concept of transaction appeared to many social workers to have a stronger potential for a firm integration of person-in-situation (Hearn 1958; Gordon 1969). Both SST and GST assume that systems of varied sizes and complexities share certain properties despite their obvious dissimilarities. Major GST concepts (von Bertalanffy 1960; Buckley 1967; Laszlo 1972; Arieti 1969) include the following:

Transaction refers to the continuous exchanges between person and environment in which each influences the other over time. The concept represents a shift in causality from the simple one-directional cause-effect to a more complex, circular causality in which cause becomes an effect, which then becomes a cause, which then becomes an effect and so on, around the loop being observed or studied over time.

Hierarchy refers to the arrangement of living systems in which each is a subsystem of the next larger system. Looking up the hierarchy, for example, a person as a system is a subsystem of the family or group system. Family and group, in turn, are subsystems of the community, and so on up the hierarchy. Looking downward, a person is a system that consists of subsystems such as respiratory, cardiovascular, etc. They, in turn, are systems that consist of subsystems such as cells, etc., and so on down the hierarchy.

By definition, a system is a set of interacting parts (subsystems) contained within a *boundary*. In order for a living system to live and develop, its boundary must remain permeable enough to permit needed exchanges with the environment, yet firm enough to maintain its integrity. It must receive inputs from the environment such as information, energy, and other resources. It must process them internally and export outputs to the environment in the form of resources to be used by other systems.

Systems and environments have mutual *feedback* processes that monitor what is going on, so they can stay within a required or optimal range of variation and avoid disorganization. In coping with life stressors, for example, the person experiences internal and external feedback which tells her, via personal comfort or discomfort and environmental approval or disapproval, whether the coping is effective.

A living system has the potential for reaching an end state independent of its starting position, or *equifinality*. Thus its end state is unpredictable, and living systems having very different initial conditions
may achieve similar end points. The opposite principle, multifinality,
suggests that similar initial states may lead to different end states
because of different inner and outer influences along the way and,
some would add (e.g., Dobzhansky 1976), differing degrees of freedom
from either or both influences.

When a system's boundary is too rigid, resources needed from the
environment are shut out, and the system proceeds toward disorganization or death (*positive entropy*). Sometimes, of course, boundaries are
open, but the environment withholds resources with the same ill
effects. Living systems seek to achieve *negative entropy*, usually by
building up reserves to counteract positive entropy over their lifetime.

An advantage of systems theories lies in their capacity to integrate living systems and their environments that are composed of other systems,
physical settings, and exist within varied cultures. Because of this capacity, systems theory led to the development of generalist and integrative
modes of practice that were welcomed by many social workers. Such
modes legitimized the worker's response to requests for assistance on
the basis of client need, rather than on the basis of professional method.

A disadvantage of both SST and GST is that they have little to say
about the development and functioning of the human bio-organism
and the personality per se. Hence, programs need to add one or more
developmental frameworks that may or may not conflict with systems
ideas. (Again, this is an opportunity for students to undertake comparative analysis of differing theories.) Another disadvantage of GST lies
in its abstractness and unfamiliar language, which seem to many social
workers to be dehumanizing, depersonalizing, and disconnected from
the realities of face-to-face practice. Also, despite the capacity of systems concepts to expand the scope of assessment by pointing to otherwise unseen points of intervention, they provide little with which to
design new interventions in work with individuals.

However, systems theories did generate new family concepts (e.g.,
Hartman and Laird 1983; Laird and Allen 1983) that led to innovative
interventions in practice with families, groups, and communities. Yet
feminist critics (e.g., Taggart 1985; Hare-Mustin 1978) reject the use of
GST in family therapy on grounds that it lacks attention to historic,
economic, political, and social contexts in which women are subordi-

nated to men in regard to status, power, and access to resources. Thus, family systems therapy is said to reinforce oppressive gender-typed family roles. Oddly, it would seem there is nothing inherent in systems theory to prevent the incorporation of oppressive contexts, and their impact, into family systems theory. The fault may lie with misunderstanding or misuse of systems theory by individual therapists.

Despite the shortcomings for practice, however, a systems approach is remarkably useful in HBSE foundation courses at both BSW and MSW levels. It guides the organization of content into an integrated, coherent, and enlightening approach to the diversity of concepts and research findings from the psychological, social, and behavioral sciences. When new or different concepts emerge, the organization can be re-formed legitimately and simply by removing discredited or obsolete concepts and substituting new ones. Hence, over their professional careers former students as continuous learners may refurbish their organization of theories-for-practice or perhaps, in some instances, even construct a new one.

An ecological framework (Germain 1991) is somewhat related to systems theories only in its use of the transaction concept. The framework is rooted in 1) theories of biological, psychological, social, and cultural adaptation (e.g., Coelho, Hamburg, and Adams 1974: Dobzhansky 1976; Dubos 1965; White 1959; Lazarus and Launier 1978); 2) a "life course" conception of human development instead of a stage model; 3) social pollutions such as poverty, oppression, abuse of power, militarism, etc.; 4) technological pollutions of communities and workplaces, and the global environment; and 5) a stress-coping paradigm (Lazarus and Folkman 1984). The organizing concepts of the approach are all transactional in nature. They are viewed as expressions of positive or negative people-environment relationships rather than as attributes of either alone.

Behavioral, Cognitive, and Cognitive-Behavioral Theories

Behavioral Theory

The behavioral approach became visible in social work practice in the late 1960s and has grown steadily ever since. However, it seems to have more to do with a practice method based on empirical research from

psychology and social work, and less to do with the interplay of biological, psychological/emotional, social, and cultural forces in human
development and behavior from conception to old age. This may
account for Gambrill's observation: "Most schools of social work do not
provide a thorough grounding in basic behavioral principles" (1987:191).
However, the number of social workers of other persuasions who use
behavioral and cognitive techniques in selected situations is growing.
Hence, it may be time for all HBSE foundation courses to include some
content on behavioral and cognitive concepts to support practice.

The behavioral approach derives in part from Pavlov's theory of
respondent conditioning. Pavlov noticed that dogs, when presented with
food (unconditioned stimulus) salivate (unconditioned response).
When he paired this stimulus-response presentation with a bell, and
then later presented only the bell without the food, the dog still salivat-
ed (now a conditioned or learned response). While much more sophisticated today, based on research and practice experience, respondent
conditioning serves as a theoretical base for contemporary behavioral
treatment of anxiety and phobias as learned (conditioned) behaviors,
most often through systematic desensitization to a noxious stimulus
(Schwartz 1983).

Behaviorism has more extensive roots in Skinner's theory of *operant
conditioning* in which operant, or voluntary, behavior(s) depend on environmental antecedent and consequent events. This is an A-B-C sequence,
that is, *antecedent* (A) events precede *behavior* (B). Behavior is followed by
consequences (C). Thus the frequency of a behavior targeted for change
can be increased by reinforcement or decreased by withholding reinforcement (punishment is not used by social workers for ethical reasons).
Refined and elaborated by clinical research and practice experience,
operant conditioning is the foundation of most contemporary behavioral
modification in social work (Schwartz 1983; Thomlison 1986).

While a person-in-environment focus is clear in behavioral modification, the meanings of both terms are quite different from their
meanings in other approaches. "Person" is primarily limited to
observable behavior and excludes the inner life. "Environment" is
limited to contingencies (behavioral events before and after the focal
behavior) that then condition the focal behavior(s). Recently, however, some behavioral social workers also include attention to significant others and social conditions (e.g., Gambrill 1987). Similarly,
behavioral and cognitive approaches now include bio-behavioral

techniques for "stress management"—the everyday hassles and annoyances at home, work, and so on. (Stress management should not be confused with the transactional "stress-coping paradigm," which is concerned with major life stressors, internal and external coping resources, and the interaction of bio-psycho-social-cultural forces in stressors and coping.)

Cognitive Theory

Included under this rubric are rational-emotive therapy and reality therapy developed by psychiatrists. However, Harold D. Werner, a social worker, has written extensively about cognitive theory and practice in social work since the late 1960s. He states,

> A cognitive approach holds that the principal determinant of emotions, motives, and behavior is an individual's thinking, which is a conscious process. The problems that clients bring to social workers are considered to be problems of consciousness. The essence of cognitive theory is that it requires the practitioner to discard the concept of an "unconscious" as the primary force in the psychic life.   (1986:91)

For Werner, cognitive theory differs from psychoanalytic theory and its emphasis on internal biologically based drives because "thinking intervenes continuously to deactivate or modify instinctual drives" (p. 105). It also differs from behavioral theory and its emphasis on externally conditioned behaviors because it includes the inner world of emotions and thoughts. A change in thinking can change learned responses.

Emotional distress can develop from faulty choices, destructive or antisocial goals, fears and anxieties, self-blame, and so on. Treatment involves helping clients to see themselves and their environments as clearly as possible. To do this, the social worker's perceptions of the person, environment, and culture must also be accurate. The worker must ensure that the client has all the facts and concepts necessary to make reality-oriented judgments to change goals and perceptions and to engage in effective problem solving (Werner 1986).

While Werner views cognitive approaches as different from behavioral ones, Thomlison (1986:138) sees cognitive theory as part of behavioral modification. He cites the following elements of cognitive theory that were identified by Robert Schwartz (1982:269): 1) information processing (acquisition, storage, and utilization of information and attention, perception, language and memory); 2) beliefs and belief systems (ideas, attitudes, and expectations about self, others, and experience); 3) self statements (private monologues that influence behavior and feelings); and 4) problem solving and coping processes to deal with problematic situations.

Cognitive-Behavioral Theory

Berlin (1980) presents a dual approach that she asserts is different from both the behavioral and the cognitive approaches. In a very important sense it is; her work takes account not only of motivation, thoughts, and feelings but of biological issues, diversity, oppression, and other influences in the larger or institutional environment as well. Hence her work is more strongly related to the person-in-environment focus of social work than behavioral approaches alone. However, as a primary emphasis in HBSE, each of these three theories would require a supplemental theory of biopsychosocial development and the influences of diversity and oppression.

Required HBSE Foundation Content

The professional foundation must provide content about theories and knowledge of human bio-psycho-social development, including theories and knowledge about the range of social systems in which individuals live (families, groups, organizations, institutions, and communities). The HBSE curriculum must provide an understanding of the interactions between and among human biological, social, psychological, and cultural systems as they affect and are affected by human behavior. The impact of social and economic forces on individuals and social systems must be presented. Content must be provided about the ways in which systems promote or deter people in the maintenance or attainment of optimal health and well-being. Content about values and ethical issues related to bio-psycho-social theories must be included. Students must be taught to evaluate theory and apply theory to client situations.

(Council on Social Work Education 1992:8)

With this statement, CSWE delineated a powerful synthesis of continuing and newly mandated content in HBSE that has a very strong potential for achieving the long-standing professional objective: a true integration of biological, psychological, social, and cultural forces in human development and behavior.

An analysis of the 1992 CPS reveals the enormity of the task faced by all programs. A vast multidisciplinary literature is available, but I cite only a few items for each element in each of the five groups as suggested resources to start. Most contain extensive bibliographies for further additions.

A. "The professional foundation must provide content about theories and knowledge of human bio-psycho-social development, including theories and knowledge about the range of social systems in which individuals live (families, groups, organizations, institutions, and communities."

1. This element requires continuance of the focus on individuals' biological, social, and psychological/emotional development from conception to old age. The choice for instructors is wide, including the stage models, object relations or attachment theories, or the life course conception. Also, attention must be given to cultural variations in the marking and management of biologically based life transitions such as puberty, adolescence, and old age, and also socially based transitions such as becoming a couple, parenthood, school roles, divorce, widowhood, and "coming out" as a gay or lesbian. The focus may be on theories of the "self," competence, adaptation, and stress and coping.

Both the 1982 and 1992 CPS emphasize the embeddedness of individuals in varied collectivities. Therefore, the following must also be considered:

2. Diversity of contemporary and emerging family forms and their form-specific family functions; the development of families over their own life course within larger environments and varied cultures; oppression and violence in family life; sibling relationships; family myths, rituals, and worldview; work roles and the significance of work and no-work to workers and their children and other family members; individual and family coping with disability or grave illness and death and other health matters (genetic principles and disease, pregnancy and childbirth).

3. Group theory, types of groups, and group purposes; how groups develop a structure of roles, functions, and communication and relationship patterns; the power of groups in society as well as their own internal power structure; and the effects of prejudicial discrimination

on formed and natural groups, including youth gangs and peer groups.

4. The kinds of organizations found in the public and/or private sector, such as social agencies, health care, and educational systems as providers of goods and services to those whom social work serves and sometimes as workplaces of social workers; characteristics of bureaucracies and their effects on clients, workers, and quality of service; bureaucratic norms that may conflict with professional norms and values; factors in organizational development and change.

5. Community theory, community dynamics, structures, and functions; rural/urban differences; formal and informal support systems; the influence on human development and functioning of such community issues as AIDS, poverty, powerlessness, institutional racism, homelessness, environmental pollution, alcoholism, illicit drugs, and crime.

B. "The HBSE Curriculum must provide an understanding of the interactions between and among human biological, social, psychological, and cultural systems as they affect and are affected by human behavior": This is an important synthesis and integrating position, and it reflects the transactional interplay of these forces that ecological and systems frameworks provide. To illustrate, a single example is put in its simplest form: *biological* maturation and varied biological states (genetic disease and principles of heredity; pregnancy and fetal development; infertility and reproductive technologies; illness, injury, and disability and the biochemical and neurological aspects of human physiology as all of these affect and are affected by *social* expectations and responses). Biological maturation and varied biological states help shape the individual's *psychological/emotional* states (perceptions, cognitions, attitudes, feelings, and emotions, and those of others in transaction with the person). Biological maturation may be marked by *cultural* norms and rituals; states of illness, injury, or physical or mental challenge may be defined and experienced differently across varied cultural patterns and practices.

In the same way, but without spelling it out here, social and psychological systems, social and cultural systems, and cultural and psychological systems can be shown to influence and help shape each other. The continuous transactions among the four systems shape human development and functioning and, in turn, are affected by human behavior. Examining women's issues and men's issues, for example, can be used to illustrate this complex interplay.

C. "The impact of social and economic forces on individuals and social systems must be presented. Content must be provided about the ways in which systems promote or deter people in the maintenance or attainment of optimal health and well-being": Positive and negative consequences of diversity (race, ethnicity, gender, age, sexual orientation, physical or mental challenge, social class, religion) for individual and family development and functioning need to be considered in the context of environmental characteristics. The latter include economic, political, and justice structures, power abuses, social conflict, prejudicial discrimination, and stigma that lead to vulnerability and powerlessness. Strengths within poor, disempowered, or vulnerable groups and their communities should also be continually in view.

Also to be considered are social institutions including foster, group, and day care, nursing homes, mental institutions, and prisons; labeling theory and theories of deviance and stigma.

D. "Content about values and ethical issues related to biopsychosocial theories must be included": Students and instructor together must examine theories and concepts presented in the course for congruence with the profession's values and ethics. Incongruence can be blatant (e.g., theories that suggest race and intelligence, or gender and moral development, are associated). Incongruence can be subtle (e.g., concepts that imply parents cause autism in their young child or cause schizophrenia in their teenager).

E. "Students must be taught to evaluate theory and apply theory to client situations": At the broadest level, the differences between biological, social, psychological, and cultural systems of thought provide an opportunity for students to analyze comparatively the structure, extent of research support, and the humanistic qualities and concerns of each theory. More narrowly, students need to explore the relationship of theories and concepts presented to the liberal arts base, the social work mission and philosophy, other foundation courses, and their own practice experiences.

Pedagogical Issues

A major emphasis on psychoanalytic theories is less clearly connected to social work's mission in society than other emphases. It is also less clearly connected to the person-in-environment focus, insofar as major attention is given to the person, chiefly to the person's intrapsychic aspects, while environment may be limited to "mother" or to a generalized "family." Thus, some faculty and some practitioners believe that a theory base for practice that focuses mainly on the individual is inappropriate for the foundation HBSE course.

Supplemental courses that present the newly mandated content, depending on how they are taught, may or may not be as effective as those that rely on a thoroughly integrated perspective throughout. For example, splitting psychoanalytic ideas and ideas of bio-social-psychological-cultural forces into separate courses may make integration of, and professional identification with, the focus on individual/collectivity-in-environment more difficult for students to achieve. By comparison, an integrated perspective can make the students' integrative tasks easier and professional identification with the content stronger. Another solution, exemplified in some schools, is to provide in the first year an integrated perspective and to offer electives in the second year in psychoanalytic theories.

Some instructors believe that all practice students must be taught Freudian ideas, ego psychology, and object relations theory, because field instructors and future employers expect this emphasis, and are not aware of or sympathetic to any other. To a certain extent that is true. Many do complain about students who are ignorant of psychodynamic concepts. But other field instructors and employers believe this is a status quo position, which must change if students are to be prepared for effective practice with the kinds of severe bio-psycho-social-cultural issues that afflict people in our contemporary world.

A long-standing question by faculties over the decades has been, "How can we possibly fit anything more into the curriculum without removing essential components?" And now there is a great deal more in the foundation HBSE courses that graduate and undergraduate programs must somehow include for accreditation and reaccreditation. The issue of fitting it all in is unquestionably a serious one, not easily solved overnight or for all time because knowledge, theory, and research continue to expand in the relevant sciences. Each program is left to work out its own solution in light of its particular mission and conditions, but it must include all the mandated HBSE foundation content.

Differentiation of MSW and BSW educational objectives and content of the HBSE foundation continues to be extremely difficult or even impossible for most if not all programs to achieve. The CPS does not specify qualitative or quantitative differences in objectives for the two levels, nor does it offer criteria on which to make distinctions. Further, a 1984 CSWE standard states, "Social workers at both the undergraduate and graduate levels must demonstrate, according to their respective levels of entry, proficiency and competence in five professional foundation areas" (Germain 1984: CPS Sect. 7.6, p. 9). How are BSW and MSW proficiency and competence in foundation HBSE to be distinguished? No clue is given.

Without guidelines for the general allocation of HBSE foundation content to each educational level, redundancy in foundation HBSE is a problem for some BSW graduates who enter graduate programs, together with the issue posed by graduate programs having to provide foundation HBSE coverage for college graduates who do not have BSW degrees. In the attempt to be helpful to programs facing these issues, a CSWE 1984 standard states,

> BSW graduates entering MSW programs are not to repeat what has been mastered in their BSW work. In order to promote the social work education continuum MSW programs are to develop policies and procedures to identify coverage and mastery and to prevent unproductive repetition. MSW programs are to establish explicit admissions procedures and policies relevant to course waivers, substitutions, exemptions, and advanced standing for BSW graduates. All such arrangements should be explicit and unambiguous.
>
> (Sect. 6.14, p. 6)

Of course, redundancy must be avoided. But is it possible that universities, especially in difficult financial straits, will view with disfavor graduate programs that accept undergraduate foundation courses in HBSE in lieu of a *supposedly* graduate-level HBSE foundation course? If the profession answers "yes," then CSWE with the help of HBSE faculty must undertake the awesome, but nonetheless essential task of differentiating between foundation content in HBSE at the two levels.

Should differentiation be achieved, however, the problem faced by MSW applicants who lack the BSW degree will remain. Here the 1984 standard is "[All MSW programs] must provide all non-BSW students with the professional foundation content on which every concentration is built" (sect. 6.13). This requirement seems to imply that graduate foundation courses are no different from undergraduate courses. Universities would hardly agree that a graduate program must provide what is BSW content taught in undergraduate programs to graduate students who lack such content. Also, granting advanced standing to BSW graduates, given the lack of differentiation, seems to imply that undergraduate work in the final two years is equivalent to the first year of graduate work. If this is the case, something is wrong with graduate programs, or with the policy.

Further, the profession is clearly not in a position to require a BSW of every applicant to MSW programs, nor is that a necessarily desirable goal. Should non-BSW students, perhaps, be required to take BSW foundation courses in HBSE before entry into the MSW program? Such a proposal is likely to be controversial, especially during periods of decreasing enrollment.

To repeat, it does seem essential that CSWE, aided by HBSE faculty, differentiate between the educational objectives and the content in foundation HBSE at the two levels, so that the integrity of each level is safeguarded and students are spared redundancy. A daunting task, but perhaps not an impossible one.

HBSE has been an essential part of social work education since the earliest "training courses" of a century ago. It has grown in the breadth and depth of content over the years, guided by the goal of providing a sound base of theories, research findings, and knowledge for effective and ethical social work practice. The HBSE foundation today also reflects advances made in practice with individuals and collectivities, and in social work administration, research, and social welfare policy and services. It also contributed to those advances—an appropriate reciprocal influence through which both the HBSE foundation and practice affect each other over time. Competing approaches and perspectives provide a needed arena for each generation of HBSE instructors and students to refine that which still serves the profession's mission well, and also to strive toward surpassing what has gone before. This is done, first, through continuous, critical examination of new theories and findings. And second, through the adoption of new theories and findings that fit still better with the profession's mission and its integrative, multidimensional focus on diverse persons(s)-in-diverse-environments.

In short, the past century of progressive development of HBSE content led to the HBSE foundation as we know it now. It also created what will be a continually evolving, fundamental, and essential element in the profession's achievements during its next century of service.

REFERENCES

Ainsworth, Mary D. Salter. 1969. "Object Relations, Dependency, and Attachment: A Theoretical Review of the Infant-Mother Relationship." *Child Development* (August):969–1025.

Anderson, Ralph E. and Irl E. Carter. 1984. *Human Behavior in the Social Environment*. 3d rev. ed. New York: Aldine.

Arieti, Silvano E. 1969. "Designated Discussion." In William Gray, Frederick J. Duhl, and Nicolas D. Rizzo, eds., *General Systems Theory and Psychiatry*, pp. 48–50. Boston: Little, Brown.

Bandler, Louise. 1963. "Some Aspects of Ego Growth Through Sublimations." In Howard J. Parad and Roger R. Miller, eds., *Ego-Oriented Casework: Problems and Perspectives*, pp. 89–107. New York: Family Service Association of America.

Belenky, M., B. Clinchy, N. Goldberger, and J. Tarule. 1986. *Women's Ways of Knowing*. New York: Basic Books.

Berger, Raymond and Ron Federico. 1985. *Human Behavior: A Social Work Perspective*. 2d ed. New York: Longman.

Berlin, Sharon. 1983. "Cognitive-Behavioral Approaches." In Aaron Rosenblatt and Diana Waldfogel, eds., *Handbook of Clinical Social Work*, pp. 1095–1119. San Francisco: Jossey-Bass.

Blanck, Gertrude and Rubin Blanck. 1974. *Ego Psychology: Theory and Practice*. New York: Columbia University Press.

——. 1978. *Ego Psychology II. Developmental Psychology*. New York: Columbia University Press.

Bloom, Martin. 1984. *Configurations of Human Behavior: Life Span Development in Social Environments*. New York: Macmillan.

——. 1992. *Changing Lives: Studies in Human Development and Professional Helping*. Columbia: University of South Carolina Press.

Bower, Tom G. R. 1976. *The Perceptual World of the Child*. Cambridge, Mass.: Harvard University Press.

Bowlby, John. 1958. "The Nature of the Child's Tie to His Mother." *International Journal of Psycho-Analysis* 39:350–373.

——. 1973. "Affectional Bonds: Their Nature and Origin." In Robert S. Weiss, ed., *Loneliness: The Experience of Emotional and Social Isolation*, pp. 38–52. Cambridge, Mass.: MIT Press.

Bruner, Jerome. 1983. *Child Talk: Learning to Use Language*. New York: Norton.

Buckley, W. 1967. *Modern Systems Research for the Behavioral Scientist*. Chicago: Aldine.

Chescheir, Marth W. 1985. "Some Implications of Winnicott's Concept for Clinical Practice." *Clinical Social Work Journal* 13(3):218–233.

Chess, Stella, P. Fernandez, and S. Korn. 1980. "The Handicapped Child and His Family: Consonance and Dissonance." *Journal of the American Academy of Child Psychiatry* 19:56–67.

Chess, Wayne A., and Julia M. Norlin. 1990. *Human Behavior and the Social Environment: A Social Systems Model*. Boston: Allyn and Bacon.

Chodorow, Nancy. 1978. *The Reproduction of Mothering: Psychoanalysis and the Sociology of Gender*. Berkeley: University of California Press.

——. 1989. *Feminism and Psychoanalytic Theory*. New Haven: Yale University Press.

Coelho, George V., David A. Hamburg, and John E. Adams, eds. 1974. *Coping and Adaptation*. New York: Basic Books.

Council on Social Work Education. 1992. *Curriculum Policy Statement for Master's Degree Programs in Social Work Education*. Alexandria, Va.

Coyle, Grace Longwell. 1958. *Social Science in the Professional Education of Social Workers*. New York: Council on Social Work Education.

Dinerman, Miriam. 1984. "The 1959 Curriculum Study: Contributions of Werner W. Boehm." In Miriam Dinerman and Ludwig L. Geismar, eds., *A Quarter-Century of Social Work Education*, pp. 3–24. Silver Spring, Md.: National Association of Social Workers.

Dobzhansky, Theodosius. 1976. "The Myths of Genetic Predestination and Tabula Rasa." *Perspectives in Biology and Medicine* 19 (January):156–170.

Dubos, Rene. 1965. *Man Adapting*. New Haven: Yale University Press.

——. 1981. *Celebrations of Life*. New York: McGraw-Hill.

Erikson, Erik H. 1950. *Childhood and Society*. New York: Norton.

——. 1959. "Growth and Crises of the Healthy Personality." In *Identity and the Life Cycle, Selected Papers by Erik H. Erikson*, pp. 50–100. New York: International Universities Press.

——. 1964. "A Schedule of Virtues." In *Insight and Responsibility*, pp. 111–134. New York: Norton.

Ewalt, Patricia L. 1983. *Curriculum Design and Development for Graduate Social Work Education*. New York: Council on Social Work Education.

Fairbairn, W. R. D. 1952. *An Object Relations Theory of the Personality*. New York: Basic Books.

Freeman, M. 1984. "History, Narrative, and Life-Span Development Knowledge." *Human Development* 27:1–19.

Freud, Anna. 1966 [1946]. *The Ego and Mechanisms of Defense*. Rev. ed. New York: International Universities Press.

Gambrill, Eileen D. 1987. "Behavioral Approach." In Anne Minahan, ed., *Encyclopedia of Social Work*. 18th ed., vol. 1, pp. 184–194. Silver Spring, Md.: National Association of Social Workers.

Ganter, Grace and Margaret Yaekel. 1980. *Human Behavior and the Social Environment: A Perspective for Social Work Practice.* New York: Columbia University Press.

Germain, Carel B. 1984. *Handbook of Accreditation Standards and Procedures.* New York: Council on Social Work Education.

——. 1990. "Life Forces and the Anatomy of Practice." *Smith College Studies in Social Work* 60 (March):138–152.

——. 1991. *Human Behavior in the Social Environment: An Ecological View.* New York: Columbia University Press.

——. 1992. *Curriculum Policy for the Master's Degree and Baccalaureate Degree Programs in Social Work Education.* Washington, D.C.: Council on Social Work Education.

Gibbs, Patty. 1986. "HBSE in the Undergraduate Curriculum: A Survey." *Journal of Social Work Education* (Spring/Summer):46–52.

Gilligan, Carol. 1982. *In a Different Voice.* Cambridge, Mass.: Harvard University Press.

Goldstein, Eda. 1984. *Ego Psychology and Social Work Practice.* New York: Free Press.

Gordon, William E. 1969. "Basic Constructs for an Integrative and Generative Conception of Social Work." In Gordon Hearn, ed., *The General Systems Approach: Contributions Toward an Holistic Conception of Social Work*, pp. 5–12. New York: Council on Social Work Education.

Gould, Roger. 1980. "Transformations During Early and Middle Adult Years." In Neil J. Smelser and Erik H. Erikson, eds., *Themes of Work and Love in Adulthood*, pp. 213–237. Cambridge, Mass.: Harvard University Press.

Greene, Roberta R. and Paul H. Ephross, eds. 1991. *Human Behavior Theory and Social Work Practice.* New York: Aldine.

Guntrip, Harry. 1969. *Schizoid Phenomena, Object Relations, and the Self.* New York: International Universities Press.

Hamburg, David A., Curtis P. Artz, Eric Reiss, William H. Amspacher, and Rawley E. Chambers. 1953. "Clinical Importance of Emotional Problems in the Care of Patients With Burns." *New England Journal of Medicine* 248(9):355–359.

Hare-Mustin, Rachel T. 1978. "A Feminist Approach to Family Therapy." *Family Process* 17 (June):181–194.

Hareven, Tamara K. 1982. "The Life Course and Aging in Historical Perspective." In Tamara K. Hareven and K. J. Adams, eds., *Aging and the Life Course Transitions: An Interdisciplinary Perspective*, pp. 1–26. New York: Guilford Press.

Hartman, Ann and Joan Laird. 1983. *Family Centered Social Work Practice.* New York: Free Press.

Hartmann, Heinz. 1958. *Ego Psychology and the Problem of Adaptation.* New York: International Universities Press.

——. 1964. *Essays in Ego Psychology.* New York: International Universities Press.

Hearn, Gordon A. 1958. *Theory Building in Social Work*. Toronto: University of Toronto Press.

Johnson, Harriette C. 1980. *Human Behavior and Social Environments: New Perspectives. Vol 1. Behavior, Psychopathology, and the Brain*. New York: Curriculum Concepts.

——, et al. 1990. "Strengthening the `Bio' in the Biopsychosocial Paradigm." *Journal of Social Work Education* 2 (Spring/Summer):109–123.

Klein, Melanie. 1950. *Contributions to Psychoanalysis*. London: Tavistock.

Kohlberg, Lawrence. 1969. "Continuities and Discontinuities in Child and Adult Moral Development." *Human Development* 12 (February):93–120.

Kohut, Heinz. 1977. *The Restoration of the Self*. New York: International Universities Press.

Kroeber, Theodore. 1963. "The Coping Functions of the Ego Mechanisms." In Robert W. White, ed., *The Study of Lives*, pp. 178–198. New York: Atherton Press.

Laird, Joan and Jo Ann Allen. 1983. "Family Theory and Practice." In Aaron Rosenblatt and Diana Waldfogel, eds., *Handbook of Clinical Social Work*, pp. 176–201. San Francisco: Jossey-Bass.

Laszlo, Ervin. 1972. *The Systems View of the World*. New York: George Braziller.

Lazarus, Richard S. and Susan Folkman. 1984. *Stress, Appraisal, and Coping*. New York: Springer.

Lazarus, Richard S. and Raymond Launier. 1978. "Stress-Related Transactions Between Person and Environment." In Lawrence A. Pervin and Michael Lewis, eds., *Perspectives in Interactional Psychology*, pp. 287–327. New York: Plenum.

Levinson, Daniel J. 1978. *The Seasons of a Man's Life*. New York: Knopf.

Lichtenberg, Joseph. 1981. "Implications for Psychoanalytic Theory of Research on the Neonate." *International Review of Psycho-Analysis* 3:35–52.

Longres, John F. 1990. *Human Behavior and the Social Environment*. Itasca, Ill.: F. E. Peacock.

Maas, Henry S. 1984. *People and Contexts*. Englewood Cliffs, N.J.: Prentice-Hall.

Mahler, Margaret S., Fred Pine, and Anni Bergman. 1975. *The Psychological Birth of the Human Infant*. New York: Basic Books.

Miller, Jean Baker. 1976. *Toward a New Psychology of Women*. Boston: Beacon Press.

Mitchell, Juliet. 1974. *Psychoanalysis and Feminism*. New York: Pantheon.

Murphy, Lois B. 1974. "Coping, Vulnerability, and Resilience in Childhood." In George V. Coelho, David A. Hamburg, and John E. Adams, eds., *Coping and Adaptation*, pp. 60–100. New York: Basic Books.

Myerhoff, Barbara and Andrei Simic, eds. 1978. *Life's Career—Aging: Cultural Variations on Growing Old*. Beverly Hills, Calif.: Sage.

Neugarten, Bernice L. 1979. "Time, Age, and the Life Cycle." *American Journal of Psychiatry* 136:887–894.

Parsons, Talcott. 1951. *The Social System*. Glencoe, Ill.: Free Press.

Piaget, Jean. 1952. *The Origin of Intelligence in Children.* New York: International Universities Press.

Pillari, Vimala. 1988. *Human Behavior and the Social Environment.* Belmont, Calif.: Brooks/Cole.

Polsky, Howard. 1969. "System as Patient: Client Needs and System Function." In Gordon Hearn, ed., *The General Systems Approach: Contributions Toward an Holistic Conception of Social Work,* pp. 12–25. New York: Council on Social Work Education.

Reamer, Frederic G. 1983. "The Free Will—Determinism Debate and Social Work." *Social Service Review* 57(4):626–644.

Riley, Mathilda W. 1985. "Women, Men, and the Lengthening Life Course." In Alice S. Rossi, ed., *Gender and the Life Course,* pp. 333–347. New York: Aldine.

Rutter, Michael. 1979. "Protective Factors in Children's Responses to Stress and Disadvantage." In Martha Whalen Kent and Jon E. Rolf, eds., *Primary Prevention of Psychopathology,* pp. 49–74. Hanover, N.H.: University Press of New England.

Sander, L. W. 1980. "New Knowledge About the Infant from Current Research." *Journal of the American Psychoanalytic Association* 28:181–198.

Schwartz, Arthur. 1983. "Behavioral Principles and Approaches." In Aaron Rosenblatt and Diana Waldfogel, eds., *Handbook of Clinical Social Work,* pp. 202–228. San Francisco: Jossey-Bass.

Schwartz, Robert. 1982. "Cognitive-Behavior Modification: A Conceptual Review." *Clinical Psychology Review* 2:267–293.

Shafer, Carl M. 1969. "Teaching Social Work Practice in an Integrated Course: A General Systems Approach." In Gordon Hearn, ed., *The General Systems Approach: Contributions Toward an Holistic Conception of Social Work,* pp. 26–36. New York: Council on Social Work Education.

Solomon, Barbara Bryant. 1987. "Human Development: Sociocultural Perspective." In Anne Minahan, ed., *Encyclopedia of Social Work.* 18th ed., vol. 1, pp. 856–866. Silver Spring, Md.: National Association of Social Workers.

Specht, Riva and Grace J. Craig. 1987. *Human Development: A Social Work Perspective.* Englewood Cliffs, N.J.: Prentice-Hall.

Sroufe, L. Alan. 1978. "Attachment and the Roots of Competence." *Human Nature* 1 (October):50–57.

Stamm, Isabel. 1959. "Ego Psychology in the Emerging Theoretical Base of Social Work." In Alfred J. Kahn, ed., *Issues in American Social Work,* pp. 80–109. New York: Columbia University Press.

Stern, Daniel. 1985. *The Interpersonal World of the Human Infant.* New York: Basic Books.

Strean, Herbert S., ed. 1971. *Social Casework: Theories in Action.* Metuchen, N.J.: Scarecrow Press.

——. 1979. *Psychoanalytic Theory and Social Work Practice.* New York: Free Press.

Taggart, Morris. 1985. "The Feminist Critique in Epistemological Perspective:

Questions of Context in Family Therapy." *Journal of Marital and Family Therapy* 11(2):113–126.

Thomas, Alexander. 1981. "Current Trends in Developmental Theory." *American Journal of Orthopsychiatry* 51 (October): 580–609.

Thomlison, Ray J. 1986. "Behavioral Therapy in Social Work Practice." In Francis J. Turner, ed., *Social Work Treatment: Interlocking Theoretical Approaches*, pp. 131–154. New York: Free Press.

Vaillant, George E. 1977. *Adaptation to Life*. Boston: Little, Brown.

von Bertalanffy, Ludwig. 1960. "The Theory of Open Systems in Physics and Biology." *Science* 111:23.

Weiss, Robert S. 1982. "Attachment in Adult Life." In Colin M. Parkes and Joan Stevenson-Hinde, eds., *The Place of Attachment in Adult Life*, pp. 171–183. New York: Basic Books.

Werner, Harold D. 1986. "Cognitive Theory." In Francis J. Turner, ed., *Social Work Treatment: Interlocking Theoretical Approaches*, pp. 91–130. New York: Free Press.

White, Robert W. 1959. "Motivation Reconsidered: The Concept of Competence." *Psychological Review* 25 (September):271–274.

Winnicott, Donald W. 1958. "Transitonal Objects and Transitional Phenomena." In *Through Pediatrics to Psychoanalysis*. London: Hogarth Press.

——. 1965. *The Family and Individual Development*. London: Tavistock.

Woods, Katherine M. 1971. "The Contributions of Psychoanalysis and Ego Psychology to Social Casework." In Herbert S. Strean, ed., *Social Casework: Theories in Action*, pp. 76–107. Metuchen N.J.: Scarecrow Press.

5

Research and Evaluation

WILLIAM J. REID

This paper can be framed by two general questions: What research knowledge and skills should be regarded as an essential part of social work education and practice? How should such knowledge and skills be taught? When examined, these broad questions dissolve into a host of more specific queries. What kind of research content should be presented and from what epistemological standpoint? What types of skills are considered basic? For example, how much emphasis should be placed on teaching students to become consumers as opposed to doers of research? And what kinds of doing and consuming should be considered fundamental? How should research teaching be integrated horizontally with other coursework taken at the same time? How should it be integrated vertically? For example, what basic-to-advanced sequences of courses make sense? Should research courses taken at the MSW level be necessarily more advanced than those taken at the BSW level?

There are no simple or straightforward answers to such questions. Although points of consensus can be found, most questions of this kind are unsettled issues in research teaching. This chapter will be one formulation of what social work students should learn about research and how they should learn it. In reaching this formulation I shall try to identify areas of agreement, clarify issues, and argue for certain positions. I shall focus on research education at the master's level but will also consider its place at the baccalaureate and doctoral levels. My goal is not to produce a definitive statement but rather some informative observations that will stimulate thinking about the what and how of research teaching in social work.

The Evolution of Research Teaching in Graduate Social Work

Research has been a part of social work from the beginnings of the profession. The scientific philanthropy movement in the late nineteenth century and the social survey movement that followed in the early decades of the twentieth were integral to the development of professional social work (Zimbalist 1955). Research courses were included in the curricula of the first schools of social work.

As graduate social work programs developed during the 1920s, research offerings generally consisted of courses in research and statistics, which culminated in an individual thesis—following academic traditions for master's study. Early teaching of research emphasized the methodology of the social sciences, which also furnished texts and teachers. Students were viewed as both potential consumers and doers of research. Moreover, study of research was seen as an essential part of preparation for practice. As Hagerty (1931:117) observed, "[Research] offers to all social workers a means of analytical approach to the puzzling problems they are bound to encounter."

By the 1950s most schools of social work required at least one research course during the first year of graduate study followed by an individual or group project during the second (Mencher 1959). Gradually group projects began to replace individual theses, and then, beginning in the sixties, the use of second-year projects of any sort began to decline. Serious questions were raised about the scientific merit of such projects and even more serious questions were raised about the large amounts of faculty and student time required to complete them relative to their results and to other curriculum needs. Increasingly it was being seen as an archaic and unproductive exercise students needed to complete in order to obtain their degrees.

The fade-out of the master's project was symptomatic of a growing pessimism about the value of research in social work education and, indeed, in social work practice itself (Austin 1986). Research was seen as lacking relevance to the needs of the practitioner. On the other hand, research that appeared to be relevant often seemed to be sending the message that social work was ineffective without giving any direction about how effectiveness might be improved (Fischer 1973). Few practitioners were involved in doing research and, as a study by Rosenblatt (1968) suggested, few made use of research as a source of knowledge.

Given the minimal participation of practitioners in research activities, it seemed pointless to prepare them to be research producers. Perhaps the main value of research teaching lay in inculcating students with a scientific attitude toward knowledge and in preparing them to be intelligent consumers of whatever useful studies might appear on the scene. Preparation for doing research seemed to make sense only for the minority of students—e.g., in community organization, administration, or research concentrations—who might be expected to use it in their work.

However, some developments were under way that would begin to change this picture. Doctoral education in social work had begun to grow in earnest in the 1960s and had began to produce faculty more knowledgeable about research and more committed to its values. Increasingly, these newer faculty had expertise in both research and other areas, which enabled them to teach research in ways more attuned to students' interests and to give research a different voice than could be supplied by just "research faculty." These newer faculty also began to edit and write research texts specifically related to social work research. It is worth noting, however, that such texts did not appear in any number until the 1980s—an indicator that efforts by social work educators to define the content of research instruction have indeed been quite recent.

Another development, one that began in the late sixties and reached fruition the following decade, was the empirical practice movement (Briar 1990). Fueled by new behavioral interventions, single-system research methods, and growing concern over accountability, it brought to direct practice, the branch of social work most estranged from research, a new scientific perspective. A strong research orientation was seen to be not only compatible with practice at the case level but as a means to strengthen it. Case problems and goals could be operationally defined, often in quantitative terms; interventions could be carefully specified and guided by case data or research-based theories; changes and outcomes could be systematically measured. In short, roles of practitioner and researcher could be integrated in ways not possible, or even imagined, in more traditional forms of practice.

One consequence of this movement was to open up new possibilities for integrating teaching of direct practice and research. Programs in which both methods were taught in an integrated manner, often in the same course, began to appear. Another consequence was the introduction of single-case methodology as a means for students to evaluate their own practice. There was renewed attention to the student as a doer of research—not so much as an investigator in traditional studies but rather as a practitioner-researcher who could do rigorous evaluations of his or her own practice. By 1982 the Council on Social Work Education (CSWE) was requiring that schools prepare students to evaluate their own practice.

Finally, more systematic approaches to research utilization and diffusion began to evolve. Rather than simply lamenting practitioners' reluctance to learn about and apply the results of research, social work researchers began to study processes of research dissemination. Use was made of the large body of research on knowledge utilization in the social sciences (Havelock 1969; Kirk 1979). Research projects and conferences on research utilization in social work education were developed (Rubin and Rosenblatt 1979; Briar, Weissman, and Rubin, 1981; Kirk and Rosenblatt 1981). There was growing interest in devising ways of translating research results into practice models (Rothman 1980; Mullen 1978; Thomas 1978). These developments stimulated new thinking about ways of making research more relevant and applicable to practice. They also introduced technology for building research into practice models. By applying these models, practitioners could utilize research indirectly.

The Current Scene

Research education in the 1990s is characterized by considerable diversity, to say the least. It seems as if every historical development in teaching research, as well as every shade of opinion about how much research should be emphasized, continues to survive in one form or another.

In a recent study, Fraser and Lewis (1993) found that much of this variation could be captured in four clusters. Certain schools (n=10) placed considerable emphasis on research and statistics in an effort to prepare students to be research doers as well as consumers—the "de rigeur approach," as the authors describe it. Another group (n=29) could be described as following a "single case plus approach," one that emphasized single-system designs and own practice evaluation. In schools using a "traditionalist approach" (n=29), emphasis was on basic research methods with scant attention paid to either statistics or to single-system methodology. Finally, "minimalist" schools (n=15) offered a scaled-down version of the traditionist approach: the goal appeared to be only a moderate level of research consumption.

Another source of variation concerns whether research or practice methods are taught in an integrated manner or separately. Fraser, Lewis, and Norman (1991) found that integrated formats were used by thirty-five of the ninety master's programs surveyed. Presumably most of these programs were also those in which the "single case plus approach" was used.

Finally, schools differ in respect to the research project. The traditional master's thesis or group project as a degree requirement persists in a small and declining minority of schools. However, in a substantial proportion of schools, almost 40 percent, all or most students carry out research projects in their field placements (Fraser, Lewis, and Norman 1990). Many of these projects are presumably own practice evaluations. By contrast, in almost a third of the schools the field placement is not used as a project site.

Given all this variation, what normative statements can be made? Most schools offer a basic research methods course, although, as suggested, these courses may vary considerably in level of sophistication. A second course in research related either to clinical or administrative practice is a common pattern. In their survey, Fraser, Lewis, and Norman (1990) found that schools require an average of about six semester hours of research coursework (including the project); four schools required as little as two hours and one required as much as thirteen.

How does this variegated picture of research offerings square with CSWE's accreditation requirements? According to its most recent curriculum policy statement for master's programs (1992), students should learn "how to apply relevant research findings to practice, . . . to demonstrate skills in quantitative and qualitative research design, data analysis, and knowledge dissemination [and] conduct empirical evaluations of their own practice interventions and those of other systems." Research curricula "must provide an understanding . . . of a scientific, analytic approach to building knowledge for practice and for evaluating service delivery" and all parts of the curriculum must strengthen this objective. Although it may be hard to imagine how programs at the lower end of investment in research education—e.g., the minimalist programs—could meet such standards, much depends on how the standards are interpreted. Fraser and Lewis's (1993) comments on the council's 1980 research standards (which are similar to those cited above) are germane: "The Guidelines are insufficiently specific. They suffer from multiple, often competing and contradictory, interpretations" (p. 87). To provide a simple illustration, skills in data analysis could mean anything from simple frequency counts to factor analyses.

Getting Specific about Research Education

The variety of perspectives on what students should learn about research and the lack of detailed accreditation guidelines support the need for the kind of specifications to be undertaken in this chapter. I shall concentrate on three areas: the subject matter of research, research skills, and integration in research teaching. Particular attention will be given to issues concerning what the essentials should be. In addition, I shall attempt to balance my conception of research essentials against other curriculum demands. By so doing I shall try to avoid the fallacy of developing an ideal program in research (or whatever) that might be completely infeasible given these demands.

The Subject Matter of Research

In this section I shall consider basic content for all students at the master's level. Before taking up the subjects to be included in foundation content, I will briefly discuss the *research paradigm* that I will use to frame the content and issues relating to this choice. The paradigm one adopts controls what topics are chosen and emphasized.

Paradigm Issues

From its inception social work research has been dominated by a single paradigm. I shall refer to it as "contemporary empiricism," following Peile (1988), but it is more usually called "postpositivism" (Guba 1990; Phillips 1990; Fraser et al. 1991). It consists of a system of assumptions and practices about the most effective ways of discovering and testing knowledge, a loosely organized and sometimes conflicted system that has evolved over centuries of human inquiry. Although its methods vary, it tends to use preplanned designs, structured instruments, and largely quantitative data to examine frequencies and relationships within specific sets of variables.

In recent years a number of alternatives to this paradigm have been proposed (for reviews, see Peile 1988; Orcutt 1990). Among these alternatives are constructivism (Gergen 1985; Witkin 1989), the heuristic model (Heineman-Pieper 1989), naturalistic inquiry (Lincoln and Guba 1985), hermeneutics (Ricoeur 1981), and new paradigm research (Reason and Rowan 1981). A common theme in these paradigms is the advocacy of qualitative methodology.

Despite the challenge posed by the alternative paradigms, contemporary empiricism has remained the dominant force in social work and social science research. There are no signs of an impending collapse. Although its worldviews and methodologies have been vigorously attacked (Heineman 1981; Imre 1984; Haworth 1984), they have also been stoutly defended (Hudson 1982; Schuerman 1982; Phillips 1987; Fraser et al. 1991). Much of the criticism has been aimed at the presumed philosophical foundations of empiricism, rather than at the working assumptions of contemporary empirical researchers, which may be quite different from, if not at odds with, those "foundations." Criticisms that empiricism has added little to social work knowledge can be countered by examples of meaningful and much used contributions it has produced (Reid 1994). Contemporary empiricism was clearly the banner of the recent and influential Task Force on Social Work Research (1991). It recommended in effect a more assiduous application of this paradigm in social work research.

Moreover, if students are to be trained to utilize research as well as to be participants in its production, they need to learn the methodology of contemporary empiricism, which accounts for all but a small fraction of present-day social work research. Otherwise they would leave educational programs decidedly ill-prepared for these research roles.

Finally, contemporary empiricism is quite compatible with the *methodology* proposed by the alternative paradigms. From the empiricist viewpoint, qualitative methodology is a legitimate means of carrying out inquiry. Like any other methods, they have their special strengths and limitations. It would be certainly possible, and, I think, desirable, to expand their use in social work research. But it would make sense to expand within an empiricist framework that would enable quantitative and qualitative methods to be used in combination

(Harrison 1994). My specification of foundation content will be framed by this kind of developing empiricism.

Knowledge, Theory, and Problem Formulation.

In order to get a grasp of what research is and how it works, it is essential to have an understanding of the nature of knowledge and theory. In particular, it is important for students to know how knowledge and theory lead to research questions and hypotheses and how research results in turn provide feedback to knowledge and theory development.

Students should be exposed to different views of knowledge, especially contrasts between contemporary empiricism and alternate paradigms. It is important for students to see that empiricism, which will be the usual organizing framework, *is* a paradigm with its own set of arguable assumptions rather than simply the voice of science. While students might be given some exposure to the epistemological debate in social work (Reamer 1993; Reid 1994), it is hard to justify, as foundation content, much reading or discussion of related literature in the philosophy of science. Dabbling in this highly technical literature is more confusing than enlightening for most students. Moreover, as Rorty (1979) has argued, it is an error to assume that knowledge of philosophy of science is needed as groundwork for understanding or justifying a research paradigm.

In empiricism, research questions or hypotheses are broken down through a familiar process: key concepts are defined theoretically and then operationally through specific indicators, which are usually quantified. The result is an ordering of the problem into variables, whose frequencies and interrelationships are then investigated through statistical analysis.

Although students need to learn this fundamental process, they also need to become aware of its shortfalls. As exponents of alternate paradigms have suggested, it can lead to fragmented analyses that ignore holistic relationships and the contexts in which they occur. In this regard it helps to view typical research processes in the empiricist framework as leading to very rough and partial pictures of reality that need to be filled out through such means as common sense, theory, practice wisdom, and qualitative methods. But to recognize the limitations of empiricism is not to reject its usefulness. All means of acquiring knowledge are limited, and truth is usually more an ideal to strive for than an absolute goal to attain.

Design

As part of learning the fundamentals of research students should become familiar with basic types of design, including experimental, quasi-experimental, exploratory-descriptive, and longitudinal designs as well as ex post facto studies that use matching or statistical controls. Designs for qualitative as well as quantitative research should be a part of this core.

However, it is not enough for students to learn about research design at an abstract level. Design should be viewed in relation to the kind of research questions that are of concern to social work. These questions flow from social work's knowledge needs, e.g., to increase understanding of problems and dynamics of individuals, families, groups, organizations, and communities and to determine the characteristics and effectiveness of service programs.

Thus, single-system and group experimental designs can be taught largely within the context of studies evaluating programs and testing service effectiveness. Although it is essential for students to have an understanding of controlled designs, equal attention should be paid to designs lacking the usual controls—for example, the AB single-system design (baseline followed by intervention) and the pre-post (intervention only) design commonly used in evaluations of demonstration projects. Complex designs more appropriate to the laboratory than the field, such as the Solomon four-group design, can probably be passed over, although it may be worthwhile to consider factorial designs, which have been used in social work field experiments.

Similarly, exploratory-descriptive designs can be taken up in relation to studies of population characteristics, to client satisfaction surveys, or in conjunction with needs assessments. Longitudinal designs can be examined as a part of strategies to study human development among other possibilities. Controlled ex post facto designs can be connected to investigations of the etiologies of social problems, as for example, in studies that compare families with a problem member (delinquent, schizophrenic, etc.) against matched "normal" controls.

Students should become familiar with ways of assessing the strengths and limitations of designs. Students should learn how designs vary in respect to their capacity to control alternative explanations (threats to internal validity) and to yield generalizable findings (external validity). It is particularly important that they grasp the distinction between causal and correlational relationships. For example, in evaluating intervention programs students frequently fall prey to the "post hoc fallacy"—if the client improves after service, the improvement must be the result of service.

The work of Campbell and his associates (Campbell and Stanley 1963; Cook and Campbell 1979), as well as a framework developed by Krathwohl (1985) are especially useful here. Another key idea is Cook's (1985) principle of multiplism—that research problems should be pursued through a variety of designs. Thus, there is a strategy in which the weaknesses of one kind of design are offset by the strengths of another.

Sampling and Generalization

A nontechnical overview of the major types of sampling plans (e.g., probability and nonprobability), together with their usual pros and cons, can lead to examination of detailed aspects of sampling and generalization as they relate to typical social work studies. Given the nature of such studies, emphasis should be on nonprobability samples and the kind of logical generalizations that can be derived from them.

Data Collection and Measurement

Content in this area should include a review of: 1) data collection methods of particular relevance to social work research, such as observation, semistructured and in-depth interviews, standardized tests, self-administered questionnaires, clinical measurement packages, participant observation, and content analysis; 2) the levels of measurement (ratio, ordinal, etc.) and commonly used scales (Likert, rank order, etc.); and 3) the concepts of validity and reliability. The principle of multiplism applies here as well: students should learn the importance of using multiple means of data collection and multiple measures, including combinations of quantitative and qualitative approaches. As with design, there needs to be application to social work contexts. How does the concept of inter-rater reliability apply to a content analysis of case records? In dealing with these complex topics it is useful to make use of certain common standards that students can readily grasp. One such is the notion of bias.

Thus, students can examine different methods of data collection from the standpoint of the kinds of biases likely to be encountered with each and what can be done to control these biases. Particular attention should be given to the tendency of clients to respond in socially desirable ways in evaluation instruments, especially clients who might think that "wrong" responses might endanger their services or benefits.

Data Analysis

In order for students to be either consumers or doers of research, they need to have some familiarity with basic elements of data analysis. These elements would include coding, construction and interpretation of simple tables, measures of association, and tests of significance. At a minimum, one or two measures of association and tests of significance can be used as models for how such measures and tests are constructed, without detailed coverage of the many variations. The distinction between statistical and substantive significance should be given special emphasis (Jayaratne 1990).

Although there is general agreement that at least some minimum of statistical content, such as described above, should be a part of the research curriculum, there are differences of opinion over how much beyond this minimum is desirable for students at the master's level. Some schools require special courses in statistics, and arguments for increasing emphasis on statistics have been advanced (Lazar 1990; Jenson, Fraser, and Lewis 1991; Glisson and Fischer 1987).

The basic argument for requiring substantial content on statistics, which is generally meant to mean one or more statistics courses, is that a reasonable degree of statistical literacy is needed to become an informed consumer of research as well as a participant in research undertakings (Lazar 1990; Glisson and Fischer 1987). An additional argument is that basic coursework in statistics is a necessary part of a vertically integrated research curriculum that would, among other things, prepare students for advanced study at the doctoral level (Jenson, Fraser and Lewis 1990; Glisson and Fischer 1987).

There is little doubt that an increased knowledge of statistics would prepare practitioners for better research consumership and participation. However, given the difficulties typically experienced by social work students in learning and retaining statistics, it is questionable that master's level coursework in the subject would really make a difference. A *considerable* amount of sophistication in statistics is necessary to critique studies using complex statistical designs, much more than students bring away from an introductory course or two. Moreover, statistics is not normally a part of the student's learning and doing professional practice in the field or work setting. The powerful sources of incentive and reinforcement these settings provide for acquiring new knowledge are not present for statistics, a main factor no doubt in students' reluctance to learn statistics and to its early departure from their memories. When other demands in the master's curriculum are taken into account, it is hard to justify statistics courses as part of a core research requirement.

A related issue is whether or not students should learn to use computers in conjunction with data analysis. Computers have, of course, a variety of functions in social work and social work education, and an argument can be made that students should attain a degree of computer literacy (Parker et al. 1987). In respect to research, however, it is difficult to support spending much time having students learn to use statistical computer programs if teaching statistics is to be primarily consumer-oriented.

Other Topics

Certain subjects that might have been included above, such as interpretation of findings, research utilization, and own practice evaluation, will be taken up as skills in the next section. I will consider here, however, two subjects whose possible inclusion into core research content raises some issues.

One of these concerns ethics in the conduct of research. Although inclusion of content of the ethics of research is an accreditation requirement, the subject often receives only passing attention. Primary emphasis should be given to issues concerning human subjects. Included here would be such topics as informed consent, risks to subjects, and protection of confidentiality. It is also important to clarify ethical questions relating to use of experimental designs with client populations, as well as designs that may be intrusive or that involve withholding or delay of service. Agencies' reluctance to use such designs is sometimes based on ethical arguments that might not hold up when closely examined. In other instances ethical quandaries emerge when none seemed apparent at first glance. Because students will become the agency decision makers of the future, it is vital that they have a chance to work through such dilemmas in their training.

The second issue has to do with research content relating to diversity —women, racial, ethnic, and other minorities. There are differences of opinion about the emphasis to be given such content in research courses and how it is to be introduced. Because a great deal of general theoretical and methodological content must be squeezed into these courses, there is not sufficient time, in my view, to deal with diversity in any depth. However, instructors can take up diversity issues in various contexts. For example, within the context of research questions and design, instructors can stress the importance of studies addressed to the needs of minority or oppressed groups. Sampling considerations can lead to a discussion of how certain groups, such as African Americans, have been deliberately excluded from research samples. Data collection methods can be examined from the standpoint of the need for their adaptation to the special needs and characteristics of minority groups. Specifically, students can learn how wording on questionnaires may be insensitive or inappropriate. Studies involving research with such groups can be used in conjunction with teaching general aspects of the research process.

Essential Skills

So far we have considered the subject matter that students should be exposed to in basic research courses. We turn now to the specific applications that students might make of this content, that is, to the skills in research that might be regarded as generic in master's level education. These skills fall basically into three groups: 1) research utilization, that is, being able to comprehend, evaluate, and make use of studies and other products of research; 2) doing research, that is, being able to carry out research tasks as part of a formal study or in conjunction with practice activities; and 3) scientific thinking, that is, the ability to apply a scientific, analytic approach to knowledge and practice. (Since this last skill can be taught throughout the curriculum, it will be discussed subsequently, within the context of integration.)

Research Utilization

Research utilization incorporates the notion of research consumption—or reading, understanding, and evaluating studies—but also includes the application of research in professional roles. Although there is general agreement on the importance of enabling students to achieve competence in research utilization, there is lack of consensus about what exactly we expect students to accomplish.

The more conservative position stresses the need for students to achieve a thorough comprehension of the research methodology used, including complex statistical techniques, and to be able to evaluate it critically. Students should be able to form their own conclusions based on the data and methods presented. Especially to be avoided are errors in the application of research, such as overgeneralizing findings. The more liberal position accepts the usefulness of partial comprehension and evaluation. The main point is that students should be stimulated to make use of research at whatever level their skills permit, even at the risk of some misapplication. It is far worse for students to not read research because "it's too difficult" or discarding possibly useful findings because of "flaws in the study."

I am inclined toward the liberal position since it is more in tune with student interests and limitations in respect to research. It is more compelling to get students involved in actively using research to the best of their ability than to require a depth of understanding and a level of critical capacity that may be beyond the reach of most.

From this standpoint I would like to spell out the kinds of skills in research utilization that may be particularly important at the master's level. First, students should know how to apply the basics of the research process reviewed earlier to the understanding and evaluation of empirical investigations. Some examples will illustrate the kind of skills I have in mind. For instance, students should be able to understand the function of an experimental design in controlling alternative explanations (extraneous variance) and to identify typical threats to internal validity found in experimental and quasi-experimental designs. They should be able to apply knowledge of matching to controlled ex post facto designs and to identify variables not matched for. They should be able to understand tables displaying frequencies and cross-tabulations, to interpret graphic presentations of time-series data, and to comprehend the functions and limitations of tests of significance. They should be able to detect common sources of error in measurement, such as social desirability and halo effects, and to make informed judgments about the reliability and validity of instruments used.

Second, students need to learn skills in utilizing studies whose methodology they may not fully comprehend. An effort here should be made in helping students get at least a conceptual grasp of advanced techniques. For example, they can learn that factor analysis is a technique for identifying clusters of variables that tend to be interrelated. Such conceptual understanding (especially with some help from the author(s) of the study) may be sufficient for a student to discern what a factor analysis has accomplished, even though the student may not understand eigenvalues, commonalities, or methods of rotation. Students should always be encouraged to go as far as they can and instructors should avoid being condescending. What should be emphasized is that knowledge of such methods is usually partial (most researchers who use factor analysis do not understand its mathematical foundations) and that partial knowledge may be adequate for the purposes at hand.

A final utilization skill has to do with students' ability to incorporate research findings into whatever systems of knowledge they will make use of in their practice (Mullen 1978). This skill can be developed in the light of newer models of research utilization in the human services. In older models it was assumed that users applied research findings directly to service problems. In studies of utilization it was found that this kind of "instrumental" utilization did not occur frequently (Weiss and Bucuvalas 1980). Of greater importance was "conceptual utilization" (Rich 1981) in which findings are combined with other sources of knowledge, including knowledge derived from personal experience. From the standpoint of conceptual utilization, studies need to be mined for results that might connect to the student's own fund of knowledge and discussed in relation to that knowledge. The strength of research findings needs to be seen in the light of other kinds of knowledge the student might have or can obtain from other sources. Thus, flawed research findings may turn out to be better evidence than—and hence preferable to—knowledge otherwise available to the student. In evaluating research findings students should learn to think in terms of how they stack up against the evidential base of alternative formulations rather than their meeting absolute criteria of scientific truth.

Doing Research

In recent years education for skill in doing research has focused on enabling students to become proficient at evaluating their own practice. As was seen earlier, the main vehicle for developing skill in this type of evaluation has been the single-system design (SSD), at least for students in direct practice (Bloom and Fischer 1982; Videka-Sherman and Reid 1990). The SSD framework has been used to organize a variety of specific skills. These include skills in use of a range of assessment devices, such as direct observation, rapid assessment instruments (Corcoran and Fischer 1987), and client self-monitoring tools (Bornstein, Hamilton, and Bornstein 1986), as well as skills in measuring change through such means as constructing graphs, calculating differences between before and after measures, goal attainment scaling (Kiresuk and Sherman 1968), and collecting evaluation data from clients and collaterals (Reid and Smith 1989). Although controlled SSDs—e.g., multiple baseline and withdrawal designs—may be taught, learning for doing tends to concentrate on simple time series, such as the AB design, the kind that students are most likely to use in applications to their own cases.

Although these skills may be taught and practiced within a case evaluation framework, they can be used for purposes other than evaluation. For example, research tools can be used just for purposes of assessment or case planning. More generally the "own evaluation" focus comprises a range of research skills that have a variety of practice applications.

In order to justify the teaching of these skills, one needs to determine the extent to which they are used in the students' postgraduate careers. Results of followups have suggested that only a small minority of graduates use full SSDs to evaluate their work—about 12 percent—but that much larger percentages use a range of SSD techniques, such as specifying goals in measurable terms and assessing client functioning through standardized instruments (Penka and Kirk 1991; Richey, Blythe, and Berlin 1987). It is difficult to evaluate such results since we have few norms by which to assess the application of *any* skill students may be taught. But the findings suggest that some elements are being used, especially measurement techniques.

These results appear to support arguments by Gingerich (1990) and Blythe (1990) that more emphasis should be placed on measurement for purposes of case monitoring, planning, and evaluation and less on complex design. These measurement skills are the ones that students are most likely to retain because they are the ones most likely to help them do a better job with clients. For this reason, if no other, they may be the most critical. Their usefulness to students can be increased with the addition of "nonbehavioral" applications (Dean and Reinherz 1986; Nelsen 1990) and qualitative methods (Reid and Davis 1987; Ruckdeschel, Earnshaw, and Firrek 1994).

Comparable skills for students specializing in areas other than direct practice have not been as well developed. Thus, for management students, the focus may be on skills in program evaluation (discussed below). However, to evaluate a program is rather different from evaluating one's own practice, which in the case of an administrator, might involve tracking the outcomes of his or her decisions or other aspects of managerial effectiveness.

The older sense of doing research—carrying out studies of clients, programs, communities, etc.—involves a larger and potentially more sophisticated array of skills than single case evaluation. The study by Fraser and Lewis (1993) referred to earlier reflects the divergence among schools in respect to whether such skills should be goals of master's curricula and, if so, to what extent. The current accreditation requirement that students be able to "perform research activities independently or as a member of a research team" is open to a wide range of interpretation. The ambivalence and inconsistency in how such skills are viewed can be clearly seen in a recent survey of curriculum priorities held by deans and directors of master's programs (Eure, Griffin, and Atherton 1987:27). When skills in doing research were cast at a high level of abstraction—for example, "skill in the generation of knowledge"—they tended to be given high priority. However, specific competencies needed to implement these abstract skills—for example, "construction of tables, graphs, and other displays"—were given quite low priority. While schools may subscribe to the ideal of training students to do research, there is reluctance to provide them with the specific tools to enable them to realize this ideal.

It may be helpful to develop some mid-range "doing" skills, less abstract than "generation of knowledge" but more general than "construction of tables." At this middle level it may be possible to identify certain skills in "operations research," or research that provides direct support to agency programs. Two types in particular come to mind: 1) the ability to carry out simple needs assessments, including key informant studies and community surveys; and 2) skills in program evaluation, including the ability to develop a before-after design, to collect and analyze simple process and outcome data—especially data based on feedback from clients—and to apply findings to program improvement. Skills at this level would serve to organize more specific competencies, such as table construction. Presumably the products of such operations research would be used in program development rather than as a basis for generating knowledge for the field, although published reports might occur in some cases as a byproduct. Other midrange skills in operations research might be added, especially for students in macro practice. These might include cost-benefit analysis and research uses of management information systems.

In my view, teaching a limited number of operational research skills would constitute a practical, attainable goal in contrast to the amorphous and overblown objective of preparing students to be generators of knowledge. While it is hoped that some MSWs would be able to do independent knowledge-building research, it is unrealistic to expect that they can be trained to do so at the master's level.

Integration

In teaching research, as well as other subjects, two kinds of integration of subject matter and skills are of particular concern. One is *horizontal integration*, or the integration of research with other subjects in the curriculum that are taught more or less concurrently. The other is *vertical integration*, or the sequencing of research courses from less to more advanced or through the three levels of social work education—BSW, MSW, and PhD. After taking up horizontal integration, again limited to the master's level, I shall turn to vertical integration in which all three levels will be considered.

Horizontal Integration

In discussing horizontal integration I shall focus on the interconnections between teaching research and practice methods, which have received the most attention in school curricula and in the literature. The purposes of this kind of integration have been to enhance student learning of research and their attitudes toward research by making it more relevant to practice and, at the same time, to teach them empirically grounded practice methods.

A variety of approaches have been used. Research and practice methods may be taught in the same course or in different courses by a single instructor or by a team. Different instructors may teach coordinated, concurrent courses. Teaching research may also be integrated with field instruction, especially around single case studies or other projects carried out in the field.

Whatever format is used, integrated approaches stress commonalities between research and practice, such as use of problem solving, hypothesis testing, data gathering, and inference making. Students might be asked to utilize the research literature to build personal practice models (Mullen, Bostwick, and Ryg 1980) or to combine a review of research relating to a practice approach with study of the approach itself. Clinical use of research methods, such as standardized instruments and observation and, more generally, of single-case evaluation techniques, provide additional examples of integration. Integration can perhaps be most fully achieved when the practice models taught are empirically based—such as behavioral approaches—although it has been possible to attain with other models of practice (Gottlieb and Richey 1980).

Integration between research and practice in field settings generally involves the carrying out of practice-related research projects or tasks. These may include program evaluations, needs assessments, single case studies, or the use of specific research methods, such as rapid assessment or observational instruments.

Most studies of integrative approaches have reported positive results in respect to such aspects as students' attitudes toward research, learning research methods, use of research-grounded practice, and perceived readiness for practice (Gottlieb and Richey 1980; Mullen, Bostwick, and Ryg 1980; Richey, Blythe, and Berlin 1987; Olsen 1990). Although in her study of an integrated curriculum, Siegel (1983) reported mixed results, including a more negative attitude toward research, she was able to identify factors associated with positive learning outcomes (Siegel 1985). For example, she found that stress on empirical practice themes in class and support of the student's research in his or her fieldwork setting contributed to better attitudes toward research.

Integrative approaches to teaching research and practice methods appear to make research more interesting and relevant to students and to enhance their learning of it. Teaching of practice may also be strengthened by the infusion of research perspectives and techniques, even practice that is "nonbehaviorial" (Wood 1980). Opportunities to apply integrative learning in the field through single case evaluations and other kinds of practice-related projects seem to be particularly important (Siegel 1985; Olsen 1990; Wodarski et al. 1991). The learning value of these projects will also be enhanced if field instructors themselves have some research skills.

Integrated approaches are not without their problems. Scheduling may be difficult. It may be hard to find appropriate combinations of faculty willing to spend the extra time coordinated teaching requires. In single-instructor or team-teaching arrangements, one method may get shortchanged, or there may not be adequate time to cover either adequately. Further study is needed to determine which integrative structures are the most cost-effective. Quite possibly much of the value of integration can be achieved in separate research and practice courses, each taught from an integrative point of view.

The integration between research and other parts of the curriculum is not limited, of course, to practice methods in the class or field. Magee (1982), for example, has described a way of integrating research and HBSE. More generally, two aspects of research can be applied throughout the curriculum. One of these is scientific thinking. Students can be taught to view knowledge with skepticism, to search for alternative explanations, to distinguish between correlational and causative relations, to identify untested assumptions and logical fallacies, to demand evidence to support assertions, to recognize the importance of corroboration in establishing truth claims, and to define phenomena in terms of specific indicators (Siegel and Reamer 1988). Although thinking of this kind is by no means limited to science—it is characteristic of any discipline that demands critical, analytic intelligence—it receives particular emphasis and refinement in scientific pursuits. Moreover, in teaching students to think scientifically, instructors can draw parallels between the kind of problem solving done in research and the kind done in practice (Grinnell and Siegel 1988).

In the second kind of general application one can make use of the research base of whatever subject is being taught. Given the need to cover a great deal of ground in the typical social work course, one would not expect that much attention could be given to individual studies. Reviews and meta-analyses of research, as well as empirically grounded theory, could play an important role, however. In discussions of such literature, issues in research methodology that might affect the knowledge base could be taken up.

Vertical Integration

In keeping with my emphasis on MSW programs I will start with some observations about sequencing of courses within the master's level.

Following this, I will examine some issues in integration across program levels, with particular attention to BSW programs.

As noted earlier, the typical sequencing of research courses at the master's level consists of a basic course followed by an advanced course. The advanced courses differ according to the student's specialization, micro or macro. This progression seems to be a reasonable one. It will be greatly beneficial if *both* courses provide some degree of integration of research and practice methods and if content and skills taught in the classroom can be applied in the field through small-scale projects related to one or both courses. I see this package as constituting the basic minimum for research training at the master's level. If this minimum were to be extended, the next addition, in my view, would be a more ambitious research project, ideally one connected to the student's field placement.

At the BSW level, research training consists largely of a single basic course in research methods. The course is often taught by an instructor without a social work background; for this reason, among others, it is usually not related to courses in practice methods (Smith, DeWeaver, and Kilpatrick 1986). Course content and emphases seem similar to the introductory master's level course (Eure, Griffin, and Atherton 1987).

According to the most recent curriculum policy statement, students graduating from BSW programs should emerge with knowledge, attitudes, and skills similar to their MSW counterparts. The main differences are that BSWs are expected to need supervision to evaluate their own practice and are not expected to carry out other research activities independently. Poulin (1989) found that the majority of program directors—60 percent—did not think that BSW programs should aim to prepare students to "contribute to the generation of knowledge for practice" (p. 287).

Since BSW students receive on the average about half the instruction in research than do MSW students, it would be expected that most similar curriculum goals, such as the ability to evaluate research studies and apply them to practice, would be achieved at a lesser level in BSW programs. Also, lack of instructors with social work backgrounds would be an obstacle to achieving goals regarding own practice evaluations.

Given the issues that have been raised, the recommendations by Smith, DeWeaver, and Kilpatrick (1986:69) make sense: that research courses should be taught by instructors with social work backgrounds, that they should be taught by the same instructors "whenever possible" as a means of fostering integration—or, I might add, by instructors working in collaboration—that students should carry out research projects, such as single case studies, within the practicum, and that the research component should be stressed in practice, human behavior, policy, and other courses. Implementation of these recommendations would enable BSW graduates to attain the CPS standards more fully and would better justify their receiving advanced credit for research in master's programs.

When research training across the three levels of social work education is examined, one is struck by lack of progression. It is only a slight exaggeration to say that the same introductory course in research methods is taught at the BSW, MSW, and PhD programs. Students moving through the three levels will almost always have to repeat the course at least once. Over the years, and in recent years particularly, some educators have proposed that research training be made progressive across the three levels (Jenson, Fraser, and Lewis 1991; Glisson and Fischer 1987). Students would take basic coursework at the bachelor's level and intermediate courses at the master's. At the doctoral level they would then be ready for truly advanced work. Students not taking a BSW would still be required to complete a comparable research course as a condition of admission to a master's program.

Although this proposal has some appeal, there are several difficulties with it. It would work best if students moved through the three levels without substantial breaks. But such is not generally the case. Typically, students interrupt their education after each level and admissions criteria for subsequent levels encourage this pattern by favoring students who have had paid social work experience. Because research learning is not reinforced during these breaks, it tends to be forgotten. Another problem concerns the basic course at the bachelor's level. The majority of students entering master's programs have not taken research courses in BSW programs. If they were required to take a substitute course, how could one be assured that these courses, which would probably cover the entire spectrum of undergraduate social science, would provide an adequate foundation? While the kind of vertical integration proposed would provide better preparation in research for beginning doctoral candidates, only a small fraction of MSWs enter PhD programs. The final, and perhaps most serious, difficulty with the proposal arises from its assumption that master's level research training should be an intermediate step in a progressive sequence. To me, it makes more sense to view the purpose of such training as providing knowledge and skills integral to the kind of practice that MSWs will perform upon graduation.

Two Kinds of Research Education

Inevitably, questions about the kind of training in research needed by all social workers become intertwined with questions about the kind of research expertise needed by the social work profession. The confounding of these really separate questions has been a source of much of the divergence on research education discussed in this paper. In this final section I shall attempt to disentangle these questions, and, at the same time, to summarize my own position about what kind of research training is needed for what purpose.

The essential distinction is between *universal* and *expert* training in research. Universal training, which is for all social work students, should, in my view, be seen as supporting the principal activities of the professional roles for which they are being prepared. At the master's level, stress should be on skills that facilitate mainline professional practice—skills in scientific thinking, research utilization, and operations research, with the latter including skills in evaluating one's own practice, in program evaluation, in needs assessment, and in doing simple descriptive-exploratory studies. To the extent possible, these skills should be taught with strong links to the kind of professional work that will be the main business of the students after graduation. From a pedagogic perspective, emphasis should be on providing students with opportunities to perform these skills both in class exercises and in the field with actual clients or in small-scale research studies. Courses throughout the curriculum should not only stress scientific thinking—a current CSWE requirement—but should also "be based on knowledge derived to the fullest extent possible from research in social work and related professions or disciplines" (Task Force on Social Work Research 1991). A similar direction should be pursued at the BSW level.

Training students in practice-relevant research skills would not provide a foundation for independent research activity of any complexity. The production of publishable research-based knowledge would not be an expected educational outcome, although the ability to participate in that production would be.

Social work's urgent need for research-based knowledge should be met largely by research experts, who should combine specialized training in research with training in one or more substantive areas. Although most of these experts would receive their specialized research training exclusively in PhD programs, such training could begin at earlier levels for *selected students*. Permitting these students to concentrate in research or to enter joint MSW-PhD programs would enable them to take advanced courses in statistics and research methodology while still at the master's level. They could then take even more advanced courses at the PhD level, in effect achieving the vertical integration proposed by the educators cited earlier.

Much more could be said about specialized training in research at both master's and PhD levels. However what has been said has perhaps served my main purpose: to be clear about the nature and function of research education for all social workers. The focus of that education should be to prepare research-oriented practitioners who will be able to use research perspectives, methods, and products in their work and to collaborate productively with research specialists to produce the hard knowledge social work so badly needs.

REFERENCES

Austin, D. M. 1986. *A History of Social Work Education*. Austin: School of Social Work, University of Texas.

Bloom, M. and J. Fischer. 1982. *Evaluating Practice: Guidelines for the Accountable Professional*. Englewood Cliffs, N.J.: Prentice-Hall.

Blythe, B. J. 1990. "Improving the Fit between Single-Subject Designs and Practice." In L. Videka-Sherman and W. J. Reid, eds., *Advances in Clinical Social Work Research*, pp. 29–32. Washington, D.C.: NASW Press.

Bornstein, P. H., S. B. Hamilton, and M. T. Bornstein. 1986. "Self Monitoring Procedures." In A. R. Ciminero, K. S. Calhoun, and H. E. Adams, eds., *Handbook of Behavioral Assessment* 2d ed., pp. 176–222. New York: Wiley.

Brekke, J. S. 1986. "Scientific Imperatives in Social Work Research: Pluralism Is Not Skepticism." *Social Service Review* 60:538–555.

Briar, S. 1990. "Empiricism in Clinical Practice: Present and Future." In L. Videka-Sherman and W. J. Reid, eds., *Advances in Clinical Social Work Research*, pp. 1–7. Washington, D.C.: NASW Press.

——, H. Weissman, and A. Rubin. 1981. *Research Utilization in Social Work Education*. New York: Council on Social Work Education.

Campbell, D. T. and J. C. Stanley. 1963. "Experimental and Quasi-Experimental Designs for Research on Teaching." In N. L. Gage, ed., *Handbook of Research on Teaching*, pp. 171–246. Chicago: Rand-McNally.

Cook, T. D. 1985. "Positivist Critical Multiplism." In W. R. Shadish and C. S. Relchardt, eds., *Evaluation Studies*. Newbury Park, Calif.: Sage.

—— and D.T. Campbell. 1979. *Quasi-Experimentation: Design and Analysis Issues for Field Settings*. Chicago: Rand-McNally.

Corcoran, K. and J. Fischer. 1987. *Measures for Clinical Practice: A Source Book*. New York: Free Press.

Council on Social Work Education. 1992. *Curriculum Policy Statement*. Washington D.C.: Council on Social Work Education.

Dean, R. and H. Reinherz. 1986. "Psychodynamic Practice and Single System Design: The Odd Couple." *Journal of Social Work Education* 22:71–81.

Eure, G. K., J. E. Griffin, and C. R. Atherton. 1987. "Priorities for the Professional Foundation: Differences by Program Level." *Journal of Social Work Education* 23(2):19–29.

Fischer, J. 1973. "Is Casework Effective: A Review." *Social Work* 18:5–20.

Fortune, A. E. 1982. "Teaching Students to Integrate Research Concepts and Field Performance Standards." *Journal of Education for Social Work* 18:5–13.

Fraser, M. W. and R. E. Lewis. 1993. "Research in M.S.W. Programs: Four Competing Perspectives." *Journal of Social Service Research* 17(3/4):71–90.

——, R. E. Lewis, and J. L. Norman. 1990. "Research Education in M.S.W. Programs: An Exploratory Analysis." *Journal of Teaching in Social Work* 4(2):83–103.

Fraser, W., M. J. Taylor, R. Jackson, and J. O'Jack. 1991. "Social Work and Science: Many Ways of Knowing?" *Social Work Research and Abstracts* 27(4):5–15.

Gergen, K. J. 1985. "The Social Constructionist Movement in Modern Psychology." *American Psychologist* 40:260–275.

Gingerich, W. J. 1990. "Rethinking Single-Case Evaluation." In L. Videka-Sherman and W. J. Reid, eds., *Advances in Clinical Social Work Research*, pp. 11–24. Washington, D.C.: NASW Press.

Glisson, C. and J. Fischer. 1987. "Statistical Training for Social Workers." *Journal of Social Work Education* 3:50–58.

Gottlieb, N. and C. Richey. 1980. "Education of Human Services Practitioners for Clinical Evaluation." In R. W. Weinbach and A. Rubin, eds., *Teaching Social Work Research*, pp. 1–12. New York: Council on Social Work Education.

Grinnell, R. M., Jr., and D. H. Siegel. 1988. "The Place of Research in Social Work." In R. M. Grinnell, Jr., ed., *Social Work Research and Evaluation*. Itasca, Ill.: F. E. Peacock.

Guba, E. G. 1990. "The Alternative Paradigm Dialog." In E. G. Guba, ed., *The Paradigm Dialog*. Newbury Park, Cal.: Sage.

Hagerty, J. E. 1931. *The Training of Social Workers*. New York: McGraw-Hill.

Harrison, W. D. 1994. "The Inevitability of Integrated Methods." In E. Sherman and W. J. Reid, eds., *Qualitative Research in Social Work*, pp. 407–422. New York: Columbia University Press.

Havelock, R. G., J. C. Huber, and S. Zimmerman. 1969. *Major Works on Change in Education*. Ann Arbor: University of Michigan Press.

Haworth, G. O. 1984. "Social Work Research, Practice, and Paradigms." *Social Service Review* 58:343–357.

Heineman, M. B. 1981. "The Obsolete Scientific Imperative in Social Work Research." *Social Service Review* 55:371–397.

Heineman-Pieper, M. 1989. "The Heuristic Paradigm: A Unifying and Comprehensive Approach to Social Work Research." *Smith College Studies* 60:1–23.

Hudson, W. H. 1982. "Scientific Imperatives in Social Work Research and Practice." *Social Service Review* 56:242–258.

Imre, R. W. 1984. "The Nature of Knowledge in Social Work." *Social Work* 29:41–45.

Jayaratne, S. 1990. "Clinical Significance: Problems and New Developments." In L. Videka-Sherman and W. J. Reid, eds., *Advances in Clinical Social Work Research*, pp. 271–285. Washington, D.C.: NASW Press.

Jenson, J. M., M. W. Fraser, and R. E. Lewis. 1991. "Research Training in Social Work Doctoral Programs." *Arete* 16:23–36.

Kiresuk, T. J. and R. E. Sherman. 1968. "Goal Attainment Scaling: A General Method for Evaluating Comprehensive Mental Health Programs." *Community Mental Health Journal* 4:443–453.

Kirk, S. A. 1979. "Understanding Research Utilization in Social Work." In A. Rubin and A. Rosenblatt, eds., *Sourcebook on Research Utilization*, pp. 3–15. New York: Council on Social Work Education.

—— and A. Rosenblatt. 1981. "Research Knowledge and Orientation among Social Work Students." In S. Briar, H. Weissman, and A. Rubin, eds., *Research Utilization in Social Work Education*, pp. 29–39. New York: Council on Social Work Education.

Krathwohl, D. R. 1985. *Social and Behavioral Science and Research*. San Francisco: Jossey-Bass.

Lazar, A. 1990. "Statistics Courses in Social Work Education." *Journal of Teaching in Social Work* 4(1):17–30.

Lincoln, Y. and E. Guba. 1985. *Naturalistic Inquiry*. Beverly Hills, Calif.: Sage.

Magee, J. J. 1982. "Integrating Research Skills with Human Behavior and Social Environment: Assessing Historical and Cultural Influences on Students' Family Structure." *Journal of Education for Social Work* 18:14–19.

Mencher, S. 1959. *The Research Method in Social Work Education*. New York: Council on Social Work Education.

Mullen, E. J. 1978. "The Construction of Personal Models for Effective Practice: A Method for Utilizing Research Findings to Guide Social Interventions." *Journal of Social Service Research* 2:45–65.

——. 1988. "Constructing Personal Practice Models." In R. M. Grinnell, Jr., ed., *Social Work Research and Evaluation*. Itasca, Ill.: F. E. Peacock.

——, G. J. Bostwick, Jr., and B. Ryg. 1980. In R. W. Weinbach and A. Rubin, eds.,

Teaching Social Work Research, pp. 30–41. New York: Council on Social Work Education.

Nelsen, J. C. 1990. "Single-Case Research and Traditional Practice: Issues and Possibilities." In L. Videka-Sherman and W. J. Reid, eds., *Advances in Clinical Social Work Research*, pp. 37–47. Washington, D.C.: NASW Press.

Olsen, L. 1990. "Integrating a Practice Orientation into the Research Curriculum: The Effect on Knowledge and Attitudes." *Journal of Social Work Education* 26(2):155–161.

Orcutt, B. A. 1990. *Science and Inquiry in Social Work Practice.* New York: Columbia University Press.

Parker, M. W., G. H. Chynoweth, D. A. Blankinship, E. R. Zaldo, and M. J. Mathews. 1987. "A Case for Computer Applications in Social Work." *Journal of Social Work Education* 23(2):57–68.

Peile, C. 1988. "Research Paradigms in Social Work: From Stalemate to Creative Synthesis." *Social Service Review* 62(1):2–19.

Penka, C. E. and S. A. Kirk. 1991. "Practitioner Involvement in Clinical Evaluation." *Social Work* 36:513–518.

Phillips, D. C. 1987. *Philosophy, Science, and Social Inquiry.* New York: Pergamon Press.

——. 1990. "Postpositivistic Science." In E. G. Guba, ed., *The Paradigm Dialog,* pp. 31–45. Newbury Park, Calif.: Sage.

Poulin, J. 1989. "Goals for Undergraduate Social Work Research: A Survey of BSW Program Directors." *Journal of Social Work Education* 25(3):284–289.

Reamer, F. G. 1993. *The Philosophical Foundations of Social Work.* New York: Columbia University Press.

Reason, P. and J. Rowan, eds., 1981. *Human inquiry.* New York: Wiley.

Reid, W. J. 1994. "Reframing the Epistemological Debate." In E. Sherman and W. J. Reid, eds., *Qualitative Research in Social Work*, pp. 464–481. New York: Columbia University Press.

—— and I. P. Davis. 1987. "Qualitative Methods in Single Case Research." In N. Gottlieb, ed., *Proceedings of Conference on Practitioners as Evaluators of Direct Practice*, pp. 56–72. Seattle: School of Social Work, University of Washington.

—— and A.D. Smith. 1989. *Research in Social Work.* 2d ed. New York: Columbia University Press.

Rich, R. F. 1981. *Social Science Information and Public Policy Making.* San Francisco: Jossey-Bass.

Richey, C. A., B. J. Blythe, and S. B. Berlin. 1987. "Do Social Workers Evaluate Their Practice?" *Social Work Research and Abstracts* 23:14–20.

Ricoeur, P. 1981. *Hermeneutics and the Social Sciences.* Translated and edited by J. Thompson. Cambridge: Cambridge University Press.

Rorty, R. 1979. *Philosophy and the Mirror of Nature.* Princeton, N.J.: Princeton University Press.

Rosenblatt, A. 1968. "The Practitioner's Use and Evaluation of Research." *Social Work* 13(1):53–59.

Rothman, J. 1980. *Social R & D: Research and Development in the Human Sciences.* Englewood Cliffs, N.J.: Prentice-Hall,

Rubin, A. and A. Rosenblatt, eds. 1979. *Sourcebook on Research Utilization.* New York: Council on Social Work Education.

Ruckdeschel, R., P. Earnshaw, and A. Firrek. 1994. "The Qualitative Case Study and Evaluation: Issues, Methods, and Examples." In E. Sherman and W. J. Reid, eds., *Qualitative Research in Social Work*, pp. 251–264. New York: Columbia University Press.

Schon, D. 1983. *The Reflective Practitioner.* New York: Basic Books.

Schuerman, J. R. 1982. "The Obsolete Scientific Imperative in Social Work Research." *Social Service Review* 56(1):144–148.

Siegel, D. H. 1983. "Can Research and Practice be Integrated in Social Work Education?" *Journal of Education for Social Work* 19(3):12–19.

——. 1984. "Defining Empirically Based Practice." *Social Work* 29(4):325–337.

——. 1985. "Effective Teaching of Empirically Based Practice." *Social Work Research and Abstracts* 21(1):40–48.

—— and F. G. Reamer. 1988. "Integrating Research Findings, Concepts, and Logic into Practice." In R. M. Grinnell, Jr., ed., *Social Work Research and Evaluation.* Itasca, Ill.: F. E. Peacock.

Smith, M. L., K. L. DeWeaver, and A. C. Kilpatrick. 1986. "Research Curricula and Accreditation: The Challenge for Leadership." *Journal of Social Work Education* 22(2):61–70.

Task Force on Social Work Research. 1991. *Building Social Work Knowledge for Effective Services and Policies. A Plan for Research Development.* Washington, D.C.: National Institute for Mental Health.

Taylor, F. A. 1990. "The Numerate Social Worker." *Journal of Social Work Education* 26(1):25–35.

Thomas, E. J. 1978. "Mousetraps, Developmental Research, and Social Work Education." *Social Service Review* 52(3):468–483.

Videka-Sherman, L. and W. J. Reid, eds. 1990. *Advances in Clinical Social Work Research.* Silver Spring, Md.: National Association of Social Workers.

Weiss, C. H. and M. J. Bucuvalas. 1980. *Social Science Research and Decision-Making.* New York: Columbia University Press.

Witkin, S. 1989. "Towards a Scientific Social Work." *Social Service Research* 12:83–98.

Wodarski, J. S., B. A. Thyer, J. D. Iodice, and R. H. Pinkston. 1991. "Graduate Social Work Education: A Review of Empirical Research." *Journal of Social Service Research* 14(3/4):23–39.

Wood, K. M. 1980. "Experiences in Teaching the Practitioner-Researcher Model." In R. W. Weinbach and A. Rubin, eds., *Teaching Social Work Research*, pp. 13–22. New York: Council on Social Work Education.

Zimbalist, S. E. 1955. "Major Trends in Social Work Research: An Analysis of the Nature of Development of Research in Social Work, as Seen in the Periodical Literature, 1900–1950." Doctoral dissertation, George Warren Brown School of Social Work, Washington University, St. Louis, Missouri.

—— and A. Rubin. 1981. "Contrasting Extremes in Research Requirements for the MSW Curriculum." *Journal of Education for Social Work* 17(2):56–61.

6
Field Education

ANNE E. FORTUNE

Field education is central to education for social work. During the field practicum in a social work agency, students learn practice skills and apply knowledge and concepts from the classroom; it is the opportunity for hands-on learning in a real situation (a characteristic of professional education). From a student's point of view, field education is the most productive, memorable, significant, and satisfying aspect of their social work education (Kadushin 1991). From an educator's point of view, field education is essential for testing students' commitment to social work and their ability to work with people, for teaching new skills and application of knowledge, and for helping students integrate the discrete parts of social work education to become competent, caring practitioners.

Because field education is so important, it merits special attention in constructing a coherent curriculum. Yet recently educators have focused on the structure and process of field education and bypassed the more fundamental question of what content should be included.

What—if any—content should be required of all social work students during the field practicum? I will approach this question by first addressing several other questions: Is there a common core that underlies all social work practice? What is the relationship between baccalaureate and graduate education? What is the best way to learn to be a social worker? This chapter briefly examines how these questions were answered in the past, then looks at what social workers do currently, and at what helps students learn in field. Current answers to the three questions are then proposed. Finally, a model of content for fieldwork is explicated: core content and skills for all social work students and specialized content for master's level students.

Historical Themes

Education for social work started as what we now recognize as field education, on-the-job training for the "friendly visitors" who provided guidance to poor families for the charity organization societies in the late 1890s. Today, social work education is university-based, and the field practicum is one part of a complex academic and experiential education. Throughout the transformation, tensions around three issues defined the content of the field practicum and its relationship to the rest of the curriculum. These issues are 1) the search for a common professional base, or whether there is a common core underlying specialized content; 2) the relationship between baccalaureate and graduate education; and 3) assumptions about the best way to learn to be a social worker.

Origins

The earliest formal social work education programs were of two types. One type expanded from the agency training programs and included freestanding or agency-affiliated programs such as the New York School of Philanthropy, associated with the New York Charity Organization Society. The other type was university-affiliated programs started by social reformers, such as the Boston School for Social Workers, sponsored by Harvard University and Simmons College. A third type was soon added: undergraduate, state schools, usually midwestern. These varying origins brought different traditions of education and fieldwork into social work education, creating issues that are still unresolved.

Programs that began as agency training programs usually focused on practical, applied skills and on the policies and procedures of the sponsoring organization. Learning was through the apprentice model, emulating experienced persons (Austin 1986; Rothman 1977). An underlying assumption was that extended contact with the poor was needed to develop understanding and caring about their needs, a set of values stressing human dignity and capacity, and proper work habits (Sikkema 1966). Programs that were not tied to a single agency, which trained workers for many agencies, of necessity had less emphasis on agency-specific knowledge and more interest in commonalities of work among agencies. The legacy of the agency-based training programs was learning by doing, learning through modeling by a primary practitioner/teacher (together the elements of the apprentice model), and the search for common elements to define the social work method.

The second stream of social work training was from the university-based programs. The early programs included courses about the problems of poverty, housed in departments of sociology and economics (Brackett 1903). Field education was through field excursions to observe rather than through actual work. This reflected the more theoretical approach of academic-based social scientists, who emphasized analysis of social conditions and broad social reform rather than assistance to individuals and families. The legacy of the university-based programs is the social reform purpose for social work, the emphasis on research and academic-based knowledge, and the emphasis on learning by observing and thinking rather than doing.

A third stream of social work training was undergraduate education in state schools. The first two streams of educational programs were primarily private, eastern, urban, and postbaccalaureate; they prepared workers for employment in religious and private philanthropic institutions (Austin 1986). Elsewhere, social work education was at the undergraduate level, in programs that tended to be public, midwestern, rural, and serving areas with different needs from the east coast. Because social service was viewed as a public, governmental responsibility rather than private philanthropy, their institutional mission was training for public service, which focused on limited decision making about eligibility rather than provision of services through the casework method (Austin 1986). Many undergraduate programs did not include fieldwork because of difficulty finding agencies in rural areas (Tufts 1923) or reluctance to offer academic credit for "work" (Hagerty 1931). The legacy of the undergraduate state schools includes the public service and rural missions, responsiveness to localized service needs, and a detachment from the developments and strictures of field education in the other streams.

The Search for Common Method(s)

Beginning with training for the charity organizations, practitioners and educators sought definition of the commonalities of social work. Mary

Richmond's definition of social casework included analysis and work with individual family situations, as well as practical assistance (Richmond 1917). However, as casework services were offered in newer settings such as hospitals, schools, or psychiatric services, narrow specialities were again defined and taught as discrete methods (Austin 1986). The Milford conferences and the report of 1929 attempted a new definition of fundamental similarities: the purpose of social casework was assisting individuals to achieve self-determined personal objectives, using Freudian developmental concepts for diagnosis and treatment of intrapsychic factors.

As social casework grew more narrow and specialized, even though recognized as generic, other approaches to social work practice such as administration, social group work, and community organization were recognized and taught as separate methods. Through the 1950s, most graduate schools offered separate methods courses.

In the 1950s through the 1970s, several forces pushed social work to include new "methods." Federal funding of education in community mental health helped shift social casework to mental health psychotherapy (Austin 1986). Discomfort with the questionable effectiveness of current service methods led to new approaches to casework such as crisis intervention, task-centered casework, and behavioral interventions. At the same time, the social unrest and political activism of the 1960s renewed interest in alleviation of social problems and in community action.

Educational innovations included organizing curricula around social problems or practice settings and combining methods such as casework and group work into direct service or micro practice (Dinerman 1984). The attempts to combine methods marked a shift from generic method to generalist method; rather than look for underlying common elements within all methods (generic), educators began to define the core of practice as knowledge of several discrete methods (generalist). The reformulations of the common base included conceptual frameworks that emphasized systems and "person-in-situation" concepts (to meld the concerns with individual functioning and social problems) and "generalist" forms of practice that emphasized interventions with different-sized client units and with varying problem loci (Austin 1986; Dinerman 1984; Schatz, Jenkins, and Sheafor 1990).

Relation Between Undergraduate and Graduate Education

Developed to meet different needs, undergraduate and graduate education were in conflict about issues such as the purpose of social service, the type of training (casework versus administration of public welfare), and independent professional status versus public administration (Leighninger 1984; Lowe 1985). In 1939 the American Association of Schools of Social Work declared that professional status required two-year graduate education and excluded from its membership the undergraduate and one-year-graduate public programs. The graduate and undergraduate program associations did not merge again until 1952 as the Council on Social Work Education (CSWE). Consequently, undergraduate curricula continued to respond to quite different markets from the graduate level, preparing workers for public sector services and general rural social services.

When undergraduate and graduate education were reunited in one organization, there were new attempts to define their relationship as an educational progression rather than preparation for differing employment markets. The idea of stages of education, with certain content preceding other content (the so-called continuum) was resisted by graduate schools, partly as a defense of their professional status (Brennen 1984). However, in 1968 the National Association of Social Workers recognized undergraduate degree holders as professionals, thus undermining the graduate schools' exclusive claim to professional status and acknowledging a common, professional base on which, presumably, a continuum could be built.

CSWE and many graduate programs have not yet accepted a continuum and the idea remains controversial. Nevertheless, since 1969, the CSWE Curriculum Policy Statement (CPS) has permitted graduate programs to grant "advanced standing" to holders of undergraduate social work degrees. And since 1982 the CPS has referred to content in "foundation" areas that are similar at undergraduate and beginning graduate levels.

The two main themes—the search for a common base and the relation between undergraduate and graduate education—come together in the attempt to define the foundation that is similar at both levels. The 1992 CPS specifies for the first time that graduates of both levels will "apply the knowledge and skills of generalist social work to practice systems of all sizes," thus specifying the type of practice approach. The earlier CPS (of 1982) specified that undergraduate practice was generalist; the shift of "generalist practice" to both levels solidifies undergraduate claims to a continuum. However, the meaning of generalist social work is still under debate. Austin (1986) suggested two meanings: 1) entry-level ability in all five social work methods identified by the 1959 curriculum study (casework, group work, community organization, administration, research); and 2) ability to apply direct practice (usually casework) methods in a variety of settings. A third important formulation is the systems perspective and intervention on multiple, hierarchical levels (Pincus and Minahan 1973; Vosler 1989), including new attempts to construct a coherent model of practice (Schatz, Jenkins, and Sheafor 1990).

Learning to Be a Social Worker

With the Milford Conference redefinition of social casework, the purpose and the means of learning in field education changed. With the focus on diagnostic understanding of individuals (rather than the family and social conditions) and on use of the casework interview to change behavior (rather than advice and practical assistance), the purpose of education was professional development of the student. There was disagreement about the meaning of professional development: personality growth through a therapeutic relationship with a supervisor or development of professional use of self (including discipline, values, and attitudes) through education by a supervisor (Sikkema 1966). In either case, field education was still tied to the individual relationship between supervisor and student, and an objective of field education was the student's productive use of supervision.

Field education at the undergraduate level was erratic. Many programs did not offer it to all or even some students (Bisno 1959). Continuing the academic, social reform tradition, the field experiences were often limited opportunities for trips or observation, with minimal participation and few educational objectives. Educators argued whether field should be included and, if so, should it be "field observation," "field experience"—learning by doing—or "field instruction" with planned educational objectives and recognized status in the curriculum (Cox 1971).

Not until 1970 was fieldwork made a *requirement* in the curricula of undergraduate members of CSWE (Schiller 1972). The earlier lack of established criteria and procedures for field instruction meant that, once fieldwork was included, undergraduate programs were not bound by the dogmas that restricted graduate field education. In the 1960s and 1970s, undergraduate field educators embraced such innovations as specific educational objectives, skills-focused instruction, competency-based education, generic models, and practice seminars (Baer and Federico 1978; Cox 1971; Dinerman 1984).

From the 1960s on, at both undergraduate and graduate levels, there was increasing acceptance that the school could control field education by setting objectives for field learning and sequencing learning opportunities. As the academy assumed greater control of fieldwork and new theories of learning were examined, the relationship between field and classroom changed. Gordon and Schutz proposed their "knowing-understanding-doing" paradigm, which renews emphasis on the role of cognition in education (Gordon and Gordon 1982; Gordon and Schutz 1969). Some saw field education as the endpoint of learning, the "doing" or the last step in a learning sequence that begins in the classroom. Others developed an articulated approach, with equal emphasis and simultaneous sequencing of the knowing, understanding, and doing, and careful integration of field and classroom with a single articulated curriculum (George 1982; Jenkins and Sheafor 1982). Schools experimented with learning centers run like small agencies, with faculty hired to act as field instructors to units of students, with group supervision, and with other approaches that reduced the dependence on a single agency-based field instructor. Recently, in a swing back to agency-based learning, these ideas of sequence and structure have been challenged by theories of andragogy that emphasize self-directed, student-centered learning and individualized learning contracts (Bogo and Vayda 1987; Davenport and Davenport 1988).

Social Work Practice and Education in the 1990s

The history of social work field education suggests many shifts that reflect changes in the employment market, in social work practice, in the relation between undergraduate and graduate education, and in notions of how to learn social work. What is the current status of practice and education? Are there similarities in today's practice that suggest underlying practice methods? Are there differences between BSW- and MSW-level practice that suggest education should be different? What aids learning in the field? This section reviews recent research on employment activities, curricula, and field education. The answers will provide the framework for a model curriculum for field education.

Job Analyses of Social Work Practice

An important source of information for curriculum construction is data on the tasks social workers perform on the job. Several content validation studies have addressed what American social workers do in their employment.

A study of workers in seventeen Virginia human service organizations identified critical knowledge and activities for baccalaureate and master's social workers (Biggerstaff and Kolevzon 1980; Kolevzon and Biggerstaff 1983). Both groups spent nearly half their time in micro activities, with assessment and individual therapy consuming the most time. Case management tasks such as case monitoring and record-keeping used 41 percent of BSW time, 32 percent for MSWs, while macro tasks like program planning and supervising others were 11 percent of BSW and 18 percent of MSW time. Overall, MSW workers needed more specialized casework skills such as family therapy or specialized therapies but also, as they gained experience, a broader array of both micro- and macro-level skills.

A larger study included over three thousand baccalaureate and master's-level social workers who had passed credentialing examinations in thirty-three states (Biggerstaff and Eisenberg 1989). BSW and MSW social workers shared a set of frequent activities (43 percent of 141 activities). These included recordkeeping, assessment, general treatment, service coordination, and referral activities. Neither group did much macro-level activity such as providing supervision, budgeting, or research. They differed on 35 percent of tasks: MSWs engaged in much more assessment and provision of direct treatment services than did the BSWs, and they provided specialized services such as complex diagnostic activity and family treatment.

Another source of data is three large studies undertaken by the National Association of Social Workers (NASW). The three samples, totaling more than 7,800 social workers, included NASW members, occupational social workers, and graduates from baccalaureate programs (Teare and Sheafor 1992b). Among direct service workers, the core or frequent activities were similar for both BSWs and MSWs and included tasks in the areas of interpersonal helping, individual and family treatment, case planning and maintenance, and professional development (Teare 1992b). Among supervisors, BSWs and MSWs were again similar, but with broader responsibilities including development of delivery system knowledge, staff supervision, and staff information exchange as well as direct service. Among administrators, there were distinct differences between BSWs and MSWs, with BSWs providing more service provision and less supervision and program development. Overall, BSWs had a broader range of activities than MSWs no matter what the position (Teare 1992a). BSWs were also spread more uniformly over problem areas and worked more with tangible problems such as substance abuse, housing, or financial need, while MSWs emphasized more abstract problems such as depression or interpersonal relationships (Teare and Sheafor 1991).

Overall, these three sources of data on social workers' employment tasks suggest both similarities and differences between BSW and MSW practice. The similarities are a primary focus on serving individuals and families, with a core of tasks related to interviewing, assessment, case planning, case management, treatment, evaluation and termination of cases, and personal professional development. This core comprises the primary job description for both BSW and entry-level MSW practitioners. The differences are that BSW-level workers generally work with more tangible problems, take a broader range of roles, and utilize more skills relating to work with communities and groups (although neither does much community work or group work). Entry-level MSW workers focus more on providing therapeutic treatment, and use more skills related to clinical diagnosis and specialized treatment approaches. Both BSWs and MSWs who hold supervisory jobs have an expanded repertoire, taking on supervisory and management tasks while retaining the core practice tasks. However, MSWs are more likely to hold supervisory positions, and MSWs almost exclusively engage in the specialized tasks of management (normally without also having practice tasks). In short, although BSWs and MSWs share a core of direct practice tasks, MSWs are more likely to focus on therapeutic services or management.

Educators' Perceptions of Important Curriculum Content

A second source of information for curriculum construction is social work educators' perceptions of content important for students. Two studies examined administrators' perceptions of foundation content and compared baccalaureate to master's respondents (Eure, Griffin, and Atherton 1987; Griffin and Eure 1985). Overall, both BSW and MSW educators believed the most important foundation content included oppression and cultural diversity, systems knowledge, human development, the relation of social policy and social problems, practice evaluation, social work ethics, critical thinking and writing skills, interpersonal skills for work with clients, and general problem-solving practice skills.

Both groups also concurred that group work and management skills were not important for the foundation (Eure, Griffin, and Atherton 1987). However, in the practice and field portions of the foundation, differences in their rankings of items suggest that MSW educators gave somewhat more weight to clinical skills and knowledge such as ecological or psychosocial treatment approaches while BSW educators gave more weight to fundamental social work values like social responsibility and diversity, collegial and agency work responsibilities, and work with community groups.

Current Curriculum Content

A third source of information for curriculum construction is what is currently taught at schools of social work. Several studies have investigated the content and organization of curricula at the BSW and MSW levels.

Individual institutions define both foundation and specialization content in their own ways. In the late 1970s and early 1980s, several studies (Bakalinsky 1982; Dinerman 1982; Hartman 1983; McCaslin 1987) found an emphasis on treatment of individuals at both BSW and MSW levels, inconsistency among schools at both levels, and, as Dinerman (1982:84) noted, a "discontinuity . . . between the BSW and MSW levels rather than a nonredundant educational continuum." Only Hartman (1983), investigating child welfare curricula, found consistent differences between levels: BSW courses were broader and more field-specific in their content while the MSW specialization courses focused on clinical treatment.

More recent studies of *overall* curricula could not be located in the published literature. However, a study of first-year MSW methods courses found "reasonable consistency in basic educational content" with a focus on clinical practice with individuals in direct practice courses (LeCroy and Goodwin 1988:47).

In field education, a major pressing issue, according to several expert panels, is identifying objectives for field (Raskin 1983, 1993; Skolnik 1989). A recent study of the criteria for student field evaluation at sixty-six MSW programs uncovered numerous discrete areas such as treatment practice skills, critical thinking, self-directed learning, leadership, caseload management, and administrative skills (Dore, Epstein, and Herrerias 1992).

Another pressing issue in field education, according to the expert panels, is determining criteria that distinguish graduate from undergraduate material (Raskin 1993; Skolnik 1989; Wayne, Skolnik, and Raskin 1989). The only current studies are of joint programs, schools with both an undergraduate and a graduate program. At one school, there were differences between BSW, MSW first-year, and MSW specialization field placements, although first-year MSW placements overlapped with BSW placements (Reeser, Wertkin, and Davis 1991). In a larger study of thirteen programs, two-thirds reported similar objectives, knowledge base or practice skills for their BSW and foundation MSW programs (Kilpatrick 1991). However, BSW fieldwork had more specific skill-oriented objectives and task-oriented skills that focused on casework and community resources, while MSW foundation field education required more independent responsibility and analytic thinking and emphasized a therapeutic knowledge base.

In short, sketchy evidence about practice and field curricula again suggests similarities between BSW and MSW foundation courses, but greater emphasis on therapeutic and individual clinical skills at the MSW level.

Research on the Outcome of Field Education

The final source of information to inform field curricula is research on the structure and outcome of field education.

The assumption that field-based learning is essential to social work education has not been tested. Other helping disciplines make "hands on" learning optional; their investigations provide some evidence for the utility of social work field education. For example, in medicine, residents who undertook a psychiatric residency were better at the medical and psychiatric aspects of patient care than those who did not (Karasu, Stein, and Charles 1978). In psychology, undergraduate students who did an internship changed more on four of thirty-six psychological traits than those who did not (Ware, Millard, and Matthews 1984). This slim evidence suggests that field education can improve practice skills but is unlikely to affect deep-seated traits.

Efforts to evaluate social work field education have focused on structural aspects such as block placements or delayed entry into the field. In the "block" placement, coursework is suspended while the student is placed full-time in an agency, usually for three to nine months. Block placements are compared to "concurrent" placements during which the student is in an agency several days a week while taking academic courses on other days (Cassidy 1982). One study found students in block and concurrent placements earned equivalent grades for field (Tsang 1988). However, in another study, students in block placements deteriorated more on social work problem-solving ability than those in concurrent placements (Davis, Short, and York 1984). In a third, graduates from block placements were more agency-oriented and less conceptual than students from concurrent placements (Ramsey 1989). Thus, concurrent placements appear to help students maintain or increase the cognitive or conceptual learning of practice.

Another structural variation is delayed entry. In delayed entry, in contrast to immediate entry, students receive structured academic preparation before entering field placement or seeing clients. In one study, delaying entry did not affect mastery of classroom content nor of practice skills (Gordon and Gordon 1989). Another study similarly found that delayed entry neither increased students' preparation for field education nor speeded up their integration into the agency, while it reduced the number of client contacts (Grossman and Barth 1991). Thus, there appear to be no benefits and potential detriment to delaying entry into field to allow pre-placement preparation.

Another way to synchronize necessary knowledge with practice experiences is matching experiences with academic content in a planned progression. At one school, students were based in a learning center and performed a sequence of tasks at various neighborhood agencies (Lewis, Howerton, and Kindelsperger [1962], described by Cassidy 1982). Although academic and field content were well articulated, there was little difference in outcome compared to the traditional field placement model.

Another structural variation is "work-study" placement, or use of the student's employment setting as a practicum site. Typically, students must be experienced and must have learning assignments different from their employment duties. Several studies have found no difference in outcome when compared to placements in nonemploying agencies (Abbott 1986; Marshack, Starr, and Haffey 1987; Powers, Hess, and Koleski 1984; Tsang 1988). Another study qualified the benefit; outcome was better if the field instructor participated in training and provided conceptual structure with process recordings (Davis, Short, and York 1984). The main drawbacks of work-study placements were to the school and the sponsoring agency, due to high turnover of practicum sites and rapid departure of newly educated employees (Haffey, Marshack, and Starr 1984; Marshack, Starr, and Haffey 1987).

These studies of sequencing class and field suggest that concurrent placement enhances conceptual learning but, beyond that, close articulation between the classroom content and field experience is not essential to learning. On the other hand, the studies of delayed entry suggest that time in the agency is not the critical variable: delayed-entry students had similar outcomes despite less time in the agency. Indeed, time spent in field agencies is often poorly used and unrelated to learning activities or performance (Korbelik and Epstein 1976; Munson 1987). However, learning activities such as client contact *are* associated with performance (Davis, Short, and York 1984; Korbelik and Epstein 1976). In sum, the important aspects of field placement are not the length of time nor precise articulation with the classroom but having field work concurrent with academic coursework and having meaningful learning experiences in the field placement.

Parameters for a Model of Field Education

This chapter began with three questions that underlie any attempt to propose content for field education: Is there a common core that underlies social work practice? What is the relationship between baccalaureate and graduate education? What is the best way to learn to be a social worker? This section proposes answers based on past and present practice and research.

Question 1: Is there a common core underlying social work practice? If yes, what is the relationship between social reform, change at the individual/family level, and change at the community/organizational level? Where does the problem or population specialist fall in?

The employment task analyses suggest common skills and content that cross-cut settings and levels. The similarities include personal professional development and a core of skills focused on serving individuals and families: interviewing, problem solving, assessment, case planning, case management, treatment, evaluation and termination of cases, and collaboration. Core content includes social work values and ethics, cultural diversity, the effects of oppression, and human behavior in the social environment. The emphasis is on working with people within existing systems. To the extent it occurs, change at the community or organizational level is on behalf of individuals. Few social workers do or are educated for social reform despite much agreement that it is important. Consequently, the model for core field curriculum includes work with client systems with minimal focus on social reform.

Both BSW and MSW social workers are problem or population specialists in that they use knowledge particular to their employment settings, for example, child protective services, health care, mental health, or substance abuse. However, the common content cross-cuts this specialized setting-specific knowledge.

Question 2: What is the relationship between undergraduate and graduate education? Does education prepare for different roles—public services or mental health, for example? Is there a "continuum," with stages and a "foundation"?

A clear, consensual distinction between undergraduate and graduate social work is not yet possible. Despite common content and skills, there are differences in practice and education. On the job, individual BSW practitioners use a broader range of skills than MSWs, but they are not generalists in the sense of working at several levels of system (Teare and Sheafor 1991). Collectively, they are more evenly distributed among practice areas than MSWs; they are not specialists in rural or public social services nor does rural or public service work differ from work done by BSWs elsewhere (Kolevzon and Biggerstaff 1983; Teare and Sheafor 1991). MSWs work more in mental health and provide more specialized therapeutic treatment. As they gain experience, MSWs are far more likely to work as supervisors and administrators than BSWs.

The education at undergraduate and graduate levels also differs, although not always in ways consonant with the job differences. BSW education is more specific to a particular field (depending on local choices of specialization) and perhaps broader in role preparation. It also includes an important element of helping students test their suitability for the helping professions. MSW education offers specialized in-depth therapeutic approaches, plus a variety of specializations—problems, populations, fields of practice, etc. Graduate education also offers specializations appropriate for experienced MSWs—management, research, social reform, etc. MSW education thus prepares practitioners for two places in the career path—beginning MSW practitioners with specialized therapeutic skills and experienced MSW practitioners with management, advocacy, and knowledge-development skills.

There is little evidence to suggest that BSW and MSW practitioners are at different stages of a single career path or educational progression. The common elements that permeate practice are not necessarily a "foundation" that can be isolated, taught as a stand-alone unit, and then built upon by the relatively simple addition of more specialized or advanced knowledge and skills. The common knowledge and skills could be imbedded in curricula built around specializations such as level of system (micro-macro), population, problem, or field of practice. To avoid confusion, I will call the common knowledge and skills "core." Under current CSWE guidelines, the core can be considered the "foundation" field curriculum; it is the basic skills and knowledge that all BSW and MSW students should learn.

Where should substantive specialization—the specific knowledge about problems or delivery systems—be placed in the field curriculum? Currently, both BSW and advanced MSW curricula often focus on narrowly defined areas. Such specializations are popular among students but are of marginal utility in the employment market. In my opinion, such substantive specialization should not be required at either BSW or MSW levels. Rapid changes in social problems and job markets quickly date specialized knowledge. Consequently, it is better to concentrate on the core skills and advanced practice content. The specialized, situation-specific content necessary to function on the job can and should be learned on the job. Thus, the model of content and skills for field practica that follows includes core and advanced material but not substantive specialization.

Question 3: What is the best approach to learning social work practice? What is the relationship between class and field?

Effective social work practice requires mastery of substantive content and its appropriate application to particular instances (such as knowledge of human behavior), mastery and application of skills (such as assessment or interviewing), and development of social work values and attitudes (such as a nonjudgmental attitude or celebrating diversity). Education for these goals includes cognitive, behavioral, and affective development. Experience in a social work agency is a good way to learn both practice skills and application of knowledge, while the practicum is an important site for affective development. Thus, field instruction is a critical component of social work education.

In relation to the overall curriculum, field education has two purposes: 1) it is a site for learning, that is, field education has its own content, curriculum, and objectives; and 2) fieldwork allows students to apply and integrate content from elsewhere in the curriculum, that is, it is linked to other parts of the curriculum. Although it is possible to structure field experiences differently, the consensus is that field education should be for an extended period in a single agency, under the guidance of a primary field instructor, who is responsible for one or more students. To enable students to balance the cognitive and affective learning, the field placement should be concurrent with coursework. And although the actual amount of time in a field placement is not important, the use of that time for meaningful content and learning activity is critical.

The model field curriculum proposed in the next section includes universal content for all students. Most current writing, including the CSWE Curriculum Policy Statement, assumes that the individual educational program should determine broad objectives and the student and field instructor then negotiate individual objectives based on andragogical principles (Bogo and Vayda 1987; Council on Social Work Education 1992; Urbanowski and Dwyer 1988). However, the task analyses reviewed above clearly indicate common skills and knowledge essential to social work practitioners. *This common content and skills should be included among the objectives for all field education, regardless of program, student or field setting.*

The means of learning—reaching the objectives—are through learning assignments (thinking and doing) and through cognitive-affective processing of those assignments (reflecting, writing, discussing, etc.). Both the learning assignments and the processing can and should be individualized, depending on the program, the agency, the field instructor, and the student. However, effective learning requires an overview, structure, continuity, and progressive experiences, even though integration and mastery may not be linear (Boehm 1959). It also requires multiple formats for presenting material, to link emotional and cognitive learning; repetition (practice) with variations to make new skills automatic and to generalize learning; and linking specifics to general strategies, to aid in recognizing principles (Cuasay 1992). The field instructor's role includes providing the necessary structure and continuity, overseeing learning experiences, creating a safe learning environment, and helping the student to generalize from the learning experiences. The field instructor-student relationship is an educational relationship, not therapeutic, although the instructor does provide guidance on professional development issues such as values, maturity, and self-awareness.

In sum, field instruction is critical to education because of the opportunity it provides for learning content and skills and for applying academic knowledge. Field instruction has its own objectives, but also includes application of material from the rest of the curriculum. Mastery of the content and skills is through meaningful learning assignments and cognitive-affective processing guided by the field instructor and classroom instructor.

A Model of Content and Skills for Field Education

The final section describes a model for field curricula that is based on several assumptions. First, although field instruction may be coordinated with other curricular areas, it has its own content, curriculum, and objectives. The objectives of field curricula include acquisition of skills and knowledge, learning how to apply knowledge, and personal development—self-awareness and use of self but not therapeutic growth.

Second, regarding common content, the model includes a core of skills and content common to BSW and MSW practice. This core is based on the studies of social work practice reviewed above. The model also includes two other sections, a preparatory level for undergraduates and an advanced level for MSW methods specialization. The BSW preparatory level is added for pragmatic reasons: many students are exploring career options and the field practicum is often the final testing ground for such characteristics as nonjudgmental attitudes and tolerance of difference. The advanced MSW level includes the content that distinguishes MSWs from BSWs on the job; it is a necessary part of graduate education, but is distinctly graduate.

Third, the model does not include substantive specialization. Specialized situation-specific knowledge is included when it is needed for responsible service delivery, but its educational purpose is to understand the context for practice or to learn how to learn. For example, a student learns the field agency's policies in order to understand how policies shape service and influence the resources offered to clients. An important role for field instructors is helping the student view specific content in this broader context.

The content is the same for all students; the learning assignments to achieve mastery will vary by school, agency, or student. Examples of learning assignments are noted, but other sources include more systematic presentations of teaching tools: Cuasay (1992) reviews principles for teaching based on new understanding of brain functioning during cognitive processing. Boehm (1959), and Dea, Grist, and Myli (1982) discuss how to develop and manage learning tasks; Jarrett (1979) offers good examples of learning tasks while Ifill (1989) focuses on learning about diversity. Baer, Fassett, and Morris (1979) and Wilson (1981) describe principles for individualizing assignments within an overall structure; Schur, Barndt, and Baum (1983) and Urbanowski and Dwyer (1988) show how to establish progressive tasks over the course of an academic year.

The model does not include a section that traditionally appears in field syllabi: the "student as learner" or "use of supervision" area that includes willingness to self-disclose in field instruction, attitudes toward the field instructor, ability to use feedback constructively, use of process recordings to learn, etc. (Urbanowski and Dwyer 1988). Such statements describe the structure or process by which students may learn, not content that should be learned or outcomes of learning.

In sum, the model for field education includes the skills and knowledge that should be included for all students in all practica at three levels, a preparation for professional commitment for baccalaureate students, a core for both baccalaureate and master's students, and an advanced level for master's students.

Preparation for Professional Commitment

The first level, preparation for professional commitment, is for students who are testing their interest and suitability for a career in social work. It includes work skills necessary to hold a job and act responsibly toward clients and colleagues, a beginning self-awareness that is essential for working nonjudgmentally with clients, understanding the social work role including its limits and the responsibility of representing an agency, and knowledge of key values and ethics that distinguish social work from other careers (Eure, Griffin, and Atherton 1987; Urbanowski and Dwyer 1988). It also includes systematic evaluation of the student's aptitude for a career in social work. Although very basic, this material is essential, particularly where the field practicum is a primary means of screening out unsuitable students (Moore and Urwin 1991).

Although many of the first-level skills precede later core skills, this level is not a separate "preprofessional" unit. The content is integrated among the learning tasks for the core, described next. Thus, to help understand the social work role, assignments related to organizational context could include interviewing staff members from several professions and comparing their perceptions in terms of roles and values. Or to clarify values while learning interviewing skills, the student might interview two hospital patients with the same illness but where one is confident of survival and the other is seeking euthanasia.

Core Content and Skills for Baccalaureate and Master's Practica

The core includes the content on practice with individuals and families that is common to BSW and MSW direct service workers (Biggerstaff and Eisenberg 1989; Biggerstaff and Kolevzon 1980; Kolevzon and Biggerstaff 1983; Teare and Sheafor 1992a). It also includes the professional development skills used by all social workers and the contextual knowledge to survive in and use service delivery organizations and community resources.

Professional Development

Commitment to social work values and ethics

Professional development, the first core area, includes content that defines social workers and characterizes professional career commitment. The first aspect of professional development is full commitment to the basic values already mentioned in the section on preparation. These include regard for individual worth and dignity, people's right to make independent decisions, assisting people to obtain resources, making institutions more humane, respect for diversity, and responsibility for ethical conduct and practice (Council on Social Work Education 1992; Loewenberg and Dolgoff 1992; Reamer 1990). Two factors distinguish the core from the preparatory level: a) students must demonstrate commitment to social work values, and b) they must be able to handle the ambiguous or conflicting ethical situations that characterize so much of practice.

Learning assignments should help students recognize ethical issues. For example, should the parents of children in a story-telling group be told that one child has AIDS? When does burden on the care-taking family members override an elderly client's right to self-determination? Assignments should also encourage students to act on social work values, as a way of increasing commitment to them. For example, the student can represent the client's wishes in a team meeting, to reinforce individuation and respect for self-determination.

Commitment to diversity and ability to work with persons from many backgrounds

A second aspect of professional development is honoring diversity and working with persons of different backgrounds, perspectives, or gifts (Eure, Griffin, and Atherton 1987). An important part of diversity is a multicultural approach to differences based on racial and ethnic background. The multicultural perspective respects differences among cultural groups and recognizes the strengths of different cultures rather than viewing one culture or perspective as superior (Chau 1990; Lister 1987). A similar approach of valuing difference, recognizing strength, and avoiding judgment based on egocentric standards should be applied to groups identified by other characteristics such as gender, sexual orientation, or physical gifts.

The traditional approach to teaching about diversity has been to include content about selected groups in various places in the curriculum, including field. This approach assumes that accurate knowledge is a necessary precursor to unbiased attitudes and actions, but it may also perpetuate stereotypes and does not help with understanding other cultures than those taught. New approaches attempt to give students tools to go beyond the specific knowledge. For example, Nakanishi and Rittner's (1992:30) inclusionary cultural model teaches stu-

dents to "recognize behaviors and attitudes most likely to be culturally influenced regardless of the specific cultural context," while Latting
(1990) increases cognitive sophistication and critical thinking to help
students avoid stereotyping reactions. Such approaches—along with
experience working with culturally diverse populations—are especially appropriate for field, where the emphasis should be on learning to
recognize and overcome cultural barriers to effective service.

All students should have at least one field placement where they
work predominantly with persons different from themselves—as
much of a cross-cultural experience as is possible. Such an experience
cannot guarantee commitment to honoring diversity, but it does
require students to experience other ways of organizing social behavior, to learn to recognize dissonances in perspective, and to test their
real commitment to social work values.

Commitment to promotion of social and economic justice

Another part of professional development is commitment to overcoming oppression, discrimination, and economic injustice. The CSWE's
Curriculum Policy Statement (1992) mandates content on certain populations-at-risk for such oppression—persons of color, women, gay
and lesbian persons—and others may be included. As with diversity,
all students should work with persons from a population-at-risk. However, if the population-at-risk is culturally different from the student,
care must be taken to avoid the risk of reinforcing stereotypes, such as,
"all Haitian immigrants are poor" or "all women are victims." Oppression and diversity have often been confused, for example, equating
racism and ethnicity. Similarly, if work with a population-at-risk is
confined to the core in master's programs, and not in specialization, a
sense of institutionalized racism or elitism may be created (Reeser,
Wertkin, and Davis 1991). Such potential risks can be avoided with
careful assignments and supervision; instructors must help students
separate the effects due to difference, class or economic structure, from
societally condoned oppression.

Commitment to promotion of justice includes an orientation to
using practice skills for the benefit of populations-at-risk. For example,
skills to make service delivery more humane should be used on behalf
of persons of color who may be stigmatized by intake procedures, or on
behalf of persons with disabilities who have been excluded by a build-

ing's physical barriers. Community organization or political action efforts should assist poor tenants or economically marginal farmers rather than suburban homeowners.

Self-awareness

A fourth aspect of professional development is self-awareness. Self-awareness as knowledge of self and of one's strengths and weaknesses is the basis for professional growth; and without accurate self-perception, the student cannot offer service ethically. It is also the foundation for establishing relationships and for using intervention approaches that rely on use of self.

Traditionally, self-awareness is enhanced through field instruction conferences and recording formats like process recording that are designed to highlight the impact of the student's behavior (Wilson 1981). Another approach normalizes emotional reactions throughout the stages of adjustment to the field agency (Grossman, Levine-Jordano, and Shearer 1991). Both approaches are reactive in that they wait until a suitable opportunity occurs. Learning assignments can also stimulate a proactive approach toward knowledge of self. For example, students may select their own assignments on the basis of what will "stretch" them the most, or assignments may be selected to challenge "blind spots" and unquestioned cultural assumptions, such as expectations of submissiveness, of kinship obligations, or of sexuality (Gladstein and Mailick 1986; Manoleas and Carrillo 1991).

Commitment to professional growth

A fifth aspect of professional development is commitment to professional growth. This is both a value—the desirability of lifelong growth—and a set of skills—or learning how to do it. The skills include self-evaluation and modification of self-presentation, transferring knowledge from one situation to another, and updating knowledge through participation in professional organizations and through learning activities such as reading current literature or using consultation. Most of the skills are ones the student is already engaged in as a learner. The only additional input in the field setting is reinforcement of the importance of continued (postgraduate) development. Some students may also need help in making conscious the processes of learning, especially those related to transferring knowledge among situations. For example, students can compare intervention techniques in different cases, to draw conclusions about when to use the techniques.

Evaluation of effectiveness

The final component of professional development is evaluation of one's own effectiveness (Eure, Griffin, and Atherton 1987). This requires consistent monitoring of effects, whether client outcome, securing material resources, or accuracy of budget projections. Despite all the introspection required of students, this area is usually neglected in field curricula. Emphasis should be placed on systematic ways of evaluating the accomplishment of tasks, for example, through goal attainment scaling, single-system designs, or performance appraisals. Recording formats that focus on outcome as well as process help students (and field instructors) to reorient toward the outcome of practice, for example, the structured clinical record (Videka-Sherman and Reid 1985).

Organizational Context

The second core area is organizational context, the knowledge and skills that enable social workers to survive in and provide effective service in an organization.

Agency mission

The first area within organizational context is understanding the agency's mission, philosophy, and policies about client service—the "public" part of an agency, open to outsiders and often publicly disseminated.

Agency structure

The second part of organizational context is the structure of the agency: the formal and informal bureaucracy, how information is channeled and decisions are made, and how to access the agency's resources for clients—the "inner workings" of the agency (Broeker and Pearson 1972). Learning tasks may be direct—interviewing staff about the structure—or indirect—analyzing inconsistencies in staff behavior. For example, at a psychiatric hospital, how do physicians' orders for patient privileges get "lost" at the implementation level (informal versus formal decision making) (Gilbertson and Winklebleck 1972)?

Functioning within a bureaucracy

Another part of organizational context is learning to function in organizations—the politics of bureaucracies including discretion, keeping goals in sight over the long haul, assessing and negotiating in situations with conflicting interests, etc. (Gummer 1990). This area is often neglected when students are—rightly—protected from the worst of internal conflicts, but it is a critical skill.

Effective functioning within a bureaucracy also includes influencing the organization to provide more effective, humane service. The most basic level includes knowledge of the strengths and weaknesses of an agency; using the formal and informal structure to increase service responsiveness; participating in the creation of a humane, service-oriented work environment (through good collegial relations, responsibility, sharing information, etc.); and attempting to change problematic procedures through discussion with supervisors or raising issues at staff meetings (Jarrett 1979; Urbanowski and Dwyer 1988). Intermediate skills include initiating formal proposals for change in policy, or systematic planning to enhance the work environment, for example, through in-service training, reorganization of work groups, or improving channels for sharing information (Gummer 1990; Holloway and Brager 1989). Advanced skills in maintaining and changing organizations are reserved for master's-level specialization. Although students must know the realities of how organizations work, it is unrealistic to expect them to oversee personnel or agency functioning during a core practicum in which they are learning foundation skills.

Recordkeeping and writing

A fourth area of organizational context is recordkeeping and writing (Bogo and Vayda 1987; Eure, Griffin, and Atherton 1987). Agency recordkeeping is an onerous, tedious task, but students must learn how to do it and how it relates to organizational maintenance and service delivery. This can perhaps be tied into content on research and data utilization for the purposes of improving service to clients.

Related to recordkeeping is writing skill: written communication that is clear, precise, concise, and professional. Students should write often, focusing on the kind of writing essential to practice: client assessments, letters to clients, reports to referral organizations, memos, etc. Such writing for practice must be distinguished from both process recording and classroom term papers, whose purposes are student learning (not communication to others) and whose requirements and skills are quite different.

Earlier I mentioned that the practicum model assumed a distinction between learning for the purpose of knowing a skill and learning for the purpose of understanding the context. The area of organizational context is an illustration of this distinction. Students write to learn the skills of professional writing and will use those skills anywhere. However, they learn the agency's internal structure to understand how the structure shapes service to clients. They will not need to know this agency's structure in the future, but they do need to know what to look for in a new organization, how to survive in organizations, and how to use the internal structure to benefit clients.

Service Delivery System Context

The third core area for both BSW and MSW students is the larger context of the community and social service delivery system. There are three levels: social policy, the community, and the community's social service delivery system.

Social policy

The first aspect of the context of service delivery is the national, state, and local policies that directly affect the agency (Eure, Griffin, and Atherton 1987). The scope and broad outlines of policy should be learned in the classroom. In field, the relevant material is the very specific knowledge necessary to provide service and the skills to assess their impact. With a few exceptions, such as mandated reporting of child abuse, the purpose of learning the policies is to understand how they affect service. For example, the assumptions about family violence underlying federal and state policies affect whether service aims for temporary protection and punishment or long-term self-sufficiency for women (Davis and Hagen 1988), and gay men are

still excluded by law from some occupations (Blumenfeld and Raymond 1988).

Knowledge of the community

The second level, knowledge of the community, includes the economic, political, social, and cultural structure of the area served by the
agency. Again, although the knowledge is essential to adequate service
provision, the purpose for the field student is to learn the importance
of the information, how to get it, and how to apply it to service. Learning tasks include "community surveys" where students observe a
neighborhood, or visits to town hall for local demographic, economic,
and political information. Knowledge of the community also includes
the relationships among community groups such as employers, political organizations, ethnic coalitions, and other powerful groups. Finally, the relation between community groups and the organization is
important: is the service agency seen as an employer or interloper?
asset or liability? resource or watchdog?

Knowledge of the local service delivery system

The third level of external context is the local social service delivery
network, including both formal (organized) and informal sources of
assistance (kinship networks, self-help, etc.). This includes knowledge
of what is available for clients: frequently used resources, less used formal resources, and the informal helping networks that buffer clients
and enable them to regain equilibrium (Fortune 1992). For example, a
client's church may provide food as well as social interaction and spiritual resources.

Another important content area is interorganizational relationships. Issues such as domain, definition of desirable clientele, funding
sources, and conflicting interests define who receives service in
which locations and who receives none at all (Tucker, Baum, and
Singh 1992). For example, private agencies may refuse certain types
of problems because third-party reimbursement (insurance) limits
service duration below what the agency perceives as necessary. Or a
nonprofit organization may change its services to conform to funding
sources' mandates. Students will not fully understand these complex
turf issues in a single field placement, but they can begin to explore

the relevance, for example, why some referrals are more feasible than others.

A final aspect of the local service delivery system is the referral and intake process for clients—how they get to the agency, how they are treated en route, who defines their problems, etc. At the direct service level, such intake networks affect the beginning processes of service. For example, a family accused of child neglect will define its problems differently than a family seeking financial assistance, even though the underlying problem of poverty is the same. Effective learning assignments are often experiential: the student may go through the process as if a client, or accompany a client to another agency.

Basic Interpersonal Skills

The fourth core area for both BSWs and MSWs is the basic interpersonal skills necessary to work collaboratively and to secure cooperation from other people.

Interpersonal communication

These include basic communication skills: the ability to be pleasant, to listen, to empathize, to communicate clearly, to elicit information and cooperation in-person and on the telephone, and to read verbal and nonverbal cues. These skills are so basic they are often overlooked. However, even interpersonally competent students may have anxieties or blind spots that reduce their effectiveness, for example, problems in dealing with authority figures or difficulty reading nonverbal cues.

Collegial relationships

A second aspect of interpersonal skills is the ability to work collegially, including cooperation, resolution of conflicts, and constructive participation in work groups (Eure, Griffin, and Atherton 1987). Too often, the emphasis on preparing practitioners for independent professional judgment results in lip service to interpersonal collaboration; students do not learn to work *with* others. Learning tasks should include assignments that cannot be completed without working with others: securing information from several departments to prepare a budget proposal or planning a teen-parenting group with a teacher.

Another part of working collegially is constructive participation in work groups such as team or staff meetings. These skills include appropriate verbal and nonverbal behavior, assessment of group dynamics, contributing to the socioemotional and task functioning of the group, and so on. Although most social workers participate in groups (even if most do not run them), participatory skills are undervalued and rarely taught. Learning tasks again involve assignments that require group participation; supervision can focus on the group processes as well as the completion of the assignment. For example, a student might analyze the dynamics of a team meeting as well as write up the client assessment that was the purpose of a particular meeting.

General Skills for Intervention with Client Systems

The fifth core area is intervention with client systems, including individuals, families, and treatment groups. Within this broad area are twelve skills that span the problem-solving process. The problem-solving framework assumes a general systems perspective, a person-in-environment focus, and an orientation to empirical practice. Beyond this, it is broad enough to include various approaches to intervention.

In general, learning assignments appropriate for intervention with client systems include responsibility for intervention, with some ongoing case contact. Variety of cases is important, to expose students to different skills and increase the chances of transfer and generalization of skills. However, despite the need for variety, "carrying cases" should not be the sole or even primary learning assignment for core field practica (despite many students' desires).

Applying knowledge of human behavior and of diversity content

The first two areas for intervention with client systems are application of knowledge of human behavior and application of knowledge of human diversity, populations-at-risk and social justice. The bulk of teaching about these subjects should be in the classroom. Field is the opportunity to *apply* the relevant knowledge in the intervention process, that is, the integration of the knowledge with the action. Thus, a student placed in a Boys and Girls Club can compare stages of development among children at the same chronological age to individualize recreational activities, then prepare activities that reflect the children's cultural heritage. Or a student may learn the developmental needs of gay adolescents starting to "come out," in order to work effectively with a support group.

Client-related interviewing skills

The third area is skills related to interviewing client systems. Most basic are the interview skills that guide the practitioner-client interaction and convey understanding and concern the core facilitative or micro-counseling skills. Initial instruction may be in the classroom or laboratory, but the skills must be applied and reinforced in the field practicum if they are to transfer to work with clients (Collins and Bogo 1986; Kopp 1990).

A more complex interviewing skill is putting the micro skills together to engage clients in a mutual problem-solving effort—establishing a relationship, "joining" a family, welcoming a group member. Learning assignments should include involuntary or resistive clients as well as receptive clients, to learn advanced skills such as confrontation or making demands for work.

A third aspect of interviewing skills is employing the skills appropriately for the culture of clients of different races, ethnicities, and genders, for example, differential use of eye gaze and silences, hand gestures, greetings, physical contact, and space. The student should communicate readily within the norms of those served by the agency. In addition, because practitioners will encounter other cultures, the student should also recognize cues that a client may be put off by an instance of culturally insensitive communication.

Assessment of client systems

The fourth area of intervention skills includes skills related to assessment of client systems. These skills include getting information from multiple sources; applying knowledge of human behavior to the specific instance; organizing and analyzing that information; and using it to formulate an assessment that includes strengths, a systems perspective, and a person-in-environment perspective. Additional assessment skills are formulating and prioritizing problems that can be worked on and viewing the definition and causation of problems from multiple perspectives rather than a single linear causation. These are complex behavioral and cognitive skills, especially integrating multiple perspectives. Consequently, learning assignments should push students to expand horizons beyond focus on a single client, for example, by interviewing collaterals even when not necessary, or reading intervention literature from contrasting theories.

Treatment planning

The fifth area of intervention is skills for treatment planning. These skills include selecting systems for intervention; setting realistic goals; developing alternative treatment plans based on the assessment; selecting a plan likely to reach the goals and appropriate for the clients' culture; and involving client systems in the decision making. As intervention progresses, planning includes modifying the treatment approach in response to evaluation of its effects. The treatment planning area reflects an emphasis on empirical practice (Reid and Smith 1989) in several respects: 1) the importance of linking treatment plans to the assessment (a topic usually neglected in practice texts); 2) the selection of treatment plans based at least in part on their probable effectiveness; and 3) the use of systematic feedback from evaluation to modify the intervention plan.

Implementation of treatment plans

The sixth area of client intervention skills is implementation of intervention plans. This includes, first, strategies for using interpersonal communication to guide the intervention interview. These often sophisticated strategies are ways of using interviewing skills to induce change in individuals' attitudes and behavior, for example, through deliberate use of confrontation, silence, or selection of level of empathy. A second type of intervention is mobilizing resources—financial, material, social, or psychological. Securing resources requires applying knowledge from other core areas to benefit the particular client system, for example, accessing the agency's financial grants (organizational context) or locating an agency to provide a home health aide (service delivery system context).

A third type of implementation skill is ability to apply a variety of specific intervention techniques. Among the possibilities are use of the relationship and of self to change individual functioning; specific approaches to problem solving such as task-centered practice; behavioral and cognitive-behavioral techniques; changing group or family dynamics; education or skills training such as parent effectiveness training (Gordon 1970); and work with collaterals. The intervention techniques must be appropriate for the clients' cultural context. For example, action-oriented responses that include a holistic view of nature may be appropriate among Native Americans (Nofz 1988).

Mastery of all possible intervention techniques is not realistic in a core practicum. Although an eclectic approach with variety gives students versatility for later practice, concentrating on a few principles enhances learning (Cuasay 1992). The school must make an informed and systematic choice of intervention skills expected from students.

Evaluation

The seventh intervention area is evaluation, including monitoring progress toward goals and assessing the effectiveness of specific intervention techniques. Single-system designs are versatile and useful, for example, simple AB designs to ensure change is taking place, more complex designs to evaluate specific techniques. These can be applied at nearly any level of client system: a child's episodes of enuresis, number of community members attending organizing meetings, contributions to United Way during different types of publicity, and so forth. Other types of evaluation such as goal attainment scaling may be useful, but "research" in the conventional experimental-design sense is not included in the core content. As part of intervention, the evaluation activities should be integrated to inform treatment planning and termination.

Termination

The eighth area of intervention skills is termination, ending intervention appropriately. The first termination skill is knowing when to terminate, given progress and realistic expectations for further progress (Fortune 1985; Fortune, Pearlingi, and Rochelle 1991). The ability to evaluate intervention effects is critical. However, decisions to end must also consider agency contexts such as difficulty of reopening cases and legal mandates to monitor a client. A second termination skill is the ability to disengage from the client system in a way that promotes the maintenance and generalization of change. This includes reducing dependence of the client system on the practitioner, "bridging" to other supports, and otherwise helping clients learn to manage on their own. The final termination skill—really a part of disengagement—is recognizing and managing reactions to ending, including positive affect and potentially negative reactions that may undermine progress.

Related to termination is transferring clients to other practitioners, often because the student leaves the agency before the client system is ready to terminate. Important skills are similar to termination—when to make a transfer, disengaging from the client system, and handling reactions (which may include anger at the disrupted relationship). Transfer skills also include helping the client establish a new relationship and appropriate consultation with the new practitioner (McRoy, Freeman, and Logan 1986).

Opportunities to learn termination skills may be limited because clients often drop out before a planned termination date. Consequently, learning opportunities may include discussion with other practitioners who are terminating or listening to tape recordings. Criteria for termination should of course be considered throughout each case, as part of the ongoing assessment of where the client system is in relation to goals.

Work with groups

The ninth intervention area is group work and teaching—elementary skills in leading socialization or educational groups such as children's recreational clubs or in-service training. Basic skills include selecting and organizing content, presenting clearly, and using group dynamics to further the purpose of the group. Much of this can be learned in the classroom through oral presentations and project work groups, but such groups in field placement allow the opportunity to concentrate on meeting group members' needs rather than the student's own learning needs. (The skills for leading clinical or work groups are reserved for the advanced level.)

Referrals and case management

The tenth area is referral skills, the ability to locate and secure services the agency does not provide. This requires knowledge of the potential resources (see the section on local social service delivery network, above), skills in negotiating with bureaucratic representatives, and the perseverance to follow up with referral agencies to ensure that services are provided as desired. The eleventh area, case management, requires similar skills, as well as management and interpersonal skills to coordinate among multiple service providers. In agencies where case management opportunities are limited, learning assignments may include cases with several concrete needs to give the student experience coordinating complex referrals.

Advocacy

The final intervention skill is advocacy on behalf of specific individuals—when practitioners "argue, debate, bargain, negotiate, and manipulate the environment on behalf of the client" (Compton and Galaway 1979:342). This is an adversarial extension of referral skills; an important skill is knowing when to use advocacy, since mistiming or misuse may damage the client's interests.

Core Content Which May Be Elsewhere in Curriculum: Basic Skills for Changing Systems

An important core area is changing systems—elementary knowledge of community organization and political action. Community organization skills include elementary skills in assessing key community actors (see section on service delivery system context), mobilizing community groups, implementing change strategies based on a locality-development model (Rothman and Tropman 1987), and disengaging without undoing the effects. Elementary skills in political action include skills to influence legislators—targeting issues and individuals, effective letter writing and personal contact—skills to ensure that "facts" used in the media are correct, and skills to mobilize voters (Zander 1990). Underlying both areas is skill in moving from the client system's private troubles to public issues, from case to cause—part of the ability of a generalist to move among units of intervention.

All students should have experience with these skills. However, in my opinion, at times it is more appropriate to offer these experiences outside the field practicum. The success of many system-change efforts relies on a critical mass of people to conduct the campaign; a class project with many students supported by a knowledgeable instructor may be more feasible than a duo of student and field instructor. The expertise and interest to oversee student projects may be more available among university-based faculty. Occasionally, opportunities occur outside either classroom or field: political action projects catalyzed by a faculty candidate for local office (Hull 1987), special events such as NASW legislative action days, or forums around timely issues like medical care reform.

The advantage of locating community organization and political action experiences in the field curricula is that it reinforces such action as an integral part of social work skills and values, particularly since system change is essential to combating injustice and oppression. It also forces field instructors and agencies to take an interest in action, thus serving a secondary educational purpose.

Whether in the classroom or practicum, all students should have hands-on learning assignments in beginning skills for community organization and political action.

Specialization: MSW Advanced or Post-MSW Content and Skills

Rather than review the content appropriate for advanced curricula and skills in depth, I would like to comment on why it is excluded from the core and where it does belong.

The first grouping is specialized skills for intervention with client systems. Four of these—assessment of need for specialized services, family treatment, group treatment, and specialized treatment techniques—are the therapeutic, mental health, or special-problem skills that most clearly distinguished BSW from MSW practitioners in the American Association of State Social Work Boards (AASSWB) employment task analysis (Biggerstaff and Eisenberg 1989). Further, in that study, the advanced clinical skills together with the general skills for intervention with client systems were the central tasks for social workers in the advanced clinical group. Consequently, in-depth experience with therapeutic and mental health interventions is reserved for the advanced, specialized, MSW-level field curriculum. The curriculum should emphasize diverse skills and theory bases and the linkage of assessment to differential intervention, to avoid the potential problem of fitting clients to the method.

Also included in the first grouping of advanced content are skills in clinical supervision. Clinical supervision logically belongs with the next group, skills for maintaining organizations, but is usually carried out by those who specialize in direct practice. It is the first and often only step into mid-level management for direct practitioners, and to be done well requires advanced clinical knowledge. Consequently, it is placed with the intervention skills. However, unless a student has experience, clinical supervision may be better left to postgraduate education. Most MSW students are too involved in their own current experience of being supervised to learn clinical supervision at the same time.

The second grouping of advanced content is specialized skills for maintaining and changing organizations and service delivery systems: a large subset of skills related to management of organizations and advanced-level community organization and political action skills. In the employment task analysis studies, the people using management skills were distinct from direct-practice social workers (Biggerstaff and Eisenberg 1989; Teare and Sheafor 1992b). Further, BSW-level social workers rarely performed them. In statistical analyses, the management skills clustered separately from other social work skills (Teare and Sheafor 1992a, 1992b). Thus, these skills are advanced, MSW-level skills but are separate from the advanced clinical skills—a different specialization.

A legitimate question is whether students who specialize in management need to have the core skills and field experiences. The data from the employment task analyses suggest that the higher-level managers do not share the same client-contact and service-provision duties of other social workers (Biggerstaff and Eisenberg 1989; Teare 1992b). Thus, management could be a separate "track" without sharing all the core social work knowledge. However, there are several reasons for requiring managers to have core social work experiences. First, in the employment task analyses, supervisors clearly bridged both direct supervision and administration in the range and content of duties (Teare 1992b). Typical career progression to administration is through such mid-level positions (often with a direct practice position first) (Holloway and Brager 1989). Thus, administrators will need the core skills and content at intermediate if not at ultimate career stages, particularly if they have not had prior social work experience. Second, a substantial proportion of new graduates from "macro" or administration concentrations do not find first jobs in that specialization (30 to 50 percent in several studies [Fortune 1986; Fortune and Hanks 1988; Radin 1976]); they will need the core skills in intervention and will be more marketable. Third, the core interpersonal skills are critical to effective management, although they may be put to different uses in consensus building, external relations, and personnel management. Fourth is an ideological position: managers should not be in control of something they do not understand. To understand social service delivery systems, managers need the core knowledge and skills, especially knowledge of service delivery and of social work values and ethics.

The final advanced grouping is knowledge development and dissemination—the research and higher education teaching traditionally carried out at the doctoral level. The doctoral level is where they belong, although a program may choose to have such a specialization at the master's level. Most importantly, neither program evaluation (a specialized system maintenance skill) nor research as knowledge development belong among the core practicum skills. Practitioners rarely use such research skills on the job. Current research training is insufficient to develop competent researchers or researchers-practitioners and there is hardly room in the curriculum to expand it. Consequently, it seems more pragmatic and efficient to reserve knowledge development for the advanced level and, in the core, to expand the research skills practitioners do need, the case evaluation skills.

This chapter has reviewed the history of field education and the current status of social work practice and education and presents conclusions in relation to three key issues: a common core does underlie social work practice; the core is similar for baccalaureate- and graduate-level practitioners, but graduate-level social workers need additional and deeper skills; and field education is part of the curriculum, with its own objectives but linked to the rest of the curriculum. On the basis of these conclusions, I proposed and explicated a model of content and skills for field education that will prepare undergraduate and graduate students for the tasks they are most likely to encounter on the job while giving them the flexibility to move into new areas as needed. Drawing from employment task analyses and curricular considerations, the model includes three levels of content: 1) preparation for professional commitment, at the undergraduate level; 2) core content and skills for both undergraduates and graduates; and 3) advanced content and skills for graduate students (therapeutic work with client systems and methods of maintaining and changing organizations and service delivery systems).

The model assumes that the core content and skills are essential to all social workers' practice and consequently should be included in field practica for all students. Learning assignments should be geared toward this content. The emphasis on universal core content is a departure from much current literature that stresses learner-centered objectives and individualized contracts. In this model, learning assignments may (and should) be individualized, but the goal—mastery of the content and skills—and the content itself are the same for all.

The model also emphasizes content that is transferable among settings. An important assumption is that nontransferable, setting-specific knowledge should be learned on the job. The assumption about transferable knowledge has two consequences: 1) the model's master's-level specializations are organized around the tasks that experienced master's-level social workers use on the job and not around populations, problems or fields of practice; and 2) when situation-specific content such as agency policy or local service delivery networks is included (as of course it must be), the purpose is to understand the context or to learn how to learn.

Field education is a central component of social work education. It is essential for testing students' abilities and commitment to work with people, for teaching real-life skills and content, and for helping students apply and integrate social work knowledge. The curriculum for field must be comprehensive and rigorous enough to prepare students for the essential tasks of practice in a world with complex, rapidly changing social problems. Yet it must be parsimonious enough to be attainable, a realistic part of an overall plan for professional education. The model in this chapter provides the framework of the essential elements of such a field curriculum, one that recognizes the realities of education and practice at the turn of the new century.

REFERENCES

Abbott, Ann A. 1986. "The Field Placement Contract: Its Use in Maintaining Comparability between Employment-Related and Traditional Field Placements." *Journal of Social Work Education* 22(1):57–66.

Austin, David M. 1986. *A History of Social Work Education.* Austin: University of Texas School of Social Work.

Baer, Betty L., Jacqueline D. Fassett, and Laura B. Morris. 1979. "The Common Purpose of the Social Work Practitioner and the Social Work Educator." In Betty L. Baer and Ronald C. Federico, eds., *Educating the Baccalaureate Social Worker: A Curriculum Development Resource Guide*, vol. II, pp. 15–31. Cambridge, Mass.: Ballinger.

Baer, Betty L. and Ronald Federico. 1978. *Educating the Baccalaureate Social Worker: Report of the Undergraduate Social Work Curriculum Development Project*. Cambridge, Mass.: Ballinger.

Bakalinsky, Rosalie. 1982. "Generic Practice in Graduate Social Work Curricula: A Study of Educators' Experiences and Attitudes." *Journal of Education for Social Work* 18(3):46–54.

Biggerstaff, Marilyn A. and Robin I. Eisenberg. 1989. *Summary Report: Job Analysis Verification Study, American Association of State Social Work Boards*. Culpeper, Va.: American Association of State Social Work Boards.

Biggerstaff, Marilyn A. and Michael S. Kolevzon. 1980. "Differential Use of Social Work Knowledge, Skills, and Techniques by MSW, BSW, and BA Level Practitioners." *Journal of Education for Social Work* 16(3):67–74.

Bisno, Herbert. 1959. *The Place of the Undergraduate Curriculum in Social Work Education*. New York: Council on Social Work Education.

Blumenfeld, Warren J. and Diane Raymond. 1988. *Looking at Gay and Lesbian Life*. Boston: Beacon Press.

Boehm, Werner. 1959. *Objectives of the Social Work Curriculum of the Future*. New York: Council on Social Work Education.

Bogo, Marion and Elaine Vayda. 1987. *The Practice of Field Instruction in Social Work: Theory and Process*. Toronto: University of Toronto Press.

Brackett, Jeffrey Richardson. 1903. *Supervision and Education in Charity*. New York: Macmillan.

Brennen, E. Clifford. 1984. "The Continuum: Multiple Levels of Social Work Education." In Miriam Dinerman and Ludwig L. Geismar, eds., *A Quarter-Century of Social Work Education*, pp. 25–46. New York: National Association of Social Workers, ABC-CLIO, and Council on Social Work Education.

Broeker, Richard C. and Edith F. Pearson. 1972. "Curriculum Guide of the Minnesota Unit." In Kristen Wenzel, ed., *Curriculum Guides for Undergraduate Field Instruction Programs*, pp. 23–87. New York: Council on Social Work Education.

Cassidy, Helen. 1982. "Structuring Field Learning Experiences." In Bradford W. Sheafor and Lowell E. Jenkins, eds., *Quality Field Instruction in Social Work: Program Development and Maintenance*, pp. 198–214. New York: Longman.

Chau, Kenneth L. 1990. "A Model for Teaching Cross-Cultural Practice in Social Work." *Journal of Social Work Education* 26(2):124–133.

Collins, Don and Marion Bogo. 1986. "Competency-Based Field Instruction: Bridging the Gap Between Laboratory and Field Learning." *Clinical Supervisor* 4(3):39–52.

Compton, Beulah R. and Burt Galaway. 1979. *Social Work Processes*. Homewood, Ill.: Dorsey Press.

Council on Social Work Education. 1992. *Curriculum Policy Statement*. Washington, D.C.: Council on Social Work Education.

Cox, Cordelia. 1971. "Characteristics of Undergraduate Programs in Social Work Education." In Lester J. Glick, ed., *Undergraduate Social Work Education for Practice: A Report on Curriculum Content and Issues.* Washington, D.C.: U.S. Government Printing Office.

Cuasay, Peter. 1992. "Cognitive Factors in Academic Achievement." *Higher Education Extension Service Review* 3(3):1–7.

Davenport, Judith A. and Joseph Davenport III. 1988. "Individualizing Student Supervision: The Use of Andragogical-Pedagogical Orientation Questionnaires." *Journal of Teaching in Social Work* 2(2):83–97.

Davis, Hope W., Jo Stallings Short, and Reginald O. York. 1984. "Achieving Quality Field Instruction in Part-Time Graduate Social Work Programs." *Clinical Supervisor* 2(1):45–54.

Davis, L. V. and Jan Hagen. 1988. "Services for Battered Women: The Public Policy Response." *Social Service Review* 62(4):649–667.

Dea, Kay L., Marah Grist, and Ruth Myli. 1982. "Learning Tasks for Practice Competence." In Bradford W. Sheafor and Lowell E. Jenkins, eds., *Quality Field Instruction in Social Work: Program Development and Maintenance*, pp. 237–261. New York: Longman.

Dinerman, Miriam. 1982. "A Study of Baccalaureate and Master's Curricula in Social Work." *Journal of Education for Social Work* 18(2):84–92.

——. 1984. "The 1959 Curriculum Study: Contributions of Werner W. Boehm." In Miriam Dinerman and Ludwig L. Geismar, eds., *A Quarter-Century of Social Work Education*, pp. 3–24. New York: National Association of Social Workers, ABC-CLIO, and Council on Social Work Education.

Dore, Martha Morrison, Bonnie Newman Epstein, and Catalina Herrerias. 1992. "Evaluating Students' Micro Practice Field Performance: Do Universal Learning Objectives Exist?" *Journal of Social Work Education* 28(3):353–362.

Eure, Gerald K., Jerry E. Griffin, and Charles R. Atherton. 1987. "Priorities for the Professional Foundation: Differences by Program Level." *Journal of Social Work Education* 23(2):19–29.

Fortune, Anne E. 1985. "Planning Duration and Termination of Treatment." *Social Service Review* 59(4):646–661.

——. 1986. "MSW Alumni of Virginia Commonwealth University School of Social Work: Employment Patterns, Professional Activities, and Curriculum Satisfaction of 1975–1984 MSW Graduates." Unpublished manuscript.

——. 1992. "Inadequate Resources." In William J. Reid, ed., *Task Strategies: An Empirical Approach to Clinical Social Work*, pp. 250–279. New York: Columbia University Press.

—— and Louella L. Hanks. 1988. "Gender Inequities in MSWs' Early Careers." *Social Work* 33(3):221–226.

——, Bill Pearlingi, and Cherie D. Rochelle. 1991. "Criteria for Terminating Treatment." *Families in Society* 72(6):366–370.

George, Aase. 1982. "A History of Social Work Field Instruction: Apprenticeship to Instruction." In Bradford W. Sheafor and Lowell E. Jenkins, eds., *Quality Field Instruction in Social Work: Program Development and Maintenance*, pp. 37–59. New York: Longman.

Gilbertson, William H. and Layne Winklebleck. 1972. "Curriculum Guide of the Washington State Unit." In Kristen Wenzel, ed., *Curriculum Guides for Undergraduate Field Instruction Programs*, pp. 204–258. New York: Council on Social Work Education.

Gladstein, Muriel and Mildred Mailick. 1986. "An Affirmative Approach to Ethnic Diversity in Field Work." *Journal of Social Work Education* 22(1):41–49.

Gordon, Thomas. 1970. *P.E.T. Parent Effectiveness Training: The Tested New Way to Raise Responsible Children.* New York: P. H. Wyden.

Gordon, William E. and Margaret Schutz Gordon. 1982. "The Role of Frames of Reference in Field Instruction." In Bradford W. Sheafor and Lowell E. Jenkins, eds., *Quality Field Instruction in Social Work: Program Development and Maintenance*, pp. 21–36. New York: Longman.

——. 1989. "George Warren Brown's Field Instruction Research Project: An Experimental Design Tested by Empirical Data." In Miriam S. Raskin, ed., *Empirical Studies in Field Instruction*, pp. 15–28. New York: Haworth Press.

Gordon, William E. and Margaret Schutz. 1969. *FIRP: Final Report Field Instruction Research Project.* St. Louis: George Warren Brown School of Social Work, Washington University.

Griffin, Jerry E. and Gerald K. Eure. 1985. "Defining the Professional Foundation in Social Work Education." *Journal of Social Work Education* 21(3):73–91.

Grossman, Bart and Richard P. Barth. 1991. "Evaluating a Delayed Entry Model of First Year Field Work." In Dean Schneck, Bart Grossman, and Urania Glassman, eds., *Field Education in Social Work: Contemporary Issues and Trends*, pp. 131–140. Dubuque, Ia.: Kendall/Hunt.

Grossman, Bart, Nancy Levine-Jordano, and Paul Shearer. 1991. "Working with Students' Emotional Reactions in the Field: An Education Framework." In Dean Schneck, Bart Grossman, and Urania Glassman, eds., *Field Education in Social Work: Contemporary Issues and Trends*, pp. 205–216. Dubuque, Ia.: Kendall/Hunt.

Gummer, Burton. 1990. *The Politics of Social Administration: Managing Organizational Politics in Social Agencies.* Englewood Cliffs, N.J.: Prentice-Hall.

Haffey, Martha, Elaine Marshack, and Rose Starr. 1984. "Costs and Benefits of Work Study vs. Traditional Field Placement Models." *Arete* 9(2):41–53.

Hagerty, James Edward. 1931. *The Training of Social Workers.* New York: McGraw-Hill.

Hartman, Ann. 1983. "Concentrations, Specializations, and Curriculum Design in MSW and BSW Programs." *Journal of Education for Social Work* 19(2):16–25.

Holloway, Stephen and George Brager. 1989. *Supervising in the Human Services: The Politics of Practice.* New York: Free Press.

Hull, Grafton H., Jr. 1987. "Joining Together: A Faculty-Student Experience in Political Campaigning." *Journal of Social Work Education* 23(3):37–43.

Ifill, Don. 1989. "Teaching Minority Practice for Professional Application." *Journal of Social Work Education* 25(1):29–35.

Jarrett, Herbert H. 1979. "Operationalizing Educational Outcomes in the Curriculum." In Betty L. Baer and Ronald C. Federico, eds., *Educating the Baccalaureate Social Worker: A Curriculum Development Resource Guide*, vol. II, pp. 93–108. Cambridge, Mass.: Ballinger.

Jenkins, Lowell E. and Bradford W. Sheafor. 1982. "An Overview of Social Work Field Instruction." In Bradford W. Sheafor and Lowell E. Jenkins, eds., *Quality Field Instruction in Social Work: Program Development and Maintenance*, pp. 3–20. New York: Longman.

Kadushin, Alfred E. 1991. "Field Education in Social Work: Contemporary Issues and Trends." In Dean Schneck, Bart Grossman, and Urania Glassman, eds., *Field Education in Social Work: Contemporary Issues and Trends*, pp. 11–12. Dubuque, Ia.: Kendall/Hunt.

Karasu, T. B., S. P. Stein, and E. S. Charles. 1978. "A Three-Year Follow-up Study of the Elimination of the Internship: A Comparative Study of Internship- and Noninternship-Trained Residents in a Psychiatric Outpatient Setting." *Archives of General Psychiatry* 17(4):1024–1026.

Kilpatrick, Allie C. 1991. "Differences and Commonalities in BSW and MSW Field Instruction: In Search of Continuity." In Dean Schneck, Bart Grossman, and Urania Glassman, eds., *Field Education in Social Work: Contemporary Issues and Trends*, pp. 167–176. Dubuque, Ia.: Kendall/Hunt.

Kolevzon, Michael S. and Marilyn A. Biggerstaff. 1983. "Functional Differentiation of Job Demands: Dilemmas Confronting the Continuum in Social Work Education." *Journal of Education for Social Work* 19(2):26–34.

Kopp, Judith. 1990. "The Transfer of Interviewing Skills to Practicum by Students with High and Low Pre-Training Skill Levels." *Journal of Teaching in Social Work* 4(1):31–52.

Korbelik, John and Laura Epstein. 1976. "Evaluating Time and Achievement in a Social Work Practicum." In *Teaching for Competence in the Delivery of Direct Services*. New York: Council on Social Work Education.

Latting, Jean Kantambu. 1990. "Identifying the `Isms': Enabling Social Work Students to Confront Their Biases." *Journal of Social Work Education* 26(1):36–44.

LeCroy, Craig W. and Cynthia C. Goodwin. 1988. "New Directions in Teaching Social Work Methods: A Content Analysis of Course Outlines." *Journal of Social Work Education* 24(1):43–49.

Leighninger, Leslie. 1984. "Graduate and Undergraduate Social Work Education: Roots of Conflict." *Journal of Education for Social Work* 20(3):66–77.

Lewis, Mary, Dorothy Howerton, and Walter L. Kindelsperger. 1962. *An Experimental Design for First Year Field Instruction*. New Orleans: School of Social Work, Tulane University.

Lister, Larry. 1987. "Ethnocultural Content in Social Work Education." *Journal of Social Work Education* 23(1):31–39.

Loewenberg, Frank M. and Ralph Dolgoff. 1992. *Ethical Decisions for Social Work Practice*. 4th ed. Itasca, Ill.: F. E. Peacock.

Lowe, Gary R. 1985. "The Graduate Only Debate in Social Work Education, 1931–1959, and Its Consequences for the Profession." *Journal of Social Work Education* 21(3):52–62.

McCaslin, Rosemary. 1987. "Substantive Specializations in Master's Level Social Work Curricula." *Journal of Social Work Education* 23(2):8–29.

McRoy, Ruth G., Edith M. Freeman, and Sadye Logan. 1986. "Strategies for Teaching Students about Termination." *Clinical Supervisor* 4(4):45–56.

Manoleas, Peter and Ernestina Carrillo. 1991. "A Culturally Syntonic Approach to the Field Education of Latino Students." *Journal of Social Work Education* 27(2):135–144.

Marshack, Elaine, Rose Starr, and Martha Haffey. 1987. "Investment or Resource Drain: An Empirical Study of the Career Patterns of Work-Study Graduates." *Journal of Continuing Social Work Education* 4(2):39–44.

Moore, Linda S. and Charlene A. Urwin. 1991. "Gatekeeping: A Model for Screening Baccalaureate Students for Field Education." *Journal of Social Work Education* 27(1):8–17.

Munson, Carlton E. 1987. "Field Instruction in Social Work Education." *Journal of Teaching in Social Work* 1(1):91–109.

Nakanishi, Manuel, and Barbara Rittner. 1992. "The Inclusionary Cultural Model." *Journal of Social Work Education* 28(1):27–35.

Nofz, Michael P. 1988. "Alcohol Abuse and Culturally Marginal American Indians." *Social Casework* 69(2):67–73.

Pincus, Allen and Anne Minahan. 1973. *Social Work Practice: Model and Method.* Itasca, Ill.: F. E. Peacock.

Powers, Gerald T., Howard J. Hess, and Raymond Koleski. 1984. "Evaluating the Relative Effectiveness of Alternative Models of Professional Education: The Weekend/Work-Study Curriculum Option." *Journal of Continuing Social Work Education* 3(1):28–32.

Radin, Norma. 1976. "A Follow-up Study of Social Work Graduates." *Journal of Education for Social Work* 12(3):103–107.

Ramsey, Patricia Campbell. 1989. "Practice Orientation of Students in Field Instruction." In Miriam S. Raskin, ed., *Empirical Studies in Field Instruction*, pp. 137–160. New York: Haworth Press.

Raskin, Miriam. 1983. "A Delphi Study in Field Instruction: Identification of Issues and Research Priorities by Experts." *Arete* 8(2):38–48.

——. 1993. "The Delphi Study in Field Instruction Revisited: Consensus of Issues and Research Priorities by Experts." In *Council on Social Work Education Annual Program Meeting* New York: Council on Social Work Education.

Reamer, Frederic G. 1990. *Ethical Dilemmas in Social Service.* 2d ed. New York: Columbia University Press.

Reeser, Linda Cherry, Robert A. Wertkin, and Eddie Davis. 1991. "Differences in Undergraduate and Graduate Practicums: Elitism, Racism, and Classism?" In Dean Schneck, Bart Grossman, and Urania Glassman, eds., *Field*

Education in Social Work: Contemporary Issues and Trends, pp. 261–271. Dubuque, Ia.: Kendall/Hunt.

Reid, William J. and Audrey D. Smith. 1989. *Research in Social Work*. New York: Columbia University Press.

Richmond, Mary. 1917. *Social Diagnosis*. New York: Russell Sage Foundation.

Rothman, Jack. 1977. "Development of a Profession: Field-Instruction Correlates." *Social Service Review* 51(2):289–310.

—— and John E. Tropman. 1987. "Models of Community Organization and Macro Practice Perspectives: Their Mixing and Phasing." In Fred M. Cox, et al., eds., *Strategies of Community Organization: Macro Practice*, pp. 3–26. Itasca, Ill.: F. E. Peacock.

Schatz, Mona S., Lowell E. Jenkins, and Bradford Sheafor. 1990. "Milford Redefined: A Model of Initial and Advanced Generalist Social Work." *Journal of Social Work Education* 26(3):217–231.

Schiller, John A. 1972. "The Current Status of Undergraduate Social Work Education." In Kristen Wenzel, ed., *Undergraduate Field Instruction Programs: Current Issues and Predictions*, pp. 3–13. New York: Council on Social Work Education.

Schur, Edith L., JoAnn Barndt, and Jan Baum. 1983. "A Criterial Structure for Graduate Field Education: A Model for Planning, Performance, and Evaluation." *Social Work Education Reporter* 31(2):6–10.

Sikkema, Mildred. 1966. "A Proposal for an Innovation in Field Learning and Teaching." In Council on Social Work Education, ed., *Field Instruction in Graduate Social Work Education: Old Problems and New Proposals*, pp. 1–22. New York: Council on Social Work Education.

Skolnik, Louise. 1989. "Field Instruction in the 1980s—Realities, Issues, and Problem-Solving Strategies." In Miriam Raskin, ed., *Empirical Studies in Field Instruction*, pp. 47–75. New York: Haworth Press.

Teare, Robert J. 1992a. Personal communication.

——. 1992b. Unpublished data.

—— and Bradford W. Sheafor. 1991. "Separating Reality from Fantasy: A Depiction of BSW Practice." In *Ninth Annual Baccalaureate Program Directors' Conference*, Orlando, Fla.

——. 1992a. "An Empirically Grounded Framework for Social Work Practice," Unpublished manuscript.

——. 1992b. "Social Work Practice and Practitioners," Unpublished manuscript.

Tsang, Nai-ming. 1988. "Factors Associated with Fieldwork Performance in a Social Work Course in Hong Kong." *Clinical Supervisor* 6(3/4):337–358.

Tucker, David J., Joel A. C. Baum, and Jitendra Singh. 1992. "The Institutional Ecology of Human Service Organizations." In Yeheskel Hasenfeld, ed., *Human Services as Complex Organizations*, pp. 47–72. Newbury Park, Calif.: Sage.

Tufts, James H. 1923. *Education and Training for Social Work*. New York: Russell Sage Foundation.

Urbanowski, Martha L. and Margaret M. Dwyer. 1988. *Learning Through Field Instruction: A Guide for Teachers and Students*. Milwaukee: Family Service of America.

Videka-Sherman, Lynn and William J. Reid. 1985. "A Structured Clinical Record: A Clinical Education Tool." *Clinical Supervisor* 3(1):45–62.

Vosler, Nancy R. 1989. "A Systems Model for Child Protective Services." *Journal of Social Work Education* 25(1):20–28.

Ware, Mark E., Richard J. Millard, and Janet R. Matthews. 1984. "Strategies for Evaluating Field Placement Programs." *Psychological Reports* 55:571–578.

Wayne, Julianne, Louise Skolnik, and Miriam S. Raskin. 1989. "Field Instruction in the United States and Canada: A Comparison of Studies." In Miriam Raskin, ed., *Empirical Studies in Field Instruction*, pp. 77–87. New York: Haworth Press.

Wilson, Suanna J. 1981. *Field Instruction: Techniques for Supervisors*. New York: Free Press.

Zander, Alvin. 1990. *Effective Social Action by Community Groups*. San Francisco: Jossey-Bass.

7

Social Work Values and Ethics

FREDERIC G. REAMER

The subject of values and ethics has been central to social work since its formal inception. Historical accounts of the profession's development routinely dwell on the compelling importance of social work's value base and ethical tenets. Over time, beliefs about social work's values and ethics have served as the principal organizing theme of the profession's mission, and as the normative linchpin in the profession's foundation.

Social work is, after all, a normative profession, perhaps the most normative of the so-called helping professions. In contrast to professions such as psychiatry, psychology, and counseling, social work's historical roots are firmly grounded in concepts such as justice and fairness. Throughout its history, social work's compass has been anchored principally, although not exclusively, by conceptions of what is just and unjust, by a collective sense of what individuals have a right to in life, and what duties they owe one another.

Although the theme of values and ethics has endured in the profession, social workers' conceptions of what these terms mean, and of their bearing on practice, have changed considerably over time. In the late nineteenth century, when social work was formally inaugurated as a profession, there was much more concern about the morality of the client than about the morality or ethics of the profession or its practitioners. Organizing relief and responding to the "curse of pauperism" (Paine 1880) were the profession's principal missions. This preoccupation often took the form of paternalistic attempts to strengthen the morality or rectitude of the poor whose "wayward" lives had gotten the best of them.

Concern about the morality of the poor waned considerably—although not entirely—during the rise of the settlement house movement in the early twentieth century, when the aims of many social workers shifted from concern about the morality, or immorality, of the poor to the need for dramatic social reform designed to ameliorate a wide range of social problems, for example, related to housing, health care, sanitation, employment, poverty, and education (Reamer 1992b).

Concern about the morality of the client continued to recede somewhat during the next several decades of the profession's life, as practitioners engaged in earnest attempts to establish and polish their intervention strategies and techniques, training programs, and schools of thought. Over time, concern about clients' morality was overshadowed by debate about the profession's very future, that is, the extent to which social work would stress the cultivation of expertise in psychosocial and psychiatric casework, psychotherapy, social welfare policy and administration, community organization, or social reform.

By the late 1940s and early 1950s, however, concern about the moral dimensions of social work practice intensified, although in rather different form. Unlike the earlier preoccupation with the morality of the client, this mid-twentieth-century concern focused much more on the morality or ethics of the profession and of its practitioners. This was a significant shift. Nearly a half-century after its formal inauguration, the profession began to develop ethical guidelines to enhance proper conduct among practitioners. In 1947, after several years of debate and discussion, the Delegate Conference of the American Association of Social Workers adopted a code of ethics. The profession's journals also began to publish articles on the subject with greater frequency. In 1959 Muriel Pumphrey published her landmark work, *The Teaching of Values and Ethics in Social Work Education*. Several other significant publications of that period included the American Association of Social Workers' *Standards for the Professional Practice of Social Work* (1952), Hall's (1952) "Group Workers and Professional Ethics," Roy's (1954) "Code of Ethics," and Johnson's (1955) "Educating Professional Social Workers for Ethical Practice" (Pumphrey 1959:12). Thus, the 1950s marked the onset of serious scholarly interest in the subject of professional ethics.

This is not to say, of course, that social workers neglected the subject prior to this period. Certainly this was not the case. Social workers have always espoused concern about a core group of central values that have served as the profession's ballast, such as the dignity, uniqueness, and worth of the person, self-determination, autonomy, respect, justice, equality, and individuation (Biestek 1957; Cabot 1973; Hamilton 1951; Joseph 1989; National Association of Social Workers 1974; Richmond 1917). In addition, there were several modest efforts earlier in the twentieth century to place ethics on social workers' agenda. As early as 1919 there were attempts to draft professional codes of ethics (Elliott 1931). In 1922 the Family Welfare Association of America appointed an ethics committee in response to questions about ethical problems in the field (Joseph 1989; Elliott 1931). Further, there is evidence that at least some social work schools were teaching discrete courses on values and ethics in the 1920s (Elliott 1931). However, the late 1940s and early 1950s rather clearly constitute a watershed period in social work when the subject of professional ethics became a subject of study and scholarship in its own right (Frankel 1959; Reamer and Abramson 1982).

Not surprisingly, in the 1960s social workers shifted considerable attention toward the ethical constructs of social justice, rights, and reform. The public and political mood of this turbulent period infused social work training and practice with concern about social equality, welfare rights, human rights, discrimination, and oppression (Emmet 1962; Lewis 1972; Plant 1970; Vigilante 1974). It is noteworthy that in 1960 the National Association of Social Workers (NASW) adopted its first code of ethics.

Perhaps the most visible expression of emerging concern about social work values and ethics was the 1976 publication of Charles Levy's *Social Work Ethics*. Although the profession's journals had by then published a number of articles on social work values and ethics, Levy's book was the profession's most ambitious conceptual discussion of the subject. This had great symbolic significance. From that point on, scholarship on social work ethics has blossomed. Levy's work, contained in *Social Work Ethics* and earlier publications (1972, 1973), helped to turn social workers' attention toward the study of overarching values and ethical principles.

The early 1980s marked yet another significant transition in social work's concern with values and ethical issues. During the 1970s there was a dramatic surge of interest in the broad subject of professional ethics. Professions as diverse as medicine, law, business, journalism, engineering, nursing, and criminal justice began to devote sustained attention to the subject. Large numbers of undergraduate and graduate training programs added courses on ethics to their curricula, professional conferences witnessed a substantial increase in presentations on the subject, and the number of publications on professional ethics increased dramatically (Callahan and Bok 1980; Reamer and Abramson 1982).

This growth of interest was due to a variety of factors. Controversial technological developments in health care and other fields certainly helped to spark ethical debate around such issues as termination of life support, organ transplantation, genetic engineering, and test-tube babies. Widespread publicity about scandals in government also triggered considerable interest in professional ethics. In addition, the introduction, beginning especially in the 1960s, of terminology such as patients' rights, welfare rights, and prisoners' rights helped shape professionals' thinking about the need to attend to ethical concepts. Finally, the well-documented increase in litigation and malpractice, along with publicity about unethical professionals, forced the professions to take a closer look at their ethics traditions and training.

Since the late 1970s a major focus in ethics scholarship, training, and education has been on the phenomenon of ethical dilemmas. Professionals have become increasingly interested in the analysis of ethical dilemmas where practitioners must make difficult choices among competing professional duties or obligations. Beginning especially in the early 1980s, social workers have been introduced to the subjects of ethical decision making and ethical theory, particularly as they pertain to the dilemmas encountered in day-to-day practice (Loewenberg and Dolgoff 1992; Reamer 1980, 1982, 1983b, 1987b, 1990; Reamer and Abramson 1982; Rhodes 1986). There has also been some renewed interest in reexamining the content of social work's value base (Siporin 1982, 1983, 1989).

The Nature of Social Work Values and Ethics

Foundation-level content on social work values and ethics is diverse. It includes four major topical areas: 1) the value base and ethical tenets of the profession; 2) ethical dilemmas in social work practice; 3) ethical decision making; and 4) ethical misconduct. Although these areas are not entirely mutually exclusive, they constitute discrete subject areas about which social workers should be knowledgeable.

The Value Base of Social Work

The clearest, most enduring content is related to core social work values that, in principle, shape and give meaning to the profession's mission. From the earliest days of social work's history, the profession has embraced a set of values rooted in concern about individual well-being and social justice. As Vigilante (1974) has said, social work values are the "fulcrum of practice."

As Timms (1983) has noted in his seminal work on social work values, discussions of values in the profession have been of three types: broad overviews of the profession and social work's mission, which include general references to "value" or "values" (e.g., Hamilton 1940; Younghusband 1967); critical assessments of social work values or of a particular value (e.g., McDermott 1975); and reports of empirical research on values held or embraced by social workers (e.g., Varley 1968).

Although there is some variation among the core values of the profession identified by different authors, there is considerable consistency. Commonly cited values are *individual worth and dignity, respect of persons, valuing individuals' capacity for change, client self-determination, providing individuals with opportunity to realize their potential, seeking to meet individuals' common human needs, commitment to social change and social justice, confidentiality, seeking to provide individuals with adequate resources and services to meet their basic needs, client empowerment, equal opportunity, nondiscrimination, respect of diversity,* and *willingness to transmit professional knowledge and skills to others* (Baer 1979; Barker 1991; Bartlett 1970; Biestek 1957; Biestek and Gehrig 1978; Goldstein 1983; Gordon 1962; Keith-Lucas 1977; Levy 1973, 1976, 1984; Morales and Sheafor 1986; Plant 1970; Pumphrey 1959; Reamer 1987b, 1990; Sheafor, Horejsi, and Horejsi 1988; Solomon 1976; Teicher 1967; Timms 1983; Wilson 1978).

Pumphrey (1959:79–80) offered one of the earliest classifications of social work values, placing them into three categories of value-based objectives. The first focused on "relating the values of the profession to those operating in the culture at large." This area concerned the compatibility between the profession's mission—for example, regarding social justice, social change, meeting common human needs—and the broader society's values. The second category focused on "internal relationships within the professional membership," for example, the ways in which the profession interprets and implements its values and encourages ethical behavior. The final category focused on "relations to the specific groups or individuals served," that is, understanding and responding to clients' values.

Levy (1973) has also provided a useful classification of the values held by the social work profession. The first of Levy's three groups includes "preferred conceptions of people," such as the belief in individuals' inherent worth and dignity, capacity and drive toward constructive change, mutual responsibility, need to belong, uniqueness, and common human needs. The second group includes "preferred outcomes for people," such as the belief in society's obligation to provide opportunities for individual growth and development, to provide resources and services to help people meet their needs and to avoid such problems as hunger, inadequate education or housing, illness, and discrimination, and to provide equal opportunity to participate in the molding of society.

Levy's third group includes "preferred instrumentalities for dealing with people," such as the belief that people should be treated with respect and dignity, have the right to self-determination, be encouraged to participate in social change, and be recognized as unique individuals.

One of the most persistent tensions in the value base of the profession concerns social workers' simultaneous commitment to individual well-being and the welfare of the broader society. As we shall see in our discussion of ethical dilemmas, social workers sometimes face difficult choices between protection of clients' individual interests and protection of the broader community's interests. There is also tension between social workers' commitment to psychotherapeutic change in individuals and families and their commitment to social change related to such phenomena as inequality, discrimination, poverty, and injustice (McCormick 1961; Reamer 1992b; Rhodes 1986; Specht 1991; Wakefield 1988a, 1988b).

A significant portion of the literature on social work values focuses on the need for social workers to clarify their own personal values. The assumption here is that practitioners' personal values exert considerable influence on their views of their clients, their intervention frameworks and strategies, and their definitions of successful or unsuccessful outcome.

With regard to social work, Pumphrey (1959) states that individuals' values are "formulations of preferred behavior held by individuals or social groups. They imply a usual preference for certain means, ends and conditions of life, often being accompanied by strong feeling" (23). Rokeach (1973) offers what has become a classic definition of "value" in his *The Nature of Human Values*: "An enduring belief that a specific mode or end state of existence is personally or socially preferable to an opposite or converse mode or end state of existence" (5).

From this perspective, it is important to distinguish among ultimate, proximate, and instrumental values. *Ultimate values* are broadly conceived and provide general guidance to a group's aims. In social work, values such as *respect for persons, equality,* and *nondiscrimination* constitute ultimate values. *Proximate values,* on the other hand, are more specific. In social work they might take the form of specific policies such as psychiatric patients' right to refuse certain types of treatment, welfare clients' right to a certain level of benefits, or ethnic minorities' right to quality health care. Finally, *instrumental values* are specifications of desirable means to valued ends. In social work, respecting clients' rights to confidentiality, self-determination, and to give informed consent would be considered instrumental values (Johnson 1989; Rokeach 1973).

Three issues related to social work values deserve special emphasis. First, social workers occasionally face tension between their own personal values and the profession's espoused values. Perhaps the best example of this conflict concerns the profession's position on abortion. NASW has adopted a position that is generally embraced by its members. According to NASW policy, women have the right to choose whether or not to abort a pregnancy, to the extent permitted by law. This is a policy that is troubling to some social workers who, usually for personal religious reasons, are opposed to abortion. This value conflict can present difficult problems for social workers opposed to abortion who are employed in settings that respect women's right to choose. Similar conflicts may arise when a social worker is providing services to a client whose cultural or religious beliefs support behaviors or activities (for example, concerning health care or the treatment of children) that run counter to the profession's or the worker's personal values (Reamer 1990; Rhodes 1986; Timms 1983).

The second issue concerns social workers' values or beliefs related to the determinants of clients' problems. Social workers repeatedly make assumptions about the causes and malleability of clients' problems and shape intervention plans accordingly (Stalley 1975; McDermott 1975;

Reamer 1983a). For example, poverty may be viewed as the outcome of a grossly unjust society that harbors discrimination, exploitation of labor, and inadequate social support, or as the result of individual sloth and laziness. Similar contrast can be offered with respect to problems such as emotional distress, crime and delinquency, unemployment, and substance abuse. While some social workers may assume that these problems are the result of structural determinants over which individuals have little, if any, control, others may assume that these problems are the byproducts of individual choice (Reamer 1983a).

Social workers' values in this regard are likely to have important bearing on their response and intervention. They may affect practitioners' beliefs about what kind of change is *possible*, and how that change can be brought about, and about what kind of assistance individuals *deserve*. A social worker who believes that a criminal (for example, a convicted child abuser) chooses his unlawful behavior (the so-called free will view) may respond very differently than would a social worker who believes that the criminal behaves as he does because of the compelling societal forces surrounding him (the determinist view). These social workers may also have different sentiments about the extent to which the offender deserves help.

Differences in social work educators' views on the free will-determinism debate are reflected in the profession's literature. Ephross and Reisch (1982), for example, found clear differences in the ideological and value orientations of introductory social work texts' authors. They conclude that

> there are clear differences among the books reviewed as to social, political, and economic content, and it seems that these differences are quite important for the education of professional social workers. In a sense, one can distribute these introductory textbooks over an ideological spectrum. The temptation is to visualize such a spectrum as covering a range from "Left" to "Right." These terms are used a bit unconventionally here; they do not imply that the authors adhere to all of the political views commonly associated with Left or Right positions. Rather, the idea is of a scale whose polar points describe conceptions of the relationship between societal forces and individual experiences. The Left pole, then, encompasses the position that individuals' lives are circumscribed and heavily influenced, if not determined, by political, economic, and institutional patterns within society. The Right pole attributes to individuals and families a great

deal of leeway to determine their individual and interpersonal experiences.   (280)

The third issue concerns the legitimacy of social work's core values.
Although social work's values have traditionally been embraced
throughout the profession's history, it would be a mistake to conclude
that they have been entirely static and unchallenged. Siporin (1982,
1983, 1989), for example, has expressed concern about what he believes
may be excessive tolerance of non-normative, libertarian views that
may lead to abandonment of personal and social responsibility. For
Siporin, social work is essentially a "moral enterprise" (1989:44), but an
enterprise that has lost some of its moral bearings in recent years, due
largely to the influence of the medical model and proprietary or entre-
preneurial models of practice: "The net effect of these trends is that
they have made for an erosion of social work morality, and of its ethical commitments. They have disrupted the balances that existed about
conflicting values, created partisan dissension among social workers
about the issues at stake, and have fragmented the consensual unity of
the social work profession" (1989:50).

Ethical Dilemmas in Social Work

In many instances, social workers' ethical responsibilities are clear and
uncomplicated. Ordinarily, social workers understand their duty, for
example, to respect clients' right to confidentiality and to protect the
general welfare of members of society. These ethical principles are set
forth rather clearly in the NASW *Code of Ethics* (1994), and there is long-
standing support for them in social work literature and practice.

On occasion, however, such duties conflict. A social worker whose
client informs her during a counseling session that he plans to harm his
estranged spouse must make a difficult choice between the client's
right to confidentiality and protection of a third party. Assuming clinical intervention fails to resolve the issue and there is evidence the
client plans to carry out his threat, the social worker must choose
between two competing duties that social workers are ordinarily
expected to fulfill.

Hence, ethical dilemmas in social work include those instances
where practitioners face conflicting duties or obligations. Three categories of dilemmas are particularly relevant to social work practice.

The first includes ethical dilemmas related to intervention with individuals, families, and groups. Prominent dilemmas in this area concern issues of confidentiality, client self-determination, paternalism, and truth-telling (Reamer 1987b, 1990). With regard to confidentiality, it is important for social workers to understand the limits of confidentiality, particularly when clients threaten to harm themselves or a third party (Arnold 1970; Promislo 1979; Reynolds 1976; Wilson 1978). Under what circumstances should social workers breach clients' right to privacy in order to protect third parties or clients from themselves?

Similar dilemmas arise with regard to clients' right to self-determination. Ordinarily, social workers respect clients' right to self-determination and help them pursue goals that are meaningful to them (Bernstein 1960; Keith-Lucas 1963; McDermott 1975; Perlman 1965). Instances arise, however, where social workers must consider limiting clients' right to self-determination, because such actions threaten to harm clients themselves or third parties. Consider, for example, a social worker whose client is a battered woman. After a period of separation from her abusive partner, who has battered the client on several prior occasions, the client informs the social worker of her intention to once again live with her partner. The social worker feels strongly that the client will, quite likely, be abused again. Empirically based literature on the phenomenon also supports the worker's hunch. To what extent should the worker respect the client's right to self-determination and help her pursue her chosen goal, as opposed to actively attempting to dissuade her from her plans to move in again with her partner?

Further, how should social workers respond to severely mentally or physically disabled clients who have decided to end their lives, because of the chronic emotional or physical pain they experience? Should social workers summarily reject the possibility of "rational" suicide and discourage clients from further consideration of the possibility? Is it ever defensible for social workers to respect the decision of a distressed, but competent, client who has decided to commit suicide?

Debate concerning the limits of clients' right to self-determination in instances when their actions seem self-destructive inevitably leads to discussion of the concept of professional paternalism. Paternalism is ordinarily defined as interference with an individual's intentions or mental state in order to protect the individual from him- or herself (Buchanan 1978; Carter 1977; Dworkin 1971; Feinberg 1971; Gert and Culver 1976; Husak 1980). Common examples of paternalism include prohibiting swimming at beaches when lifeguards are not on duty, requiring members of certain religious groups to receive life-saving blood transfusions, permitting involuntary civil commitment to a psychiatric facility, and legislating against suicide.

Social workers face several types of ethical dilemmas involving paternalism (Reamer 1983a). First, there are those instances when social workers decide whether to physically interfere with clients for their own protection. Should a social worker require a resourceful, but troubled, homeless individual to go to a shelter against her wishes, when the temperature is below freezing?

Second, there are those instances when social workers decide whether to withhold information from a client, because of a belief that the client's knowledge of that information will be harmful. Is it justifiable, for example, for a hospital-based social worker to withhold information from a critically ill patient that his child was just killed in an automobile accident? Is paternalism, in the form of withholding personally relevant information, justified in order to protect the hospital patient from harm?

Third, there are those instances when social workers decide whether to deliberately give clients inaccurate information, or to lie to clients, in order to protect clients from harm. Is it justifiable, on paternalistic grounds, for a social worker to lie to a child about the reason for her father's arrest by the police, in order to preserve, as much as possible, the child's relationship with her father? Is it permissible to give inaccurate information to a suicidal client in an effort to prevent suicide?

A special problem social workers face in these circumstances concerns the distinction between paternalism and pseudopaternalism (Reamer 1983a). Pseudopaternalism occurs when social workers use the language of paternalism to justify limiting clients' right to self-determination, when, in fact, the paternalistic interference is driven by some ulterior motive. An example is admitting a homeless individual to a shelter, against his wishes, primarily to remove this "nuisance" from the street, while arguing that placement in the shelter is "for his own good." Another example is withholding disturbing information from a client, on the grounds that "he can't handle it," when the principal reason may be that the social worker is reluctant to deal with the distress the sharing of the information may cause.

Dilemmas involving paternalism frequently raise issues concerning the phenomenon of truth telling. Although social workers are typically inclined to be truthful with clients, there may be times when it may seem that truth telling would be harmful (Bok 1978). Whether deception can ever be justified is an important matter to debate.

The second major category of ethical dilemmas in social work pertains to the ways in which practitioners design and administer social welfare policies and programs (Reamer 1987b, 1990). One of the most enduring dilemmas social workers face concerns the allocation of limited or scarce resources. Social workers often control the distribution of resources such as emergency beds or food, treatment sessions, service vouchers, and program funds.

There is considerable debate among social workers as to the ethical criteria that should be used to allocate such resources. In fact, various criteria are used. Program services, for instance, may be distributed equally, with equal shares granted to eligible parties. Or, they may be distributed based on the principle of equality of opportunity, in the form of a lottery or first-come, first-served. In contrast, program services may be allocated on the basis of client need—with those in greatest need receiving higher priority—or based on clients' ability to pay for the services. Further, some programs may allocate services based on affirmative action principles, with oppressed or minority clients receiving higher priority (Coulton, Rosenberg, and Yankey 1981; Reamer 1990; Reid and Billups 1986).

Social workers also encounter dilemmas concerning their duty to obey laws, agency rules, and public- or private-agency regulations. In all states, for example, social workers are required to report suspected cases of child abuse and neglect to protective-service officials. Despite this mandate, however, social workers sometimes do not report such cases, on the grounds that they are in a better position than public officials to intervene effectively or they do not want to betray the client's trust.

Complicated ethical dilemmas also arise with respect to compliance with regulations. Many social service agencies, for instance, depend on reimbursement for their services from insurance carriers or other third-party payers. To receive reimbursement, agency staff typically need to provide insurers with documentation of reimbursable services provided. Because some of the agency's services may not be reimbursable under the insurer's guidelines, social workers may struggle with their obligation to provide truthful claims information. The viability of the agency and its services may be at stake.

Ethical dilemmas of a different sort pertain to agency policy concerning actual services provided. A sectarian agency, for example, may prohibit abortion-related counseling. This may present a dilemma for a social worker who is pro-choice and who feels a professional obligation to inform clients of all their legal options.

Ethical dilemmas concerning the design and administration of social welfare policy and programs also involve broad regional or national issues. For example, social workers may be involved in debate about the ethics of mandatory HIV testing of psychiatric patients or prison inmates, workfare programs involving single mothers with young children, the development of group homes for the retarded against local residents' wishes, and cutbacks in public spending on substance abuse treatment programs. In these instances, there are complex ethical issues concerning policies on privacy, coercion, and the role of the state in the provision of social welfare.

The third broad category of ethical dilemmas involves relationships among professional colleagues. The most common, perhaps, concerns instances when social workers encounter impaired or incompetent colleagues. In these circumstances—when a social worker has evidence that a colleague is abusing alcohol, drugs, or clients, for example—there are troubling ethical issues involving "whistle blowing" (Barry 1986; Bok 1980; Nader, Petkas, and Blackwood 1972; Peters and Branch 1972; Reamer 1990). Under what circumstances is whistle blowing justifiable? What conditions should first be met? How much professional and personal risk should the whistle blower be willing to assume?

Ethical dilemmas can also arise in relationships among colleagues with respect to the use of deception. Social service providers may be competitors with one another, and such competition may sometimes tempt administrators to engage in deceptive practices to win new grants or undermine competitors' advantage, in order to ensure their own agency's fiscal health or survival. Deception may also be contemplated in order to surreptitiously gather information to document wrongdoing allegedly engaged in by colleagues.

It is particularly important for social workers who face ethical dilemmas to critically examine the political and ideological context surrounding them, in addition to addressing the immediate, case-specific problem (Rhodes 1986; Timms 1983). There is no question that ethical dilemmas often reflect the political leanings and ideological orientations of involved parties. Ethical dilemmas related to the allocation of scarce health care resources, for example, may call for social action to challenge the prevailing distribution of responsibility between the public and private sectors for such essential services. Ethical dilemmas related to the use of coercion with homeless people or welfare recipients may warrant aggressive social change efforts to challenge the way a Western capitalist nation provides, or fails to provide, for its most vulnerable citizens. It is often difficult to separate the ethical and political aspects of such dilemmas.

Ethical Decision Making

One of the more important developments in scholarship on social work values and ethics has been the relatively recent emphasis on ethical decision making. Until the early 1980s, there was very little discussion in the social work literature on decision-making guidelines, frameworks, or ethical theory. Instead, the literature focused primarily on the nature of social work values and value conflicts.

In the early 1980s, a small group of social work educators began to explore the relevance of ethical theory and concepts to the decisions practitioners must make when faced with ethical dilemma. Not surprisingly, similar developments were taking place in other professions.

The format has been fairly consistent across professions. Scholars typically offer an overview of traditional ethical theories—theories of *metaethics* and *normative ethics*—and apply them to practice-based circumstances. Metaethics includes analysis of the meaning of ethical terms or language and the derivation of ethical principles and guidelines. Typical metaethical questions include: What do we mean by the terms *right* and *wrong*, or *good* and *bad*? What criteria should we use to judge whether someone has engaged in unethical action? How should we go about deriving ethical principles to guide individuals who struggle with moral choices?

Some philosophers, known as cognitivists, believe that it is possible to identify objective criteria for determining what is ethically right and wrong, or good and bad. Others, however, question whether this is possible. These so-called noncognitivists argue that such criteria are inevitably subjective, and ethical principles merely reflect our own individual biases and preferences. Some social workers may believe that it is possible to establish universal principles upon which to base ethical practice, perhaps in the form of a code of ethics or "God-given" tenets. Other social workers may reject this view, arguing instead that ethical standards for social work depend on cultural practices, political climate, contemporary norms, and other contextual considerations. This is a debate between what is sometimes called "absolutism" and "relativism" in ethics (Stace 1975).

In contrast to metaethics, which can be a rather abstract endeavor, questions of normative ethics tend to be of special concern to social workers because of their immediate relevance to professional practice. In particular, applied ethics concerns the application of ethical principles and concepts to ethical dilemmas that arise in professional work. Such guidance is especially useful when social workers face conflicts among duties they are ordinarily inclined to carry out, or what the philosopher W. D. Ross (1930) refers to as *prima facie* duties. The prima facie duty that takes precedence over others is one's *actual* duty. Thus, in the example described above, the social worker who must choose between respecting a client's right to confidentiality and protecting a third party from harm would be interested in using theories of normative ethics in order to help make this choice. Another example is whether to break a law when doing so seems to be in a client's best interest, or whether to allocate scarce resources in a way that gives preferential consideration to clients of color, consistent with affirmative action goals, but in a way that consequently limits aid to some more needy clients.

Theories of normative ethics are generally grouped under two main headings. *Deontological* theories (from the Greek *deontos*, "of the obligatory") are those that claim that certain actions are inherently right or wrong, or good and bad, without regard for their consequences. Thus, a deontologist—the best known being Immanuel Kant, the eighteenth-century German philosopher—might argue that telling the truth is inherently right, and people therefore should never lie to clients. The same might be said about keeping promises made to colleagues, upholding contracts with vendors, obeying a mandatory reporting law, and so on. For deontologists, rules, rights, and principles are sacred and inviolable. The ends do not necessarily justify the means, particularly if they require violating some important rule, right, principle, or law (Frankena 1973; Hancock 1974; Williams 1972).

One well-known problem with this deontological perspective is that it is often easy to imagine conflicting arguments using similar language about inherently right (or wrong) actions. Thus, one can imagine a deontologist arguing that all human beings have an inherent right to be told the truth, and that any form of lying constitutes a violation of this right. However, another deontologist might argue that truth telling that results in a client's death (for example, where a truthfully bleak prognosis may lead a vulnerable client to commit suicide) is inherently wrong.

The second major group of theories, *teleological* theories (from the Greek *teleios*, "brought to its end or purpose"), takes a very different approach to ethical choices. From this point of view, the rightness of any action is determined by the goodness of its consequences. For teleologists, it is naive to make ethical choices without weighing potential consequences. To do otherwise is to engage in what the philosopher Smart (1971) refers to as "rule worship." Hence, from this perspective (sometimes known as *consequentialism*) the responsible strategy entails an attempt to anticipate the possible outcomes of various courses of action and to weigh their relative merits (Frankena 1973; Hancock 1974).

There are two major teleological schools of thought, egoism and utilitarianism. *Egoism* is a form of teleology that is not typically found in social work; according to this point of view, when faced with conflicting duties one should maximize his or her own respective good. In contrast, *utilitarianism*, which holds that an action is right if it promotes the maximum good, has historically been the most popular teleological theory and has, at least implicitly, served as justification for many decisions made by social workers.

According to the classic form of utilitarianism—as originally formulated by Jeremy Bentham and John Stuart Mill—when faced with conflicting duties one should perform that action that will produce the greatest good. In principle, then, a social worker should engage in a calculus to determine which set of consequences will produce the greatest good. Thus, a utilitarian would argue that violating a client's right to confidentiality in order to protect a third person's welfare is justifiable, in order to bring about a greater good (assuming, of course, that protecting a third person from harm is considered more compelling than protecting privacy). Similarly, a strict utilitarian might argue that tearing down a section of a town's dilapidated housing, and displacing its residents, is justifiable if it leads to economic revival of the entire neighborhood.

One form of utilitarian theory is known as *good-aggregative utilitarianism* (Gewirth 1978a), according to which the most appropriate action is that which promotes the greatest total or aggregate good. Second, there is *locus-aggregative utilitarianism*, according to which the most appropriate action is that which promotes the greatest good *for the greatest number*, considering not only the total quantity of goods produced but also the number of people to whom the goods are distributed (Gewirth 1978a). The distinction between these two forms of utilitarianism is important when one considers, for example, whether to distribute a fixed amount of public assistance in a way that tends to produce the greatest aggregate satisfaction (which might entail dispensing relatively large sums to relatively few people) or produces the greatest satisfaction for the greatest number (which might entail dispensing smaller sums of money to a larger number of people).

One problem with utilitarianism is that this framework, like deontology, sometimes can be used to justify competing positions. Thus, while one utilitarian might argue that razing dilapidated housing would produce a net gain in social benefit, another utilitarian, who assigns different weights to the factors involved, or even enters different factors into the equation, might argue that the harm produced by displacing residents of a community could never be outweighed by an urban renewal plan.

Some philosophers argue that it is important and helpful to distinguish between *act* and *rule* utilitarianism (Gorovitz 1971). According to act utilitarianism, the rightness of an action is determined by the goodness of the consequences produced in *that* individual case, or by that particular act. One does not need to look beyond the implications of this one instance. By contrast, rule utilitarianism takes into account the long-run consequences likely to be produced if one generalizes from this one instance, or treats it as a precedent. Thus, an act utilitarian might justify violating a mandatory reporting law if it can be demonstrated convincingly that this would result in greater good (for example, if the social worker will continue to work closely with the family to prevent further neglect or abuse, in a way that, allegedly, would not be possible if the case were reported to local protective service officials). A rule utilitarian, however, might argue that the precedent established by this deliberate violation of the law would generate more harm than good, regardless of the benefits produced by this one particular violation. That is, a rule utilitarian might argue that the precedent might encourage other workers to take matters into their own hands rather than reporting suspected abuse or neglect to local protective service officials, and that this would, in the long run, be more harmful than helpful.

A key problem with utilitarianism, then, is that different people are likely to consider different factors and weigh them differently, in light of their different life experiences, values, political ideology, and so on. In addition, when taken to the extreme, classic utilitarianism can justify trampling on the rights of a vulnerable minority in order to benefit the majority. In principle, a callous utilitarian social worker could argue that the social costs produced by placement of "annoying," but competent, homeless individuals in shelters against their wishes is outweighed by the public benefit (removal of "public nuisances" from the streets). In light of countless instances throughout history where the rights of minorities have been insensitively and gratuitously violated to benefit the majority, social workers have good reason to be concerned about such strict applications of utilitarian principles.

Perhaps the best-known proposed alternative to utilitarianism is presented in John Rawls's (1971) *A Theory of Justice*. Rawls's theory assumes that individuals who are formulating a moral principle by which to be governed are in an "original position" of equality and that each individual is unaware of his or her own attributes and status that might produce some advantage or disadvantage. Under this "veil of ignorance" it is assumed that individuals will derive a moral framework, which Rawls calls the "difference principle," that ultimately protects the least advantaged based upon a ranked ordering of priorities. Rawls also makes a distinction between *natural* duties—fundamental obligations such as helping others in dire need or not injuring other people—and *supererogatory* actions—actions that are commendable and praiseworthy, but not obligatory, such as donating one's time to an agency's bake sale. Other philosophers have also offered theories about the most appropriate way to rank-order conflicting duties. Donagan (1977) argues in *The Theory of Morality* that when choosing among duties that may result in harm, one should be guided by the principle of *minima de malis eligenda*—when you must choose between evils, choose the least. Gewirth (1978b) argues in *Reason and Morality* that conflicting duties can be rank-ordered based on the goods involved (Reamer 1990). Duties concerning such goods as life itself and health (what Gewirth calls "basic" goods) take precedence over duties concerning such goods as protecting privacy or more comfortable living conditions beyond what is essential ("additive" or "nonsubtractive" goods).

Although it is important for social workers to have a firm grasp of classic ethical theory, and of its relevance to professional practice, it is also important for social workers to understand the limitations of this theory. No one should expect that mastery of these theoretical constructs will provide one-stop solutions to complex moral and ethical problems in practice. To the contrary, ethicists with different theoretical and ideological leanings often produce different interpretations of ethical dilemmas. As Macklin (1988) aptly observes, rarely does ethics

> offer "one right answer" to a moral dilemma. Seldom can a philosopher arrive on the scene and make unequivocal pronouncements about the right thing to do. Yet, despite the fact that it has no magic wand, [ethics] is still useful and can go a long way toward "resolving the issues," once that phrase is properly understood. . . .
>
> As long as the debate between Kantians and utilitarians continues to rage and as long as the Western political and philosophical tradition continues to embrace both the respect-for-persons principle and the principle of beneficence, there can be no possible resolution of dilemmas traceable to those competing theoretical approaches. But the inability to make a final determination of which theoretical approach is ultimately "right" does not rule out the prospect for making sound moral judgments in practice contexts, based on one or the other theoretical perspective.
>
> The choice between utilitarian ethics and a deontological moral system rooted in rights and duties is not a choice between one moral and one immoral alternative. Rather, it rests on a commitment to one moral viewpoint instead of another, where both are capable of providing good reasons for acting. Both perspectives stand in opposition to egoistic or selfish approaches, or to a philosophy whose precepts are grounded in privileges of power, wealth, or the authority of technical experts.   (52, 66–67)

Ethical Misconduct

The final content area that is essential for social workers to master concerns unethical conduct in professional practice. Regrettably, reports of ethical misconduct among social workers have been on the rise (Berliner 1989; Bernstein 1981; Besharov 1985; Levine 1976; McCann and Cutler 1979; Reamer 1989, 1992a, 1994 [in press]).

Professional malpractice is generally considered a form of negligence, applied to professionals who are required to perform in a manner consistent with the *standard of care* in the profession, that is, the way an ordinary, reasonable, and prudent professional would act under the same or similar circumstances (Cohen 1979; Cohen and Mariano 1982; Hogan 1979; Rinas and Clyne-Jackson 1988). Social work malpractice typically occurs when four conditions exist: 1) a social worker owes a duty to a client (for example, to obtain informed consent before disclosing confidential information); 2) there is a breach of the duty (the social worker discloses confidential information to a public agency without the client's permission); 3) the client suffers an injury (the client experiences financial hardship when benefits are terminated by the public agency following the unauthorized disclosure of confidential information); and 4) there is a causal connection between the breach of the duty and the injury (the social worker's failure to obtain informed consent resulted in the termination of benefits and, hence, the client's financial hardship).

Malpractice generally occurs as a result of a social worker's active violation of clients' rights (known variously as acts of commission, misfeasance, or malfeasance), or as a result of a social worker's failure to perform certain duties (acts of omission or nonfeasance). Some of the more common acts of commission include sexual impropriety with clients, inappropriate disclosure of confidential or private information (for example, in hallway conversations or to colleagues in other agencies), invasion of privacy, defamation of character, falsification of records, fraud, assault and battery, use of inappropriate treatment techniques, client harassment, inappropriate termination or extension of treatment, improper referral, breach of contract, violation of civil rights, wrongful removal of children, and abandonment of clients. Some of the more common acts of omission include failure to obtain informed consent, protect third parties, consult with or refer a client to a specialist, provide adequate supervision of staff or clients, restrain impaired clients, prevent client suicide, and adequately diagnose and treat clients' problems.

Some malpractice claims result from genuine mistakes or inadvertent oversight on the part of social workers (for example, forgetting to have a client sign an informed consent form), or from a deliberate decision to risk a claim (for example, a social worker decides to divulge confidential information to protect a third party from harm). In many cases, however, malpractice claims allege unethical behavior and professional misconduct.

Professional misconduct often reflects some form of practitioner impairment. It may involve a failure to provided competent care or an explicit violation of ethical standards in the profession. Impairment may take such forms as providing flawed or inferior psychotherapy to a client, sexual involvement with a client, or failure to carry out one's duties as a result of substance abuse or mental illness. It may result from personal stress related to a practitioner's marriage, relationships, emotional and physical health, and finances, or from environmental stress related to concern about employment security, working conditions, and educational demands (Deutsch 1985; Guy, Poelstra, and Stark 1989; Kilburg, Kaslow, and VandenBos 1988; Kilburg, Nathan, and Thoreson 1986; Pope, Tabachnick, and Keith-Spiegel 1988).

Social work's first national acknowledgement of the problem of impaired practitioners was in 1979 when NASW released a public policy statement on the topic of alcoholism and alcohol-related problems (NASW 1987:32–36). By 1980 a small nationwide support group for chemically dependent practitioners, Social Workers Helping Social Workers, had formed. In 1982 NASW established the Occupational Social Work Task Force, which was charged with developing a "consistent professional approach for distressed NASW members" (NASW 1987:7). In 1984 the NASW Delegate Assembly issued a resolution on impairment, and in 1987 NASW published the *Impaired Social Worker Program Resource Book*, prepared by the National Commission on Employment and Economic Support, to help practitioners design an impaired social worker program.

Unfortunately, little is known about the prevalence of impairment and ethical misconduct among social workers. In contrast to a number of other helping professions, such as psychology, psychiatry, counseling, and medicine, the social work literature contains little discussion of the extent and nature of unethical conduct engaged in by impaired practitioners (Reamer 1992a).

Pedagogical Issues

There have been several ambitious attempts to highlight the need to educate social workers about values and ethics. The earliest landmark publication on the subject was Pumphrey's (1959) volume, *The Teaching of Values and Ethics in Social Work Education,* published as a report of the Council on Social Work Education's (CSWE) Curriculum Study. As the author stated in her introduction:

> When this part of the Curriculum Study was projected in the fall of 1956, preliminary perusal of class materials, educational committee reports and professional literature indicated that no comprehensive effort to define the exact content of this part of the total learning experience had ever been attempted. . . . In contrast to other curriculum areas which had benefited from years of detailed course and sequence formulation, repeated experimentation, and testing in beginning practice, very little previous group thinking or codified and critically appraised educational experience was available for examination. (Pumphrey 1959:3)

Pumphrey set out to assess the ways in and extent to which content on professional values and ethics was being conveyed to social work students. She gathered data systematically from eight schools of social work in order to determine prevailing views concerning social work values and ethics, how they are applied in practice, and strategies for conveying this content to social work students. Pumphrey interviewed faculty and students, audited classes, examined curriculum materials, school catalogs, committee reports, and read students' papers and course evaluations. Pumphrey also gathered survey data from other accredited schools of social work concerning instruction on values and ethics, and conducted a content analysis of widely used social work texts and journals.

Pumphrey concluded that content on values and ethics needed to be strengthened considerably. She found that while the subject of values was pervasive throughout social work instruction, students were, by and large, not receiving systematic instruction on professional ethics: "As a whole, faculty members were much more prepared to discuss the teaching of abstract value formulations than to hazard opinion about teaching ethics. This seemed to be a reflection of the primitive and generalized state of professional ethical formulations" (Pumphrey 1959:32).

Pumphrey formulated a set of educational objectives that, in her judgment, should guide instruction on social work values and ethics. They addressed the need to include content on the nature of values; similarities and differences among clients', social workers', and society's values; the relationship between values and social workers' assessments and interventions; the relevance of professional codes of ethics; and the nature of value conflicts (Pumphrey 1959:81–118).

Despite Pumphrey's vigorous advocacy, education related to social work values and ethics—both in social work practice settings and schools—continues to be idiosyncratic. Although some social service agencies provide staff with training on values and ethics, many do not. Although some schools and departments of social work provide systematic instruction on these subjects, many do not.

In fact, one might argue that over time the proportion of social work education programs devoting explicit attention to this content area has shrunk. In 1931 Elliott reported that 7 of 29 schools (24 percent) offered discrete courses on values and ethics. In 1955 Johnson reported that 15 of 27 member schools of the Council on Social Work Education (56 percent), which had enrollments of 60 or more full-time students, taught ethics in a special course. In 1975, sixteen years after the publication of Pumphrey's widely circulated report, Meinert conducted a content analysis of more than 2,500 course descriptions from bulletins of schools of social work for the year 1975. He found that only 19 course descriptions (less than one percent) contained the words *values*, *ethics*, *morals*, *beliefs*, or *philosophy*. And, in 1989, Black and colleagues found that only 7 out of 73 graduate social work programs (10 percent) offered a discrete course on ethics. Although instruction on values and ethics does not necessarily need to take place in a discrete course, and may be taught very effectively as part of other courses in the curriculum, the decline over the years in the number of programs offering a course on this subject may indicate that students are not being exposed to this content systematically. Whether this material ought to be taught in a discrete course, as opposed to incorporating it into other courses (such as policy, practice, human behavior, and research courses), is debatable (Reamer and Abramson 1982).

It seems clear that practitioners in the field and students in educational programs need comprehensive, deliberate exposure to a wide range of subject areas related to values and ethics. As discussed above, the four general content areas that must be conveyed include: 1) the value base and ethical tenets of the profession; 2) ethical dilemmas in social work practice; 3) ethical decision making; and 4) ethical misconduct. More specifically, content on the value base and ethical tenets of the profession should include examination of the profession's traditional values and value base, including its codes of ethics (for example, the NASW Code of Ethics, the National Association of Black Social Workers Code of Ethics, and the National Federation of Societies for Clinical Social Work Code of Ethics), the formation of personal values and values clarification, and conflicts among clients', workers', the profession's, and society's values. Content on ethical dilemmas should include systematic review of the nature of ethical conflicts and choices that arise in direct practice with individuals, families, and groups, in the design and administration of social welfare policy and programs, and in relationships among professionals. Content on ethical decision making should acquaint practitioners and students with various schools of thought regarding ethical theories and principles, particularly with respect to their political implications and their application to ethical dilemmas encountered in practice (that is, the relevance of theories and principles of metaethics and normative ethics).

Finally, it is essential for social workers to learn how to recognize and prevent ethical misconduct, and to be familiar with the liability and malpractice risks associated with professional practice. Training should provide systematic exposure to the forms of negligence that arise in social work, and with ways to prevent malpractice and liability. This may include specific information concerning how to prevent, for example, inadvertent disclosure of confidential case material, defamation of character, civil rights violations, inadequate supervision, or improper referral. It may also include an overview of forms, symptoms, and causes of professional impairment, along with appropriate intervention strategies (Reamer 1992a).

Clearly, the depth of the material presented to practitioners and students should be adjusted to their level of training and education. Undergraduate-level practitioners and students should be exposed to all four content areas, but the level of detail and conceptual sophistication may be somewhat lower than that presented to master's or doctoral-level practitioners and students. For example, while undergraduate-level practitioners and students should be acquainted, in general, with utilitarianism and deontology as prominent schools of thought drawn on in ethical decision making, instructors and trainers may want to avoid ambitious, fine-grained analysis of debates concerning the merits of different cognitivist and noncognitivist theories of metaethics; these may be more appropriate for master's and especially doctoral-level practitioners and students. Similarly, while undergraduate-level practitioners and students should be acquainted with the problem of ethical misconduct and malpractice among impaired practitioners, sophisticated discussion of theories of tort liability should probably be reserved for more advanced audiences.

Education and training on values and ethics should address a number of overarching objectives. In general, they should seek to familiarize practitioners and students with the wide range of value and ethical issues in the profession and equip them with the conceptual and analytic skills needed to address these issues (Callahan and Bok 1980; Reamer and Abramson 1982). As the CSWE Curriculum Policy Statement (1992) asserts, "Students must acquire specific knowledge about social work values and their ethical implications and demonstrate their application in professional practice. Students must develop an awareness of their personal values and clarify conflicting values and ethical dilemmas" (Principle 6.2). Specifically, such instruction should:

1. *Stimulate awareness of ethical issues and dilemmas.* The bulk of social work training is devoted to the cultivation of knowledge and skills related to intervention with individuals, families, groups, communities, and organizations. It is important for practitioners and students to have a greater appreciation of the value and ethical dimensions of practice. In addition to developing technical skills and knowledge, educators, administrators, and supervisors must seek to enhance practitioners' and students' ability to recognize and grapple with the value and ethical features of practice.

2. *Developing analytical skills.* Practitioners and students must learn a variety of analytical tools and conceptual frameworks to enable them to assess value and ethical issues in social work. In addition to learning ethical theories and principles, practitioners and students should become proficient in the use of inductive and deductive logic, to enable them to offer cogent arguments and recognize logical fallacies. Discussions about values and ethics, and about the beliefs we hold concerning what is right and wrong, or good and bad, are often emotionally charged; although it is important to retain the emotional elements of discourse about values and ethics, it is essential that practitioners and educators hold one another to principles of rational discourse and debate.

3. *Eliciting a sense of moral obligation and personal responsibility.* After all, social work is a normative profession, one whose agenda ultimate-

ly has political purposes and implications. Practitioners are not neutral, value-free observers of the human condition. Instead, the profession has a longstanding tradition of commitment to values related to justice, fairness, altruism, and human dignity. Instruction on values and ethics must do more than equip practitioners and students with conceptual and analytical skills. It must also nurture and strengthen their determination to embrace the profession's values and promote activities and policies that are consistent with them. Although social workers may disagree about the operationalization of these values, in the final analysis, practitioners' expression of these values constitutes the profession's principal mission.

4. *Tolerating and resisting disagreement and ambiguity*. This objective may seem contradictory. In fact, however, there are times when it is appropriate for social workers to tolerate disagreement and ambiguity surrounding value and ethical issues, and times when they must resist them. For example, debate about different mechanisms for distributing scarce resources, or about the limits of confidentiality when a client threatens a third party, is likely to generate considerable disagreement. This is an inherent feature of debate about values and ethics, and it is unlikely that consensus about such matters will ever be achieved. Reasonable, thoughtful people can disagree about these sorts of issues.

At the same time, however, there are issues about which social workers should strenuously resist disagreement, particularly when the profession's deep-seated values are challenged. Public or agency policies that discriminate against social workers' clients—for example, if women on AFDC are threatened with the loss of custody of their children primarily because of their welfare status, or if residents of a low-income community are displaced without due process to make way for a for-profit commercial enterprise—must be challenged vigorously. In such instances, there is no room for ambiguity.

Enduring Issues

There is no question that social work's grasp of value and ethical issues in the profession has matured, especially since the mid-1970s. Although the profession has always been preoccupied with its value base, only recently has there been a sustained, in-depth effort to explore the relationship between ethical dilemmas in practice and ethical analysis and theory.

In spite of this considerable progress, much work remains to be done. First, both social work students and practitioners need to be acquainted with content on values and ethics more deliberately and systematically. Although social work students are typically introduced to content on social work values, many do not receive in-depth instruction on ethical dilemmas, ethical decision making, ethical theory, and ethical misconduct. It is essential that these subjects become a standard component in social work education.

Similarly, only some agency-based and private practitioners have received systematic instruction on this content. Although agencies and professional social work organizations (for example, state chapters of NASW, clinical societies) are offering institutes and workshops on professional ethics with increasing frequency, these offerings tend to be sporadic. Both social service agencies and professional organizations ought to mount ambitious in-service training and institutes, on a regular basis, to ensure that social workers are equipped to identify and address ethical issues encountered in practice.

It is also important for social workers to enhance their involvement in agency-based discussions of ethical issues. Many agencies have established "institutional ethics committees" (IECs) and "institutional review boards" (IRBs) to explore ethical issues in their respective settings and to provide colleagues with an opportunity to consult with one another about ethical issues in practice (Reamer 1987a). In hospitals, for instance, IECs have existed at least since the 1920s to provide opportunities for health care professionals, including social workers, to exchange ideas about ethical issues related, for example, to termination of life support, organ transplantation, blood transfusion, and abortion. Since the 1960s, many organizations have sponsored IRBs to review ethical issues related to research and the use of human subjects (Cohen 1982; Levine 1984; Randal 1983; Veatch 1977).

IECs and IRBs have assumed several different functions, depending on their organizational context and sponsor. Among the most important functions is that of educating staff about ethical issues germane to the host agency. Training sessions might be devoted specifically to issues that arise in the delivery of clinical services to individuals, families, and groups (for example, limits on the right to give informed consent or to confidentiality). Other sessions might focus on ethical issues relevant to agency policy and administration, such as criteria for making budget cuts or allocating scare agency resources.

Ethics committees also take an active role in formulating agency policy, for example, reviewing and revising client grievance procedures, informed consent guidelines, or confidentiality policy. Finally, some committees also offer case consultation and review, either as a case is unfolding or retrospectively. Although ethics committees' judgment on case-specific issues is generally not binding, it may help staff and clients to identify and sort out pertinent ethical issues.

In addition to these efforts to increase social workers' involvement in the formulation of ethics policy and in case consultation, the profession also needs to confront two additional ethical issues. The first concerns social workers' efforts to help clients address their *own* moral and ethical dilemmas (Timms 1983:8–9). As I noted earlier, in the late nineteenth and early twentieth centuries, social workers were concerned about moral aspects of clients' lives. However, this concern had much more to do with clients' morality than with their personal struggles to address moral and ethical dilemmas in their lives. As Siporin (1975) has observed:

> Along with essential material and social resources that social workers make available, they also need to make available the value system and ethical principles that can aid clients to resolve their dilemmas. This calls for a focus with clients on their philosophic beliefs and value commitments or conflicts, and direct aid to them in clarifying and choosing adaptive and positive, self-fulfilling philosophies and life styles. (88)

It is one thing, for example, for a sectarian family service agency to struggle with its own policy on abortion counseling. It is quite another for staff of that agency to understand how best to help clients who are struggling with the moral dimensions of their personal decisions about abortion. Similarly, it is one thing for hospital staff to develop institutional policy on withdrawal of life support for impaired infants. It is quite another for hospital-based social workers to understand how best to help parents who are struggling with the moral dimensions of their personal decisions about withdrawal of life support.

As Goldstein (1987) notes, such exploration is one of the neglected moral links in social work practice: "It is concerned mainly with how moral principles serve as guides or rules for the way people think and make choices about and actively cope with both the extraordinary and commonplace problems of everyday living" (182). This is exploration focused on clients' efforts to determine what is ethically or morally right or wrong, or just and fair, in their own lives. It forces the social worker to examine and understand his or her role with respect to helping clients follow their own moral compass.

Finally, it is essential for social workers to continually examine the moral and political purposes of the profession. In recent years, there has been vigorous debate about whether social work has lost its sense of moral "calling," such that the profession's longtime commitment to the poor and most vulnerable has been traded in by many practitioners for allegedly more lucrative, less stressful psychotherapeutic work with a more affluent clientele (Reamer 1992b; Specht 1991).

In fact, social work has always struggled with the nature of its mission. For example, every serious account of social work's evolution explores the persistent tension between "case" and "cause," between the amelioration of individual suffering and social change designed to bring about structural reform. There has always been debate about the nature of social work's commitment to the poor and victims of oppression, as opposed to those who are more advantaged and what some have described as the "worried wealthy."

Now, however, the stakes seem especially high. Between 1975 and 1985, for instance, the number of clinical social workers in the U.S. increased from 25,000 to 60,000 (an increase of 140 percent), placing social workers first in the list of professional groups providing mental health services, followed by psychiatrists, clinical psychologists, and marriage and family counselors. During roughly the same period (1972–1982), there was an 18 percent decline in the number of NASW members employed in the public sector, in federal, state, and local human service agencies. This was accompanied by a remarkable increase in social workers' employment in private sectarian and proprietary (for-profit) agencies—increases of 132 and 264 percent, respectively (Reamer 1992b). Although one cannot assume that clinical social workers in private settings are less committed to work with poor and oppressed clients, there is some risk that the shift of social workers out of public-sector agencies and into private agencies has led to a decline of social work services delivered to our society's most vulnerable members.

Certainly, this movement may stem in part from a significant decline, especially beginning in the 1970s, in government funding of and commitment to social service programs, and, hence, a decline in the number of attractive jobs in the public sector. Social workers may have simply borne the brunt of the broader culture's weakened commitment to poor and oppressed groups. Nonetheless, the pattern has forced many social workers to closely examine the moral purposes of the profession, particularly with respect to its historic preoccupation with the least advantaged.

Since the profession's inception, the subject of values and ethics has been at the heart of social work practice. What began as a rather moralistic concern about the character and rectitude of the profession's clients has evolved into a more sophisticated grasp of a wide range of troubling and troublesome ethical issues facing practitioners, encompassing complex questions concerning the value base of the profession, ethical dilemmas in practice, ethical decision making, ethical misconduct among social workers, and the moral purposes of the profession. Knowledge and scholarship on values and ethics has evolved and matured, casting light on a critically important series of questions about the normative aims and integrity of the profession. Through it all, the topic of values and ethics has endured as a keystone in social work's foundation.

REFERENCES

American Association of Social Workers. 1952. *Standards for the Professional Practice of Social Work.* Supplement to July 1952 *Social Work Journal,* Part II. New York: American Association of Social Workers.

Arnold, Selma. 1970. "Confidential Communication and the Social Worker." *Social Work* 15:61–67.

Austin, Kenneth M., Mary E. Moline, and George T. Williams. 1990. *Confronting Malpractice.* Newbury Park, Calif.: Sage.

Baer, Betty. 1979. "Social Work Practice." In Betty Baer and Ronald Federico, eds., *Educating the Baccalaureate Social Worker: A Curriculum Development Resource Guide,* vol. 2. Cambridge, Mass.: Ballinger.

Barker, Robert L. 1991. *The Social Work Dictionary,* under the word "values." 2d ed. Silver Spring, Md.: National Association of Social Workers.

Barry, Vincent. 1986. *Moral Issues in Business.* 3d ed. Belmont, Calif.: Wadsworth.

Bartlett, Harriet M. 1970. *The Common Base of Social Work Practice.* New York: Columbia University Press.

Berliner, Arthur K. 1989. "Misconduct in Social Work Practice." *Social Work* 34(1):69–72.

Bernstein, Barton E. 1981. "Malpractice: Future Shock of the 1980s." *Social Case-work* 62:175–181.

Bernstein, Saul. 1960. "Self-Determination: King or Citizen in the Realm of Values?" *Social Work* 5(1):3–8.

Besharov, Douglas S. 1985. *The Vulnerable Social Worker*. Silver Spring, Md.: National Association of Social Workers.

Biestek, Felix P. 1957. *The Casework Relationship*. Chicago: Loyola University Press.

—— and Clyde C. Gehrig. 1978. *Client Self-Determination in Social Work: A Fifty-Year History*. Chicago: Loyola University Press.

Black, Phyllis N., Elizabeth Kennedy Hartley, Joanne Whelley, and Cordelia Kirk-Sharp. 1989. "Ethics Curricula: A National Survey of Graduate Schools of Social Work." *Social Thought* 15(3/4):141–148.

Bok, Sissela. 1978. *Lying: Moral Choice in Public and Private Life*. New York: Pantheon.

——. 1980. "Whistleblowing and Professional Responsibility." *New York University Education Quarterly* 11:2–10.

Buchanan, Allen. 1978. "Medical Paternalism." *Philosophy and Public Affairs* 7:370–390.

Cabot, Richard C. 1973 [1915]. *Social Service and the Art of Healing*. Washington, D.C.: National Association of Social Workers.

Callahan, Daniel and Sissela Bok, eds. 1980. *Ethics Teaching in Higher Education*. New York: Plenum Press.

Carter, Rosemary. 1977. "Justifying Paternalism." *Canadian Journal of Philosophy* 7:133–145.

Cohen, Cynthia. 1982. "Interdisciplinary Consultation on the Care of the Critically Ill and Dying: The Role of One Hospital Ethics Committee." *Critical Care Medicine* 10:776–784.

Cohen, Ronald J. 1979. *Malpractice: A Guide for Mental Health Professionals*. New York: Free Press.

—— and William E. Mariano. 1982. *Legal Guidebook in Mental Health*. New York: Free Press.

Coulton, Claudia J., Marvin J. Rosenberg, and John Yankey. 1981. "Scarcity and the Rationing of Services." *Public Welfare* 39(3):15–21.

Council on Social Work Education. 1992. *Curriculum Policy Statement for Master's Degree Programs in Social Work Education*. Alexandria, Va.: Council on Social Work Education.

Deutsch, C. 1985. "A Survey of Therapists' Personal Problems and Treatment." *Professional Psychology: Research and Practice* 16(2):305–315.

Donagan, Alan. 1977. *The Theory of Morality*. Chicago: University of Chicago Press.

Dworkin, Gerald. 1971. "Paternalism." In Richard A. Wasserstrom, ed., *Morality and the Law*, pp. 107–126. Belmont, Calif.: Wadsworth.

Elliott, L. J. 1931. *Social Work Ethics*. New York: American Association of Social Workers.

Emmet, Dorothy. 1962. "Ethics and the Social Worker." *British Journal of Psychiatric Social Work* 6:165–172.

Ephross, Paul H. and Michael Reisch. 1982. "The Ideology of Some Social Work Texts." *Social Service Review* 56:273–291.

Feinberg, Joel. 1971. "Legal Paternalism." *Canadian Journal of Philosophy* 1:105–124.

Frankel, Charles. 1959. "Social Philosophy and the Professional Education of Social Workers." *Social Service Review* 33:345–359.

Frankena, William K. 1973. *Ethics*. 2d ed. Englewood Cliffs, N.J.: Prentice-Hall.

Gert, Bernard and Charles M. Culver. 1976. "Paternalistic Behavior." *Philosophy and Public Affairs* 6:45–57.

Gewirth, Alan. 1978a. "Ethics." In *Encyclopedia Britannica*. 15th ed.

——. 1978b. *Reason and Morality*. Chicago: University of Chicago Press.

Goldstein, Howard. 1983. "Starting Where the Client Is." *Social Casework* 64:264–275.

——. 1987. "The Neglected Moral Link in Social Work Practice." *Social Work* 32(3):181–186.

Gordon, William E. 1962. "A Critique of the Working Definition." *Social Work* 7:6.

Gorovitz, Samuel, ed. 1971. *Mill: Utilitarianism*. Indianapolis: Bobbs-Merrill.

Guy, James D., Paul L. Poelstra, and Miriam Stark. 1989. "Personal Distress and Therapeutic Effectiveness: National Survey of Psychologists Practicing Psychotherapy." *Professional Psychology: Research and Practice* 20(1):48–50.

Hall, L. K. 1952. "Group Workers and Professional Ethics." *The Group* 15(1):3–8.

Hamilton, Gordon. 1940. *Theory and Practice of Social Casework*. New York: Columbia University Press.

——. 1951. *Social Casework*. 2d ed. New York: Columbia University Press.

Hancock, Roger N. 1974. *Twentieth-Century Ethics*. New York: Columbia University Press.

Hogan, Daniel B. 1979. *The Regulation of Psychotherapists: A Review of Malpractice Suits in the U.S.*, vol. III. Cambridge, Mass.: Ballinger.

Husak, Douglas N. 1980. "Paternalism and Autonomy." *Philosophy and Public Affairs* 10:27–46.

Johnson, Arlien. 1955. "Educating Professional Social Workers for Ethical Practice." *Social Service Review* 29(2):125–136.

Johnson, Louise C. 1989. *Social Work Practice: A Generalist Approach*. 3d ed. Boston: Allyn and Bacon.

Joseph, M. Vincentia. 1989. "Social Work Ethics: Historical and Contemporary Perspectives." *Social Thought* 15(3/4):4–17.

Keith-Lucas, Alan. 1963. "A Critique of the Principle of Client Self-Determination." *Social Work* 8(3):66–71.

——. 1977. "Ethics in Social Work." In *Encyclopedia of Social Work* 17th ed. Washington, D.C.: National Association of Social Workers.

Kilburg, Richard R., Florence W. Kaslow, and Gary R. VandenBos. 1988.

"Professionals in Distress." *Hospital and Community Psychiatry* 39(7): 723–725.

Kilburg, Richard R., Peter E. Nathan, and Richard W. Thoreson, eds. 1986. *Professionals in Distress: Issues, Syndromes, and Solutions in Psychology*. Washington, D.C.: American Psychological Association.

Levine, Carol. 1984. "Questions and (Some Very Tentative) Answers About Hospital Ethics Committees." *Hastings Center Report* 14:9–12.

Levine, R. S. 1976. "Social Worker Malpractice." *Social Casework* 56:466–468.

Levy, Charles S. 1972. "The Context of Social Work Ethics." *Social Work* 17:95–101.

——. 1973. "The Value Base of Social Work." *Journal of Education for Social Work* 9:34–42.

——. 1976. *Social Work Ethics*. New York: Human Sciences Press.

——. 1984. "Values and Ethics: Foundations of Social Work." In Sidney Dillick, ed., *Value Foundations of Social Work*. Detroit: Wayne State University School of Social Work.

Lewis, Harold. 1972. "Morality and the Politics of Practice." *Social Casework* 53:404–417.

Loewenberg, Frank M. and Ralph Dolgoff. 1992. *Ethical Decisions for Social Work Practice* 4th ed. Itasca, Ill.: F. E. Peacock.

McCann, Charles W. and Jane Park Cutler. 1979. "Ethics and the Alleged Unethical." *Social Work* 24:5–8.

McCormick, Mary. 1961. "The Role of Values in Social Functioning." *Social Casework* 42:70–78.

McDermott, F. E., ed. 1975. *Self-Determination in Social Work*. London: Routledge and Kegan Paul.

Macklin, Ruth. 1988. "Theoretical and Applied Ethics: A Reply to the Skeptics." In David M. Rosenthal and Fadlou Shehadi, eds., *Applied Ethics and Ethical Theory*. Salt Lake City: University of Utah Press.

Meyer, Robert G., E. Rhett Landis, and J. Ray Hays. 1988. *Law for the Psychotherapist*. New York: W. W. Norton.

Morales, Armando and Bradford W. Sheafor. 1986. *Social Work: A Profession of Many Faces*, 4th ed. Boston: Allyn and Bacon.

Nader, Ralph, Peter J. Petkas, and Kate Blackwood, eds. 1972. *Whistle Blowing*. New York: Grossman.

National Association of Social Workers. 1974 [1929]. *The Milford Conference Report: Social Casework, Generic and Specific*. Washington, D.C.: National Association of Social Workers.

——. 1994. *Code of Ethics*. Rev. ed. Silver Spring, Md.: National Association of Social Workers.

——, Commission on Employment and Economic Support. 1987. *Impaired Social Worker Program Resource Book*. Silver Spring, Md.: National Association of Social Workers.

Paine, Robert Treat, Jr. 1880. "The Work of Volunteer Visitors of the Associated Charities Among the Poor." *Journal of Social Science* 12:113.

Perlman, Helen Harris. 1965. "Self-Determination: Reality or Illusion?" *Social Service Review* 39(4):410–421.

Peters, Charles and Taylor Branch. 1972. *Blowing the Whistle: Dissent in the Public Interest*. New York: Praeger.

Plant, Raymond. 1970. *Social and Moral Theory in Casework*. London: Routledge and Kegan Paul.

Pope, Kenneth S., Barbara G. Tabachnick, and Patricia Keith-Spiegel. 1987. "Ethics of Practice: The Beliefs and Behaviors of Psychologists as Therapists." *American Psychologist* 42(11):993–1006.

Promislo, Estelle. 1979. "Confidentiality and Privileged Communication." *Social Work* 24:10–13.

Pumphrey, Muriel W. 1959. *The Teaching of Values and Ethics in Social Work Education: A Project Report of the Curriculum Study*, vol. 13. New York: Council on Social Work Education.

Randal, J. 1983. "Are Ethics Committees Alive and Well?" *Hastings Center Report* 13:10–12.

Rawls, John. 1971. *A Theory of Justice*. Cambridge, Mass.: Harvard University Press.

Reamer, Frederic G. 1980. "Ethical Content in Social Work." *Social Casework* 61(9):531–540.

——. 1982. "Conflicts of Professional Duty in Social Work." *Social Casework* 63(10):579–585.

——. 1983a. "The Concept of Paternalism in Social Work." *Social Service Review* 57(2):254–271.

——. 1983b. "Ethical Dilemmas in Social Work Practice." *Social Work* 28(1):31–35.

——. 1987a. "Ethics Committees in Social Work." *Social Work* 32(3):188–192.

——. 1987b. "Values and Ethics." In *Encyclopedia of Social Work* 18th ed. Silver Spring, Md.: National Association of Social Workers.

——. 1989. "Liability Issues in Social Work Supervision." *Social Work* 34(5):445–448.

——. 1990. *Ethical Dilemmas in Social Service*, 2d ed. New York: Columbia University Press.

——. 1992a. "The Impaired Social Worker." *Social Work* 37(2):165–170.

——. 1992b. "Social Work and the Public Good: Calling or Career?" In P. Nelson Reid and Philip R. Popple, eds., *The Moral Purposes of Social Work*. Chicago: Nelson-Hall.

——. 1993. *The Philosophical Foundations of Social Work*. New York: Columbia University Press.

——. 1994. *Social Work Malpractice and Liability*. New York: Columbia University Press.

——. 1995 (in press). "Malpractice and Liability Claims Against Social Workers: First Facts." *Social Work*.

——. 1995 (in press). *Social Work Values and Ethics*. New York: Columbia University Press.

—— and Marcia Abramson. 1982. *The Teaching of Social Work Ethics*. Hastings-on-Hudson, N.Y.: The Hastings Center.

Reid, P. Nelson and James O. Billups. 1986. "Distributional Ethics and Social Work Education." *Journal of Social Work Education* 22(1):6–17.

Reynolds, Mildred M. 1976. "Threats to Confidentiality." *Social Work* 21: 108–113.

Rhodes, Margaret L. 1986. *Ethical Dilemmas in Social Work Practice*. London: Routledge and Kegan Paul.

Richmond, Mary. 1917. *Social Diagnosis*. New York: Russell Sage Foundation.

Rinas, Joan and Sheila Clyne-Jackson. 1988. *Professional Conduct and Legal Concerns in Mental Health Practice*. Norwalk, Conn.: Appleton and Lange.

Rokeach, Milton. 1973. *The Nature of Human Values*. New York: Free Press.

Ross, W. D. 1930. *The Right and the Good*. Oxford: Clarendon.

Roy, Agnes. 1954. "Code of Ethics." *The Social Worker* 23(1):4–7.

Schutz, Benjamin M. 1982. *Legal Liability in Psychotherapy*. San Francisco: Jossey-Bass.

Sheafor, Bradford W., Charles R. Horejsi, and Gloria A. Horejsi. 1988. *Techniques and Guidelines for Social Work Practice*. Boston: Allyn and Bacon.

Siporin, Max. 1975. *Introduction to Social Work Practice*. New York: Collier-Macmillan.

——. 1982. "Moral Philosophy in Social Work Today." *Social Service Review* 56:516–538.

——. 1983. "Morality and Immorality in Working with Clients." *Social Thought* 9(4):10–28.

——. 1989. "The Social Work Ethic." *Social Thought* 15(3/4):42–52.

Smart, J. J. C. 1971. "Extreme and Restricted Utilitarianism." In Samuel Gorovitz, ed., *Mill: Utilitarianism*. Indianapolis: Bobbs-Merrill.

Solomon, Barbara. 1976. *Black Empowerment: Social Work in Oppressed Communities*. New York: Columbia University Press.

Specht, Harry. 1991. "Point/Counterpoint: Should Training for Private Practice Be a Central Component of Social Work Education?" *Journal of Social Work Education* 27(2):102–107.

Stace, Walter. 1975. "Ethical Absolutism and Ethical Relativism." In Karsten J. Struhl and Paula Rothenberg Struhl, eds., *Ethics in Perspective*. New York: Random House.

Stalley, R. F. 1975. "Determinism and the Principle of Client Self-Determination." In F. E. McDermott, ed., *Self-Determination in Social Work*. London: Routledge and Kegan Paul.

Teicher, Morton. 1967. *Values in Social Work: A Re-examination*. New York: National Association of Social Workers.

Timms, Noel. 1983. *Social Work Values: An Enquiry*. London: Routledge and Kegan Paul.

Varley, Barbara K. 1968. "Social Work Values: Changes in Value Commitments from Admission to MSW Graduation." *Journal of Education for Social Work* 4:67–85.

Veatch, Robert M. 1977. "Hospital Ethics Committees: Is There a Role?" *Hastings Center Report* 7:22–25.

Vigilante, Joseph L. 1974. "Between Values and Science: Education for the Profession or is Proof Truth?" *Journal of Education for Social Work* 10:107–115.

Wakefield, Jerome C. 1988a. "Psychotherapy, Distributive Justice, and Social Work, Part I. Distributive Justice as a Conceptual Framework for Social Work." *Social Service Review* 62:187–210.

——. 1988b. "Psychotherapy, Distributive Justice, and Social Work, Part II. Psychotherapy and the Pursuit of Justice." *Social Service Review* 62:353–382.

Williams, Bernard. 1972. *Morality: An Introduction to Ethics*. New York: Harper and Row.

Wilson, Suanna J. 1978. *Confidentiality in Social Work: Issues and Principles*. New York: Free Press.

Younghusband, Eileen. 1967. *Social Work and Social Values*. London: Allen and Unwin.

8

Confronting Social Injustice and Oppression

DAVID G. GIL

Social workers are required by their *Code of Ethics* "to promote social justice . . . with special regard for disadvantaged or oppressed groups and persons." The *Code of Ethics* does not specify, however, the meanings of social justice and oppression, as if these meanings were self-evident. Yet social justice can not be promoted, nor can oppression and social injustice be overcome, unless their meanings, sources, and dynamics are first clarified. This chapter attempts such a necessary clarification, regardless of potentially controversial and unsettling implications.

Unraveling these meanings, sources, and dynamics is, however, fraught with difficulties, because oppression tends to be more effective in achieving its apparent ends—enforcement of exploitation, social injustice, and constraints on liberty—when its victims, as well as its perpetrators, are not conscious of the social dynamics involved, when the victims perceive their conditions as "natural" and inevitable, and, especially, when they share illusions of being "free." Throughout much of human history, denial and rationalization of oppression and social injustice, and their validation as sacred and secular "law and order," may actually have been the most effective weapons in the defense and legitimation of unjust ways of life that tended to benefit primarily privileged social groups and classes. Students of oppression and social injustice and of their opposites should therefore explore not only the meanings and dynamics of these phenomena but also their own consciousness and values, the perceptions of their needs and interests, their possible denials of oppression and injustice, as well as their unexamined, taken-for-granted justifications of established, oppressive, and unjust ways of life.

Understanding oppression and social injustice seems especially important for social workers, since the conditions that cause people to seek help from social services are usually direct or indirect consequences of oppressive and unjust social, economic, and political institutions, and since the profession of social work is ethically committed to promote social justice. Insights into oppression and social injustice, and into ways of overcoming them, are therefore essential aspects of the foundations of social work knowledge.

Assumptions

The following related assumptions underlie this exploration:

1. Oppressive relations within and among human societies, and unjust ways of life enforced and shaped by such relations, are results of human choices and actions throughout social evolution. While not contrary to human nature, oppression and injustice are not inevitable expressions of it. This key assumption is supported by the existence, throughout history, of human groups and entire societies whose internal and external relations were shaped by values of equality, liberty, solidarity, and cooperation, rather than by dynamics of oppression and injustice (Kropotkin 1956; Maslow and Honigman 1970).

2. Societies that initiated oppressive relations and unjust conditions on small scales and local levels tended to extend such relations and conditions also beyond their populations and territories. Such oppressive practices and tendencies intensified gradually and acquired momentum as a result of cycles of resistance by victims and reactive repression by perpetrators, as well as through competition for dominance among different oppressive and exploiting societies. Eventually, oppression and injustice penetrated and permeated most branches of humankind, all over the globe.

3. Oppressive relations and unjust conditions, and the coercive processes by which they were established, maintained, and extended within and beyond societies, came to be reflected not only in social, economic, cultural, and political institutions, and in all spheres of everyday life, but also in the consciousness and behavior of their victims and perpetrators.

4. Oppression and injustice and their gradual expansion were never,

nor are they now, inevitable. People have often challenged these destructive practices and conditions, and are likely to do so again, by organizing liberation movements and spreading critical consciousness—a prerequisite for collective action toward fundamental social change (Freire 1970). Such movements have usually encountered resistance in the past, and are likely to encounter it again in the future, from individuals and social classes committed to conserve ways of life they consider compatible with their perceived needs and interests. The outcomes of conflicts between challengers and defenders of oppression and injustice are unpredictable.

Meanings and Defining Characteristics of Oppression, Social Injustice, and their Opposites

Oppression refers to relations of domination and exploitation—economic, social, and psychologic—between individuals; between social groups and classes within and beyond societies; and, globally, between entire societies. Injustice refers to discriminatory, dehumanizing, and development-inhibiting conditions of living (e.g., unemployment, poverty, homelessness, and lack of health care), imposed by oppressors upon dominated and exploited individuals, social groups, classes, and peoples. These conditions will often cause people to turn to social services for help.

Oppression seems motivated by an intent to exploit (i.e., benefit disproportionally from the resources, capacities, and productivity of others), and it results typically in disadvantageous, unjust conditions of living for its victims. It serves as *means* to enforce exploitation toward the *goal* of securing advantageous conditions of living for its perpetrators. Justice reflects the absence of exploitation-enforcing oppression; it implies liberty, while oppression-induced injustice involves discriminatory constraints on liberty (see definitions of key concepts later in this section).

To individuals, groups, classes, and societies that oppress and exploit others, and impose upon them unjust conditions of living, their policies and practices tend to make sense. For in the consciousness of perpetrators of oppression, their attitudes and actions seem, by and large, compatible with the pursuit of socially sanctioned, legitimate goals, and with the internal logic of established social, economic, cultural, and political institutions. How and why, one wonders, did human societies evolve ways of life in which oppression and injustice came to be taken for granted and considered legitimate and appropriate?

To answer this complex and disturbing question, one needs to examine the evolution of the following *key dimensions* of social life and the values underlying them:

- stewardship (i.e., development, management, control, and ownership) of natural and human-created resources;
- organization of work and production;
- exchange of products of human work, and distribution (i.e., indirect exchanges) of goods and services, and civil and political rights and responsibilities.

For in any human group, at any time, the combined effects of these key dimensions of social life, and of the values underlying them, shape the quality of human relations and the conditions of life of individuals and social classes, be these relations and conditions nonoppressive and just or oppressive and unjust (Gil 1992).

By focusing the analysis of oppression, injustice, and their opposites on these key dimensions of social life and the values underlying them, I do not mean to disregard other social, psychological, historical, and cultural dimensions of social relations and living conditions. I merely intend to stress that, regardless of the role such other dimensions may play in maintaining and reproducing these relations and conditions, oppression and injustice can neither be fully understood, nor overcome at their roots, apart from systems of resource stewardship, work and production, and exchange and distribution. For these systems and their underlying values constitute always the very core of any mode of social life, and they must, therefore, be changed significantly, if an oppressive and unjust mode of life is to be transformed into its opposite.

Furthermore, work and exchange seem to be fundamental processes, not only of human social organization, but of all forms of life in nature. Living beings, from single cells to complex organisms, are never self-contained, but assure their existence by interacting with other organisms and nonorganic substances in their environment. This is how they generate, obtain, and transmit materials and energy necessary for individual and species survival. These essential, life-sustaining interactions in nature may be understood as the universal model of work and exchange. Organisms that cease to engage in such life-sustaining interactions are dying. Work and exchange seem, therefore, a sine qua non of all life, and their organization and institutionalization are essential for human survival and societal continuity. Accordingly, systems of work and exchange are valid foci for the analysis of oppression and injustice, as well as for efforts to overcome these dehumanizing practices and conditions.

Stewardship of resources, work and production, and exchange and distribution can be, and have actually been, organized by different societies, in different times and circumstances, in nonoppressive and just ways, in accordance with values of equality, liberty, mutualism, cooperation, and community. Conversely, they can be, and have been, organized in oppressive and unjust ways, in accordance with values of inequality, domination, exploitation, competition, and selfishness (i.e., disregard for others and community).

The defining characteristics of nonoppressive and oppressive societies and work systems, and of just and unjust systems of exchange and distribution, are suggested here:

1.*Societies and work systems are non-oppressive*, when all people are considered and treated as equals, and, therefore, have equal rights and responsibilities concerning (a) the stewardship of resources; (b) decisions affecting the control, organization, design, substance, quality, and scope of production; and (c) the amount and types of work they perform. Under such truly democratic conditions, everyone would enjoy the same level of liberty, and would be subject to the same level of constraints and expectations concerning work.

2. *Societies and work systems are oppressive*, when people are not considered and treated as equals, and therefore do not have equal rights and responsibilities concerning the key dimensions of social life. Under such inherently undemocratic conditions, different people, and different groups and classes, are entitled to different levels of liberty, and are subject to different levels of constraints and expectations concerning work. Establishing and maintaining unequal levels of rights and responsibilities concerning stewardship of resources and production, and unequal levels of liberty, constraints, and expectations concerning work, is usually not possible without overt and covert coercion, i.e., "societal violence" (Gil 1989).

3. *Systems of exchange and distribution are just*, when terms of exchange (measured in units of human work and natural and human-created resources invested in products of work), are consistently fair

and balanced, i.e., nonexploiting; when everyone's individual needs and potential are considered and treated as equally important; and when all people are treated flexibly as equals, relative to their individual needs, in the distribution of concrete and symbolic goods and services, and civil and political rights and responsibilities (Barry 1973; Rawls 1971; Tawney 1964).

4. *Systems of exchange and distribution are unjust*, when terms of exchange are consistently discriminatory, unfair, and unbalanced, i.e., exploiting; when the needs and potential of members of certain groups and classes are deemed more important than those of others; and when these individuals, groups, and classes receive routinely preferential treatment, relative to others, in the distribution of concrete and symbolic goods and services, and civil and political rights and responsibilities. Establishing and maintaining unjust modes of exchange and distribution are usually predicated upon overt and covert coercive processes, in the same way as establishing and maintaining oppressive social and work systems.

Oppression and injustice tend to vary among societies in levels of intensity, from very low to very high. These variations reflect underlying differences in values, and in degrees of inequality with respect to the key dimensions of social life, in particular societies at particular times. The higher the degrees of inequality, the higher also are likely to be the levels of coercion necessary to enforce inequality, as well as the levels of conflict, resistance, and reactive repression. An important function of social services throughout history has been to modify and fine-tune the intensity of oppression and injustice in societies, and to ameliorate their destructive consequences for human development. Social services were, however, never meant to eliminate oppression and injustice and their consequences.

Variations are not possible, however, concerning social justice and nonoppressive relations, which, by definition, are predicated upon equal rights and responsibilities with regard to the key dimensions of social life. Equal rights and responsibilities, obviously, can not vary by levels, because equality is not a continuum, but the zero point on the continuum of social inequality.

When politicians and social work leaders, in public policy discourse, nevertheless advocate "more equality," as they often illogically do, what they actually mean are lower levels of inequality, privilege, and deprivation, but not real social equality and elimination of discrimination, privilege, and deprivation. Reductions of inequality, discrimination, privilege, and deprivation are, of course, welcome improvements in the quality of social life, but should not be mistaken for an end to oppression and the establishment of justice. The quality of social life will continue to be affected by the dynamics and logic of oppression and injustice, as long as some level of inequality concerning the key dimensions of social orders will be "conserved," and dominant social values will remain essentially unchanged.

Historically, societies that developed nonoppressive social and work systems tended to evolve just systems of exchange and distribution, while societies that developed oppressive social and work systems tended to evolve unjust systems of exchange and distribution. These typical associations between nonoppressive social and work systems and just systems of exchange and distribution, on the one hand, and oppressive and unjust ones, on the other, suggest causal links between oppression and injustice, and nonoppressive social relations and justice. These associations suggest and reflect also the presence or absence of overt and covert coercion or societal violence, which has been used throughout history, and continues to be used in our time, by socially dominant groups, classes, and peoples, from local to global levels, in order to establish, maintain, and legitimate privileged conditions of living for themselves. People have always been unlikely to submit of their own free will to discriminatory, development-inhibiting, nonegalitarian practices concerning stewardship of resources and work, and to unjust, exploiting terms of exchange and distribution. Accordingly, it does not seem possible to ever establish and maintain such systems and conditions of living through truly democratic processes, and without at least some measure of overt and covert coercion or societal violence.

It follows from these theoretical considerations that whenever significant inequalities are prevalent in a society concerning the key dimensions of social life, such as unemployment, relative poverty, homelessness, inadequate education and health care, and distinctions and discrimination by social class, race, sex, and age—the gamut of conditions that bring people to various social services—its ways of life involve oppression, exploitation, and injustice; its people are not free in a meaningful sense; and its political institutions are essentially undemocratic, coercive, and structurally violent, in spite of formal elections and misleading claims, such as "being part of the free world."

Sources and Dynamics of Oppression and Social Injustice: Historical Notes

Contrary to widely held, taken-for-granted beliefs, oppression, exploitation, and injustice are not inevitable, "natural" characteristics of human life. The study of social evolution reveals that these practices did not become firmly established in human societies until some ten thousand years ago, following the discovery, development, and spread of agriculture, animal husbandry, and crafts, which gradually generated a stable economic surplus. These new conditions facilitated the emergence of complex divisions of work, of occupational and social castes and classes, and of spatial and social differentiations of societies into rural peasant communities and urban centers. Since the human species originated more than three hundred thousand years ago, the last ten thousand years are a relatively short period, and should not be perceived erroneously as our entire history (Eisler 1987).

For many millennia, from the emergence of the human species until the agricultural revolution, people tended to live in small and isolated, nomadic communities that subsisted by gathering, fishing, and hunting. The internal organization of these societies was usually based on egalitarian, cooperative, and communal principles, and did not involve systematic oppression, exploitation, and injustice.

People's resources during these early stages of evolution consisted of their human capacities, their accumulated experiences and orally transmitted knowledge and traditions, and the natural wealth of the territories they inhabited. Stewardship over these resources was exercised collectively toward the goal of meeting everyone's survival needs. Work roles were barely differentiated, as nearly everyone had to participate in securing the basic necessities for survival. Whatever division of work did emerge, tended to be based on age, sex, physical conditions, and individual capacities, but not, as during later stages of social evolution, on discriminatory social criteria, such as family, clan, tribe, race, religion, caste, or class.

Exchanges of work products and the distribution of goods and services tended to be balanced and egalitarian, i.e., non exploitative. In the course of their lives, most people contributed to, and received from, aggregate social production about as much as others. Civil and political rights and responsibilities also tended to be shared equally and to be linked to age, sex, and capacities. People enjoyed roughly equal liberties, and they were subject to roughly equal constraints concerning their work and activities.

These essentially egalitarian modes of resource stewardship, work and production, and exchange and distribution seem to have required little coercion beyond child rearing, socialization, and conformity-inducing public opinion. For, under conditions prevailing in these early societies, people seem to have been self-motivated to work, as their work was typically linked directly to their real interests—the satisfaction of basic needs.

Levels of conflict within societies seem to have been low during the early stages of evolution, as everyone's needs were deemed equally important, and were met accordingly, subject to limits set by the resources and collective productivity of societies. Also, since the gathering, hunting, and fishing mode of production necessitated nearly everyone's participation to assure provisions for basic needs, few opportunities existed for the emergence of crafts and the generation of a stable economic surplus—the disposition and appropriation of which became a potential source of conflicts during later stages of social evolution.

Finally, apart from their egalitarian, cooperative, and communal value premises, the ways of life of early human societies were not conducive to establishing systems of economic exploitation such as slavery, serfdom, or wage labor. Their simple technologies, typically, did not enable people to produce, in the course of their lives, significantly more than they consumed for their subsistence. They were therefore unable to generate a stable economic surplus for appropriation and exploitation by others—the material basis and precondition for the emergence of systems of oppression.

I do not mean to idealize here the ways of life of early human groups, nor to advocate a return to that primeval stage of social evolution, in order to overcome oppression, exploitation, and injustice in contemporary societies. I also do not suggest that human relations were then entirely free from oppressive tendencies, especially in relations between men and women, between older and younger persons, and between members of societies and strangers they encountered. I am also aware that relations between different societies were not always peaceful then.

However, from what has been learned by anthropology, archaeology, and history about this very long, pre-agricultural and preliterate period of human evolution, oppression, exploitation, and injustice in relation to the key dimensions of social life, as perpetrated routinely by many societies over the past ten millennia, were not institutionalized policies and practices. We could, therefore, derive important insights from the values and ways of life of these early human communities, and thus enhance our ability to overcome oppression, exploitation, and injustice in contemporary societies.

What conditions and forces have brought about radical transformations of the relatively static, continuously self-reproducing, traditional patterns of life of early human societies? Likely answers to this important historical question are implicit in the existential imperative of the human condition to assure a steady flow of suitable, life-sustaining necessities from a society's environment, while conserving also that environment's regenerative capacities. Humans must always maintain a rough balance between their survival needs and their abilities to satisfy these needs in particular environments, given their particular levels of scientific and technological development. This essential balance may be upset by unchecked population increases relative to the carrying capacity of a society's territory. When such imbalances occurred and reached critical levels, human groups could not survive and continue living in their traditional ways, unless they expanded their territories or migrated to different ones. Survival could also be assured by discovering and developing new technologies and new ways of life that enabled people to reestablish an adequate balance between their growing numbers, needs, and environmental resources.

Many early human communities, whose population increases were insignificant for a long time, eventually experienced accelerated increases in their numbers, which did upset the essential balance between them and their environments. Some of these societies, in different parts of the globe, at about the same time (some eight to ten millennia ago), overcame the threats to their survival by discovering and developing agriculture and animal husbandry, and initiating thereby a new era of social development with new challenges, opportunities, choices, and risks.

The introduction of agriculture and animal husbandry had revolutionary consequences for the ways of life of nomadic societies that developed them, and for their internal and external relations. Gradually, they began to establish sedentary peasant communities that were able to generate a relatively reliable and ample food supply. Because of this increase in productivity, it was no longer necessary for everyone to participate in food production, and growing numbers of people could, henceforth, pursue alternative occupations and roles. In time, this led to "divisions of labor" between manual and mental work, and to the emergence of social and occupational castes and classes including peasants, artisans, and traders; priests, scholars, professionals, and artists; civilian administrators, soldiers, and ruling elites. Occupational differentiations and specializations led gradually also to spatial differentiations—the emergence of cities and neighborhoods—and to social, economic, political, and cultural differentiations, all of which resulted in differences in ways of life, consciousness, interests, values, and ideologies among subgroups of societies.

These multifaceted developments reflect a gradual transformation, following the spread of agriculture, of the egalitarian, cooperative, and communal systems of resource stewardship, work and production, and exchange and distribution of hunting and gathering societies, into alternative systems. The new systems involved tendencies toward expropriation, fragmentation, and concentration concerning resource stewardship, and increasingly complex divisions of labor, which began to yield a significant economic surplus—the material base and precondition for the emergence of oppression, exploitation, and injustice. These changes concerning resource stewardship and work and production led also to corresponding significant changes in modes of exchange and distribution, and in overall social organization, values, and ideologies. Illustrations of these developments are the ancient civilizations of Mesopotamia and Egypt (Durant 1935; Garraty and Gay 1972).

To be sure, these developments took centuries and millennia, and involved, at any stage, many choices, none of which were ever inevitable. Indeed, different societies, which developed agriculture and animal husbandry in different regions of the globe, at different times, made different choices and developed different patterns of resource stewardship, division of work, and exchange and distribution, which also gave rise to different sets of values and ideologies.

Before tracing the emergence and institutionalization of oppression, exploitation, and injustice—the most widespread consequence of the agricultural revolution—it is important to note that not all societies that developed agriculture developed systems of oppression. Some societies used the economic surplus resulting from their increased productivity toward enhancing the quality of life for all their members, and they continued to manage resources, to organize work and production, and exchange and distribution in accordance with egalitarian, cooperative, and communal values. Illustrations of this tendency have been identified by anthropologists and historians among native peoples in America, Africa, and elsewhere. Many of these "native societies" preserved essentially nonoppressive and just ways of life until, and often beyond, the violent conquests of their lands by colonizing European empires (Farb 1968; Zinn 1980).

The ways by which oppression and injustice were established as dominant modes of social life, following the development of agriculture, have varied among societies. Two main related and interacting types may be distinguished:

1. exploiting strangers, i.e., other societies and their people; and

2. exploiting fellow citizens within societies.

Historically, societies that have practiced exploitation and oppression have usually done so at home and abroad, as both types involve similar assumptions, value premises, and ideologies, and as internal and external human relations interact with, and influence, one another. It is nevertheless useful to differentiate conceptually between external and internal exploitation and oppression, and to analyze their emergence separately, since they do differ in origins.

Exploiting and Oppressing Strangers

Agricultural products ripening in the fields and gardens of societies that had preceded others in developing this new mode of production and survival technology, seem to have attracted pre-agricultural societies to invade the peasant settlements around harvest time, in order to appropriate their products, especially if population increases were threatening the food supply of the invading societies. These invasions were the beginnings of warfare between societies, motivated by efforts to achieve control over economic resources. Invasions of ancient European peasant communities by Asian nomadic tribes, the Kurgans, illustrate this process (Eisler 1987).

While these violent encounters probably made sense in the consciousness of those involved, in spite of high costs in human life, they were clearly not inevitable. The discoverers of agriculture may have been ready to share their knowledge, technology, and skills peacefully with others, as native peoples have actually done in the Americas when European explorers and conquerors first arrived.

The invasions of peasant communities around harvest time resulted gradually in their coercive enslavement by nomadic peoples, who became accustomed to securing their food supplies by appropriating the fruits of other people's work, and who apparently preferred living by marauding to acquiring agricultural technologies in order to produce their own food. Invasions to expropriate the products of peasant communities did initially not result in enslavement, as the invaders tended to kill the people of the invaded communities. However, with time they realized the advantage of keeping these people alive and coercing them to continue raising crops and to turn over much of their products to the invaders. Eventually, nomadic societies not only coerced entire conquered communities to continue farming and turn over their surplus products, but they captured and exiled men and women from conquered communities, to enslave them and exploit them sexually in the communities of their captors.

One can identify the typical elements of oppression and injustice in these early relationships between nomadic warrior peoples and peasant communities, over whom they gained dominance coercively, and whom they subsequently enslaved. The motivating factor of the interaction is obviously economic exploitation of the victims. This is accomplished by gaining control over their basic resources—their territories, and forcing them to perform work, which the dominant society is unwilling to do, and to turn over the surplus product of this work, exclusive of what is necessary for the subsistence of the enslaved communities.

With time, social, psychological, and ideological dimensions evolved around the economic roots of oppressive and exploitative relationships: the prestige of work performed by enslaved people declined relative to the prestige of activities engaged in by the dominant people, regardless of the objective importance of the work and activities; and the status and prestige of dominated, enslaved workers declined relative to that of members of dominant societies. These perceptions of the relative status and prestige of work and workers became internalized in the consciousness of everyone involved in exploitative and oppressive relations, and they became the core of discriminatory ideologies and practices concerning different social groups, castes, classes, and peoples. Phenomena such as sexism, racism, anti-Semitism, ethnocentrism, and so forth, are contemporary manifestations and expressions of this very ancient tendency. (Social work's consistent struggles against contemporary discriminatory practices reflect the earlier noted function of the profession, to modify the intensity of oppression and injustice, but not to eradicate their sources in the fabric of society.)

Imposing oppressive relations and unjust conditions on other societies in order to exploit their natural resources, the potential of their people to work, and their human-created goods and services, as was done on relatively small scales by marauding nomadic peoples following the agricultural revolution, has gradually become the model for building colonial empires during antiquity, the Middle Ages, and modern times. Historical details have varied from case to case but institutional principles and practices concerning stewardship of resources, work and production, and exchange and distribution have remained essentially the same throughout history, and so have the social, psychological, and ideological dimensions, as well as the secular and religious rationalizations and justifications for exploitation, oppression, injustice, and discrimination (Frank 1977; Magdoff 1977).

Exploiting and Oppressing Fellow Citizens

Oppression and injustice emerged, following the spreading of agriculture, within many but not all societies, as a possible consequence of occupational, social, and spatial differentiations. Whether or not these differentiations resulted in oppressive relations and unjust conditions seems to have depended largely on the terms of exchange that were established between peasants in rural communities and people pursuing newly emerging crafts and other occupations and roles, mainly in urban centers.

If exchanges were just, i.e., fairly balanced, in terms of human and material resources invested in respective products and services, then relations between a society's peasantry and social groups pursuing other occupations, and living mainly in cities, could evolve along voluntary, noncoercive, nonoppressive, and synergetic patterns, with everyone benefiting equally (Maslow and Honigman 1970).

If, on the other hand, exchanges were unjust, i.e., imbalanced, establishment and maintenance of such conditions required typically physical and ideological coercion, that is, oppression and domination or societal violence. In these situations, urban dwellers were bent upon exploiting the peasantry, and gradually also each other, as occupational specializations and social differentiations multiplied, and as each occupational and social group or class aspired to appropriate as much as possible of the aggregate economic surplus by consistently claiming, and struggling for, privileged shares of available goods and services.

Unjust and oppressive societies, which are based on coercively maintained exploitative exchanges among people and classes engaging in different occupations and performing different social roles and enjoying different levels of rights, responsibilities, and liberty, were not as stable and change-resistant, as pre-agricultural, egalitarian, cooperative, and communal societies. They were changing continuously, as a result of gradually intensifying competition and conflicts among individuals and social and occupational groups, who gained control over different shares of resources and different roles in the work system, and who consequently were able to command different shares in the distribution of goods and services, and civil and political rights and power.

During early stages of the emergence of unjust and oppressive relations, following the establishment of societies based on agriculture and crafts, the egalitarian, cooperative, and communal values, ideology, and consciousness of pre-agricultural societies were gradually transformed into their opposites. These value changes toward inequality, competition, and selfishness were conducive to the ongoing development and stabilization of occupationally, spatially, and socially fragmented and stratified societies.

Once inequalities concerning resources, social and occupational roles, and goods, services, and rights were established in a society, they tended to be perpetuated, since individuals and groups who controlled disproportionally larger shares of resources and access to preferred work were in advantageous positions to assure continuation of these privileges, and even to increase them. Also, emerging legal and political institutions tended to reflect established societal inequalities and power relations among competing interest groups and classes, and were therefore unlikely to upset temporary equilibria among them.

The processes, dynamics, and logic of conflict and competition within societies apparently originated in insignificant initial inequalities in exchanges among individuals and occupational and social groups, which barely required coercion. However, the emerging tendency to legitimate, institutionalize, and increase initial, minimal inequalities did require coercion. This resulted usually in resistance from victimized groups, to which privileged groups reacted with intensified coercion. The vicious circle of oppression and exploitation, resistance, and repression intensified with time, as people tended to focus on, and to react to, the latest violent stages in the circle, but did not trace the sources of these destructive interactions, and therefore lacked insights for reversing their course, and moving in alternative, constructive, nonexploitative directions.

It may be difficult to accept the hypothesis that minimal, initial inequalities within human societies, concerning the key dimensions of social life, have eventually led to contemporary, massive inequalities within and among societies. While analogies do not prove anything, it may nevertheless be of interest to reflect on the latest hypotheses and supportive discoveries of cosmology, according to which massive galactic structures evolved out of minimal variations in densities and temperatures in the smooth physical medium of the early universe.

The tendency for inequalities to intensify in societies, once they are initiated on a small scale, has an important implication for social workers and others who advocate reductions rather than elimination of inequalities: as long as inequalities, at any level, are considered legitimate and are being enforced by governments, competitive interactions focused on restructuring inequalities tend to continue among individuals, social groups, and classes, and a sense of community and solidarity is unlikely to evolve.

One reason for the constant intensification of coercion in unjust and oppressive societies was that the motivation of people to work declined in proportion to the increase in exploitation. Work discipline had, therefore, to be assured by ever more overt and covert coercion. Hypocritical expectations concerning a "work ethic" became typical elements of socialization, and of religions and ideologies which interpreted and justified established, inegalitarian conditions of life and work. And socialization and indoctrination were routinely backed up by elaborate systems of submission-inducing rewards and sanctions, and by open and secret police and military forces, the instruments of "legitimate violence" within inegalitarian societies, and among societies of unjust and exploitative world systems.

The history of the origins and development of oppression and injustice within and among societies over the past ten thousand years is essentially a series of variations on the theme of coercively initiated and maintained exploitative modes of resource stewardship, work and production, and exchange and distribution. This history is a tragic one indeed. The mere mention of coercive work systems such as ancient and recent slavery, feudal serfdom, and early and contemporary industrial and agricultural wage labor, brings to mind images of toiling people transformed, not by their own choice, into dehumanized "factors of production," dominated and exploited by tyrants and slave masters, absolute rulers and aristocracies, and individual and corporate, capitalist employers. Such work systems could never have been established and perpetuated without massive coercion and violence in the form of civil and foreign wars, genocide, murder, torture, imprisonment, starvation, destitution, discrimination, unemployment, and the ever-present threat of these and other oppressive measures (Pope John Paul II 1982; Tucker 1978).

Contemporary Manifestations of Oppression and Injustice

The foregoing conceptual and historical analysis suggests insights into contemporary manifestations of oppression, exploitation, and injustice, as well as into philosophical and political dimensions of liberation movements pursuing the eradication of injustice and the emergence of truly democratic, nonoppressive, just societies. The analysis also sheds light on social work's ameliorative orientation and regulatory function.

Existing manifestations of oppression, exploitation, and injustice within societies, as well as in worldwide relations, are typically experienced, perceived, and challenged as supposedly discrete, unrelated phenomena, such as racism, anti-Semitism, sexism, ageism, and discrimination by sexual orientation, disabilities, religions, etc. However, in spite of their social, psychological, political, and historical uniqueness, these different manifestations of discrimination appear to have common ancient sources, and they continue to interact, intersect, and overlap. They have all been shaped for centuries by the dynamics and logic of occupational and social caste and class differentiations of ancient and recent slavery, medieval feudalism and colonialism, early and advanced capitalism, chauvinism, and economic imperialism.

Contemporary racism, which refers to oppression, exploitation, and injustice resulting from discriminatory attitudes and practices toward racial and ethnic minorities, derives from the ancient practice of invading the domains of other societies in order to exploit and appropriate their resources and products, and to capture and enslave their people.

In spite of important objective and subjective differences, the experiences of native American peoples, coercively imported slaves from Africa, Hispanic and Asian immigrants and migrant workers, and Jews and other ethnic groups fleeing poverty, persecution, and pogroms in Europe, reflect the practices and dynamics of economic, social, and psychological domination and exploitation imposed by many societies upon "strangers," ever since the development of agriculture.

Oppression, exploitation, and injustice by social class, on the other hand, which usually intersect and overlap with the dynamics of racism, derive from early processes of occupational, social, and spatial differentiations among fellow citizens within societies, and from subsequently coercively established and maintained, continuously expanding and intensifying inequalities among social groups, concerning resource stewardship, work and production, and exchange and distribution.

In spite of ideologically shaped illusions of democracy and liberty in people's consciousness, contemporary social class structures under advanced capitalism, like social castes and strata before them, involve overtly and subtly enforced exploitation and injustice with regard to the key dimensions of social life. Formal and informal criteria for access and promotions within and between occupational classes, and the fact that at the bottom of the class structure are usually people who participate only marginally in the work system, and who experience, therefore, severe material deprivations, tend to result in fierce competition among individuals and social groups. This economically induced, and politically manipulated, competition tends to become a major arena for conflicts between individuals and social groups, victimized by subjectively discrete types of discrimination.

Manifestations of domination of women by men occurred already among some pre-agricultural societies and thus predate the emergence of institutionalized oppression and exploitation by race and social class. Such early domination of women seems to have evolved in relation to biological aspects of the life process and the organization of work, since childbearing, breastfeeding, and the care of offspring caused real limitations on women's activities. Women seem to have assumed major responsibilities for children very early in social evolution, before the role of men in procreation came to be fully understood. Early forms of domination of women by men, before societies were able to generate a stable economic surplus, and before societal values changed from equality, cooperation, and community toward their opposites, did, however, not yet involve as severe economic exploita-tion and injustice as during later stages of social evolution.

While in some pre-agricultural societies men tended to dominate, this tendency was by no means universal during that early stage. Rather, many societies revered women as the source of all life. Women were presumed to possess superior powers, and were therefore accord-ed leading social and political responsibilities. This tendency was reflected symbolically in early myths and religions, which assigned central roles to goddesses.

Sexism, as we know it today—institutionalized oppression and exploitation of women—emerged only following the agricultural revo-lution, along, and in interaction, with invasions by nomadic, patri-archic peoples, the spread of warfare, the enslavement of conquered societies, the economic and sexual exploitation of captured strangers, and the emergence of occupational and spatial differentiations and social and economic stratifications within societies. All these develop-ments came to be reflected in major value shifts toward inequality, domination, exploitation, competition, and selfishness; in the spread-ing of patriarchic patterns of social organization; and in corresponding myths, religions, and ideologies.

Sexism evolved gradually into a nearly universal practice. Its mani-festations, however, have varied in form and intensity, throughout his-tory among societies and cultures. Moreover, sexism has always inter-acted with other forms of oppression and exploitation, including race and social class, and it can therefore neither be fully understood nor overcome apart from all other manifestations of injustice.

Discrimination against homosexual men and women seems rooted in ancient fears of behavioral differences and related tendencies to oppress strangers and minorities; and in tendencies to enforce confor-mity with patriarchic patterns of social organization and with patterns of sexual relations compatible with the conservation of patriarchy. Contemporary oppression and injustice toward homosexual men and women, while still rooted in psychological fears of, and resistance to, different and usually repressed sexual tendencies, intersects and inter-acts now with all other dimensions of discrimination that permeate the incessant struggles for survival, advantage, and dominance in the com-petitive context of class structures of advanced capitalism.

Contemporary discrimination against aged persons reflects a recent challenge to, and partial reversal of, early societal tendencies toward domination of younger people by their elders. Like the early domination of women by men, the dominance of older people in early societies was rooted in biological dimensions of the life process and of the organization of work. An added, objective element of that domination was the wealth of experience—and of knowledge and skills—acquired by the elderly over the course of life. Finally, since life for most people was relatively short then, aged individuals were few in numbers, and were therefore revered. The gradual reversal of the dominant status of the elderly reflects several important developments during recent centuries, including:

1. a relative decline in knowledge and skills of older people, as younger age groups benefited from an acceleration of innovation in science and technology disseminated through formal education; and

2. a relative decline in the overall size of the workforce in the context of competition for access and promotion, which resulted in delayed entry for the young, and earlier separation of the aged.

A countervailing force to these developments is a relative increase in the size of the aged population as a result of an overall prolongation of life, and a related increase in their political influence. As a contemporary phenomenon, ageism intersects with the other dimensions of oppression and injustice in the prevailing competitive societal context, and cannot be understood and dealt with apart from that context.

Biological, Psychological, and "Victim-Blaming" Perspectives on Oppression and Social Injustice

So far, this analysis has used sociocultural, economic, and historic-evolutionary perspectives. Some further perspectives for the interpretation of oppression and social injustice are noted later, some complementary to, and others in conflict with, the former perspectives.

Freud and other psychoanalysts have posited a biologically based human tendency toward aggression in social and sexual relations, which is expressed in violent and oppressive relations between individuals and social groups. Freud even suggested an inherent "death drive" (Freud 1959; Storr 1968).

Konrad Lorenz and other ethologists who studied animal behavior concluded that aggressive impulses, and struggles for domination and territory, are biologically innate to some degree. They drew analogies from observations of animals to humans, in interpreting violence and oppressive relations on individual and social levels (Lorenz 1966).

The biological dimension of human behavior and social relations stressed by psychoanalysis and ethology is an appropriate complement to a social-cultural and historic-evolutionary perspective on violence, domination, oppression, and injustice. However, one must not infer inevitability from biologically given possibilities. While human capacities for aggression, competition, and violence are supported by massive evidence, so are the capacities for love, care, cooperation, and mutual support. Freud, and especially Lorenz and many of their followers, seem to view biological possibilities apart from social and cultural dynamics, rather than in close interaction with them. It is these latter dynamics, however, that influence human choices between biologically possible destructive and constructive behaviors.

There seems to be a further fallacy in Lorenz's extrapolation from animal behavior to humans. Animal behavior is genetically determined to a significantly larger extent than human behavior. As a result of biological evolution, human genetic programs have become less specific and more open, along with gradual increases in the functional capacities of the human brain. Humans are able to, and must choose, individually and collectively, specific patterns of life among biologically possible alternatives, since few specific patterns are imprinted in their genetic makeup, with the exception of certain reflexes. Social designs and their cultural transmission have, therefore, come to replace, in the case of the human species, predominantly genetic transmissions of patterns of life of animal species. Accordingly, while humans do have biological capacities to act and relate destructively, and have often chosen to do so, they also have biological capacities to act and relate constructively, have often chosen to do so, and can do so again.

Psychological perspectives on oppression and injustice tend to consider fear and resentment of strangers, and of differences in them, and related attitudes of ethnic and social class superiority, apart from economic motivations and social-cultural interactions throughout history. Such ahistoric, reductionistic, psychological interpretations tend to fragment oppression and injustice into supposedly discrete types, based on symptoms rather than causes, such as racism, anti-Semitism, sexism, and other discriminatory practices, each to be overcome on its own terms. While symptom-focused psychological analyses, and reform efforts derived from them, are not without merit, their effectiveness to enhance understanding toward overcoming oppression and injustice seems limited.

A final perspective on oppression and social injustice to be noted here reflects a conservative, "victim-blaming" ideology (Ryan 1971). According to this perspective, since civil and political rights have been legally equalized, unjust conditions experienced by individuals and social groups are now due mainly to their own lack of motivation, initiative, and sense of responsibility, and to their allegedly inferior capacities, rather than to prevailing oppressive social structures and dynamics. Moreover, neoconservative policy analysts such as Charles Murray argue that social welfare programs, designed to ease, not to eliminate, the consequences of oppression and injustice for its victims (e.g., Aid to Families with Dependent Children), are actually the cause of "welfare dependency." Based on such fallacious arguments, they suggest abolishing all income support programs for people in poverty, and forcing them to expose themselves to the discipline of the labor market (Murray 1984; Cloward and Piven 1992).

"Victim-blaming" interpretations, too, disregard the history of relations among different social, occupational, and ethnic groups and classes, and the destructive long-term effects of past oppressive interactions on individual and social development. Moreover, these interpretations confuse formal, legal equality with substantive social equality and equality of economic opportunity, and they tend to mistake effects for causes.

Toward Liberation from Oppression and Injustice

While oppression and injustice on local and global levels can, and should, be reduced significantly through appropriate reforms, such as the transition policies noted later in this discussion, *real liberation from these dehumanizing phenomena is predicated upon eradication of their sources and therefore requires radical transformations of key dimensions of social life and underlying values and ideologies, rather than merely marginal, or even "liberal," modifications.*

Accordingly, since the sources of oppression and injustice have been traced to coercively established and maintained inequalities concerning the stewardship of resources and the organization of work, the exchange and distribution of goods and services, and the allocation of civil and political rights and responsibilities, all geared to economic, social, and psychological domination and exploitation of some individuals and groups by others, *establishment of just and nonoppressive societies requires the elimination of these systemic inequalities.* Furthermore, since the coercive establishment, perpetuation, and intensification of these inequalities has also led to the emergence of value systems and ideologies stressing inequality, domination, competition, selfishness, and ethnocentrism, *liberation requires a recommitment to alternative values and ideologies, stressing equality, liberty, cooperation, and human solidarity.* And finally, since oppression and injustice have evolved through interactions of coercively wrought changes in social institutions and corresponding changes in people's consciousness, *liberation requires a counterprocess of interactions of noncoercive changes in consciousness and corresponding democratic transformations of social institutions.*

While social workers have historically been advocates of social justice as an abstract ideal, they have lacked clarity concerning the institutional sources and dynamics of oppression and injustice, and commitment to their elimination. Growing insights into these phenomena and into strategies for overcoming them should make it possible for social workers to integrate the pursuit of social justice into their theories, practice, and social and political actions.

What would be some major characteristics of liberated, truly democratic societies, whose institutions will have been shaped by values of equality, liberty, cooperation, and human solidarity, rather than by values of inequality, domination and exploitation, competition, and selfishness? Such alternative societies would pursue optimum development for their own people, as well as for people anywhere on earth. Social institutions would be designed in ways conducive to meeting everyone's biological, psychological, social, and economic needs. Resources and production would be managed democratically. People would control their work as "masters of production," rather than be dominated and exploited by individual and corporate employers as "factors of production." The ancient, dehumanizing, development-inhibiting, and mind-killing division of intellectual and physical work would be overcome. All people would be free to choose their work and prepare for it. Socially necessary work not chosen voluntarily by enough people would be done by everyone on rotation. Work would also be in harmony with nature and be adapted to requirements implicit in global demographic developments. Ecological and demographic considerations would assure conservation of natural resources, avoidance of all waste, and commitment to high-quality, durable products. Exchanges of products of work would be fair and balanced, and distribution of goods and services, and of civil and political rights and responsibilities, would reflect egalitarian principles, as well as individual needs and capacities. Structures and processes of governance would be truly democratic, nonhierarchic, decentralized, horizontally coordinated, and geared to protecting the equal rights, and serving the real interests, of everyone living now and in the future (Gil and Gil 1987).

Struggles against oppression and injustice by women, gays and lesbians, Native Americans, racial, ethnic, and religious minorities, occupationally and economically marginal classes, poor and homeless people, the elderly, and people with disabilities reflect the politics of interest group competition rather than the politics of universal human liberation. Interest group competition within inegalitarian social orders does not directly challenge established institutional patterns and values. Its goals are merely to reduce the consequences of systemic oppression and injustice for specific groups. Such efforts will often shift these consequences onto other groups but will not affect the sources and dynamics of oppression.

The goals of the politics of human liberation, on the other hand, are to transcend the trap of competitive politics that, by implication, legitimate and reinforce established, oppressive, and unjust social institutions. Human liberation can be attained only by pursuing cooperatively the common interests of all people rather than competitively the fragmented interests of separate oppressed groups. Human liberation involves creating jointly, and sharing equally, an entirely new, development-conducive social order and aggregate social product rather than securing for one's group ever larger shares of the existing, development-inhibiting, dehumanizing social order and aggregate product.

To bring about such radical changes in social institutions and values, and to shift from the politics of interest group competition to the politics of human liberation, requires the building, both locally and globally, of social movements committed to intense, nonviolent political action over a long time. Such long-term commitment seems necessary because the movements would have to overcome oppression and injustice that have evolved over many centuries and are now permeating social institutions and people's consciousness all over the globe. Obviously, the institutional and ideological products of centuries of social evolution cannot be reversed easily and quickly. Intense activism, involving community organizing by means of consciousness-expanding dialogue, seems necessary because working for radical social changes against tremendous odds will require the secular equivalent of missionary work. And nonviolent approaches seem essential, not only for ethical but also for theoretical and practical reasons because the vicious circle of oppression, resistance, and repressive violence cannot be broken and transcended by participating in it and thus actually reinforcing it.

Social workers can, of course, participate in building movements for radical social change. They have done so in the past and, as discussed below, radical social workers have recently organized an association, the Bertha Capen Reynolds Society, in order to pursue collectively the development of social-change-oriented approaches to practice and theory.

Movements for radical social change must, however, never disregard the deprivations and suffering of people due to existing unjust conditions, and should pursue not only the long-term goals of comprehensive liberation. Rather, they should actively advocate transition policies or "non-reformist reforms," whose implementation seems feasible within established social and legal systems, but would test and expand their usual limits (Gorz 1964). Such transition policies should be designed to significantly reduce oppression and injustice in the short term, to challenge prevailing social arrangements, and to serve as stepping stones toward the long-term goals of comprehensive human liberation.

Excellent sources for such transition policies are the "Economic Bill of Rights," proposed by President Franklin Roosevelt in his State of the Union message to Congress on January 11, 1944, and the "Universal Declaration of Human Rights," adopted without dissent by the United Nations on December 10, 1948, with the active support of the United States, and with the able leadership of Eleanor Roosevelt (Harvey 1989; Wronka 1992).

Roosevelt's Economic Bill of Rights was meant to complement the civil and political rights guaranteed by the first ten amendments to the U.S. Constitution—the original Bill of Rights—with legally enforceable guarantees of essential economic rights. His proposal included rights to useful paid employment, adequate income, and decent housing; adequate medical care and the opportunity to achieve and enjoy good health; adequate protection from the economic fears of old age, sickness, accident, and unemployment; a good education; fair terms of trade for the agricultural products of farmers; and freedom from unfair competition and domination by monopolies at home and abroad.

While President Roosevelt's initiative to enact such a bill was not successful, the United Nation's Universal Declaration of Human Rights, which is gradually being perceived as *customary international law*, includes nearly all the economic rights Roosevelt advocated in 1944. It is, in fact, the first international document on human rights that does not involve the fallacious assumption that civil and political rights can be assured and exercised in the absence of economic rights. It therefore asserts civil and political rights, not apart from, but in the context of comprehensive economic rights (United Nations Center for Human Rights 1992).

Movements committed to the pursuit of social justice and nonoppressive human relations at home and abroad should put on the political agenda as initial steps toward their long-range goals proposals to expand U.S. constitutional rights in keeping with the economic rights contained in both the UN declaration and Roosevelt's farsighted proposals. In advocating such transition policies, they might steer the political discourse away from conventional interest group competition toward the politics of universal human rights, which represent the real interests of every human being and every social group. They might also initiate in this way a powerful, durable political alliance of all oppressed groups, and of all people committed to social justice and comprehensive human rights, in place of temporary, tactical coalitions of conventional politics.

Social Work and Social Services and Oppression and Social Injustice

Having discussed so far the meanings, sources, and dynamics of oppression and social injustice, and strategies to overcome them, we can now examine the relations of social services with institutionalized oppression and social injustice, and with their victims and perpetrators. These relations have evolved over centuries and millennia and are therefore complex and often contradictory.

Social work and social services would probably never have evolved at all unless oppression and injustice had first become normal aspects of social life. The institutionalization of these dehumanizing phenomena undoubtedly preceded the emergence of social services and social work. For these latter may be understood as societal responses, designed to stabilize oppressive social orders by "fine-tuning" their unjust conditions in order to facilitate the survival of their victims and regulate their behavior, as well as to protect those social classes that benefit socially, psychologically, and economically from oppressive practices (Piven and Cloward 1971). In this context, social work and social services seem important components of an array of conscious-ness-shaping and social control mechanisms necessary for the maintenance of coercively established, exploitative, and unjust systems of resource stewardship, work, exchange, and distribution.

Another no less significant social tendency, which has influenced the response of social work and social services to oppression and injustice, derives from consistent resistance and struggles by oppressed social groups, classes, and peoples to the perpetrators and agents of oppression, as well as from a deep, spontaneous inner yearning for social justice. This tendency, which is reflected in ancient sacred texts and in prophetic, anti-establishment traditions and movements within many religions (e.g., contemporary "liberation theology"), has in the course of history given rise to systems of ethics, individual and orga-nized charity, liberal policy reforms aimed at reducing oppression and injustice, and radical social movements and radical theory and practice in social work and social services, aimed at eradicating the sources and dynamics of oppression and injustice.

The conditions that cause people to seek help from social workers and social services are invariably consequences of oppression and injustice. While these links are fairly obvious in situations such as unemployment, poverty, hunger, homelessness, and educational and occupational marginality, they may be less obvious in situations involving delinquency and crime, developmental deficits, substance abuse, mental and physical ills, emotional and relational difficulties, and domestic violence. However, in-depth study of these situations, and of individuals and groups of people involved, typically reveals direct or indirect links to the dynamics of oppression and injustice. Illustrations of such direct and indirect links are increases in the inci-dence of domestic violence, alcoholism, and mental breakdowns fol-lowing rises in unemployment (Brenner 1984; Gil 1970).

While not all social and emotional difficulties that bring people to social services would immediately vanish were oppression and injus-tice eliminated, many certainly would. Moreover, those social and emotional difficulties unaffected by the elimination of oppression and injustice would likely become more amenable to treatment and resolution in just societies.

In spite of strong links between oppression and injustice and the conditions that cause people to seek help from social services and social workers, professional schools of social work and social services were not expected by their accrediting body, the Council on Social Work Education (CSWE), to include the study of oppression and injustice in their curricula before 1983. The CSWE Curriculum Policy Statements of 1952, 1962, and 1969 did not mention the concepts of oppression and social injustice, although they noted links between destructive social and economic conditions and the problems that motivate people to seek help. They also stressed social work values that imply commitment to human dignity and development, and to the promotion of progressive reforms of social policy.

The 1982 Curriculum Policy Statement is the first one that referred specifically to the promotion of "social and economic justice" (4.1), and noted that "social workers hold that people should have equal access to resources, services, and opportunities" (5.1). Under the heading "Special Populations," the statement noted that "the profession has also been concerned about the consequences of oppression" (7.3) and that "curricula must give explicit attention to the patterns and consequences of discrimination and oppression" (7.4).

It would seem from these excerpts in a section on special populations that discrimination and oppression were viewed in a fragmented way with regard to women, minorities, and other discrete social groups, rather than in the context of overall economic exploitation through coercively maintained social and occupational divisions and class structures. However, the statement required, in a general section, that students "acquire frameworks for analyzing social and economic policies in the light of the principles of social and economic justice" (7.10).

A 1992 revision of the CSWE Curriculum Policy Statement is clearer than the 1982 statement concerning oppression and injustice, and stresses the responsibility of schools of social work to teach about social justice and about approaches to overcome oppression. Since oppression and injustice increased significantly during the 1980s, both institutionally and ideologically, any increase in clarity and commitment concerning these issues is certainly a welcome development. However, like the 1982 policy statement, the 1992 revision reflects the fallacious assumption that discrimination, oppression, and injustice affecting women, minorities, and other discrete social groups can be overcome without eradicating their sources in the occupational and social class divisions of contemporary capitalism.

Social policies and social services have hardly been affected in recent decades by the progressive Curriculum Policy Statements concerning oppression and social injustice. Rather, recent "reforms" of these policies and services reflect ultra-conservative ideologies, which do not even aim to ameliorate oppression and unjust conditions, as "liberal" policies tend to do.

As for recent social work practice, it helps people to adapt as best as they can to existing unjust conditions rather than to support efforts to change these conditions in accordance with human rights standards and people's needs. Practice, as well as policies and services, thus appears to move in opposite directions from social work education standards, a glaring contradiction that causes severe ethical dilemmas for the profession.

Some social workers, however, are resisting dominant practice trends and are developing alternative, "radical" approaches. The essence of these approaches is to facilitate the emergence of critical consciousness by helping people trace links between their personal troubles and the dynamics of oppression and injustice. Once people come to realize that not they, but prevailing social and economic forces are very often the sources of their difficulties, and once they discover that established social arrangements are neither sacrosanct nor inevitable, but are human-evolved and coercively maintained, they can also realize that they could organize and struggle together against oppression and injustice. Radical social workers identify with people's yearning for social justice rather than with institutions and social services that promote submission and adaptation to unjust conditions. Hence they are on the side of the victims of injustice and support them in organizing resistance. Radical social workers and other human services practitioners have recently organized the Bertha Capen Reynolds Society, and have established the *Journal of Progressive Human Services* to pursue collectively the development of alternative practice approaches and of corresponding practice theories (Brake and Bailey 1980; Corrigan and Leonard 1978; Fisher 1980; Galper 1975, 1980; Gil 1976, 1979; Reynolds 1975, 1985; Wagner 1990; Wineman 1984; Withorn 1984).

Emancipatory Pedagogy

To conclude, some comments are indicated concerning teaching about these phenomena. Such teaching involves intellectual as well as experiential dimensions. To facilitate real learning, the experience of students should support their intellectual efforts, for in studying oppression and injustice, form and structure become substance, and the medium is indeed the message (McLuhan 1967).

Universities and professional schools are important components of contemporary oppressive and unjust social orders. They facilitate the maintenance and ideological justification of elitist social systems, and they credential new members of their elites. Their own rules and practices in relation to students, as well as to teachers, involve certain oppressive and unjust aspects.

When teaching about oppression and injustice in universities, teachers should acknowledge and analyze the oppressive and unjust aspects of their institutions, and should try to transform their own classes and seminars into "liberated spaces," to the extent that the limits of "academic freedom" permit. To accomplish this, teachers should surrender to students responsibility and control over their own learning, by eliminating teacher-set requirements and assignments and by encouraging students to set these themselves. Similarly, students, with advice from teachers, should evaluate their learning and also grade their own work, as long as grading is required by their schools. The role of a teacher in a nonoppressive context should be that of facilitator, adviser, and resource, rather than of "expert," authority, and judge. Learning should occur through collective, dialogical explorations, rather than through top-down instruction. If teachers will consistently yield control to students over their education, students will have real opportunities to experience and explore the meanings and dilemmas of responsibility and freedom, and they will be able to study the conceptual issues of oppression and injustice, not as mere abstractions, but as concrete issues of social relations in everyday life (Burstow 1991; Freire 1970).

Social workers, their profession and educational institutions, and the settings in which they practice are caught up in a difficult dilemma with regard to oppression and social injustice. This dilemma derives from the fact that people's lives in our society and many other societies are influenced, directly or indirectly, by the dynamics of past and present oppression and injustice. The profession of social work, too, is rooted in these dynamics, and its practice and the issues practitioners deal with, as well as its service settings and educational institutions, are continuously impacted upon by these dynamics.

Yet, in contradistinction to many other professions, social workers are not only influenced by the dynamics of oppression and injustice but are also mandated by their curriculum policies and their code of ethics to study and overcome them. Unfortunately, the more one studies oppression and injustice, the more one realizes the vastness of the task of overcoming their dynamics. Social workers are consequently in the painful situation of being not only affected by these dehumanizing dynamics but also of being fully conscious of them, and feeling challenged, as well as overwhelmed, by their special responsibility to confront and overcome them.

There are no easy answers to this dilemma, and certainly no personal answers. There is also no way out of the dilemma by denying or disregarding the realities of oppression and injustice. Knowledge once gained will remain with us, on conscious or unconscious levels. The most appropriate response may be to confront and examine these issues together with others. Socrates' view that "an unexamined life is not worth living" seems relevant here. By creating support groups among social workers and other practitioners in the human services to search cooperatively for appropriate ethical, professional, and political responses, we are most likely to deal constructively with the central dilemma of our lives and work.

REFERENCES

Barry, Brian. 1973. *The Liberal Theory of Justice*. London: Oxford Universitry Press.
Brake, Mike and Roy Bailey, eds. 1980. *Radical Social Work and Practice*. London: Arnold.
Brenner, Harvey. 1984. *Estimating the Effects of Economic Change on National Health and Wellbeing*. Washington, D.C.: U.S. Government Printing Office.
Burstow, Bonnie. 1991. "Freirian Codifications and Social Work Education." *Journal of Social Work Education* 27(2):196–207.
Cloward, Richard A. and Frances Fox Piven. 1992. "The Myth of Dependence." *Democratic Left* 20(4) (July/August):5–6.

Corrigan, Paul and Peter Leonard. 1978. *Social Work Practice Under Capitalism*. London: Macmillan.

Durant, Will. 1935. *The Story of Civilization. I: Our Oriental Heritage*. New York: Simon and Schuster.

Eisler, Riane. 1987. *The Chalice and the Blade*. New York: Harper and Row.

Farb, Peter. 1968. *Man's Rise to Civilization*. New York: Avon.

Fisher, Jacob. 1980. *The Response of Social Work to the Depression*. Cambridge, Mass.: Schenkman.

Frank, Andre Gunder. 1977. *World Accumulation, 1492–1789*. New York: Monthly Review Press.

Freire, Paulo. 1970. *Pedagogy of the Oppressed*. New York: Herder and Herder.

Freud, Sigmund. 1959. *Collected Papers*. New York: Basic Books.

Galper, Jeffrey. 1975. *The Politics of Social Services*. Englewood Cliffs, N.J.: Prentice-Hall.

——. 1980. *Social Work Practice: A Radical Perspective*. Englewood Cliffs, N.J.: Prentice-Hall.

Garraty, John A. and Peter Gay, eds. 1972. *The Columbia History of the World*. New York: Harper and Row.

Gil, David G. 1970. *Violence Against Children*. Cambridge, Mass.: Harvard University Press.

——. 1976. *The Challenge of Social Equality*. Cambridge, Mass.: Schenkman.

——. 1979. *Beyond the Jungle*. Cambridge, Mass.: Schenkman.

——. 1989. "Work, Violence, Injustice, and War." *Journal of Sociology and Social Welfare* 16(1) (March):39–53.

——. 1992. *Unravelling Social Policy*, 5th ed. Rochester, Vt.: Schenkman.

——. 1993. "Beyond Access to Medical Care: Pursuit of Health and Prevention of Ills." *Evaluation and the Health Professions* 16(3):251–277.

—— and Eva A. Gil, eds. 1987. *The Future of Work*. Cambridge, Mass.: Schenkman.

Gorz, Andre. 1964. *Strategy for Labor*. Boston: Beacon Press.

Harvey, Philip. 1989. *Securing the Right to Employment*. Princeton: Princeton University Press.

John Paul II. 1982. *Encyclical on Human Work*. Boston: Daughters of St. Paul.

Kropotkin, Peter. 1956. *Mutual Aid*. Boston: Porter Sargent.

Lorenz, Konrad. 1966. *On Aggression*. London: Methuen.

McLuhan, Marshall. 1967. *The Medium Is the Message*. New York: Bantam.

Magdoff, Harry. 1977. *Imperialism: From the Colonial Age to the Present*. New York: Monthly Review Press.

Maslow, Abraham H. and John J. Honigman. 1970. "Synergy: Some Notes of Ruth Benedict." *American Anthropologist* 72 (April):320–333.

Murray, Charles. 1984. *Losing Ground: American Social Policy, 1950–1980*. New York: Basic Books.

Piven, Frances Fox and Richard A. Cloward. 1971. *Regulating the Poor*. New York: Pantheon.

Rawls, John. 1971. *A Theory of Justice*, Cambridge, Mass.: Harvard University Press.

Reynolds, Bertha C. 1975. *Social Work and Social Living*. Washington, D.C.: National Association of Social Workers.

———. 1985. *An Uncharted Journey*. Hebron, Conn.: Practitioners Press.

Ryan, William. 1971. *Blaming the Victim*. New York: Pantheon.

Storr, Anthony. 1968. *Human Aggression*. New York: Atheneum.

Tawney, R. H. 1964 [1931]. *Equality*. London: Allen and Unwin.

Tucker, Robert C. 1978. *The Marx-Engels Reader*, 2d ed. New York: Norton.

United Nations Center for Human Rights. 1992. *Teaching and Learning About Human Rights: A Manual for Schools of Social Work and the Social Work Profession*. New York: United Nations.

Wagner, David. 1990. *The Quest for a Radical Profession: Social Service Careers and Political Ideology*. Lanham, Md.: University Press of America.

Wineman, Steven. 1984. *The Politics of Human Services: Radical Alternatives to the Welfare State*. Boston: South End Press.

Withorn, Ann. 1984. *Serving the People: Social Services and Social Change*. New York: Columbia University Press.

Wronka, Joseph. 1992. *Human Rights and Social Policy in the 21st Century*. Lanham, Md.: University Press of America.

Zinn, Howard. 1980. *A People's History of the United States*. New York: Harper and Row.

9

Diversity and Populations at Risk: Ethnic Minorities and People of Color

ELAINE PINDERHUGHES

"How am I going to help poor black families when I feel so helpless myself?," complained a social work student. "The problem in working with black families is that the therapist begins to feel as overwhelmed as the client," observed a well-known family therapist. The confusion and sense of entrapment manifested by these two social work practitioners has been a common response in work not only with African American individuals and families but other clients who are people of color or ethnic minorities. The urgent need for training that would prepare all social workers to work effectively with such populations, and to work generally with any client who is culturally different, was recognized by the Council on Social Work Education as early as 1971. Indeed, it has seemed mandatory that social work, with its focus on context and environmental dynamics in the assessment of people's needs and problems, and on the solutions that must be sought, would include the cultural factor. Social work has, in fact, provided leadership among the helping professions in the demand for cultural competence in training and in the development and implementation of curricula that ensure the development of skill for working effectively with ethnic minorities and people of color.

The most recent curriculum policy statement of the Council on Social Work Education (1992) requires 1) that students must be prepared to understand and appreciate cultural and social diversity; and 2) that content must be provided on the experiences, needs, and responses of minorities of color and other groups who "have been subjected to institutionalized forms of oppression."

In the general population ethnic minorities and people of color are rapidly increasing in numbers (U.S. Census 1991; U.S. Department of Labor 1988). Indeed, it is estimated that in the year 2059, when persons born in 1994 will be 65 years old, a majority of U.S. citizens will trace some lineage to Africa, Asia, and South America (White 1992). Currently the U.S. population includes not only the more rapidly reproducing populations that are Native American, African American, Asian American, and Hispanic American, but immigrants from Mexico, the Caribbean, South America, Asia, the Near East, and Africa.

A brief definition of terms is important here. *Culture* generally refers to the ways of living that people devise to meet biological and psychosocial needs. These patterns are handed down from generation to generation, acquire symbolic value, and become incorporated as a system of expectations about norms for how people should think and behave. *Ethnicity* refers to connectedness based on these commonalities that have evolved as a result of shared identity and history based on religion, nationality, and so on. *Race* is often used interchangeably with ethnicity, although they are technically different in meaning (Davis and Proctor, 1989), and culture is often used to refer to both. Race, while a biological term, takes on ethnic meaning if specific ways of living have evolved for members of that biological group. Race is thus embraced in the notion of ethnicity, as seen in the use of the term white Anglo-Saxon Protestant, or black when referring to African Americans.

Ethnic minorities and *people of color* refers to persons who are primarily nonwhite, that is, are from groups whose origin is, for example, Native American, African, Asian, or Latino. Some experts include among those identified as ethnic minorities persons from European ethnic groups such as Italian, Irish, and so on, or who are Jewish; I do not, although it is certainly important for social workers to incorporate knowledge about such ethnic groups into their practice.

Work with ethnic minorities and people of color requires skills in cultural competence. To be effective, work must be consistent with the profession's goals of enhancing the social functioning of clients, of strengthening clients' abilities to cope with their realities, and of improving the quality of their lives. This means that a primary objective should be assisting ethnic minorities of color to remain positively connected with their cultural group and at the same time to live in both their cultural environment and the mainstream.

This also means that social workers must pay attention to culture as a factor in problem formation, problem resolution, and in the helping process itself, which includes assessment, relationship development, intervention, and evaluation of outcome. The specific perspectives, capacities, competencies, and abilities that facilitate such effectiveness, and which are mandatory for cultural competence, include:

1. knowledge of the specific values, beliefs, and cultural practices of clients;

2. the ability to respect and appreciate the values, beliefs, and practices of all clients, including those culturally different, and to perceive such individuals through their own cultural lenses instead of the practitioner's;

3. the ability to be comfortable with difference in others and thus not be trapped in anxiety about difference or defensive behavior to ward it off;

4. the ability to control, and even change, false beliefs, assumptions, and stereotypes, which means one will have less need for defensive behavior to protect oneself;

5. the ability to think flexibly and to recognize that one's own way of thinking and behaving is not the only way; and

6. the ability to behave flexibly. This is demonstrated by the readiness to engage in the extra steps required to sort through general knowledge about a cultural group and to see the specific ways in which knowledge applies or does not apply to a given client. These steps take extra time, effort, and energy (Hodges 1991; Pinderhughes 1989).

Development of these skills is basic to preparation for work with persons of any cultural background, including clients who are ethnic minorities and people of color. Training to ensure such mastery requires a curriculum that addresses both cognitive and attitudinal growth in students. While most experts agree there is no well-conceptualized cultural content in the social work curriculum, there is some consensus that a culturally sensitive theoretical framework for practice with ethnic minorities and people of color must attend to: 1) the cultural reality of ethnic minorities; 2) the significance of minority status; 3) the influence of environmental systems on their cultures; 4) the imperative that ethnic minorities and people of color become bicultural; 5) the significance of socioeconomic status; and 6) the significance of language (DeVore and Schlesinger 1991; Ho 1987; Lum 1986; Chau 1991). In addition, the delivery of this content must enable the student to include herself and her culture as a major factor in the cultural helping encounter (Pinderhughes 1989).

Core theories and concepts that should be included in the content on ethnic minorities and people of color include the following: systems theories, ecological concepts, constructivism, and concepts that explain how culture operates in human functioning, including those explaining minority-majority status, stereotyping and discrimination, racism, difference, culture, ethnicity, race, and power dynamics. This discussion will focus first on concepts that explain general cultural processes as a context for understanding ethnic minorities and people of color. Because it is my opinion that ethnic minorities and people of color can only be understood accurately when seen in the context of their relationship to the larger social system, which also includes the majority group, there will also be some focus on the latter.

Societal Dynamics: History as Context

"All men are created equal and endowed with certain inalienable rights to life, liberty and the pursuit of happiness." Thus reads the Preamble to the Constitution of the United States of America. For generations the ideology of the melting pot has pressed people to interpret "equal" as meaning "alike," and "alike" as personifying "white American middle class." Native Americans and descendants of slaves and immigrants all learned in countless ways that the persons viewed as having the most value and power in the U.S. have been those who embraced the homogenization of the melting pot. From the time of the Civil War through the era of the expansion of the West, and subsequently during the growth of urbanization and industrialization, this thrust toward homogenization urged would-be adherents to give up their ethnicity and abandon their pre-American cultures. To belong and to be embraced, people were encouraged to change their names, disavow old-country values, beliefs and language, relinquish familiar cultural practices (Greeley 1976:5), and become generally ashamed of any identity that was less than "100 percent red-blooded American." Solomon (1976:176) has suggested that "the proponents of the melting pot theory could be terribly cruel to ethnics who would not melt." The pressure to adopt this sameness existed on every level of the American social system, remaining strong until the 1960s.

Historically, the value system underlying social service delivery, even within the field of social work, was based on this melting pot ethic. Problems identified as significant to white middle-class persons were assumed to be the appropriate yardsticks for understanding and delivering services to everyone. The definition of problems, the theoretical constructs that determine assessment and intervention methods, the strategies devised, the programming of services, and even the evaluation of outcomes had been developed in terms of what was appropriate for the white American middle class.

When blacks, who over the years (along with other people of color) had sought acceptance into this melting pot, realized during the civil rights movement that they would always be excluded because they could not change their skin color, they launched a determined effort to change this negative identity that Americans had forced upon them and which had been used as a basis for exclusion. In this undertaking, they struggled to develop pride, power, and a positive sense of identity outside of the melting pot. That effort sparked the desire of other peoples of color to do the same.

In responding to the demands of blacks and other people of color that they be viewed in terms of their strengths, coping efforts, and cultural adaptations rather than via projections and stereotypes, white ethnics also insisted on such recognition. Their claim to power and movement toward reaffirmation of cultural identity was seen to reflect more than a simple reaction to the cry of oppressed or minority groups; it was in fact "one of the standard forms of political expression for all people" (Fieldstein and Giordano 1976). Now recognized as a significant source of group identification and an important factor in the values, family pattern lifestyles and behaviors that have persisted over generations, ethnicity has become identified as a vital force in America (McGoldrick 1982). McGoldrick (1982:4), referring to Greeley's study of cultural influence, states:

> Ethnicity remains a vital force in this country, a major form of group identification, and a major determinant of family patterns and belief systems. . . . There is increasing evidence that ethnic values and identification are retained for many generations after immigration (Greeley 1969, 1978, 1981) and play a significant role in family life and per-

sonal development throughout the life cycle (Lieberman 1974; Teper 1977; Gelfand and Kutzik 1979). Second-, third-, and even fourth-generation Americans, as well as immigrants, differ from the dominant culture in values, lifestyles, and behavior.

Experts hail the rediscovery of ethnicity as a signal that the country is beginning at last "to come to terms with the religious, racial, ethnic, and geographic diversity that exists within its boundaries" (Greeley 1976:6). And they embrace it as a welcome antidote for the sense of powerlessness, impotence, and rootlessness that pervades American life (Fieldstein and Giordano 1976). The rediscovery of ethnicity's validation of group connectedness and positive cultural identity for everyone has provided a means of bestowing meaning and identity in a society grown complex and impersonal (Sanders 1975). The focus on ethnicity also nourishes attributes urgently needed in people today: psychological security, capacity for understanding, and appreciation of difference.

The movement of blacks, other people of color, and white ethnics to reclaim and redefine themselves positively and to press for power in the political arena also mobilized nonethnic groups. In their demands for recognition, such groups have broadened the idea of cultural group beyond the concept of national origin, religion, race, or language to include the notion of interest groups and shared lifestyle. Such groups include persons who have also been denied access to political power: women, gays and lesbians, the handicapped, and the elderly. All of these groups have been engaged in a positive self-redefinition and in the development of strategies for gaining power and access to resources. Despite the activity and ferment of these various groups, some contend that the melting pot ideology remains entrenched. For, it is claimed, occupants of the seats of influence in our government agencies, educational and social service institutions, and in industry still wield their power according to "melting pot" values.

In the human service professions of health, mental health, social services, and education, the thrust toward pluralism in America has led to profound changes. Hospitals, health and mental health settings, and social agencies are now attempting to structure services that are sensitive to cultural preferences of patients and clients. In educational settings, schools are now pressed to offer multicultural education and to include in the curriculum content on a variety of ethnic and racial groups. Prior to the civil rights movement, the major emphasis in terms of environmental understanding had been on class determinants. In the field of social work, as far back as 1975, Giordano and Levine (1975) identified ethnic as well as class determinants as significant in understanding people's problems. They argued that the health, mental health, and social service needs of large numbers of Americans would best be met by organizing services within the natural and structural systems of working-class ethnic communities.

An ongoing debate emerged as to whether class identity has been more significant than ethnicity and race in the programming and utilization of services. Nevertheless, this emphasis on the "culture of poverty," which constituted the first attempts to focus on ethnic minorities, did give more attention to the issue of what kind of supports existed for minorities as they interacted with mainstream culture (Banfield 1974; Lewis 1966). However, this focus was based on a deficit model and tended to stress the negative and dysfunctional, ignoring the positive aspects of culture (Chau 1991; DeVore and Schlesinger 1991).

For example, the presentation of black culture and reality commonly projected a perception of blacks that failed to recognize the perceptual distortions involved and the source of them: the lens of the white American middle class (Tidwell 1990). Since Billingsley's landmark book in 1968, there have been persistent efforts by experts to point out the need for training that recognizes the strengths of blacks and prepares service providers to enhance those strengths.

Over time, as other people of color joined blacks in pressing for recognition and power in the larger social system, curriculum planners began to incorporate content on all of them, under the rubric of minority. It was suggested that a focus on minority provided an understanding that minority means another level of categorization beyond that associated with the ethnic group. Based on subordination and oppression by the dominant group, minority status, it was argued, embraced certain commonalities that needed to be identified and understood.

Some members of these groups objected to being lumped together, expressing concern that the uniqueness of each group would be lost in that effort. Many felt that the focus on oppression and powerlessness ignored the strengths of the group and failed to attend to their vitality and ability to prevail (Chau 1991; Lister 1987). However, as the universal significance of culture gained credibility, training programs added specific content on a wide variety of ethnic groups, giving rise to a concern for the phenomenon of "incremental ethnicity" or the "willy nilly addition to curricula" of information on a multitude of groups (Fieldstein and Giordano 1976). Objections to this state of affairs centered on the virtual impossibility of offering content on every ethnic population relevant to the location of a given social service delivery program or educational institution.

Some experts were reiterating an often-heard objection to the teaching of material on specific ethnic groups, namely, that it led to a view of a particular group as homogeneous and failed to account for the differences within the group, thus constituting another form of stereotyping. Various experts articulated the need for theoretical constructs that cut across the various groups, identifying universals and making the bewildering array of differences more manageable (Landau 1982). Moreover, debate persists concerning "whether it is cultural difference (the ethnocultural perspective) or structural deficiency (the minority perspective) that accounts for the problems encountered" by minorities and people of color (Chau 1991:26).

In the unclear atmosphere of shifting demand that has characterized training efforts related to work with minorities and people of color, practitioners and administrators have struggled to cope with the complexities and to keep pace. Education and training programs have spanned the problem and special needs areas of health, mental health, social welfare, and education. They are offered in professional schools, at service sites, and in a variety of continuing education formats and have been accompanied by administrative efforts to increase representation from these populations. The knowledge, skill building, and technical assistance offered to service providers and students have expanded rapidly. Ideas have been borrowed from training programs in intercultural communication that prepare people to function in the international arena for institutions and agencies such as the U.S. Army, the diplomatic corps, and multinational corporations (Brislin and Pedersen 1976).

Conceptual Frameworks and Theoretical Perspectives

Understanding of several key concepts is essential for social workers to fully grasp the significance of ethnicity and diversity. These include the relevance of cultural values, systems theory, culture as part of an ecological process, constructivism, difference, and power.

Value Orientation Theory

An understanding of the minority reality must be built upon theoretical approaches that explain cultural dynamics generally and the condition of ethnic minorities and people of color specifically. The concept of culture is a complex one. The province of anthropologists, sociologists, psychologists, and other social scientists, it has been a topic of disagreement among scholars who have gotten entangled in the intricacies of its processes. One approach to understanding is that of value orientation theory (Spiegel 1982), which brings order and some organization to the bewildering array of cultural differences that exist among people. Developed by anthropologist Clyde Kluckholn, the theory identifies five universals around which the value orientations and values of cultural groups are organized. These include how they value time, activity, man's relationship to man, man's relationship to nature, and the nature of man. For each of these value orientations there are several choices, for example, Americans often emphasize future time, Africans emphasize past time, and Puerto Ricans emphasize the present. Values grow out of these emphases, from which follow beliefs, cultural practices, norms, and so on. Americans who emphasize the future and autonomy in relationships embrace values that center on planning, achievement, the accumulation of wealth, and development of self. Latinos who emphasize the present and hierarchy in relationships value spirituality and respect of authority.

Value orientation theory can facilitate students' awareness of the difference in values between the American mainstream and the cultures of the world, between themselves and their clients, and the significance of this for the expectations of client and helper. It makes crystal clear the vastly different views that exist for persons of different cultures concerning many of the phenomena about which social workers concern themselves. For example, a Latino father who sees it as his duty to protect his adolescent daughter may not understand a social worker's effort to help him accept her attempts to be like her American peers: dating alone, living away from home, or becoming sexually active. A Cambodian client may think taking a biopsy of her child's tumor might release spirits while a Western social worker might define refusal to consent to a biopsy as medical neglect. Similarly, a worker may assume that all clients want to be asked to give informed consent to treatment, when members of some cultural groups find the whole idea quite odd and inappropriate. The use of value orientation theory helps students understand how the way the client is assessed, the helping strategies chosen, and the process and criteria used to evaluate the outcome of treatment are based on values that may be very different from those of the client. It also crystallizes clients' vulnerability to problems in relating, communicating, and interacting that are embodied in the helping encounter and that can jeopardize the work when client and helper have different cultural backgrounds. This approach also clarifies the commonality among minorities in their emphasis on collaterality and collective values such as the family, kinship, clan, and church (Anderson 1992; Ho 1987).

The cultural model of ethnic-sensitive practice emerges from this theoretical phenomenological approach. According to Longres (1991), the value orientation model is considered most effective for understanding immigrants and refugees and less useful in explaining the situation of ethnic minorities and people of color who have been exposed to the dominant culture. Issues related to majority-minority status and situations where ethnicity, race and/or class overlap in the lives of minorities are seen as largely unaccounted for as these factors influence and are influenced by each other and must be taken into account in any understanding of culture. (Elsewhere, using this value orientation framework as a base, I have conceptualized a "victim system culture" that, as a response to oppression, appears to be shared to some degree by all ethnic minorities as well as other victims of oppression [Pinder-hughes 1982b, 1985].)

Systems Theory

While Kluckholn's theory encourages a focus on strengths and adaptation made by the cultural group and is excellent for delivering a comparative view of culture, its phenomenological nature renders it static and inattentive to the interactive, systemic aspects of culture. Only systems theory, and concepts that explain ecological process and power dynamics, can fully explain these complex phenomena that operate to create the realities of ethnic minorities of color. These theories and concepts give attention to larger societal processes (including those on an international level) as well as to those governing individual, family, and group/community functioning and the way in which these various levels influence and are influenced by one another. A systems perspective emphasizes the interdependence of the many areas of human functioning that affect and are affected by culture. With such an approach, observers acknowledge "systems above, below and beside the problem they have chosen to work on" (Bochner 1982:7). What becomes key is the relatedness of the individual; the family as a group; the family as a part of the social system; the value orientation of the individual, family, subgroup, or social system; the geographical setting; and the interpretation of all these systems and processes that operate in a mutual, reverberating, and reciprocal manner (Papajohn and Spiegel 1976). While the most significant are the social system value orientations, the circular way in which all these factors influence and are influenced by each other must be taken into account in any understanding of culture.

Culture as Part of an Ecological Process

Culture was earlier defined as the sum total of ways of living built up by a group of human beings and transmitted from one generation to another. It refers to practices such as values, norms, beliefs, attitudes, folkways, behavior styles, or traditions that enable the survival of the group as a whole and of the individuals within, becoming key factors in the formation of both group and individual identity. Giordano and Levine (1975:5) observe that components of the broader environment:

> nurture, transmit, and teach the symbols of communication, values and norms of behavior, rewards and punishments. They also provide a means of feedback. All this is culturally determined, solidifying a communal bond, a sense of belonging, identity formation and self-esteem. Therefore, two identities are established—self and group— which are etched at birth and expressed more on an unconscious than conscious level. The tenacity of this process becomes embedded in the very preservation of life itself.

The survival of the group and its members is best assured when the environment (defined as all that is external to the individual and family, including the neighborhood, peer group affiliations, church, school or employment, governmental and economic institutions, etc.) provides appropriate resources at the appropriate time in an appropriate way. Necessary resources, defined as protection, security, support, and supplies, ensure biological, cognitive, emotional, and social development. Lack, distortion, or excess in these environmental nutrients cause stress and conflict resulting in disorganization and malfunctioning on individual, group, and societal levels (Germain 1979). The interaction between the environment—whether depriving or nourishing—and the group, family, and individual is mediated by culture. On each of these levels, and in light of both environmental deficiencies and resources, culture is a contributor. This multilevel systemic interaction has been identified by a number of observers, including Chestang (1976), Germain (1979), and Papajohn and Spiegel (1976).

The mediation function of culture is best understood through the concept of social role, which links the individual with family, group, and society via the culturally patterned behaviors that cut across these various levels of functioning. Ecosystem theory offers an understanding of the individual in relation to a natural support system of family, friends, neighbors, and community (Ho 1987). Social roles program individuals to adopt behavior that is complementary to that of other persons in these systems while also satisfying inner needs and drives. Personality and ego functioning develop, and the self evolves through the unfolding of internal processes as stimulated by the environment. Key among environmental stimuli for a given individual are persons enacting roles that are culturally programmed. On the various levels of human functioning—that is, family, group, and larger social system—culture, through social roles, acts as a mediator, determining life cycle tasks and determining what is appropriate mastery of them (Carter and McGoldrick 1980; DeVore and Schlesinger 1981).

Changes that occur in the interaction of the cultural group with the larger environment jeopardize the established reciprocity and complementarity in culturally programmed roles. Immigration, urbanization, industrialization, and other environmental processes such as exploitation, oppression, or ethnic/racial conflict can bring about such changes, pressing people to take on different values and roles in order to cope. These shifts threaten the balance that has existed in role function, jeopardizing both family and individual functioning.

Constructivism

All of the ideas examined above are incorporated in the concept of constructivism. According to this key concept, culture is viewed as the most influential determinant of meaning in the events and experiences of people. Culture carries within it history, beliefs, ways of doing things, and processes of communication that give meaning to an individual's experiences, both intimate and public (Fisher 1991). This perspective is implicit in Sue's (1978) concept of "world view." A systemic notion that illuminates the interaction of the internal and the external in human functioning, constructivism's central premise is that the reality that humans perceive is created by them (Fisher 1991). Knowledge is constructed based on the meaning people attribute to their experiences. Taking responsibility for the meaning given to one's experience (and thus for the reality that one creates) means acknowledgment of the role of choice in that meaning. Thus, unlike objectivism, which posits that there are correct ways of knowing and absolute solutions to problems, constructivism endorses the existence of multiple truths and multiple realities. It challenges the claims of Truth embodied in Western thinking and the privilege of power that results when others accept such claims. Avoiding the trap of the "expert" and of the stance of oneself as right and others as wrong, constructivism suggests that each body of knowledge is equally valid when taken from within its own frame of reference (Fisher 1991:20).

From this perspective, because we are responsible for our own constructions of reality and because each person's individual reality is valid, our interactions with others are guided by a stance of nonintrusiveness and nonjudgmentalism. One then strives to clarify the basis (the context) for a given individual's position, which opens up the possibility of generating clarity concerning similarities and differences between one's position and that of another. Immediately there exists an opportunity for negotiation. These ideas naturally endorse flexibility, being able to tolerate ambiguity and uncertainty, being able "to let go of the security of the known and to embrace the flow of events" (Fisher 1991:9).

Some experts, however, have criticized constructivism, insisting that it generates uncertainty, undermines order, and, on a political level, represents a call for anarchy. Fisher (1991:21) insists that the contrary is true: "Constructivism is a call for respecting every person's meaning as valid and for negotiating the power (that accrues with the acceptance of that meaning) rather than assuming it." Critics also suggest that constructivism can validate bias and stereotyped perceptions of others, depending on its use.

Applied to social work practice, the constructivist approach requires the social worker to search for and pursue the meanings assigned by the client that are culturally determined and explain his or her experience. It supports the sharing of knowledge and understanding between client and practitioner, with problematic situations being addressed as "negotiated explorations rather than as situations requiring the application of preconceived interventions" (Fisher 1991:9). At all times the social worker seeks to connect with the client's frame of reference and is aware of the part she is playing in the reality experienced by the client.

Difference: Stereotyping, Discrimination, Deviance, Racism, the Societal Projection Process

The differences that exist between two people of different cultures who interact, the result of the complex, interactive processes described above, may cause them to perceive the world and each other vastly differently. The perception of difference in others, whether based on beliefs, language and behavior, or appearance, impels each to categorize himself and others as "we" and "they" (Bochner 1982). This categorization becomes the basis for prejudice, stereotyping, discrimination, and racism, phenomena that have been studied extensively by social psychologists.

Concepts that explain this response to difference all focus on the key role of anxiety. Stereotyping has been explained in various ways: 1) as a generic norm of behavior; 2) as a result of competition for scarce resources; 3) as a result of the process of "deindividuation," that is, when people are not known or not visible, they are not seen as individuals; and 4) as a result of the violation of laws of interpersonal distance. Brislin (1981) suggests that prejudice or prejudging another has been explained as having the purpose of 1) easing adjustment because it is behavior that is rewarded; 2) defending the personality against harsh realities concerning the self and thus protecting self-esteem; 3) providing a vehicle for reaffirming prized values related to religion, society, and so on; and 4) providing a mechanism for organizing many social stimuli. Consequently, prejudice and prejudging are commonly employed by majority group members in their interaction with persons of color (and vice versa) as anxiety-reducing mechanisms.

The "we-they" categorization that characterizes prejudice has also been explained as a human issue reflected in "the universal presence of enemies and allies," to be understood as emerging from developmental processes of the human mind and intrapsychic processes relating to identity (Volkan 1991). The "we-they" categorization has also been identified as a "useful habit of mind" (Berlin 1990:46) and also as having a basis in physiological development. Psychophysiological processes in humans are believed to program a drive to dichotomize perceptions and behavior (Pinderhughes 1986). According to this view, physiological functioning is believed to be responsible for perceptions that take the form of paired complementarities such as "good-bad" and "we-they." Early developmental conflicts can influence the use of projections on others and societal projections to gain relief from anxiety (May 1976).

Somewhat related to these ideas is the notion of social deviance, which refers to behavior that is viewed as contradictory to the social norm. Social systems, declare some social scientists, maintain stability by identifying certain persons or behaviors as deviant. In defining what is not acceptable, the system uses deviance to separate the normal from the non-normal, thus reinforcing boundaries within systems (Coser 1956). All of these societal processes that constitute anxiety-reducing mechanisms—stereotyping, discrimination, prejudice, deviance—entail projection upon another.

There is little agreement among experts as to whether the relationship between persons who are culturally different determines or is determined by the existence and content of the stereotypes held. Klineberg (1982) identifies a circular process in which stereotypes function in both capacities. Scholars also disagree as to whether conflict is inevitable between people of different cultures and as to whether intimacy and getting to know the culturally different can automatically reduce bias. Multicultural societies do exist in which persons of culturally different groups live in relative harmony despite the hypothesis that intercultural conflicts are inevitable. Switzerland, Hawaii, and New Zealand have been identified as examples (Bochner 1982; Klineberg 1982).

While stereotypes can play a key role in the relationships that develop between persons who are culturally different, they can also determine the meaning assigned to the differences, themselves determining minority-majority status. For in combination with the mechanism of stratification, stereotypes aid in creating structures in the social system that circumscribe people's life chances, lifestyles, and thus their cultural responses (Berger and Federico 1985). In this situation, a dominant group uses biological, psychological, or cultural characteristics to differentiate others from itself. Through the mechanism of stratification, the group puts the differentiated (the "other" group) in the subordinate position, isolating them and barring necessary access to resources, thus reinforcing dominance for itself. This stratification is institutionalized into social structures so that the expectations generated by the dominant group concerning tasks and functions appropriate for the subordinate group have a profound effect upon the conditions of the subordinates, as well as those who are dominant. Power thus becomes a central factor in these dynamics.

Racism in the U.S. has operated in this manner to influence the realities, life chances, and lifestyles of ethnic minorities and people of color. Racism is defined as the existence of structural arrangements in the social system that allow access to resources by the dominant group, and not by the subordinate group, based on belief in the superiority of the former.

Thus, the status assignment of people to dominant and subordinate groups, or to majority and minority groups, which is erected through power arrangements and maintained by social structures such as racism, helps determine how people are viewed, how they view themselves, their access to resources, and their response to these conditions. Hopps (1982) suggests that true understanding of minority status requires understanding of the various levels of oppression endured by the group. Longres (1982:8) suggests that minority status exists when "subordinated groups whose right to self-determination in community life—that is, whose culture, traditions, and economic and social well-being—is at any point in time jeopardized." According to this definition, Longres lists African Americans, Native American, Mexican Americans, and Puerto Ricans, and questions whether some of the newer immigrants of color may be added in time. The key issue, no matter the level of oppression and who is identified as minority or majority, appears to be that of dominance and subordination. Power, therefore, becomes a primary factor in cultural process. Klineberg (1982) suggests that stereotypes are forms of rationalization to maintain the status quo and justify domination and immoral behavior on the part of persons in power: "There is no doubt in my mind that stereotypes are indeed shaped by social, economic, political and historical antecedents, and that they are used in order to justify the subjugation, exploitation and even elimination of others" (Klineberg 1982:48).

Race signifies biological heritage and thus is not technically a cultural phenomenon. It takes on a cultural significance as a result of the social phenomena described above. Stratification and stereotyping contribute to the meaning assigned to class status as well as to racial categorization. For both the dominant and subordinate groups, class status as well as racial categorization can determine life chances, coping responses, and lifestyles.

Ethnic/racial structures and identity are further mediated by "distinctive dispositions and behaviors" directly resulting from status related to work identity, degree of wealth, and the values placed on them (DeVore and Schlesinger 1991). Debates abound as to the influence of class in comparison to race in the circumstances of ethnic minorities and people of color. Davis and Proctor (1989) suggest that the determining factor in the subordinate status of ethnic minorities is race. Kessler and Neighbors (1986) cite their research which shows that race has a high correlation with psychological distress, especially among the poor. Cultural background thus can be seen to embrace racial categorization, ethnic belonging, social class, and minority-majority group status (Brislin 1981). Key concepts that shed light on these processes include the societal projection process, ethnicity, race, ethclass, biculturalism, the dual perspective, and sociocultural dissonance.

Societal Projection Process

The concept of the societal projection process also explains these dynamics. Particularly illuminating in terms of minorities of color, since they are identified as among the victims of this process, this notion suggests that one group, the beneficiaries in a society, perceive and treat another group, the victims, as inferior or incompetent, thereby providing stability for themselves. Bowen (1978) wrote:

> These groups fit the best criteria for long-term, anxiety relieving projection. They are vulnerable to become the pitiful objects of the benevolent, over sympathetic segment of society that improves its functioning at the expense of the pitiful. Just as the least adequate child in a family can become more impaired when he becomes an object of pity and sympathetic help from the family, so can the low-

est segment of society be chronically impaired by the very attention designed to help. No matter how good the principle behind such programs, it is essentially impossible to implement them without the built-in complications of the projection process. Such programs attract workers who are over sympathetic with less fortunate people. They automatically put the recipient in a "one down," inferior position and they either keep them there or get angry at them.   (445)

On the basis of this concept, it can be hypothesized that these victim groups are maintained in relatively powerless positions where they serve as a balancing mechanism for the systems in which they exist. They provide stability for the beneficiaries because, excluded and kept separate, they are used as receptacles for much of the tension, conflict, contradiction, and confusion that exists within the various systems. Such stability is illustrated in the interactions between ghetto communities and suburbs.

From this view, in becoming systems balancers and tension relievers in the social system, persons of color, as victims, must learn to live with stress, conflict, and contradiction. They must find ways to cope with the powerlessness that is mobilized and to empower themselves. Coping responses vary from time to time and from victim to victim, but can become a fundamental part of the culture developed by the group. Culture represents people's responses to the political, economic, and social realities they face (Navarro 1980)—responses in the form of values, social roles, norms, and family styles that grew out of efforts to cope and achieve a sense of power. These dynamics apply likewise to beneficiaries, that is, white, middle- and upper-class people whose responses also take on cultural meaning. Such an understanding allows for appreciation of the creativity and complexity involved in cultural responses and for appreciation of the subtleties and nuances that characterize cultural differences that, rich and varied as they are, become understood in terms of the strengths they embody (Green 1982). It also crystallizes the significance of power in cultural processes (Pinderhughes 1989).

Cultural Identity

On an individual level, cultural belonging involves processes, both conscious and unconscious, that satisfy a deep psychological need for a sense of historical continuity, security, and identity (Giordano and

Levine 1975). Cultural belonging refers to a sense of connectedness with the world that can be seen as both vertical and horizontal, external and internal. Vertical connectedness refers to one's linkage with time and history, one's continuity that is "based on a preconscious recognition of traditionally held patterns of thinking, feeling, and behaving" (Arce 1982:137). Horizontal connectedness involves present linkage to others who share these same ways of thinking and belonging in the world. It thus constitutes a bridge to all that is external. Through these vertical and horizontal linkages, cultural identity guards against emotional cutoff from the past and psychological abandonment in the present.

A cultural sense of self is key to healthy self-esteem, for culture forms part of an individual's own self-representation and contributes to the sense of cohesiveness, sameness, and continuity that is the essence of psychological integrity (Erikson 1968). Gehrie (1979) has stated:

> The internal experience of a cultural sense of self is a major factor contributing to the balance of the self-esteem system. In this respect, the significance of culture is internal, and forms part of an individual's own self-representation. Feelings about parents, children, and other important persons, in addition to their psychological role in development, act as culture-carriers, and contribute to the formation of the person's own internal sense of self. In such a manner, culture comes to play a fundamental role in human development from the inside, in addition to its well-known role in behavior and socialization. (170)

There is a direct relationship between how one feels about one's ethnic or cultural background and how one feels about oneself, for a positive sense of ethnicity can be an important factor in one's emotional stability (New York Institute on Pluralism and Group Identity 1980). Being secure in one's own cultural identity enables one to act with greater freedom, flexibility, and openness to others of different background (McGoldrick 1982).

Thus, an integration of concepts explaining cultural dynamics that are basic to understanding ethnic minorities and people of color suggests the following: culture is a factor in the interactive processes between individuals, their families, their groups, and their environment; in the assignment of people's life chances and lifestyles by their social structures; in how people are viewed and how they view themselves; in the cohesiveness and solidarity of groups and the manner of survival; in the structure and process of family dynamics; in the development of personality and ego functioning, including the sense of cohesiveness and the stability of the self, in the coping mechanisms evolved, and the identity achieved.

Difference

As suggested above, difference and how it operates in human functioning is critical knowledge for work with ethnic minorities and people of color. The experience of difference from another is caused by a variety of conditions and human attributes of which culture is only one (Davis and Proctor 1989). Bochner (1982) identifies others, such as beliefs, language, behavior, and appearance, and elsewhere I discuss the significance of sex role, sexual orientation, socioeconomic status or class, size, and handicap (Pinderhughes 1989). Experiences related to being different in these ways usually occur very early in one's life and become associated with a variety of feelings, many of which remain strong, predominantly negative, and influential in people's behavior. Davis and Proctor (1989:4, quoting Rosenbaum [1986]) state: "Perceiving dissimilarities between one's self and others is believed to have potent and often adverse effects for those individuals involved."

There are several explanations for this predominantly negative response to difference. One centers on the fact that difference carries an implication of comparison and thus inequality. It seems we must place a *value* on the difference and see it in terms of "better than" or "less than," evoking inferences of both power and negativity. We seem unable to view "different from" as meaning merely "not the same as," which means that one of the two differing subjects must be seen negatively.

American values compound this tendency for difference to be associated with a differential in power. They emphasize competition, winning, and being "number one," and they promote the importance of "better than," the use of comparisons, ranking, and stratifying, and do not encourage respect for uniqueness or difference except in the sense of being "the best." "American" thus not only symbolizes power in the sense of all ethnocentric bias, but also in the sense that the values themselves carry the meaning of "better than."

Compounding the discomfort stemming from the negative value placed on difference, or perhaps making for greater vulnerability to it, are residuals from early developmental struggles. One hypothesis suggests that being different evokes a sense of aloneness, isolation, and abandonment that signifies absence of connection to others and threatens the sense of psychological wholeness and intactness that people need. This fairly automatic response to difference, the hypothesis suggests, triggers old reactions related to mastering of the early developmental task of separation-individuation. The child's struggle to develop a self that is separate from mother is marked by anxiety, rage, a sense of helplessness, and intense ambivalence that diminish when mastery is achieved. For most people, however, this struggle is never completely resolved. Somewhat connected is the hypothesis that holds that the negative feelings people direct to others who are different have their genesis in anger and anxiety stemming from early narcissistic injuries where rejection and failure of object mirroring have caused a deep sense of abandonment and exclusion.

Residuals from these early developmental experiences compound the automatic tendency of people to react to unfamiliarity in others, and to things not understood, with confusion, fear, and anxiety. They push people to deal with the not knowing that is associated with difference through the use of ready explanations, such as "old wives' tales," myths and stereotypes, and through projection.

Projection, a well-known device for allaying anxiety, is also closely connected to the issue of power. The use of stereotypes and projection can been seen as "power behaviors"—since they are characterized by a stance that often elevates the self above the other through the perception of "badness" and negativity in that other.

Ethnicity

As mentioned above, ethnic and racial identity are primary sources of people's experience of themselves as different from others. Identity based on ethnicity is a manifestation of a person's linkage through time and via history to others who share the same way of seeing and behaving in the world and is thus a bridge to all that is external. At the same time, ethnicity is profoundly connected to one's internal sense of sameness and continuity, becoming the essence of psychological integrity, self-worth, and self-value, all factors that mark healthy emotional and social functioning (Erikson 1968).

The significance of ethnic identity to many people is illustrated in the excitement, energy, and even pleasure that is associated with their ethnic background. People need to feel predominantly positive about who they are and about the groups to which they belong (Pinderhughes 1989). A pervasive sense of denigration, shame, guilt, pain, or even ambivalence can undermine this much needed predominantly positive valuation of self. When people feel positive about who they are and to whom they belong, they are free to interact positively with those who are different, to respect the culture of those who are different, and are less frightened and "up tight" about difference (McGoldrick 1982).

When people feel predominantly negative about their cultural background and their self-worth is threatened, they experience pain, anger, shame, guilt, and other uncomfortable reactions whenever they are in contact with those who are culturally different. Conflict, or a strong sense of ambivalence, arouses similar reactions. People will strive mightily to avoid feeling this discomfort and will engage in a variety of maneuvers such as denying who they are, avoiding any circumstances that remind them of this, isolating and disconnecting themselves from their cultural group, and spending a lot of energy disproving the stereotypes projected on them and/or their group.

It is important to note that the status assignment of one's ethnic group can significantly influence the ethnic meaning that people develop, making power a key element in ethnic process. Both high and low assignment can contribute positive as well as negative meaning. For example, Anglo-Saxon identity is far more idealized in this country than is the ethnic identity of people of color. Members of high-status groups experience a sense of value, entitlement, and privilege that can contribute to high ethnic self-regard, but they may also experience a sense of denigration and negativity due to guilt, pain, and confusion related to their high status. In contrast, low-status groups, particularly ethnic minority groups, constantly struggle with societal denigration and the negative responses engendered, requiring them to exert extensive effort to function in ways that are not destructive to themselves and their sense of themselves.

The presence of culturally different others can mobilize in persons who are uncomfortable and confused concerning their cultural identity the anxiety and discomfort that they have internalized concerning who they are. They become so preoccupied with managing that discomfort that they are not free to interact with others in ways that promote comfortable and respectful relationships. The confusion, guilt, shame, anger, and/or sense of worthlessness they have internalized about their ethnic background compound that automatic anxiety that people often have in relation to difference.

Race

Race constitutes another level of difference and of cultural identity for ethnic minorities. It is best understood when considered separately from ethnicity. Originally referring to biological origin and physical appearance, the concept of race is more inclusive than ethnicity, embracing a number of ethnic groups within a given racial category. Race has now acquired a social meaning in which biological differences, through the mechanism of stereotyping, have become markers for status assignment within the social system. As discussed above, complex power-assigning social structures reinforce the status assignment of racial groups, creating life opportunities, lifestyles, and quality of life that cause race to have cultural meaning and, at the same time, reinforce myths and distortions about both majority and minority groups. The anxiety that is mobilized by difference in general, and by ethnic differences in particular, can become heightened when the difference is racial. Understanding racial meaning and learning to manage the unhelpful responses that one can develop to ease the anxiety is a difficult process. Nevertheless, in our society, where diversity is so rapidly escalating and where the primary differences will be between whites and ethnic minorities of color, understanding is mandatory for social workers.

Much of the anxiety and resistance associated with racial meaning and behavior is related to the pain it arouses. Elsewhere (Pinderhughes 1989) I discuss the reactions of many whites, for example, when they attempt to identify their reactions to racial difference. They may respond with anger, attacking, and avoidance behavior, such as focusing on good deeds they have done, on mistreatment of themselves by persons of color, or terrible acts of others (not themselves) against people of color. Eventually they focus on what parents, teachers, and other adults taught them as children about race, but they are often very reluctant to discuss current attitudes or actions. Resistance can be enormous. The ease with which this can occur is illustrated by the Greenson et al. (1982) description of therapists' resistance to accepting the experiences reported by an African-American analytic trainee-patient as real, not fantasies or the sign of paranoia. His resistance to information that contradicted his own beliefs about African Americans was apparently a protection against the shame and guilt stemming from his white identity that were mobilized in the interaction.

The pain behind this reluctance is usually connected to the guilt and shame associated with privileged position. And since racial identity can also contribute to one's sense of self as worthwhile, it is critical for white people, for example, to figure out what they need to do to feel positive about being white. Usually this involves acknowledging the reality of the benefit that accrues from being white, taking responsibility for one's behavior so that one can feel valued as a white, and becoming comfortable and flexible in relationships with people of color. Knowledge concerning these dynamics and how they apply to the self is critical for work with ethnic minorities and people of color.

Persons of color must know themselves and manage the negative responses, in the form of anger and avoidance, that they have internalized as a result of their cultural experiences. The confusion of immigrant persons of color about the matter of race and their lack of preparation for the depth of racial antagonism in this country, which can leave significant scars, must be understood. What people of color are most reluctant to examine, however, is how they have internalized racism and collude in its perpetuation. The major issue they seek to avoid is that of skin color. Behind their resistance is exceptional pain and guilt.

People of color must, therefore, learn how to cope with the negative feelings they carry and learn to behave in ways that are not destructive to themselves and their goals. Managing their realities requires that they be strong, clear-minded, able to process complexities, flexible, and able to manage their feelings, no matter how intense. Not so easily understood, but just as important, is the fact that while persons of color need to be able to engage in a sorting through process concerning any given interaction where negative feelings are mobilized, so too must any white person who aims to interact comfortably and effectively with them. Closeness to people of color requires helping professionals to acquire the ability to tolerate pain: both the pain that is universally experienced by people of color and the discomfort of whites that is associated with their privileged status. This situation means that the skills needed by ethnic minorities and people of color to cope with their realities (that is, being strong, clear-minded) are also needed by whites who interact with them.

Mastery of content related to systems dynamics and their relationship to concepts such as majority-minority status, difference, deviance, ethnicity, and race lays a foundation for understanding several additional key concepts.

Ethclass

The concept of ethclass (DeVore and Schlesinger 1991) refers to the combined effect of ethnicity/race and class membership upon the values, life chances, and vicissitudes that confront ethnic minorities. Class exerts considerable influence on the significance and meaning of cultural identity, again demonstrating the importance of power in human functioning. While there have been attempts to show that class is a more potent force than race, Kessler and Neighbors (1986) present evidence concerning the primary significance of race, particularly for the poor.

Biculturalism

The concept of biculturalism is the ability to live with some degree of comfort in the world of the mainstream and also in the minority world. Ability to be bicultural facilitates psychosocial well-being and may even reflect unusual strength, flexibility, and competent functioning (Pinderhughes 1982b). Bicultural socialization (De Anda 1984) facilitates biculturalism, which occurs when minority persons are able to become bilingual; have exposure to persons who serve as models, mediators, and translators to teach and guide; receive feedback upon their efforts to adapt to the expectations of the mainstream; and develop problem-solving skills that enable coping with the realities of the mainstream.

The Dual Perspective

The dual perspective suggests that ethnic minorities of color live in two environments: the larger dominant environment that is the mainstream, and the immediate nurturing environment that consists of family and neighborhood (Norton 1978). The latter can lend support and neutralize the destructive effects of the former. The significance of the family and the neighborhood as mediating factors in the denigration and negative experiences of ethnic minorities and people of color with the larger society must always be taken into account (McRoy 1990).

Sociocultural Dissonance

Sociocultural dissonance (Chau 1989) highlights the significance of cultural transition in the experience of ethnic minorities. Transitions related to immigration, migration, and societal value changes create unique vulnerabilities. Consequences include conflicts in values as reflected in role, relationship, and identity conflicts, loss of support systems that can provide nurturance and can neutralize the effects of prejudice, discrimination, and racism (Pinderhughes 1989).

Power

Power is an overarching concept that helps to focus on the systemic nature of strength and control in human functioning (Pinderhughes 1989). It especially helps to clarify the relationship between ethnic minorities of color and the majority group. It is therefore a concept that is key to understanding both groups, their interaction in general and how this affects the role of social work. As we have seen, power is a factor in the systemic processes that create and maintain majority-minority status, such as stereotyping, discrimination, racism, and the societal projection process. It is also significant in the meaning and responses associated with difference generally and with ethnicity and race particularly. As Chau (1992:32) suggests with respect to ethnic minorities, culturally related issues of power, authority, and control are involved in intergenerational, spousal, and kinship situations as well as in superior-subordinate and worker client-interactions. Longres' (1991) status model of ethnic-sensitive practice also emphasizes the significance of power in its identification of ethnic and racial stratification systems as pivotal in the troubles and realities of ethnic minorities and people of color.

Pervasive though it is in human functioning and in the helping endeavor, power has remained a dirty word, avoided as a focus in social work training. Power may be defined as the capacity to influence for one's own benefit the forces that affect one's life space. Basch (1975:513) contends that "throughout life, the feeling of controlling one's destiny to some reasonable extent is the essential psychological component of all aspects of life." Thus, the perception of oneself as having some power over the forces that control one's life is essential to one's mental health. Powerlessness is painful and people seek to avoid feeling powerless by behavior that will create a sense of power (McClelland 1975).

Power and powerlessness thus become critical in people's lives. Power exists on an individual level in terms of mastery; on an interactional level in terms of dominance-subordinance; on a group and family level in terms of status, leadership, influence, and decision making; and on an institutional level in terms of authority. These dynamics define and give significance to the existence of majority groups, minority groups, and other groups that differ in terms of race, ethnicity, and other distinguishing characteristics. Through social structures, the majority or dominant group maintains its power by excluding subordinates who have been differentiated and stratified; by denying them access to resources; by setting up expectations, tasks, and functions that affect the lifestyles, life chances, and quality of life for both themselves—the dominant ones—as well as for the subordinate groups; and by determining the way in which both groups view themselves and each other.

As I suggested above, power not only is significant to the creation and maintenance of designations of social-group belonging, but also is critical to other levels of human functioning, which are directly affected by the circular feedback processes that operate among them. In addition, social-group status, whether majority or minority, is a consequence of power arrangements, and, in turn, is a factor in perceptions of self and others.

How people respond to perceptions that they have or lack power must be understood by social workers. The specific behavioral responses that are manifested are often intricately connected with the problems clients bring. For example, as individuals, minority people of color react to being tension relievers, anxiety reducers, and victims in the social system by behaviors that aim to provide them a sense of power. Many of them struggle not to accept the projections of the powerful that they are incompetent, dumb, crazy, a stud, sexual, or dependent. Considerable effort is expended to ward off a sense of powerlessness. People adopt behaviors in which they identify with the aggressor (which leads to feelings of self-hatred); are guarded (seen by the powerful as being paranoid); strike out (seen by the powerful as being violent); and are oppositional, passive-aggressive, or autonomous (seen by the powerful as being stubborn). It is important to consider that the dependency response to conditions of powerlessness does not mean ethnic minorities and people of color desire it; instead, they may adopt dependency to get a sense of power or to be close to persons who actually have power (McClelland 1975). They may also try to get a sense of power by assuming the negative attributions of the dominant society in an exaggerated way, for example, by being a super-stud, super-dumb, or super-dependent. Although reactive, these behaviors, which Chestang (1976) identified as paradoxical mechanisms, also have meaning because they facilitate a feeling that one is the initiator.

The process that creates these mechanisms is the same as the process that marks paradoxical communication. All of these behaviors, which need to be understood by social workers as adaptive responses to the powerlessness engendered by environmental pressures and discrimination, are too often seen as signs of deficiency and ignored (Chau 1991). Adaptive though they are, such behaviors are also maladaptive and often become extremely costly. While being dependent, oppositional, passive-aggressive, and autonomous can provide a sense of power, such behaviors may encourage one to react rather than act. If one is unable to function except in a reactive way, this can prevent one from developing the ability to assume leadership, exercise initiative, make choices, and behave in a self-differentiated way.

Persons who have power experience it as gratifying and pleasurable, are able to affect systems, and create opportunities for themselves, take responsibility, and exert leadership. However, they may also be fearful (of those who are powerless or of losing their power), angry, and guilty. Having the power to define the powerless, they can also project onto the powerless their own unacceptable attributes, such as laziness, sexuality, dirtiness, and so on. These tendencies may be repressed and projected, and then are perceived as existing in the powerless. These projections are then used to provide justification for maintaining power and control over these victims. Persons in power then can blame the powerless for assuming these projections. If the powerless fail to assume these projections, those in the more powerful roles can perceive them as having done so anyway or can get angry at them (Bowen 1978).

Other behaviors that result from having a position of power include being controlling and/or dominating, expressing arrogance, and displaying paranoia; these behaviors may result from delusions of superiority, grandiosity, and an unrealistic sense of entitlement. Such behaviors create a very real vulnerability to having distorted perceptions and being unable to realistically assess one's own reality and that of the powerless. Holding on to the power because of its gratification encourages isolating, avoiding, and distancing from the victims of one's power position, which results in a comfort with sameness and an intolerance of differences. This intolerance, in turn, results in rigidity and lowered self-differentiation.

Having power can create or satisfy a psychological need to have a victim, someone to scapegoat and control in order to maintain one's equilibrium. When these behaviors are exaggerated, they can lead to the justification of aggression against the powerless, to dehumanizing behavior, and, in extreme cases, to pleasure at human suffering (Ordway 1973; Pinderhughes 1989). Understanding these dynamics must be a major focus in the training of social workers, who may also be beneficiaries in the societal projection process. The systemic aspect of power is evident in the use of projections by the powerful upon the powerless to justify holding power over the powerless, in the opportunity for the powerful to arrange certain aspects of reality so that perceptions of the powerless appear true, and in the trap of feeling uncomfortable at the injustice of having power but of being unwilling to give up the power because of its benefits.

In summary, these notions concerning the dynamics of power have relevance for understanding diversity for several reasons. First, they pertain to every relationship that is marked by a consistent power differential. For example, they apply to the relationship between women and men, as well as the relationship between the majority culture and ethnic minorities. Subordinate groups are understood not only in relation to the symbols of their culture, but also in relation to the majority group and the effect of the interaction between the majority culture and the culture of specific ethnic minority groups.

Second, understanding power dynamics facilitates a focus on the strengths and adaptational aspects of ethnic minority groups and on the goals, dynamics, and interactional patterns of the majority group. Only a focus on power, which has been avoided largely because of its negative connotation in American society (Kipnis 1967), will enable this understanding.

And finally, while it is necessary to understand the dynamics of ethnicity and/or race in and of themselves, a focus on power dynamics makes it clear that combinations of ethnicity, race, gender, and socioeconomic status can mean double or even triple jeopardy for individuals. Hence, one can conceptualize levels and degrees of powerlessness. For example, the situation of poor ethnic minority females entails powerlessness based on poverty, ethnic minority status, and the female role. These concepts also facilitate awareness of the self from a power perspective.

Whether social workers are members of the majority group or an ethnic minority group, they are pressed to understand the importance to themselves of their status as beneficiaries or victims of the societal projection process. This understanding has significance for everyone seeking to interact comfortably with others or to change their own entrapment in destructive patterns of interaction with ethnic minorities and people of color. It is critical for victims who seek to change their victimization so that they can have some control over significant aspects of their lives, and for beneficiaries who wish to control their personal vulnerability to paranoid and distorted thinking, to become more flexible, less rigid, more human, and to be able to manage their vulnerability to reinforcing the powerlessness of persons who are victims (for example, minorities, the poor) of the societal projection process. How power concepts can be applied to the helping encounter and the design and delivery of services will be discussed below.

Ethnicity and Minority Status in the Design and Delivery of Services

White Middle-Class Model as the Norm

Culture-free service delivery is nonexistent (Navarro 1980). The differences in values, norms, beliefs, lifestyles, and life chances that exist between the client and the social worker can extend to every aspect of the delivery system, which is itself a cultural phenomenon.

The programming of service delivery, the structuring of services for people, the engagement of clients in the help-giving process, the degree to which clients use services, the assessment and treatment of problems, and the evaluation of outcomes, are all in some way influenced by cultural values and traditions. Culture determines what clients see as a problem, how they express it (that is, whether symptoms are somatic, behavioral, or affective, what specific symptoms clients manifest), who they seek out for help, what they regard as helpful, and the intervention strategies they prefer (McGoldrick 1982).

There is now recognition of the degree to which such concerns have been traditionally ignored so that the needs and problems identified as significant to white middle-class persons have been assumed to be the norm for understanding and delivering services to everyone. The use of the white middle class as a yardstick has resulted in inappropriate and even destructive service delivery to ethnic minorities and people of color. In many instances where services have been sought and ethnic persons have been accepted for treatment, premature termination has been common. Use of the white middle-class model of helping has reinforced ignorance of cultural variations in people. It has also encouraged failure to assess the impact of environmental forces on individual functioning, and a disinclination to direct intervention to environmental as well as internal phenomena.

Failure to use a framework that emphasizes the significance of systemic and environmental determinants of people's problems can be oppressive to clients, leading to symbolic violence and cultural imperialism (Ivey 1981). Approaches based on this failure are designed to help clients feel better about being powerless as a result of systemic or environmental influences, and thus constitute a form of social control that sustains the status quo.

Culturally Sensitive Service Delivery

There has been surprisingly little empirical study of the influence of cultural difference on ultimate treatment outcome or actual client change. Despite this fact there is, according to Davis and Proctor (1989), voluminous literature suggesting that many ethnic minorities prefer helpers of the same cultural background; helpers are less comfortable with clients of different backgrounds; cultural difference does interfere with the helping relationship due to patterns of distrust and concealment that are culturally conditioned, and to differences in cultural values and realities; minorities receive less adequate treatment than whites; and minorities are more likely to receive pathological labels.

Nonetheless, experts claim that skilled and sensitive professionals can work effectively with culturally different clients, provided that 1) workers can establish a sense of trust and familiarity; 2) workers have experience in work with cultural difference; and 3) the service delivery system is responsive (Davis and Proctor 1989).

Service delivery that is effective should be based on assessment and intervention that accords significance to people's strengths and coping styles, to the reciprocal interaction between people, their groups, neighborhoods, and the larger social system, and to the mediating role of culture in this ecological process. Service delivery so designed will enable clients to gain some control over their environment and to establish a society for themselves that maintains self-esteem (Chau 1991; Comas Dias 1988; De Anda 1984; Gutierrez 1990; Longres 1991; Monteil and Wong 1983). Moreover, such service delivery will embrace the notion that the state of being mentally healthy is facilitated by a positive sense of connectedness with one's own cultural group (Gary 1978; Gomez 1982). It will, therefore, incorporate goals to validate, preserve, and enhance clients' *chosen* cultural identity in order to facilitate healthy relationships and group interaction; accord respect to the client's belief system as a link between him and his cultural group and as a way of providing meaning to his individual experience. The concept of empowerment (Solomon 1976), which mandates this stance, requires that efforts also be directed toward environmental insufficiencies. This requires knowledge of the community, its needs and services, and knowledge of how to intervene in the various environmental systems on behalf of clients.

Validation of the client's cultural identity demands that the service provider consider the variations that exist within a culture and the way in which cultural shift and change can enhance strength, connectedness, and a sense of identity, and, as well, lead to conflict and stress. Experts suggest that dilemmas in service delivery that are created by these variations can be met head on if services are structured so that clients have choices in terms of their degree of acculturation or assimilation (DeVore and Schlesinger 1991; Gomez 1982; Jenkins 1981). Programs should offer choices in preferred forms of help, that is, matching programs with people in different ethnic, social, and economic circumstances. There should be available three models of service delivery: 1) regular social services based on "conventional" American models; 2) independent services based on traditional ethnic practices; and 3) new types of strategies and programs that are more culturally appropriate, combining aspects of conventional American and traditional ethnic models.

The location of services, the choice of staff, the scheduling of activities, and the intervention strategies used should all be consistent with these goals, which entail equal respect for all groups and a commitment for social change, the involvement of the community in service delivery and planning, and, where necessary, the utilization of bicultural staff (Ho 1987; Jenkins 1981; Lum 1986; Valdez and Gallegos 1982).

The necessity that services should manifest congruity of goals with those of the client's cultural background means that social workers must understand the language or be able to name the problem with the right terminology and appropriate sense of causality consistent with the client's view; use treatment strategies consistent with the cultural values and expectations concerning privacy, self-disclosure, and the context of service delivery, including traditional healers and indigenous helping activities where appropriate; and be directed toward environmental insufficiencies. Social workers must also be particularly sensitive to the referral route as an indication of the powerlessness being experienced by ethnic minority clients (DeVore and Schlesinger 1991; Gary 1978; Solomon 1976).

Services rendered under mandated, nonvoluntary circumstances may not empower these clients but, rather, may reinforce the sense of powerlessness they experience on a daily basis that is connected with their cultural group's status in society. For example, despite the fact that such services may be desperately needed, a Latino mother required by the school to seek mental health services for her acting-out son, an African-American male who must seek alcoholic counseling as a condition of employment, or a Haitian father who must join a group of abusing parents because his punishment of his daughter is considered physical abuse, all may experience these referrals as coercion or more-of-the-same oppression.

Cultural competence requires that social workers use their understanding of power dynamics not only to neutralize the powerlessness of their ethnic minority clients and build on their strengths, but also in relation to themselves. That is, knowledge of power dynamics should be used by social workers to facilitate appropriate management of the power implicit in their helping role that permits them to assess, intervene, and give or withhold resources. This requires social workers to manage their own personal power needs so that gratification of them is not sought through the exercise of their professional power role. The power differential that exists between practitioners and their clients is such that it can be, and too often has been, exploited by helpers to meet their own needs for personal power and esteem (Heller 1985; Pinderhughes 1989). The rapid escalation in situations being reported where social workers have sexually abused their clients illustrates this potential (Reamer 1992). Role power used to bolster the image of the helper constitutes "perhaps the most infamous of therapy abuses" (Heller 1985:161).

In the cross-cultural helping encounter the risk of exploitation that is inherent in the helper role becomes compounded. The power implicit in the helper's role may also enhance the aggrandizement that is associated with his or her own cultural group identity. The tendency to exploit this double power role in work with clients from less valued cultural groups, to use this power to satisfy personal need, is far greater than one may think. The significance of this for clinical activity is explained, as noted earlier, by the concept of the societal projection process, which suggests that the dominant group in a society can, through projection upon a less powerful group (the victims), relieve anxiety and reduce tension in itself, thereby improving its functioning.

Thus, in the helping encounter practitioners who are members of dominant, beneficiary groups (white, male, middle or upper class, or other groups with high status assignment) can exploit their aggrandized cultural group status, relieving anxiety and reducing tension for themselves when they work with persons from victim groups (people of color, poor, female, or other groups with low status assignment). Exploitation occurs whenever social workers engage in behavior that perpetuates clients' aggrandized perception of the helper while permitting clients to continue to view themselves as incompetent and powerless. Intervention is only truly effective when these perceptions of clients are changed and clients learn to see themselves as competent and persons of value.

It is important for social workers to understand these risks and the purpose of the exploitative behaviors that they can engender; such understanding enhances practitioners' capacity to control them. Such control and management of personal responses to clients who are culturally different, particularly minorities, frequently require special training (Pinderhughes 1989).

The training for cultural competence that social workers need, and the content that must be mastered, should prepare them to be flexible in thinking and behavior and thus enable them to adapt their work styles to the values, expectations, and preferences of their culturally different clients. They should be able to choose from a variety of strategies that are useful for the range of cultural groups, social classes, levels of education, and levels of acculturation that exist among clients to work effectively, even though the values underlying these expected behaviors may be vastly different from their own and from those which have been the foundation for traditional assessment and intervention approaches. Practitioners should take the time and make the effort to manage these complexities that are embodied in cross-cultural work. They should be prepared in assessment, for example, to consider within the general framework of knowledge about the client's cultural group how the client is unique, and be capable of deciding the meaning of the behavior under scrutiny—for instance, whether it is a response to migration, is functional within the culture despite the fact that it appears pathological to the social worker, and to what degree this culturally based behavior is maladaptive. With such training, social workers can engage in extra steps and use the additional energy that is required to demonstrate the necessary flexibility that characterizes such thinking because they have faced and can manage any personal anxiety that is associated with being different, with discomfort about their cultural background, and with their own power needs.

Culturally competent training will help social workers to understand and manage their own power needs and responses, thus enabling them to be less threatened when strategies are called for that require practitioners to function in a less hierarchical, more power-sharing fashion. Such management will facilitate engagement with little difficulty in the mutual, reciprocal, open, and self-disclosing approach to helping that is expected by people who belong to certain cultural groups. These responses are generally consistent with the cultural values and expectations of many Native Americans, Puerto Ricans, and African Americans. They are also necessary for interaction with others whose experiences with personal and social powerlessness have been such that they *cannot* be engaged, and cannot begin to change their collusion with victimization without the appropriately timed use of strategies that place them at least sometimes in a power role.

Because negative responses to difference are under firm control, social workers who have become culturally competent are less liable to manage their own discomfort by automatically viewing culturally different behavior in clients as a sign of incompetence. In becoming self-aware, understanding their own issues and power needs, they will not be immobilized by discomfort concerning their beneficiary role in the helping process. Because they do not seek comfort in the stereotypes, the bias, the distorted beliefs, and the societal structures on which these projections are based, social workers trained in this way are able to look honestly at the effects of their own ethnic, racial, or other significant identity, are free to see clients in the context of their culture, in the presence or absence of societal supports, and can see them as knowledgeable and blocked from access, or trapped in positions where environmental insufficiency must be seen as a factor in the etiology of the problem and in the solutions that must be sought. Social workers can build on these supports that, if dysfunctional, will need to be strengthened. Should the dysfunction prove intractable, practitioners must be committed to creating and finding new supports. Social workers who have developed such awareness and self-management can respect their clients' struggles to find ways to be strong, to feel valued, to raise competent, strong, loving children despite the hostile environment in which they are trapped and despite their role as tension relievers within the social system that channels anxiety to themselves as victims, while freeing helpers who are beneficiaries. And most of all, social workers so prepared are free to engage in empowerment efforts such as community activities, advocacy, and systems change that seek to bring about an equalization of the power differential between their client groups and their own.

Pedagogical Issues

Notwithstanding the current Council on Social Work Education mandate, there is dissatisfaction on the part of many experts with education for practice with ethnic minorities and people of color in terms of the actual presentation of content on this population in the curriculum. The debate concerning where to place such content in the curriculum, whether in discrete courses or in an integrated fashion throughout, has been, for all practical purposes, resolved by the CSWE mandate. But the truth is that faculty whose expertise does not extend to this content have been puzzled about how and where to include it effectively. Content on culture, ethnic minorities, and people of color has relevance *in every topical area* and faculty must be assisted in their effort to focus on this content with breadth and in depth. In human behavior courses the content fits in well when combined with content on systems concepts, ecological process, and human development. For example, in teaching about systemic process and the recursive dynamics that characterize it, the transactional nature of culture is a useful illustration, particularly with respect to the nonstatic, changing, and evolving nature of culture, a phenomenon that is shaped by external forces and by individuals within each given group (Pinderhughes 1988). In human behavior courses, developmental theory should never be taught without inclusion of content on the way in which human growth and development may be unique for specific ethnic and racial groups—how a stage of development is valued by a particular cultural group or the specific nature of the behavior that is expected from individuals, family members, and others. For example, the value placed on autonomy and individualism in Western culture may mean that a white American mother may respond differently to her toddler struggling with mastery of the separation-individuation task than an immigrant Latino mother whose culture values collaterality and affiliativeness far more (DeVore and Schlesinger 1991).

In social work practice courses, content on minorities and people of color should be included in the teaching of all phases of the intervention process, with particular attention to assessment, relationship building, and intervention strategies. Moreover, culture should be a factor to be considered in all of the problem areas studied, for example, child abuse, substance abuse, aging, mental illness, and poverty.

Similar integration of this content should occur in other courses as well. Social welfare policy courses should examine the implications of programs and policies for cultural and ethnic groups, the history of discrimination affecting various groups, minorities' participation in the legislative process, and so on. Social work research and evaluation courses should examine, for example, the extent to which needs assessments have been conducted with samples drawn from ethnic minorities and the appropriateness of various data collection techniques (such as in-person interviews or self-administered questionnaires) with different cultural groups.

One school's attempt at integration placed the concepts of difference and power as overarching themes that traversed the required practice curriculum. With these concepts introduced early, in order to explain how difference and power operate in human functioning, a context was created that invited ongoing consideration of issues related to ethnic minorities, people of color, and other populations whose situations label them as different and whose problems result from lack of power on a variety of levels.

Educators all agree that the highly emotional nature of cultural content requires teaching approaches that facilitate affective as well as cognitive learning (Chau 1991; Gitterman 1991; Pinderhughes 1989). Opportunities for students, trainees, and professionals to participate in *in vivo* experiences that foster emotional understanding is critical. Such strategies are needed to help learners transcend the biases all people have and facilitate management of discomfort stemming from difference.

Experiential learning can capture the complexities of the cultural process; enable students to develop awareness of their own biases that block empathy with the culturally different; and facilitate the capacity to risk oneself in work with those who are different (Pinderhughes 1989; Pla-Richards 1991). Role playing, group exercises focused on self and others' awareness of differences in cultural behavior, assignments focused on examination of one's own cultural experiences, planned interactions with members of the cultural group under study, and field education are among the mechanisms now used. Gitterman (1991) describes how the process of collaborative communication used in the classroom, along with the model of risk taking by the instructor, can help students to transcend racial differences that may block their learning. Even instructors who are skilled in group process may need assistance in preparation for the risk taking that such collaborative learning often requires.

At all levels of social work training, attitudinal as well as cognitive preparation is needed. At the baccalaureate level, students should be prepared to examine their own cultural predispositions and manage unhelpful attitudes and responses at the same time that they develop cognitive familiarity with the culture of the groups they work with and the tasks they are expected to master at this level of cross-cultural competence. In addition to this preparation, students at the master's level must acquire knowledge in greater depth and breadth. They must be prepared to include culture as a factor in every aspect of their work, including practice evaluation. For example, in planning a design to evaluate practice outcome, the choice of measures should be culturally appropriate and outcome should be considered in the light of cultural dynamics. Students must develop comfort with assessing and managing the complexities of culture that affect their more specialized roles and tasks.

At the doctoral level, students should be assessing theories for their validity in reference to ethnic minorities and people of color, becoming expert in the application of cultural principles to their particular areas of expertise, and preparing to apply the principles of culturally relevant research to their task of developing theory.

Issues and Controversies

Despite the fact that little definitive research exists that tests the validity of many of the themes and concepts being employed to explain the realities of ethnic minorities and people of color, there is general agreement concerning their usefulness. Debates are still occurring, however, as to whether the problems encountered by these populations should be addressed in terms of structural deficiency of the social system or in terms of cultural differences that require the support of strengths and adaptations (Chau 1991; Williams 1990). Nearly every theorist emphasizes the significance of the structural deficiencies of the social system in the consideration of the problems of these populations, and intervention in the form of advocacy is nearly always stressed. However, an even stronger focus on social change and intervention at community, larger social system, and social policy levels is typically urged, with efforts centered on prevention and early intervention, education, socialization, cultural community development, and advocacy research (Chau 1991; Logan, Freeman, and McRoy 1990; Longres 1991).

The issue of changes needed in the social system to improve the quality of life of minorities and people of color and, thus, to prevent many of the problems they bring, is in fact the single most intractable issue in education and practice. For years calls have been sounded for examination of how much "efforts are directed to structural reform and how much to alleviating the effects of structural imbalance" (Washington 1982:108), and for change in institutional arrangements and social stratification (Chau 1991; Longres 1991). As Chau (1991:29) observes, "attempts to create programs and services which are culturally responsive are often doomed by systemic resistance to change in the form of hostile responses and bureaucratic hurdles, thus reinforcing services, programs and strategies that fit the client into mainstream systems and avoiding attempts to engineer the changes that must occur in the larger society."

Social work is seen by some as having failed to develop either basic theory or the practice technology to bring about change in many of the problems of ethnic minorities and people of color, especially poverty. Critics allege that social work, having turned much of its attention inward in the direction of individual psychotherapy and private practice, has deserted ethnic minority communities whose members are advised to "seek other alternatives" (Williams 1990:90).

The dissatisfaction with the gaps in and ineffectiveness of theory extends also to the dearth of research on outcomes of interventions. Refinement is needed in all these areas. Corrective efforts should take the form of research initiatives that focus on individuals and families within this population and the strengths, survival strategies, and coping skills that are used by its members to negotiate life issues and the problems attendant to membership in their cultural group. Research findings on functional coping provide sound bases for developing practice theory that can prescribe and facilitate the support of strengths and adaptations, and can identify when and under what circumstances various strategies focused on culture should be used.

Advocacy research, a process wherein there is support from the researcher for the worldview or cultural perspective of the client(s) under investigation, is also imperative. How the culture of the client(s) shapes the entire process of study, from hypothesis construction, pretest, and observation to the interpretation of the data must receive attention (Rogler 1989). The necessity for such rigor in setting up and conducting research has been made painfully clear by minority theorists (Chau 1991; Tidwell 1990; Washington 1982; Williams 1990) who identify past research that has judged and blamed the subjects under study, reinforcing bias and serving as a basis for intervention that further entraps and disempowers ethnic minorities and people of color. Remedies include the use of ethnographic studies rather than survey research (Logan, Freeman, and McRoy 1990), "direct immersion in the culture of the study, especially making use of participant observation, and interviews with knowledgeable informants" (Rogler 1989:297), and throughout the process of internal and external review an ongoing self assessment of the value system underlying the research (Tidwell 1990). Only then can we be assured that theory will emerge that will serve as the basis for policy initiatives that are just and professional practice that is humane (Tidwell 1990).

The massive changes occurring in our nation and the world, and the increasing salience of culture on the political scene, make the development of cultural competence an ever more important priority in social work education. In this context, further clarification and redefinition of old theories explaining social work with ethnic minorities and people of color, formulation of new theories, along with integration of both old and new theories across the curriculum, require a major commitment from educators. If students are to be prepared for effective functioning in the twenty-first century, such a commitment is essential.

REFERENCES

Anderson, J. 1992. "Family Centered Practice in the 1990s: A Multicultural Perspective." *Journal of Multicultural Social Work* 1(4):17–29.

Arce, A. 1982. "Cultural Aspects of Mental Health Care for Hispanic Americans." In A. Gaw, ed., *Cross-Cultural Psychiatry*. Littleton, Mass.: Wright-PSG.

Banfield, E. C. 1974. *The Unheavenly City Revisited*. Boston: Little, Brown.

Basch, M. 1975. "Toward a Theory that Encompasses Depression: A Review of Existing Causal Hypotheses in Psychoanalysis." In J. Anthony and T. Benedek, eds., *Depression and Human Existence* p. 513. Boston: Brown.

Berger, R. and R. Federico. 1985. *Human Behavior: A Perspective for the Helping Professions*. 2d ed. New York: Longman.

Berlin, S. 1990. "Dichotomous and Complex Thinking." *Social Service Review* 64:46–59.

Bochner, S., ed. 1982. *Culture in Contact*. New York: Pergamon Press.

Bowen, M. 1978. *Family Therapy in Clinical Practice*. New York: Jason Aronson.

Brislin, R. 1981. *Cross Cultural Encounters*. New York: Pergamon Press.

—— and P. Pederson. 1976. *Cross Cultural Orientation Programs*. New York: Gardner.

Carter, E. A. and M. McGoldrick. 1980. *The Family Life Cycle: A Framework for Family Therapy*. New York: Gardner Press.

Chau, K. 1989. "Sociocultural Dissonance Among Minority Populations." *Social Casework* 70(4):224–230.

——. 1991. "Social Work with Ethnic Minorities: Practice Issues and Potentials." *Journal of Multicultural Social Work* 1(1):29–39.

——. 1992. "Educating for Effective Group Work Practice in Multicultural Environments of the 1990s." *Journal of Multicultural Social Work* 1(3):57–74.

Chestang, L. 1972. *Character Development in a Hostile Environment* (Occasional Paper No. 3). Chicago: University of Chicago School of Social Service Administration.

——. 1976. "Environmental Influences on Social Functioning: The Black Experience." In P. Cafferty and L. Chestang, eds., *The Diverse Society: Implications for Social Policy*. Washington, D.C.: National Association of Social Workers.

Comas-Dias, L. 1988. "Cross-Cultural Mental Health Treatment." In L. Comas-Dias and E. Griffith, eds., *Clinical Guidelines in Cross-Cultural Mental Health*. New York: Wiley.

Coser, L. A. 1956. *The Functions of Social Conflict*. New York: Free Press.

Davis, L. and E. Proctor. 1989. *Race, Gender and Class: Guidelines for Practice with Individuals, Families and Groups*. Englewood Cliffs, N.J.: Prentice Hall.

De Anda, D. 1984. "Bicultural Socialization: Factors Affecting the Minority Experience." *Social Work* 29(2):101–107.

—— and V. Riddel. 1991. "Ethnic Identity, Self-Esteem, and Interpersonal Relationships among Multiethnic Adolescents." *Journal of Multicultural Social Work* 1(1):83–98.

DeVore, W. and E. Schlesinger. 1991. *Ethnic Sensitive Social Work Practice*. 2d ed. New York: Merrill.

Erikson, E. 1968. *Identity: Youth and Culture*. New York: Norton.

Fieldstein, D. and J. Giordano. 1976. "The New Pluralism and Social Work Education." Paper presented at annual meeting of Council on Social Work Education, March.

Fisher, D. 1991. *An Introduction to Constructivism for Social Workers*. New York: Praeger.

Foster, M. and L. Perry. 1982. "Self Valuation among Blacks." *Social Work* 27(1):60–66.

Gary, L. 1978. *Mental Health: A Challenge to the Black Community*. Philadelphia: Dorrance.

Gehrie, M. 1979. "Culture as Internal Representation." *Psychiatry* 42(5):165–170.

Germain, C. 1979. *Social Work Practice: People and Environment*. New York: Columbia University Press.

Giordano, J. and I. Levine. 1975. *Mental Health and Middle America: A Group Identity Approach*. Working Paper Series No. 14. New York: Institute on Pluralism and Group Identity.

Gitterman, A. 1991. "Working with Difference: White Teacher and African American Students." In R. Middleman and G. Wood, eds., *Teaching Secrets: The Technology of Social Work Education*. New York: Haworth Press.

Gomez, A. 1982. "Puerto Rican Americans." In A. Gaw, ed., *Cross Cultural Psychiatry*. Littleton, Mass.: Wright-PSG.

Greeley, A. 1976. "Why Study Ethnicity?" In P. Cafferty and L. Chestang, eds., *The Diverse Society: Implications for Social Policy*. Washington, D.C.: National Association of Social Workers.

Green, J., ed. 1982. *Cultural Awareness in the Human Services*. Englewood Cliffs, N.J.: Prentice Hall.

Greenson, R., E. Toney, P. Lim, and A. Romero. 1982. "Transference and Countertransference in Inter-Racial Psychotherapy." In Bass, Wyatt, and Powell, eds., *The AfroAmerican Family: Assessment, Treatment, and Research Issues*. New York: Grune and Stratton.

Gutierrez, L. 1990. "Working with Women of Color: An Empowerment Perspective." *Social Work* 35(2):149–153.

Heller, D. 1985. *Power in Psychotherapeutic Practice*. New York: Human Sciences Press.

Ho, M. K. 1987. *Family Therapy with Ethnic Minorities*. Beverly Hills, Calif.: Sage.

Hodges, V. 1991. "Providing Culturally Sensitive Intensive Family Preservation Services to Ethnic Minority Families." In E. Tracy, D. Haapala, Kinney, J. and P. Pecora, eds., *Intensive Family Preservation Services: An Instructional Sourcebook*. Cleveland: Mandel School of Applied Social Sciences, Case Western Reserve University.

Hopps, J. 1982. "Oppression Based on Color" (editorial). *Social Work* 27(1):3–5.

——. 1984. "Minorities of Color." *Encyclopedia of Social Work*. 18th ed. Silver Spring, Md.: National Association of Social Workers.

Ivey, A. 1981. "Counseling and Psychotherapy: Toward a New Perspective." In A. J. Marsella and P. Pederson, eds., *Cross-Cultural Counseling and Psychotherapy*. New York: Pergamon.

Jenkins, S. 1981. *The Ethnic Dilemma in the Human Services*. New York: Free Press.

Kessler, R. and H. Neighbors. 1986. "A New Perspective on the Relationships among Race, Social Class and Psychological Distress." *Journal of Health and Social Behavior* 27(6):107–115.

Kipnis, D. 1967. *The Powerholders*. Chicago: University of Chicago Press.

Klineberg, O. 1982. "Contact Between Ethnic Groups: A Historical Perspective of Some Aspects of Theory and Research." In S. Bochner, ed., *Cultures in Contact*. New York: Pergamon Press.

Landau, J. 1982. "Therapy with Families in Cultural Transition." In M. McGoldrick, J. Pearce, and J. Giordano, eds., *Ethnicity and Family Therapy*. New York: Guilford Press.

Lewis, O. 1966. *La Vida: A Puerto Rican Family in the Culture of Poverty*. New York: Random House.

Lister, L. 1987. "Curriculum Building in Social Work Education: The Example of Ethnocultural Content." *Journal of Social Work Education* 23(1):31–39.

Logan, S., E. Freeman, and R. McRoy, eds. 1990. *Social Work Practice with Black Families*. New York: Longman.

Longres, J. 1982. "Minority Groups: An Interest Group Perspective." *Social Work* 27(1):7–14.

——. 1991. "Toward a Status Model of Ethnic Sensitive Practice." *Journal of Multicultural Social Work* 1(1):41–56.

Lum, D. 1986. *Social Work Practice with People of Color*. Monterey, Calif.: Brooks-Cole.

McClelland, D. 1975. *Power: The Inner Experience*. New York: John Wiley and Sons.

McGoldrick, M. 1982. "Ethnicity in Family Therapy: An Overview." In M. McGoldrick, J. Pearce, and J. Giordano, eds., *Ethnicity and Family Therapy*. New York: Guilford Press.

McRoy, R. 1990. "Cultural and Racial Identity in Black Families." In S. Logan, E. Freeman, and R. McRoy, eds., *Social Work Practice with Black Families*. New York: Longman.

May, G. 1976. "Personality Development and Ethnic Identity." In P. Cafferty and L. Chestang, eds., *The Diverse Society: Implications for Social Policy*. Washington, D.C.: National Association of Social Workers.

Mokuau, N. 1991. "Ethnic Minority Curriculum in Baccalaureate Social Work Programs." *Journal of Multicultural Social Work* 1(3):57–74.

Monteil, M. and P. Wong. 1983. "A Theoretical Critique of the Minority Perspective." *Social Casework* 64(2):112–117.

Navarro, V. 1980. "Panel on Culture and Health." Symposium on Cross Cultural and Transcultural Issues in Family Health Care. University of California, San Francisco.

New York Institute on Pluralism and Group Identity. 1980. *News from the Committee*.

Norton, D. 1978. *The Dual Perspective*. New York: Council on Social Work Education.

Ordway, J. 1973. "Some Consequences of Racism for Whites." In C. Willie, B. Brown, and B. Kramer, eds., *Racism amd Mental Health*. Pittsburgh: University of Pittsburgh Press.

Papajohn, J. and J. Spiegel. 1976. *Transactions in Families*. San Francisco: Jossey-Bass.

Pinderhughes, C. 1986. "The American Racial Dilemma: A Social Psychiatric Formulation." *American Journal of Social Psychiatry* 6(2):107–113.

Pinderhughes, E. 1982a. "Black Genealogy: Self Liberator and Therapeutic Tool." *Smith College Studies for Social Work* 52(2):93–106.

——. 1982b. "Family Functioning of Afro-Americans." *Social Work* 27(1):91–96.

——. 1985. "Race, Ethnicity, and Class as Practitioner and Client Variables." In M. Day, ed., *The Socio-Cultural Dimensions of Mental Health*. New York: Vantage Press.

——. 1988. "The Significance of Culture and Power in the Human Behavior Curriculum." In C. Jacobs and D. Bowles, eds., *Ethnicity and Race: Critical Concepts in Social Work*. Silver Spring, Md.: National Association of Social Workers.

——. 1989. *Understanding Race, Ethnicity and Power*. New York: Free Press.

Pla-Richards, M. 1991. "Connected with Difference: Black Teacher—White Students." In R. Middleman and G. Wood, eds., *Teaching Secrets: The Technology of Social Work Education*. New York: Haworth Press.

Reamer, F. G. 1992. "The Impaired Social Worker." *Social Work* 37(2):165–170.

Rogler, L. 1989. "The Meaning of Culturally Sensitive Research in Mental Health." *American Journal of Psychiatry* 146(3):296–303.

Rothenberg, P. 1988. *Racism and Sexism: An Integrated Study.* New York: St. Martin's Press.

Sanders, D. 1975. "Dynamics of Ethnic and Cultural Pluralism." *Journal of Education for Social Work* 11(3):95–100.

Schinke, S., M. Moncher, G. Holden, M. Orlandi, and G. Botvin. 1992. "Preventing Substance Abuse among Native American Youth." In C. LeCroy, ed., *Case Studies in Social Work Practice.* Belmont, Calif.: Wadsworth.

Solomon, B. 1976. "Social Work in Multiethnic Society." In M. Sotomayor, ed. *Cross Cultural Perspectives in Social Work Practice and Education.* New York: Council on Social Work Education.

Spiegel, J. 1982. "An Ecological Model of Ethnic Families." In M. McGoldrick, J. Pearce, and J. Giordano, eds., *Ethnicity and Family Therapy.* New York: Guilford.

Sue, D. 1978. "World Views and Counseling." *Personnel and Guidance Journal* 458–462.

Tidwell, B. 1990. "Research and Practice Issues with Black Families." In S. Logan, E. Freeman, and R. McRoy, eds., *Social Work Practice with Black Families.* New York: Longman.

U.S. Census. 1991. *Statistical Abstract of the United States.* Washington, D.C.: U.S. Department of Commerce.

U.S. Department of Labor. 1988. "Opportunity 2000: Creative Affirmative Action Strategies for a Changing Workforce." Indianapolis: Hudson Institute.

Valdez, T. and G. Gallegos. 1982. "The Chicano Familia in Social Work." In J. Green, ed. *Cultural Awareness in the Human Services.* Englewood Cliffs, N.J.: Prentice Hall.

Volkan, V. 1991. "USSR 1991: Ethnicity and Political Change." *Mind and Human Interaction* 3:1–2.

Washington, R. 1982. "Social Development: A Focus for Practice and Education." *Social Work* 27(1):104–109.

White, B. 1992. Address to New Jersey Chapter, National Association of Social Workers, March.

Williams, L. 1990. "Working with the Black Poor: Implications for Effective Theoretical and Practice Approaches." In S. Logan, E. Freeman and R. McRoy, eds., *Social Work Practice with Black Families.* New York: Longman.

10

Diversity and Populations at Risk: Women

NANCY R. HOOYMAN

With women forming 51 percent of the world population, two-thirds of social work clients, and the majority of social workers, the importance and relevance of the inclusion of content on women would seem self-evident. Yet content on women remains uneven throughout social work curricula: in some instances, relegated to specialized electives, in others defined as part of the foundation curriculum but not always apparent to students. And even fewer schools of social work incorporate a feminist perspective in their curriculum structure, content, and teaching. One reason for the slow and uneven integration of women's content may lie in the nature of the profession itself: although men tend to be concentrated at the top of the career ladder, social work is largely a woman's profession, doing for women what is largely viewed as underpaid and undervalued women's work (Morell 1987). Forming the numerical majority of social work students, workers, and clients, women have nevertheless lacked the power to ensure that their needs and interests are consistently advanced by social work education and practice. Yet integration of such curriculum content is essential to equip practitioners with an adequate knowledge base and egalitarian attitudes in order to empower or increase the personal, interpersonal, and political power of the women with whom they work (Vinton 1992; Gutierrez 1990).

This chapter begins by reviewing the historical development of content on women within social work and education practice. The major conceptual frameworks and theoretical perspectives that are relevant to foundation curricular content—women's issues, nonsexist and feminist perspectives—will be discussed, highlighting the ongoing debate among them. After critiquing these prevailing conceptual frameworks and briefly reviewing relevant pedagogical issues, I will close with a discussion of strategies to promote such content.

Historical Development

Although women are the majority of both service providers and recipients of social services, the social work profession has been slow to develop practice strategies or curriculum initiatives that reflect women's life experiences. In 1973, NASW targeted social conditions and populations at risk, with women as the lowest priority among these populations. In the same year, CSWE's *Report from the Committee on Objectives and Strategies*, presented at the Delegate Assembly, began to implement regulations regarding curriculum content on women. In response to the women's movement and pressure to consider women's viewpoint on social problems, the CSWE Board in 1977 adopted the standard on women, which was codified as 1234B. In 1982, CSWE issued its *Curriculum Policy Statement for Master's Degree and Baccalaureate Degrees in Social Work Education*. Standard 7.3 mandated that social work curricula must provide content on the "experiences, needs and responses of special populations and people who have been subjected to institutionalized forms of oppression." Standard 7.5 spoke specifically to women: "The program shall make specific, continuous efforts to assure enrichment of the educational experience it offers by including women in all categories of persons related to the program and by incorporating content on women's issues into the curriculum" (CSWE 1991). The 1992 curriculum policy statement includes women under populations at risk, as follows: "The curriculum must provide content about people of color, women, and gay and lesbian persons." In addition, structural factors that affect women as clients, educators and students are recognized by "such content must emphasize the impact of discrimination, economic deprivation and oppression upon these groups" (CSWE).

The current CSWE Evaluative Standard 13 on Women is intended to ensure that curricula and institutional practices in social work education reflect the major changes in the roles and responsibilities of individuals and institutions that have occurred in our society. For example, students are expected to be knowledgeable about the implications of changes in women's roles and responsibilities for social work practice.

Similarly, the policies and practices of the social work program and the institution of which it is a part should uphold the rights of women and reflect their status in society. Thus Evaluative Standard 13 provides a frame of reference for evaluating compliance with the standards on women in policies, procedures, and patterns of institutional staffing, policies and procedures in student recruitment and student body composition, and curriculum. All curricular components should incorporate current knowledge about women, the contributions of women to society, and the elimination of gender-biased stereotyping. The fact that compliance to this standard does not require separate, discrete courses is relevant to the discussion below regarding the integration of content on women into foundation courses.

A review of the literature from 1974 to 1992 reflects the slow progress regarding the extent and quality of content on women in graduate and undergraduate social work curricula. Most early initiatives, for example, were specialized courses: "Social Perspectives on the Status of Women in Society" reflected the typical women's studies approach of the early 1970s, by investigating cultural definitions of appropriate sex-role behavior and resultant personality characteristics divided along gender lines (Meisel and Friedman 1974); master's level policy courses on women were developed to integrate theories of human behavior, social structure, and social policy (Brandwein and Wheelock 1978); and advanced research courses were revised to enhance students' awareness of gender as a source of bias in research, and to help them identify how their own sexual stereotyping affects the selection of research topics and the interpretation of results (Rosenman and Ruckdeschel 1981). Separate courses were advocated as the focal point for curriculum development, for student interest and for legitimacy of content. Within the larger societal context of seeking to obtain the legal protection of women's equal rights, these curricular efforts reflected a practice perspective that women's issues or problems required a specialized response (Norman and Mancuso 1980; Gottlieb 1980; Social Work Practice in a Sexist Society 1980). Along with the issue of separation vs. integration of content, other dilemmas in these early efforts revolved around the themes of sexism vs. racism, cognitive vs. experiential learning, and women only vs. coeducational enrollment (Brandwein and Wheelock 1978).

Other early initiatives reflected a concern that specialized courses could become isolated or relegated to inferior status, thereby having little or no effect on the total curriculum. Because of this, it was argued that an integrative approach within foundation courses, particularly within HBSE and policy sequences, was needed (Lowenstein 1976; Gottlieb 1987). A potential danger of the integration approach, however, is that content may become lost, buried, or less visible. Reviews of course outlines and bibliographies found little content or readings on women, raising questions about the effectiveness of such infusion efforts. When faculty and students were questioned about the adequacy of content on women in the curriculum, only 7 percent thought issues were adequately covered and 47 percent thought the presentation of such content was sexist (Price et al. 1979). It appears that the major and rapid changes in the social conditions of women during the 1970s and 1980s had comparatively little effect on the education of social workers (Bernard and Gottlieb 1987). In fact, despite the knowledge explosion about women in the 1970s and 1980s, many educators and students alike often insist there is a lack of social science and social work literature on the status of women available to include in courses.

Such assertions are disputable, given the growing body of literature about social problems facing women and about social work practice with women. Norman and Mancuso's *Women's Issues and Social Work Practice* (1980) was one of the first social work texts that addressed the impact of institutionalized sexism upon women, examining women and aging, interpersonal violence, substance abuse, racism, and lesbianism as well as women's experiences with health and mental health system and income maintenance programs. In 1981, Berlin and Kravetz urged that social workers design, implement, evaluate, and disseminate interventions to eliminate the oppression of women and suggested content areas (Berlin and Kravetz 1991).

Norman and Mancuso acknowledged the paradox that social work, known as a "women's field," is among the last of the so-called helping professions to recognize the impact of institutionalized sexism on social work practice and policy. Their explanation for this paradox is that while women comprise the majority of persons in the profession, social work executives, administrators, and educators are primarily men. Men "have planned its policies, determined its academic curriculum, directed its practices, and decided where and for whom its monies are to be spent" (Norman and Mancuso 1980:4). Until the mid-1980s, many male social work leaders still viewed women as a "special interest group" within the profession, rather than recognizing that women are the profession.

Given this domination by men, it was not surprising that not until 1980 was a woman, Maryann Mahaffey, elected president of the National Association of Social Workers—twenty-five years after the founding of the organization—nor that a national conference on women and social work was not held until 1981. The NASW National Commission on Women's Issues and the CSWE Commission on the Role and Status of Women began actively addressing gender inequities within the profession in the early 1980s. Nevertheless, gender stereotypes still have persisted in social work texts and journal articles; women remain less likely to be tenured and frequently have lower ranks and salaries in both agencies and academia; men and women faculty often have different work assignments, with women often carrying heavier loads, particularly related to the practicum; and some social services still encourage dependency and reinforce sex-stereotypical behaviors for female clients (Sowers-Hoag and Harrison 1991). Despite growing research on sexism, social workers also have been criticized for their lack of understanding of the dynamics of sexism, oppression, and violence against women, an understanding which is essential to working effectively to empower women (Stout 1991; Kravetz 1982; Quam and Austin 1984).

Some of the themes reflected in the early practice literature on women were the expansion from a narrow Freudian base for "treatment" with women, which tended to define individual women as "the problem"; the usefulness of informal social networks, particularly within the neighborhood and community, for providing services to women; the need for legislation affecting women, especially the Equal Rights Amendment; the importance of women as role models and mentors; and beginning recognition of the ways in which class, age, race, ethnicity, gender, and sexual orientation impact on personality and behavior.

Along with an increasing acknowledgment of the effects of sexism on women as clients and practitioners, innovative and, in some cases, alternative agencies were developed in the late 1970s and early 1980s, presumably to serve women more effectively, compared to traditional social service bureaucracies (Gottlieb 1980). Women's organizations, frequently operating in an egalitarian and consensual model and relying upon consciousness-raising techniques, were assumed to be more responsive to women's needs both as clients and social workers than were formal bureaucratic organizations characterized by rigid hierarchies. Many of these women's organizations, however, faced obstacles related to funding, to staff retention, and to external legitimation for untraditional models for decision making (Hooyman and Cunningham 1986; Morgenbesser 1981; Rothschild-Witt 1979).

In the past decade, the practice literature has reflected growing awareness of problems that differentially affect women—poverty, interpersonal violence, rape, sexual assault, sexual harassment, teen pregnancy, sexually transmitted disease and AIDS, and aging. What is striking, however, given the critical problems faced by women, is the relatively few books and journals devoted specifically to women in social work or that include content on women on an ongoing basis. To date, the *Journal of Social Work Education* has not published special issues on women, and the number of discrete articles on issues affecting women has increased only slightly since the 1970 and early 1980s (Quam and Austin 1984). Much of the early research focused on the predominance of male authors in social work publications, salary inequities within the profession, and the performance of women in traditional family roles rather than on nonsexist or feminist approaches to women's diverse needs. In addition, the needs of older women, women of color, or lesbians were rarely addressed (Abramovitz 1978; Quam and Austin 1984).

Another practice shift reflected in the literature includes efforts to define and differentiate feminist social work practice from traditional practice models (Kirst-Ashman 1992; Bricker-Jenkins and Hooyman 1986; Bricker-Jenkins, Hooyman, and Gottlieb 1991; Wetzel 1986; Van Den Bergh and Cooper 1986). Feminist practice aims to remove all forms of oppression, but particularly patriarchy, and approaches all issues in terms of their public and political dimensions and their implications for women. A feminist practitioner therefore advocates for individual as well as societal change, and can function within both alternative women's organizations and large bureaucracies. Recent analyses of feminist practice also seek to identify and act upon the intersections of racism, classism, heterosexism and sexism. Despite efforts to develop an empirical base for feminist practice and some students' eagerness for feminist models, few schools of social work teach anything about feminist practice. In fact, some students and faculty alike may resist the use of the term *feminist*, fearful that they will be labeled as radical or irrelevant (Kirst-Ashman 1992; Tice 1990; Bricker-Jenkins, Hooyman, and Gottlieb 1991).

To make resource materials on women's issues and feminist practice more readily available to educators and practitioners, a number of texts and CSWE monographs have presented bibliographies and assignments related to women for inclusion in core or foundation curriculum as well as for specialization by intervention, population, or by problem or service context (Burden and Gottlieb 1987; Van Den Bergh and Cooper 1986; Gottlieb 1987). Kravetz (1982) provided an overview of the content on women from the social science and social work literature that needs to be incorporated into social work curricula to provide a substantive and nonsexist knowledge base concerning women. Her review focused on the role of women in the social work profession, sexism in social welfare policies and services, and nonsexist practice methods with women. Hooyman, Summers, and Leighninger (1988), under the auspices of CSWE's Commission on the Role and Status of Women, surveyed all schools of social work about course content on women and compiled a monograph of sample course syllabi. The CSWE Women's Commission has continued to collect and disseminate such exemplary syllabi.

Aiming to transcend the ongoing debate in the 1980s about integration of women's content in the foundation vs. a separate course approach, Abramovitz et al. (1982) presented a continuum of options for integrating nonsexist content on women into social policy curriculum. Providing options rather than a single approach reflects a recognition that some schools and faculties are more ready to change than others as well as the importance of starting such change efforts by building on existing resources, including current course syllabi. Options were organized around dimensions and choices: the nature of the mandate to instructors, the degree of comprehensiveness of content about women, and the allocation of curriculum time or space to women's issues.

Under the minimal option, which appears to be characteristic of many schools of social work, content on women is not specifically required by the program (other than the CSWE standards); rather, the instructor has discretion about whether and how to include such content. This option tends to result in piecemeal and irregular inclusion of content. When included, content is not systematically related to overall course objectives. For example, a minimal approach in a policy course might include the occasional use of exemplary policies and programs relevant to women, a discussion of discrimination against women and current events related to women, or the opportunity to write a paper on women's issues. However, all social policies would not be analyzed through the lens of gender, nor would feminist models for policy change be proposed.

With the moderate option, the mandate for content inclusion is sanctioned by a schoolwide policy explicitly stating such content as necessary and important; content is presented comprehensively and systematically integrated into lectures and discussions rather than left to the instructor's discretion. References to women's issues in course descriptions, syllabi, bibliographies, and assignments are explicit; and courses about women are listed in the school bulletin, thereby complying with the accreditation standard on women. Although content on women is an integral component of historical, theoretical, and practice units of instruction and thereby linked to social work knowledge, values, and skills under the moderate option, it nevertheless is often limited to only a few introductory courses or to specialized electives.

The maximal option moves beyond this by a systematic integration of content on women in all required courses as well as the development of more electives on women's issues. Implementation of a feminist perspective in terms of curriculum content, structure, and pedagogy as well as in the organizational culture would be an example of the maximal option and is described more fully below. This option appears rarely, if ever, to have been effectively pursued. A 1992 review of the *Journal of Social Work Education* from 1983 to 1990 did not find any additional articles on efforts of schools of social work to include content on women in the required curriculum; in fact, it appears that the amount of such content within foundation courses has actually declined as the 1980s progressed, a period in which the social science knowledge based on women expanded, while backlash against women's gains occurred (Vinton 1992).

Barriers to Change

This historical review highlights the apparent paradox of the limited progress of integrating content on women into the educational preparation for a women's profession. Where progress has occurred, the problems of women are often couched in individual terms, overlooking the shared experiences of women in a patriarchal and racist society (Gutierrez 1990, 1992). Before attempting to integrate content into foundation courses that examines the systemic causes of women's oppression, the readiness of the educational system for change has to be created. The unevenness of schools' responses to meeting the accreditation standard regarding women's content suggests the persistence of profound barriers to such changes. An understanding of these barriers is an essential step toward faculty beginning to agree on both the importance, the nature, and the structure of content on women.

One primary barrier is faculty resistance, often veiled under the guise of academic freedom, to the mandating of a particular point of view. Whenever new content is introduced into a curriculum, faculty may find it difficult to hear others critique their teaching for serious flaws or omissions. Some may react with a sense of inadequacy, feeling paralyzed because any effort seems too little or too late. Others may view such content as a special topic, hoping or assuming that someone else will take care of it. To master the interdisciplinary nature of the new scholarship on women means that many faculty have to enter fields of study foreign to their area of expertise. Needless to say, to incorporate effectively the rapidly emerging body of new material on women is time-consuming, challenging faculty to "retrain" or "retool" around content that some may perceive as a "fad." Other faculty, concerned by the small number of male students, may feel pressure to reinforce the male presence in the profession. Similarly, they may view gender-related content of interest and relevance only to women.

Some may believe that the "really big problems" of social work—poverty, racism, AIDS, chronic physical and mental illness, for example—are more important than and unrelated to nonsexist practice or attention to women's distinctive needs, and fail to see how women are disproportionately affected by these growing social problems. Although considerable work remains regarding the integration of content on race and racism into social work curricula, there appears to be more professional agreement to take a clear stance and to identify a clear social work position than is true with regard to sexism (Bernard and Gottlieb 1987). More than twenty years after the beginning of the women's movement, some faculty, perhaps influenced by the current backlash against women, may believe that "women's problems have been taken care of." Confronted with multiple demands on limited curricular space, faculty may perceive that knowledge about women or sexism is not sufficiently important to warrant inclusion.

The value- and emotion-laden content about gender-based inequities can also be a source of resistance. Sexism is an issue that affects all of us personally, with gender being the one permanent difference experienced by *all* members of a society. Other special populations, such as racial or sexual minorities, may be perceived as "outside the self." But, because of the universal and personally emotional character of sex differences, it is impossible to place oneself apart or to be objective about sex role content. To integrate content on women successfully into foundation curriculum requires changes of a profound nature. Any analysis of sexism in society at large has to include also an assessment of one's own personal and professional life and an honest willingness to challenge and to modify one's own values and belief systems. Such an awareness may also highlight contradictions between what is espoused in the classroom and what occurs in one's personal life with regard to relationships with partners and children (Bernard and Gottlieb 1987; Abramovitz et al. 1982). Students undoubtedly mirror similar sources of resistance, particularly a reluctance to examine the implications of sexism for their own personal and professional lives. An underlying cause of such resistance may be structural, e.g., the fact that men remain overrepresented among tenured faculty, deans, and, in some instances, agency directorships, even though men are underrepresented as social work students and consumers.

Conceptual Frameworks

The CSWE standard provides no particular theoretical framework within which women are studied, resulting in wide variability in how schools approach and meet the accreditation standard for inclusion of content on women. The three primary conceptual frameworks relevant to the foundation content on women are: women's issues, nonsexist, and feminist perspectives. All of these contrast with traditional models of practice in which differences between males and females are viewed as natural and immutable, with male standards as the yardstick for what is normal and healthy, and females judged in relation to male needs and criteria (Abramovitz 1987; Brickman 1984). For example, models of social science research have typically treated women as the "other," studying the human condition from a male viewpoint and women as a special population. As a result, theory and research that constitute the social work knowledge base may ignore, misunderstand, misrepresent, or mystify the roles, needs, and interests of women (Abramovitz 1987). It is against this traditional model, which underlies most social work education and practice through the 1980s, that we turn to examining and critiquing three alternatives.

Women's Issues or "Add a Woman and Stir" Approach

The women's issues model, which appears to be most common, emerged in the 1970s, with an emphasis on overcoming bias and sex discrimination and gaining equity and inclusiveness for women in society (Brickman 1984). This has often been referred to as "add the women and stir" philosophy or "slice of the pie" approach, whether the goal was to increase the number of women in positions traditionally dominated by men; to enhance women's access to a "slice of the traditional pie" of career success; or to expand services to low-income women. Unfortunately, such incremental changes generally took place within existing social systems and served to maintain the status quo, both within society and social work education.

Although social work learning and practice were, to some extent, reexamined in the 1970s and early 1980s on the basis of new knowledge about women, content on women was generally incorporated into the "mainstream" of social work curriculum and presumed the traditional structure and content of the foundation curriculum. Simply adding content on women to classes, such as a session on women at the end of the course, or attaching readings to the bibliography, is compensatory rather than change-oriented, however (Andersen 1987). As a result, course materials built on a women's issues approach often fail to examine the implications of gender for the rest of the course content and to analyze adequately the paradigms that govern and constrict the social work knowledge base (Tice 1990).

Similarly, compensatory content tends to focus on ways for women to overcome internal barriers to their equality. These psychological obstacles, such as role conflicts, personal attitudes, passivity, and lack of confidence, are presumed to result from women's socialization to traditional gender-based roles. Interventions are directed toward women themselves rather than at systemic or structural factors; power is defined on an individual basis and as an individual trait. Successful women in traditionally male positions are pointed to as proof that women can be equal to men in the labor force (Gordon 1992; Brickman 1984). As an example of this individualistic approach, assertiveness training, popular in the late 1970s, presented women with a male model of individual success and upward mobility; lack of assertiveness and caring for others were viewed as female deficiencies rather than as products of structured power relations. This social skills learning approach has been widely criticized, however. For example, the psychological and behavioral qualities that women have acquired through developmental experiences, such as caregiving, should not be rejected but instead defined as socially valuable qualities, ones that women must maintain and men must develop. Accordingly, person-centered interventions should not aim to rid women of their concern for others, but rather to free such concern from being placed at the service at their own subordination (Morell 1987; Hooyman 1991).

As another example of the "add a woman and stir" approach, management training for women has tended to focus on women's acquiring rational or linear thinking, autonomy, and the ability to compartmentalize—skills based on a male-oriented model of administration (Brickman 1984; Hooyman 1991). Women were expected to "dress for success" or "think like a man" in order to move into higher-level positions. In contrast, a feminist approach identifies the strengths that women bring to management positions, including attention to interpersonal communication and process, intuitive and creative problem solving, and concern and compassion for others. Feminism is not about individual mobility up the corporate ladder, so that women with proper credentials will succeed while others will not. Rather it is about institutional norms and practices that deny women access to essential resources. Instead of women adapting to male norms of organizational behavior, women who draw upon their own strengths, experiences, and processes can enhance the larger organizational environment for both women and men by supporting the integration of personal and professional concerns (Bricker-Jenkins, Hooyman, and Gottlieb 1991; Gordon 1992).

In summary, treatment of women as a special population with special issues tends to focus on women's weaknesses and to isolate them, thereby representing little progression from the traditional orientation toward women as "other" or the "second sex" (Abramovitz 1987; Freeman 1990). By not taking account of underlying power dynamics and the need for structural changes, such individualistic approaches toward the problems faced by women ignore their life experiences of oppression. Personal issues, for both men and women, need to be viewed in a political context so that solutions extend from the individual to the organizational and institutional, as identified below in the nonsexist and feminist approaches to change.

Nonsexist Perspective or Equal Rights Model

In contrast to a women's issues approach, a nonsexist perspective recognizes the structural factors inherent and universal within sexism; an underlying assumption is that the dysfunctional system of sex role stereotyping devalues and discriminates against women and that the power differentials between women and men are explicit (Bernard and Gottlieb 1987). It is recognized that the range of problems experienced by women are rooted in and influenced by societal expectations for women's behavior and in societal restrictions on their life possibilities. Likewise, nonsexist service delivery systems would not reinforce societal stereotypes about women or men.

Guidelines for nonsexist practice tailored toward the needs of women have been formulated by Kravetz (1982). For example, problem assessment and goals are not to be based on culturally prescribed sex role behaviors; similarly, behaviors that do not meet cultural expectations, such as a woman choosing not to care for an older relative or not to bear children, should not be viewed as pathological or deviant. It is growth-producing for women to evaluate the ways in which social norms and roles and structural realities influence their experiences. Women's consciousness-raising and support groups are a way to deemphasize the authority of the expert or professional, help group members share and understand collective experiences that have influenced them as women, and facilitate their respect and trust for each other. Under a nonsexist approach, interventions address individual, interpersonal, and institutional barriers—female socialization, sex role conflicts, gender-based segregation of jobs, wage discrimination, biased attitudes of employers, and sexual harassment—all factors that limit women's aspirations and constrain their professional choices.

Rather than question the fundamental assumptions of the structure of professional practice or education, a nonsexist approach attempts to strip it of its sexist overlay. It is believed that necessary changes can take place through resocialization and reeducation within the context of the current social order as "revised." Key to the nonsexist model is the concept that those with authority set and apply standards of "fairness." Since males are the normative standard against which behavior and functioning are measured, social conditions and socialization processes need to be altered so that women can enjoy similar benefits and "be the same" as men. Equal rights tend to be discussed on an abstract level, rather than in terms of women's daily reality and life experiences (Bricker-Jenkins and Hooyman 1986).

The tenets of the nonsexist perspective can perhaps best be illustrated in terms of research. An example of how sexism has permeated research is reflected in the knowledge base underlying gerontological social work. Even though women form the majority of elderly, women were not included in any of the major longitudinal studies on aging until 1978, presentations on women were nearly absent from many major conferences on aging, and relatively little social work research has been undertaken on issues that affect only or disproportionately women, such as menopause, breast and uterine cancer, estrogen replacement therapy, poverty, and living alone. Nonsexist research recognizes that stereotypical thought and institutional sexism have permeated the entire research process with regard to a wide range of social problems, including the formulation of research questions, definition of concepts, operationalization of variables, selection of samples and analyses of findings. It aims to ensure that questions and issues of interest to both men and women are studied, research results fairly interpreted, and alternative explanations offered, when appropriate. With regard to the above example, a nonsexist approach in gerontological social work research would assure that women's concerns are addressed, and that women are proportionately represented in any samples of the elderly. However, nonsexist research, as compared to feminist research models described below, does not challenge the logical empirical and positivist assumptions nor the worldview of the traditional patriarchal perspective that underlie many traditional research designs (Van Den Bergh and Cooper 1986; Bernard and Gottlieb 1987).

Another variation of a nonsexist approach has been defined as "liberal feminism." From this perspective, the origins of women's oppression are due to the lack of equal civil rights and opportunities, and the learned psychology associated with sex-role socialization. Women's

liberation and egalitarian gender relations will be achieved when sexist discrimination is eliminated and women have the opportunity to
pursue their individual development as fully as do men. The means to
achieve these ends, such as the efforts to secure the passage of the
Equal Rights Amendment, include social and legal reform; policies to
create equal opportunity and establish individual civil rights so that no
one is denied access to resources because of gender; and reeducation
about sex-role socialization (Freeman 1990).

Closely related to a nonsexist perspective is the explicit utilization of
gender as a variable in teaching and practice (Abramovitz 1987). Such
an approach aims to make students aware of gender as a critical variable affecting social work practice, research, policy formulation, and
the organization and delivery of social services. Students are provided
with new information about women's experience, and develop the
skills to recognize and eliminate sexist stereotypes when they assess
clients, design service programs, examine social policies, and evaluate
research studies. Theories of human and social development are refor-
mulated through the use of nonsexist research questions, concepts, and
methods. Attention is paid to how ideologies of women's role as the
"other" or the "private woman" reinforce and reflect prevailing arrangements, such as the private–public gender division of labor that affects
women's familial and professional roles.

To simply add a unit, chapter, lecture, or course on women or to consider gender as a primary variable along with minor revisions to the traditional core curriculum, however, leaves untouched the paradigmatic
norms that have the effect of either marginalizing or excluding women
or treating them as a monolithic category (Tice 1990). Although a nonsexist approach tries to redress injustice, it does not fundamentally challenge the current power structure that overvalues men and masculine
traits in the public sphere and that undervalues women and feminine
traits within the private sphere. In the end, it "mainstreams" content on
women into the curriculum. But scholarship on women should "not be a
tributary that merges into the main river. Rather, the feminist perspective should rechannel the river" (Stimpson and Cobb-Kressner 1986:52).

What is needed to achieve a gender-inclusive curriculum is to go
beyond the "add a woman and stir" or nonsexist approaches to curricular reform. A women's issues or nonsexist component in social work
curricula is not equivalent to a component on feminist theory, practice,
or research. Instead, feminist theory and analysis presume a profound

rethinking of the foundations of social work knowledge and, accordingly, of education and practice (Andersen 1987; Freeman 1990). While the aim of nonsexist and women's issues perspectives are equity and inclusiveness for women, a feminist approach aims to create a method of education and practice designed to engage all persons in the process of personal and political transformation (Bricker-Jenkins and Hooyman 1986; Wetzel 1986; Van Den Bergh and Cooper 1986; Bricker-Jenkins, Hooyman, and Gottlieb 1991).

Feminist Perspective

Although a number of schools of social work utilize a women's issue or nonsexist perspective in their curricula, few schools, if any, explicitly incorporate feminism in their teaching structure, content, or process. To do so would fundamentally alter the way that practice issues are conceptualized and studied, beginning with an examination of the analytical category of patriarchy. Not surprisingly, a feminist perspective in schools or departments of social work is often regarded as marginal, peripheral, "radical," anti-male, or anti-power. In the past decade, some educators and students have unfortunately narrowly defined and, in turn, rejected feminism, failing to recognize that its evolving and comprehensive nature encompasses analyses not only in terms of gender but also race and class. Such narrow definitions have meant that exposure to feminist knowledge, values, and skills in social work curricula tends to be largely achieved through an incremental process of self-selection (Hudson 1985).

Composed of three interrelated dimensions—theory, practice, and research—feminism starts from the assumption that the prevailing standpoint of social reality and knowledge about it have, by and large, been sexist (Krane 1991). According to feminist theorists, sexism refers to a picture of social reality, shaped and influenced by a male perspective known as androcentricity (man as the norm) (Eichler 1987, 1988). Because we live in an androcentric social, political, and intellectual environment, women have been absent or invisible and their experiences—their reality and ways of making sense of the world—have been misrepresented (Cummerton 1983; Hawkesworth 1989). What has been asserted as universal knowledge and truth are "metanarratives," which feminists reject for being reductionist and ahistorical. Metanarratives falsely universalize white middle-class males as normative, while peripheralizing the diverse experiences of women, minorities, and the poor as the "other" (Andersen 1987; Mascia-Lees, Sharpe, and Cohen-Ballerino 1989; Fraser and Nicholson 1988). Similarly, essentialistic thinking about the social construction of gender as fixed, natural, and absolute reduces complex relations to fixed binary oppositions (male/female; good/bad; either/or).

Feminists advocate a "deconstructive" strategy that questions the validity of such universals and leads to theories that are nonuniversalistic, self-conscious about perspective and values, and open to the multiplicity and diversity of experiences by gender, race, class, and culture (Haraway 1988). To reject the binary conceptualization of "man" and "woman" or "white man including white woman" is to move to a conception of gender as one strand among others, while also attending to class, race, ethnicity, age, and sexual orientation. This process then opens up the possibility of diversity among men and women in specific historical, social and cultural constructs (Fraser and Nicholson 1988; Hurtado 1989).

Rather than accept a worldview based on male experience or on helping women to acquire male privileges (as in the women's issues approach), the feminist model is grounded in an alternative worldview that is fundamentally different from that rooted in our culture and profession. Feminist discourse provides a way of seeing and thinking about women's issues that is built on women's experiences (Hartsock 1979; Spender 1985). Women are the central figures, not the second sex (Brickman 1984).

Yet feminism is not concerned only with women's issues, nor is it inherently anti-male; its goal of self-actualization and its focus on oppression cross-cut concerns shared by women and men. For example, an examination of both sides of the power structure reveals the negative effects of too little power on women and too much power on men. By bringing the traditional strengths of women, such as responsiveness, relatedness, and flexibility, from the private realm of the home into the public arena of the marketplace—in other words, by women's qualities becoming public—this power imbalance can be redressed (Wetzel 1986; Brickman 1984). Similarly, feminist practice is designed to engage all persons in the process of fundamental personal and political transformation by changing institutionalized structures and beliefs that support inequality and by creating new structures that empower individuals (Goldberg-Wood and Middlemann 1989; Bricker-Jenkins, Hooyman, and Gottlieb 1991). Feminism originates in a "belief in the worthiness of all to have an opportunity to develop to their fullest" (Bricker-Jenkins [in press]). Embracing both personal and social change, feminism as a collective activity aims to eliminate all hierarchies in which one category of human beings dominates or controls another, thereby releasing collective power for the welfare of all (Morell 1987). It provides a mode of analysis and action that can and must contend with all the "isms" that threaten human well-being (Bricker-Jenkins, Hooyman, and Gottlieb 1991).

Suggesting that feminism is a lens through which to view diverse groups' experiences of oppression, an increasing number of feminist scholars from a wide range of disciplines are articulating conceptual models encompassing the intersection of racism, classism, and sexism rather than viewing them as separate systems (Gordon 1990; Collins 1991; Anzaldúa 1990; Arnott and Matthaei 1991). Nevertheless, the different developmental, historical, and socialization experiences of white women and women of color mean that issues of minority women, who view the world through the primary lens of race, diverge from mainstream white middle-class feminist perspectives. Although this chapter cannot begin to grapple with the complexities of intersections among the isms, courses taught from a feminist perspective do provide an arena in which to examine the differences among each group's reality as well as their common experiences with structural gender-based oppression (Crawley 1992). Through personal awareness of oppression and identification with other human beings, altered definitions of self, social reality, relationships and their accompanying behavior among men and women from diverse backgrounds can also change. With a feminist lens, diversity of all kinds is valued as a source of strength (Lincoln and Koeske 1987; Morell 1987; Bricker-Jenkins, Hooyman, and Gottlieb 1991).

As a mode of analysis, a way of asking questions about existing structures and behaviors and searching for answers by gleaning political insights from analyses of personal experiences, feminism does not represent fixed political conclusions nor a right or wrong way. In fact, a theme in feminist theory is the recognition of the diversity of definitions, and one of its strengths has been a lack of orthodoxy or a fixed creed. Feminist ideas are constantly evolving and adapting to the diverse experiences of women and are subject to continual self-scrutiny, challenge, and revision (Hartsock 1979). The underlying bond, however, is agreement that personal problems are affected by injustices inherent in patriarchy and that women's oppression and subordination must be eliminated.

What does a feminist perspective mean for social work education and practice? To guide the development of a more inclusive curriculum in its transformative phase, an essential question is "what is the core content of my discipline and how would it have to change to reflect the fact that women are a majority of the world's population, and that race, sex, and class stratification have structured social life?" (McIntosh 1988; Tice 1990). As noted above, opposition to essentialistic and universalistic thinking provides avenues for transforming the social work knowledge base and professional practice. Rather than focusing only on white male experience as the norm or women as a unitary group, a feminist approach to curriculum would examine a multiplicity of women's experiences, identifying differences as well as commonalities in order to understand how the intersections of class, race, sexual orientation, and gender affect the diverse range of women's ways of knowing (Luttrel 1989; Tice 1990).

To implement a feminist perspective in social work education is to alter the way in which the curriculum is organized, the pedagogy used, and the larger organizational structure of schools of social work. Most social work curricula, particularly at the master's level, are dichotomous in their basic structure. The social work profession is itself built on a foundation of dualities, such as individual adaptation and social change and humanistic values and scientific methods of development (Berlin 1990). Consistent with the feminist rejection of binary conceptualizations, curriculum restructuring would remove the false dichotomies and artificial separations that have traditionally characterized social work education: specialist vs. generalist, direct vs. indirect, research vs. practice, empirical vs. nonempirical, macro vs. clinical, individual vs. social change, theory vs. practice, policy vs. practice, process vs. product, present vs. future, professional vs. client, expert vs. student (Van Den Bergh and Cooper 1986).

With its guiding principle of the unity of all living things, events, and knowledge, feminism would seek to eliminate such polarities by transforming social work curriculum to be more integrated, generalist and holistic (Wetzel 1986; Morell 1987). For example, social work students frequently view research as "out there," irrelevant to practice. In a feminist model, research is not an end in itself, but an integral component of practice, a process of evaluating effort and outcome. Similarly, at a practice level, the scientist/practitioner can simultaneously maintain fidelity to feminist values and flexibly use a range of knowledge-generating methods, including both naturalistic and traditional scientific methods (Ivanoff, Robinson, and Blythe 1987). Nor can policy, when taught from a feminist perspective, be separated from practice and from clients' daily lives. Instead, the personal and political are inextricably interconnected. Likewise, an advanced generalist curriculum at the master's level is more consistent with feminism's emphasis on personal and social change, on methods for linking case-to-class-to-cause, and on achieving unity through diversity.

To integrate a feminist perspective into social work curricula requires a congruence of content with process and of cause with function (Morell 1987; Wharf 1990; Moreau and Leonard 1989; Lecomte 1990). Curriculum purpose and process are inseparable; the why of social work is also its how (Morell 1987). Similarly, the classroom structure cannot be separate from the process. A feminist approach goes beyond content and analysis to deal with issues of authority and control, including a commitment to nonoppressive relationships in the learning setting (Bricker-Jenkins and Hooyman 1984). Feminist theory and practice cannot be taught simply by lectures as one-way flow of communication, or the "banking principle of education," in which students are treated as empty vaults in which expert teachers deposit information (Freire 1976). Since the isolation of student and faculty groups is inherent in traditional competitive models of learning, both groups need to develop collective and empowering structures of working together. The professional distance traditional between teacher and student can be reduced by more participative and egalitarian co-learning systems. In such systems, the classroom is seen as a collaborative learning enterprise to which both students and teachers contribute through dialogue (Burstow 1991). In turn, the learning and change process experienced by social work students should parallel values and skills to be applied in their own work with clients.

One way to reduce the traditional distance between student and teacher as well as to avoid reinforcing gender stereotypes and marginalizing women is for the teacher to be both a facilitator and resource person. This also means that the teacher must be willing to share openly his or her own values and conflicts, to be honest regarding skill limitations and dilemmas, to acknowledge that no one, including the teacher, is ever completely free of biases. Teaching from a feminist perspective is an emotional, not just an intellectual engagement, oriented to developing an atmosphere of respect, trust and community (Tice 1990).

To avoid replicating the marginalization of women that still occurs in the larger society, teachers need to be attentive to subtle inequities in teacher-student exchanges as well as to how the physical arrangement of the room affects collaborative learning. They must be careful to avoid differential treatment in the classroom, such as not calling on, or interrupting women and minorities, or letting white male students dominate the discussion. Although incidents of racism and sexism will undoubtedly emerge in open class discussions, a goal should be to create classrooms that do not replicate hierarchy and oppression. A feminist curriculum provides the content and process whereby students can confront and work through their biases.

To do so, the teaching approach also needs to be congruent with the students' own personal experiences and life changes. This then suggests the value of experientially based learning, beginning with the learner's experiences and proceeding through reflection and discussion to theory and action. Such consciousness-raising techniques foster the integration of personal and professional concerns. Critical to students' developing a social consciousness (a sense of their own and others' oppression) and a social analysis (an understanding of why this occurs) are curriculum opportunities for them to explore their own values, assumptions, biases, and roots in light of the social structures in which they live. Accordingly, a classroom structured on feminist principles encourages self-reflection and critical thinking, including reading and writing critically as part of learning to think in new ways (Bunch 1983; Tice 1990). Likewise, students need opportunities to construct knowledge as well as to learn about things, to question and critically examine what they study, and to link new information and ideas to their own life experiences. Through small-group exercises, discussions and reporting out, students can pose questions, listen to, react, and comment on each others' statements and ideas. To critique themselves, their relationships, and their histories and then to connect their experiences to those of others is essential to students' understanding that personal and social change is a continuous process over time (Bricker-Jenkins 1983; Van Den Berg and Cooper 1986). Through personal awareness of oppression and identification with other human beings, students can sense a unity with others different from themselves (Lincoln and Koeske 1987).

Assignments can also be structured in ways to decrease any disassociation of the personal and affective from the cognitive. Use of oral histories and biographies, community narratives, and ethnographies can foster an awareness and appreciation of women's diversity (Barry 1989; Tice 1990). Students need chances to process and apply what they are learning rather than to memorize theoretical constructs and "facts." When writing term papers, students tend to pull together facts with others' opinions rather than to make their own effort at analysis. As an alternative to such papers, writing a journal can be useful in analyzing and thinking about others' ideas as well as developing one's own. Journals also provide a mechanism to integrate cognitive and affective learning, in other words, to relate personally with course content. Action projects move students beyond reflection, recognizing that action is necessary to transform institutions and values (Bunch 1983; Schniedewind 1983).

Restructuring the classroom to support collective and empowering ways of working together as learners is consistent with a feminist approach to education and practice. Cooperative assignments and projects, structured time for feedback, simulations, reflection and sharing, and group development and team building can strengthen such collective support and activity. The teacher and, in turn, the students become facilitators of group process. Students who experience self-directed learning, the ongoing use of learning contracts and structured feedback, and ways to utilize such critiques will be acquiring skills that they can then transfer to work settings.

Not only should there be consistency between content and structure, but also between the classroom and the larger organizational environment. Attempts to implement feminist values in social work curriculum occur within the context of large hierarchies, which value objectivity, competition, and individual merit. Administrative structures, funding sources and mandates, and policy regulations are structural constraints to implementing a feminist perspective within a social work school or department. Admittedly, few social work units can alter the larger university or college context. Nevertheless, within schools or departments, there can be deliberate efforts to create an open and equitable work climate that legitimizes a feminist approach as a goal and a process. Increasing participatory decision making does not imply structurelessness; rather, the democratic structure provides meaningful opportunities for student, faculty, and staff leadership and participation.

This does not mean, however, that there are no power differences between students and faculty. The faculty member's leadership and power are essential to creating an arena in which students can *learn* to take responsibility for themselves and the group. Instructors can also model the sharing of leadership and reflection and feedback through team teaching (Schniedewind 1983). In sum, the classroom and school context should try to mirror the kind of community in which we would like to live (Lecomte 1990; Tice 1990).

Even with efforts to create a supportive environment within the school or department of social work itself, a number of barriers may persist. University-wide course approval processes, for example, tend to perpetuate paradigms of the dominant culture. Fiscal crises, and the accompanying pressure to produce quantifiable results that are affecting nearly all institutions of higher learning, can serve to further the status quo and to discourage administrators or faculty from trying new approaches. Given these larger institutional barriers along with the time necessary for faculty to rethink fundamentally how they teach, faculty may fear risks to their careers. Pressured to publish as well as to quantify student evaluations, they may experience burnout if administrative support and resources for such changes are absent. Although the CSWE *Accreditation Standards* are an external mandate to increase content on women in the curriculum, attempts to meet the standards' intent by counting the number of readings and topics on women in course syllabi can conflict with a feminist approach that emphasizes process. In fact, the widely spread (mis)perception that feminism is peripheral to social work practice and education can, in itself, be a major barrier.

Students may themselves be resistant to a feminist approach. In fact, they may challenge the validity of the concept of feminism itself, holding onto traditional definitions of gender-appropriate behavior (Kirst-Ashman 1992). Concerned with graduating with the skills and knowledge to enhance their employability in recessionary times, they may request a "cookbook" approach to education and be uncomfortable with a more self-reflective and active learning style. Just as faculty may experience an incongruence between feminist theory and practice in the classroom and their personal lives, students will be challenged to change their own behavior by acting differently in their relationships with others. Given our socialization in a sexist and racist society, such change is difficult for all us. But it may occur through consciousness-raising techniques, personal experiences based on new ways of relating to one another, or simply through the pragmatics of self-protective mechanisms. Feminist models for change must be part of both classroom and field-based learning. This next section briefly proposes some ways of implementing a feminist perspective in courses on research, practice, social policy and HBSE as well as in the practicum. Consistent with a feminist perspective on process and change, these are not absolutes but rather guidelines to be revised and expanded by faculty, students, and practicum instructors.

A Feminist Research Course

Feminist research models have been widely advanced in the professional literature (Cummerton 1983; Gottlieb and Bombyk 1987). Hartsock maintains that the goal of "making conscious the philosophy embedded in our lives" will alter the way in which the goals of research courses are phrased and content is structured (1979:65). Social work research models have been largely derived and adopted from the social sciences, implicitly accepting many of the empirical assumptions of the social sciences. The primary assumption has been that of "positivism" or "neopositivism": the belief that scientific knowledge must be definable, measurable, and testable and that the observer must be objective or value-neutral about her observations. This tradition, by emphasizing rationality, impersonality, prediction and control, "value free" objectivity, and quantification, has tended to divide the empirical world into subject/object (Rosenman and Ruckdeschel 1981).

Feminist researchers are attempting to create research paradigms and methods that can accommodate to the multidimensional processes of life and that will supplement positivist research (Bricker-Jenkins [in press]). A feminist perspective places structural issues at center stage in every step of the research problem-solving process. As a result, feminist research is political in purpose and in method and, in fact, becomes a method of practice. A feminist research course would begin by challenging the prevailing assumption that the research process is value neutral and would show how presumed objectivity can serve as a subtle cover for ideological bias (Rosenman and Ruckdeschel 1981).

Students would be expected to think critically about the lenses, personal biases, and values by which they view social reality; they would learn that what is known cannot exist apart from those who are the "knowers" and that there are many truths (Hartsock 1979; Spender 1985; Bricker-Jenkins [in press]).

Valuing the subjective and nonrational does not mean abandoning objective information (Wetzel 1986). However, it does recognize that there is no truly objective data, since all data depend upon specific individuals, their relationships with one another, and thus the context of the research enterprise (Krane 1991). Therefore, the process of examining contrary evidence, ensuring the rigorous reporting of research findings and clarifying underlying values is central to "objectivity" (Eichler 1988).

Similarly, feminist research does not presume the use of only qualitative methods. Quantitative methods are not inherently antifeminist; instead, they can serve feminist research agendas, such as documenting trends that indicate the oppression of women, or aggregating statistical findings to advocate for policy changes (Wetzel 1986; Gottlieb and Bombyk 1987; Ivanoff, Robinson, and Blythe 1987). Research *for* women rather than *on* women, feminist research is a method of action for change, not an end in itself (Cummerton 1983). Although every claim made in the name of feminism is not legitimate, once reason and evidence provide support for a feminist claim, that claim is intended to replace, not coexist, with androcentric claims (Harding 1986).

The goal of a feminist research course in the foundation curriculum is not necessarily that students adopt a feminist perspective. Rather, they should be able to identify the lenses through which they view social issues and then begin to scrutinize accepted theoretical frameworks and modes of practice for their potential biases and often concealed assumptions of social reality. As noted above, feminism assumes that all knowledge is infused with values, and that we are constantly creating reality (Bricker-Jenkins, Hooyman, and Gottlieb 1991). The unmasking of the sexist as well as the racist, classist, and heterosexist underpinnings of the knowledge bases in empirical accounts of social issues must be systematic and explicit, because these "isms" rarely emerge in forms other than those that suggest that social reality and issues are simply the way things are (MacKinnon 1987). Within a foundation research course, this process of value identification and analysis of the source of values that underlie objective and quantifiable research is critical.

A second stage, best accomplished in an advanced research course, is to begin to build a body of research-based knowledge about women for the social work profession. Selecting a topic that focuses on women, students would bring to bear a perspective different from those traditionally used. In doing so, they would learn that women's experiences and accounts of social reality have been repeatedly negated or distorted. There is a need to document and understand the essential differences in the ways in which men and women perceive the world, resolve the dilemmas of daily life, and relate to others (Krane 1991; Davis 1986). Ideally, such a course would not end with simply a research report, but with an action plan for changing the conditions under study (Bricker-Jenkins and Hooyman 1986).

A Feminist Practice Course

Feminist social work practice rejects theoretical perspectives and interventions that implicitly or explicitly support a secondary status for women (Valentich 1986). Feminist theory offers a social structural framework for the assessment of social functioning and the design and implementation of practice interventions. But a feminist practice course is not a "cookbook" approach to developing skills as tools, nor is there one model of teaching feminist practice. The findings from a 1985 survey of feminist practitioners, funded by NASW and sponsored by the National Commission on Women's Issues, provide a beginning framework for defining the goals and methods relevant to teaching a practice course from a feminist perspective (Bricker-Jenkins, Hooyman, and Gottlieb 1991; Bricker-Jenkins and Hooyman 1986; Bricker-Jenkins [in press]). Not surprisingly, this survey found that few of the participants had learned about feminist practice in a school of social work. In fact, when practitioners were asked what readings had most influenced the development of a feminist perspective, they responded in terms of women's art, poetry, music, biographies, and autobiographies. Feminist practice is rooted in women's culture as both a network of social relationships and the artistic and symbolic representation of those relationships (Bricker-Jenkins and Hooyman 1986).

The goal of feminist practice is both personal and social change; we change ourselves as we change the world as we change ourselves. Aiming to identify the social, political, and cultural origins of the client's distress, private issues are approached in terms of their public and political dimensions, or the personal as political. There is a shifting from a deficit or pathological model to one based on strengths and growth. As one participant in the feminist practice study stated, "There are no private solutions to collective problems." Accordingly, policy cannot be separated from practice, but both are inextricably interconnected in feminist education (Bricker-Jenkins and Hooyman 1984).

The feminist practitioner uses a variety of methods, moving from case to class to cause: assessment based on clients' strengths; consciousness-raising as both content and method; process-oriented, collaborative, respectful, and nonjudgemental problem solving; noncoercive conflict resolution; validation of the nonrational; partnership between worker and client in the discovery of solutions; and attention to dimensions of human experience, such as the physical and spiritual, that are often neglected in conventional practice (Hudson 1985; Bricker-Jenkins and Hooyman 1986). When instructors draw upon similar methods in their teaching, the way in which a course on feminist practice is taught can then model the process for doing feminist practice.

The students' active involvement in a participatory learning process can enhance their understanding of a feminist approach to the problems facing their clients. Practice theory and method should be consonant with the experiences of both workers and clients; likewise, the teaching of feminist practice is congruent with the students' and faculty's experiences. Since feminist practice is rooted in women's experience with oppression, students in a feminist practice course must examine their own life experiences with oppression. Because women's strengths, histories, conditions, and developmental patterns have been suppressed, students must have the opportunity to discover and engage these characteristics. Having learned that process, they will be better able to mobilize the strengths of individuals, groups, and communities with whom they work.

A Feminist Social Policy Course

The social problems central to a foundation social policy course are women's issues: poverty and underemployment, the lack of dependent care policies for women as caregivers across the life span, inadequate health care, interpersonal violence, and threats to reproductive rights. Given the disproportionate representation of women as social service recipients, a foundation social policy course should begin by analyzing why this occurs. This question can be answered by an analysis of how the underlying values and belief system of individualism and private responsibility determine what our society defines as social problems; the social environment's impact on social policies affecting women in terms of sex roles; and historical trends in which women were the early implementers and makers of social policy, but whose work has since been devalued. In addition to students' acquiring knowledge about the background of social policy and of current problem areas, such as the feminization of poverty, that result from that context, they also need to attain an understanding of how social policy can be changed to enhance women's lives. Such an analysis is conducive to developing policy and practice strategies to empower women to take control over their environment and thus to experience personal political power (Burden 1987).

A feminist policy course would encompass not only the context and outcome of social policy, but also bring to bear a different perspective on the process of policy formulation and change. Ironically, many women social workers have resisted moving into the macro arena of policy change because of their perceptions of the policy process dominated by the "good old boys" and as closed to or alien to women. In fact, women's tendency to choose working directly with individuals or families rather than to enter administrative or policy positions reflects an unfortunate dichotomy into female/male practice arenas. This split has meant that women have not been well represented in the policy-making arena that directly and critically impacts the lives of women as clients.

A feminist perspective on the policy process would emphasize the importance of fully involving those who are impacted by the policies. In instances of policies affecting women, this often means being more responsive to groups previously denied full access to decision making. Interpersonal skills of listening, empathy, consensus building, negotiation, and conflict resolution would contrast markedly with the power plays, "backroom deals," and manipulation that have often dominated the traditional policy-making arena. Women involved in the policy-making process are more likely to have been directly and daily involved in issues affecting families—education, day care, health care, mental health, child welfare—and to recognize the need for policies, such as dependent care, family and medical leave for new parents and adult children caring for the elderly, and home health care that are related to women's traditional roles as caregivers in family and society. Students could be asked to critique the traditionally "male" nature of the policy process. An alternative assignment could be to interview women and men in policy-making positions to observe whether there are differences in how they approach the policy process.

In a feminist policy process, criteria for assessing the impact of policies would include taking account of the differential effects by gender in terms of inequities and discrimination. For example, a feminist analysis of health care policies would recognize how Medicare and Medicaid differentially impact upon women, implicitly expecting women to be the primary caregivers of dependent persons, even when this necessitates women's leaving the labor force and thus being adversely affected by reduced income and retirement benefits. Such an analysis of the human costs among the unpaid providers of services would contrast markedly with a traditional cost-benefit analysis of tax dollars expended and saved. Students could be asked to prepare a written impact analysis, bringing to bear both feminist and more traditional perspectives to the process of problem definition, goal setting, and policy formulation, implementation, and evaluation. Through such an analysis, students would become more aware of the potential for change and the importance of social workers with a feminist perspective within the political arena.

A Feminist HBSE Course

The feminist concept of the personal as political is central to foundation HBSE courses that are intended to bridge content on human development with macro analyses of culture and of economic political and organizational structures. Most HBSE courses draw upon an analysis of human development within a systems or ecological framework. From a feminist perspective, any analyses of factors affecting human behavior across the life span must address both internal (i.e., biological differences, learning theory that focuses on the socialization of women with respect to gender identity, roles, values, and worldviews) and external or environmental factors (i.e., occupational sex segregation, income maintenance systems, and social policies such as Social Security) that underlie the power imbalance of women and men in our society. For example, women's underemployment and poverty cannot be explained simply in terms of their socialization to caregiving roles; an analysis that takes account of external factors would also recognize how the historical separation of paid work from the home, the higher Social Security benefits accorded to families where the woman has assumed the traditional homemaker role, and inadequate child care all limit women's abilities to be financially independent (Burden and Gottlieb 1987). These differences then result in differential access to power for men and women across the life span in our society. In other words, students must be encouraged to bring a political analysis to bear upon human behavior and to consider the implications of political-social factors for social work with individuals, families, and groups.

In a feminist HBSE course, the role of gender along with race and class must be examined at every phase of the life span: infancy and childhood, adolescence and young adulthood, and adulthood and aging, and how the interaction of these factors results in powerlessness, particularly among low-income women of color. This feminist analysis should encompass the limitations of traditional theories of personality and human development that have been based primarily upon men, particularly the theoretical formulations of Freud, Erikson, Kohlberg, and Levinson. Theories of gender-differences in human development, which result in different values systems, life experiences, and ways of defining reality, particularly the work of Gilligan and Chodorow, should be central to this critical analysis.

Throughout a feminist HBSE course, the emphasis should be on the impact of structural inequities upon women and men, not on individual deficiencies. In fact, individual differences in personality, values, and worldviews should not be viewed as pathological. Instead, diversity should be celebrated as a positive, not as something to be merely tolerated. In their assignments, students should be expected to utilize both sociopolitical and individual analyses in understanding human behavior and its implications for social work practice with diverse client groups.

Feminist Practicum Models

Similar to the process of empowerment in the classroom, field instructor-student relationships based on trust can provide opportunities for students to experience empowerment within the context of gender-informed practicum instruction. Through this process, students may learn techniques for enhancing the potential of those with whom they work. Just as a feminist approach would seek to eliminate status distinctions and polarities in the classroom, a feminist practicum setting would ensure options for students and field instructors to experience mutuality in their relationships. The field instructors' willingness to share power, to value a personal-professional connection with the student, and to respectfully view the student as competent can build a sense of connectedness and partnership with each other. The modeling of such behavior challenges students to develop ways to translate these dimensions into student-client interactions as well (Lazzari 1991).

Through practicum training programs and orientations, schools need to analyze what is conveyed to field instructors about faculty's perceptions of students and the field. As with the classroom-based curriculum, the content and process of the educational relationship must be congruent. A feminist approach to practicum would convey the value of choices and options for both students and clients to analyze their current circumstances and roles and to make changes to better meet their needs. Such an approach, however, is likely to be incompatible with the more centralized practicum planning procedures characteristic of most schools of social work, where administrative or faculty control of the decision-making process is emphasized.

Strategies for Change

As noted above, a women's issues or nonsexist approach within social work curricula may be a necessary step in the development of content on women, but it should not be the final step. Simply adding women to a course title, or attaching readings on women to bibliographies, or relegating a discussion on women to a final class session does not serve to reduce the marginalization of women as secondary. Nor does having women faculty necessarily assure the integration of content. Admittedly, both the women's issues and nonsexist approach can inform students of the conditions and issues faced by women as clients and as primary providers of social services in our society. Within such an approach, students can learn about the ways in which women have experienced discrimination. They can become more sensitive to the ways in which the social construction of gender affects their interactions with each other and with their clients. But as long as person-centered interventions aim to change individual women rather than to alter fundamentally the social, economic, and political structures that limit women's choices, students and faculty may (inadvertently) fall into the trap of blaming women for the problems facing them.

Developing a curriculum based on feminist values is a process as well as a product in which the structure, content, and experiences of learning are systematically changed (Bunch 1983). Since for feminists our theory is our practice and our practice is our theory, we model as faculty what students need to practice in the field. In a feminist curriculum, students are not presented with a "cookbook" approach to knowledge and skill development, but rather are active participants in the learning process. Similarly, to conclude this chapter by listing feminist skills or knowledge that all students should learn is contrary to feminism as an approach that itself is constantly evolving and changing. The intent of "sharing a body of knowledge" should be superseded by an emphasis on analysis/synthesis, methods of discovery, and the translation of values into practice. A feminist approach to teaching and learning models consciousness-raising processes, which involve social consciousness and analysis, group process, critical thinking, and self-reflection in goal setting; systematic ways to incorporate evaluation and feedback; the continuous interplay of the personal as political; and congruence between the classroom experience and other academic structures, such as advising students and faculty development initiatives. Through a participatory learning process, students experience the values, skills, and processes of personal and social change that they can, in turn, apply in their own work.

As one of the participants in the 1985 Feminist Practice Project so vividly noted, "We are all in process" (Bricker-Jenkins and Hooyman 1986). A feminist curriculum is not an end in itself but is constantly evolving and changing. That process can, however, be facilitated by changes in the structure of the curriculum, such as eliminating false dichotomies of macro vs. practice skills that do not fit with the reality of feminist social work practice; by leadership on the part of the dean or director to create an organizational environment that supports and empowers faculty, staff, and students; and by faculty who feel empowered by their increased participation in their work and learning environment and who will move beyond a "women's issues" or nonsexist approach to a feminist perspective throughout the foundation curriculum.

REFERENCES

Abramovitz, M. 1978. "Social Work and Women's Liberation: A Mixed Response." *Catalyst* 3:96.

——. 1987. "Making Gender a Variable in Social Work Teaching." *Journal of Teaching in Social Work* 1(1):29–52.

——, T. J. Hopkins, V. Olds, and M. Waring. 1982. "Integrating Content on Women into the Social Policy Curriculum: A Continuum Model." *Journal of Education for Social Work* 18(1) (Winter):29–34.

Andersen, M. 1987. "Changing the Curriculum in Higher Education." *Signs: Journal of Women in Culture and Society* 12(2):222–254.

Anzaldúa, G. 1990. *Making Face, Making Soul: Haciendo Caras–Creative and Critical Perspectives by Women of Color.* San Francisco: Aunt Lute Foundation Books.

Arnott, T., and J. Matthaei. 1991. *Race, Gender, and Work.* Boston: South End Press.

Barry, K. 1989. "Biography and the Search for Women's Subjectivity." *Women's Studies International Forum* 12(6):561–577.

Berkun, C. S. 1984. "Women and the Field Experience: Toward a Model of Non-sexist Field-based Learning Conditions." *Journal of Education for Social Work* 20(3) (Fall):5–12.

Berlin, S. 1990. "Dichotomous and Complex Thinking." *Social Service Review* 64(1):46–59.

—— and D. Kravetz. 1981. "Women as Victims: A Feminist Social Work Perspective." *Social Work* 26:447–449.

Bernard, D. and N. Gottlieb. 1987. "Conditions for Non-Sexist Education." In D. Burden and N. Gottlieb, eds., *The Woman Client*, pp. 13–24. New York: Tavistock Press.

Brandwein, R. A. and A. E. Wheelock. 1978. "A New Course Model for Content on Women's Issues in Social Work Education." *Journal of Education for Social Work* 14(3) (Fall):20–26.

Bricker-Jenkins, M. In press. *The Changer and the Changed Are One: An Introduction to Feminist Social Workers and Their Practice.* New York: Columbia University Press.

——. 1983. *Feminist Ideology and Organization.* New York: Fordham University Graduate School of Social Work (monograph).

—— and N. Hooyman. 1984. "Feminist Pedagogy in Education for Social Change." *Feminist Teacher* 2(2):36–42.

——, eds. 1986. *Not For Women Only.* Silver Spring, Md.: National Association of Social Workers.

—— and N. Gottlieb, eds. 1991. *Feminist Social Work Practice in Clinical Settings.* Newbury Park, Calif.: Sage.

Brickman, J. 1984. "Feminist, Nonsexist, and Traditional Models of Therapy: Implications of Working With Incest." *Women and Therapy* 3(1) (Spring):49–67.

Bunch, C. 1983. "Not By Degrees: Feminist Theory and Education." In C. Bunch and S. Pollack, eds., *Learning Our Way*, pp. 248–260. Trumansburg, N.Y.: The Crossing Press.

Burden, D. 1987. "Women and Social Policy." In D. Burden and N. Gottlieb, eds., *The Woman Client*, pp. 25–40. New York: Tavistock Press.

—— and N. Gottlieb. 1987. "Human Behavior in the Social Environment: The Knowledge Base." In D. Burden and N. Gottlieb, eds., *The Woman Client*. New York: Tavistock Press.

Burstow, B. 1991. "Freirian Codification and Social Work Education." *Journal of Social Work Education* 27(2):196–207.

Collins, B. G. 1986. "Defining Feminist Social Work." *Journal of Social Work* 31:214–219.

Collins, P. H. 1991. *Black Feminist Thought: Knowledge, Consciousness, and the Politics of Empowerment*. New York: Routledge.

Council on Social Work Education, Commission on Accreditation. 1991. *Handbook of Accreditation Standards and Procedures*. Alexandria, Va.: CSWE.

——. 1992. *Curriculum Policy Statement*. Alexandria, Va.: CSWE.

Crawley, B. K.-J. 1992. "Gender Issues and Women of Color: What Their Portraits Reveal." Presentation at the Council on Social Work Education, APM, Kansas City.

Cummerton, J. A. 1983. "Feminist Perspective on Research. What Does It Help Us to See?" Presented at the Annual Program Meeting of the Council on Social Work Education, Fort Worth, Texas.

Davis, L. V. 1986. "A Feminist Approach to Social Work Research." *Affilia* 1(1) (Spring):32–47.

Eichler, M. 1987. "The Relationship Between Sexist, Non-Sexist, and Woman-Centered and Feminist Research in the Social Sciences." In G. Nemiroff, ed., *Women and Men: Interdisciplinary Readings on Gender*, pp. 21–53. Montreal: Fetzhenry and Whitside.

——. 1988. *Nonsexist Research Methods: A Practical Guide*. Boston: Allen and Unwin.

Fraser, N. and L. Nicholson. 1988. "Social Criticism Without Philosophy: An Encounter Between Feminism and Postmodernism." *Theory, Culture and Society* 5:373–394.

Freeman, M. L. 1990. "Beyond Women's Issues: Feminism and Social Work." *Affilia* 5(2) (Summer):72–89.

Freire, P. 1976. *Education For Critical Consciousness*. New York: Herder and Herder.

Gilroy, J. 1990. "Social Work and the Women's Movement." In B. Wharf, ed., *Social Work and Social Change in Canada*. Toronto: McClelland and Stewart.

Goldberg-Wood, G. and R. Middleman. 1989. *The Structural Approach to Direct Practice in Social Work*. New York: Columbia University Press.

Gordon, L., ed. 1990. *Women, the State, and Welfare*. Madison: University of Wisconsin Press.

Gordon, S. 1992. *Prisoner of Men's Dreams. Striking Out for a New Feminist Future.* Boston: Little, Brown.

Gottlieb, N., ed. 1980. *Alternative Social Services for Women.* New York: Columbia University Press.

——, ed. 1981. *New Knowledge About Women: A Selected Annotated Bibliography for the Human Behavior and Social Environment Curriculum in Social Work Education.* Washington, D.C.: Council on Social Work Education.

——. 1987. "Dilemma and Strategies in Research on Women." In D. Burden and N. Gottlieb, eds., *The Woman Client,* pp. 53–66. New York: Tavistock.

—— and M. Bombyk. 1987. "Strategies for Strengthening Feminist Research." *Affilia* 2(2) (Summer):23–35.

Gutierrez, L. 1990. "Working With Women of Color: An Empowerment Perspective." *Social Work* 35:149–153.

——. 1992. "Empowering Ethnic Minorities in the Twenty-First Century: The Role of Human Service Organizations." In Y. Hazenfeld, ed., *Human Services As Complex Organizations.* Newbury Park, Calif.: Sage.

Haraway, D. 1988. "Situated Knowledges: The Science Question in Feminism and the Privilege of Partial Perspective." *Feminist Studies* 14(3):575–597.

Harding, S. 1986. *The Science Question in Feminism.* Ithaca, N.Y.: Cornell University Press.

Hartsock, N. 1979. "Feminist Theory and the Development of Revolutionary Strategy." In Z. Eisenstein, ed., *Capitalist Patriarchy and the Case for Socialist Feminism,* pp. 56–77. New York: Monthly Review Press.

Hawkesworth, M. E. 1989. "Knowers, Knowing, Known: Feminist Theory and Claims of Truth." *Signs* 14:533–557.

Hooyman, N. 1991. "Supporting Practice in Large-Scale Bureaucracies." In M. Bricker-Jenkins, N. Hooyman, and N. Gottlieb, eds., *Feminist Social Work Practice in Clinical Settings.* Newbury Park, Calif.: Sage.

—— and R. Cunningham. 1986. "An Alternative Administrative Style." In N. Van Den Bergh and L. B. Cooper, *Feminist Visions for Social Work,* pp. 163–186. Washington, D.C.: National Association of Social Workers.

——, A. Summers and L. Leighninger, eds. 1988. "Women Working Together: A Collection of Course Syllabi About Women." *Council on Social Work Education. Commission on the Role and Status of Women in Social Work Education.*

Hudson, A. 1985. "Feminism and Social Work: Resistance or Dialogue?" *British Journal of Social Work* 15:635–655.

Hurtado, A. 1989. "Relating to Privilege: Seduction and Rejection in the Subordination of White Women and Women of Color." *Signs: Journal of Women in Culture and Society* 14(4):833–855.

Ivanoff, A., E. Robinson, and B. Blythe. 1987. "Empirical Clinical Practice from a Feminist Perspective." *Social Work* 32:417–424.

Kirst-Ashman, K. K. 1992. "Feminist Values and Social Work: A Model for Educating Nonfeminists." *Arete* 17(1):13–26.

Krane, J. 1991. "Feminist Thinking as an Aid to Teaching Social Work Research." *Affilia* 6(4) (Winter):53–70.

Kravetz, D. 1982. "An Overview of Content on Women For the Social Work Curriculum." *Journal of Education for Social Work* 18(2) (Spring):42–49.

Lazzari, M. M. 1991. "Feminism, Empowerment, and Field Education." *Affilia* 6(4) (Winter):71–87.

Lecomte, R. 1990. "Connecting Private Troubles and Public Issues in Social Work Education." In B. Wharf, ed., *Social Work and Social Change in Canada.* Toronto: McClelland and Stewart.

Lincoln, R. and R. D. Koeske. 1987. "Feminism Among Social Work Students." *Affilia* 2(1) (Spring):50–57.

Lowenstein, S. 1976. "Integrating Content on Feminism and Racism into the Social Work Curriculum." *Journal of Education for Social Work* 12(1):91–96.

Luttrel, W. 1989. "Working-Class Women's Ways of Knowing: Effects of Gender, Race and Class." *Sociology of Education* 62:33–46.

McIntosh, P. 1988. *White Privilege and Male Privilege: A Personal Account of Coming To See Correspondence Through Work in Women's Studies.* Working Paper 189. Wellesley, Mass.: Wellesley College Center for Research on Women.

MacKinnon, C. A. 1987. *Feminism Unmodified: Discourses on Life and Law.* Cambridge, Mass.: Harvard University Press.

Mascia-Lee, F., P. Sharpe, and C. Cohen-Ballerino. 1989. "The Postmodern Turn in Anthropology: Cautions From A Feminist Perspective." *Signs: Journal of Women in Culture and Society* 15(1):7–31.

Meisel, S. S. and A. P. Friedman. 1974. "The Need for Women's Studies in Social Work Education." *Journal of Education for Social Work* 10(3):67–74.

Moreau, M. and L. Leonard. 1989. *Empowerment Through A Structural Approach to Social Work. A Report From Practice.* Ottawa: Carleton University School of Social Work.

Morell, C. 1987. "Cause is Function: Toward a Feminist Model of Integration for Social Work." *Social Service Review* (March):144–155.

Morgenbesser, M. 1981. "The Evolution of Three Alternative Social Service Agencies." *Catalyst* 11:71–83.

Norman, E. and A. Mancuso. 1980. *Women's Issues and Social Work Practice.* Itasca, Ill.: F. E. Peacock.

Price, R. P., S. A. Foster, C. Curtis, and J. Behling. 1979. "Student and Faculty Perceptions of Women's Content in the Curriculum." *Journal of Education for Social Work* 15(3):51–57.

Quam, J. and C. Austin. 1984. "Coverage of Women's Issues in Eight Social Work Journals." *Social Work* 29(4):360–365.

Rosenman, L. and R. Ruckdeschel. 1981. "Catch 124B: Integrating Material on Women Into the Social Work Research Curriculum." *Journal of Education for Social Work* 17(2):5–11.

Rothschild-Witt, J. 1979. "The Collective Organization: An Alternative to Rational-Bureaucratic Models." *American Sociological Review* 44:509–527.

Schniedewind, N. 1983. "Feminist Values: Guidelines for Teaching Methodology in Women's Studies." In C. Bunch and S. Pollack, eds., *Learning Our Way*, pp. 261–271. Trumansburg, N.Y.: The Crossing Press.

Scott, J. 1988. "Deconstructing Equality-Versus Difference: Or the Uses of Post-Structuralist Theory for Feminism." *Feminist Studies* 14(1):33–50.

Social Work Practice in a Sexist Society: Proceedings of the First NASW Conference on Social Work Practice with Women, September 14–16, 1980. Washington, D.C.

Sowers-Hoag, K. M. and D. F. Harrison. 1991. "Women in Social Work Education: Progress or Promise?" *Journal of Social Work Education* 27(3):320–328.

Spender, D. 1985. *For The Record: The Making and Meaning of Feminist Knowledge.* London: Women's Press.

Stimpson, C. and N. Cobb-Kressner. 1986. *Women's Studies in the United States: A Report to the Ford Foundation.* New York: Ford Foundation.

Stout, K. 1991. "A Continuum of Male Control and Violence Against Women: A Teaching Model." *Journal of Social Work Education* 27(3):305–319.

Sutton, J. A. 1982. "Sex Discrimination Among Social Workers." *Social Work* 27(3):211–217.

Tice, K. 1990. "Gender and Social Work Education: Directions for the 1990s." *Journal of Social Work Education* 26(2):134–144.

Valentich, M. 1986. "Feminism and Social Work Practice." In F. J. Turner, ed., *Social Work Treatment*, pp. 564–589. New York: Free Press.

Van Den Bergh, N. and L. Cooper. 1986. *Feminist Visions for Social Work.* Silver Spring, Md.: National Association of Social Workers.

Vinton, L. 1992. "Women's Content in Social Work Curricula: Separate But Equal?" *Affilia* 7(1) (Spring):74–89.

Wetzel, J. W. 1986. "A Feminist World View Conceptual Framework." *Social Casework* 166–73.

Wharf, B., ed. 1990. *Social Work and Social Change in Canada.* Toronto: McClelland and Stewart.

11

Diversity and Populations at Risk: Gays and Lesbians

BERNIE SUE NEWMAN

An informed understanding of diversity is essential to the knowledge base of social work practice. Knowledge about populations who are different from imposed American societal norms such as white, heterosexual, temporarily able-bodied, Christian, or male is a critical part of the foundations that form the basis of social work. These populations are not only most at risk for societal oppression; but the presence of diverse communities enriches the cultural and communal quality of the entire society.

Oppression comes in too many forms to enumerate here. Removal and restriction of civil rights, consistent nonequity in the economic, political, and legal systems, and violence based on hate and prejudice are all experienced by oppressed groups, such as African Americans, Asian Americans, women, lesbians and gays, and disabled people. The richness that diverse populations add to a society is also too much to exemplify. The cultures and political and social communities of African Americans, Hispanics, Asian Americans, and Jewish Americans enhance the lives of individuals and families. Feminist analyses of and approaches to social problems add significantly to many professional fields. The strengths of the gay and lesbian community in organizing a gay pride movement and the network of responses developed in response to HIV/AIDS have contributed to the social welfare and political systems.

All social workers need an informed critical perspective on issues of oppression and diversity. Content on sexual orientation is a critical component of these issues. Studying the basis for oppression across populations can lead to a better understanding of the common elements of oppression along with unique experiences for each group. For example, basic commonalities of many oppressed groups exist, such as power structure arrangements and differentness based upon an imposed norm. However, differences in history and characteristics of the group must also be understood, such as a history of slavery and brutality experienced by the African-American community. For lesbian and gay people, a history of invisibility, stigma, and rejection, often on the basis of moral judgments, makes distinct this population's experience of oppression. An awareness and appreciation of diversity and a knowledge and understanding of issues of oppression contribute to the foundations of social work knowledge.

Historically, however, diverse populations have been excluded from the social work knowledge base. Conceptual frameworks, practice models, and empirical studies have largely been based upon middle-class white male heterosexual models of behavior (Billingsley 1970; Chestang 1972; Davis 1986; Norton 1978; Sands and Richardson 1985; Tice 1990). Formal supports for attention to diversity and oppression have developed largely because of organized efforts of subgroups of social workers in the profession who have advocated for this content. In 1982 accredited schools of social work were first required to include content on women and ethnic minorities of color in their curriculum (Council on Social Work Education 1982, Standard 7.5). Inclusion of content on lesbian women and on gay and lesbian people of color could naturally have flowed out of this requirement, but this content has not usually been included in the curricula of schools of social work (Gunter 1987; Humphreys 1983; Knight 1991). Not only has lesbian and gay content been neglected but social work education has failed to become fully inclusive of other gender and ethnic minorities of color issues (Compton 1974; Knight 1991; Proctor and Davis 1983; Tice 1990). Some individuals and groups in both schools of social work and practice settings have treated knowledge about sexual orientation and lesbian and gay issues as requisite for social work practice. But these settings where inclusion of lesbian and gay people occurs are in the minority. Although no national survey of agencies has been published, it would appear that only a few agencies require in-service training about lesbian and gay issues. One of the first agencies to focus on social service needs of a lesbian and gay population was the Institute for the Protection of Lesbian and Gay Youth founded by Hetrick and Martin in the 1960s. However, aside from a small percentage of agencies that create an open, informed atmosphere about sexual orientation, few encour-age staff or clients who are lesbian, gay, or bisexual to raise critical issues that affect their lives.

Some agencies serving adolescents have begun to include training that addresses lesbian and gay youth. A small but growing number of schools of social work have begun to require content on lesbian and gay issues in the human behavior sequence; some individual schools have passed policies to mandate this content as part of their required curriculum. Grassroots organizing by groups of social workers and other professionals concerned about gay and lesbian issues have devel-oped in many communities.

Social work educators and practitioners have made critical contri-butions to the development of a theoretical and empirical knowledge base about the lesbian and gay population for social work practice. Arguments for inclusion of content in practice and educational settings were voiced in the 1970s and 1980s (Berger 1977; 1983; Dulaney and Kelly 1982; Gramick 1983; Humphreys 1983; Newman 1989; Tully and Albro 1979). Studies showing some evidence that attitudes toward and practice with lesbian and gay clients can be positively influenced through training provided in an agency setting (Schneider and Trem-ble 1985–86) or through coursework in a university setting (Larsen, Cate, and Reed 1983; Serdahely and Ziemba 1984) were published in the same period. Conceptual and empirical models for understanding social work theory, practice and research issues regarding sexual ori-entation have been provided in the social work literature in the last twenty years (examples are Berger 1980, 1982a, 1982b, 1990b; Hall 1978; Hidalgo, Peterson, and Woodman 1985; Icard 1986; Lewis 1980; Lewis 1983; Moses and Hawkins 1982; Pierce 1989; Potter and Darty 1981; Poverny and Finch 1985, 1988b; Schneider and Tremble 1986; Waters 1986; Woodman 1992).

Some national-level organizational supports have developed over the years. The National Association of Social Workers (NASW) 1979 *Code of Ethics* included sexual orientation as an unacceptable basis for discrimination, and one that social workers should act to prevent and eliminate (NASW 1979). Recently, the Council on Social Work Educa-tion Curriculum Policy Statement (CPS) has identified content on les-bian and gay persons as foundation knowledge. In the first CPS pub-lished in 1962, no mention of this population was made. In the 1982 standard 7.5, sexual orientation was suggested as an area of knowledge necessary for an understanding of diversity and oppression, but it was not required. The present CPS, published in 1992, requires inclusion of lesbian and gay content in the standard on populations-at-risk.

The effects of this requirement will likely not be noticeable for several years. However, prior to this mandate, most schools of social work had not included content on lesbian and gay issues (Gunter 1987; Humphreys 1983; Knight 1991). In a 1983 survey of California schools of social work, Humphreys reports that the most frequent method used by faculty members to discuss homosexuality was when a student brought up the issue. Of those schools that reported explicit attempts to include curriculum content on lesbian and gay issues, the majority limited their efforts to the distribution of bibliographies on homosexuality. Knight (1991) reports that content on lesbians was not typically included in the content on women in the schools she surveyed.

Some have suggested that the social science foundations of social work theory and practice often exclude diverse populations. Conceptual frameworks and theories of human behavior have most often been based on white, male, middle-class, heterosexual perspectives, for example, Erikson's "eight stages of man" (Erikson 1963) or definitions and theories of family development, such as Carter and McGoldrick's (1989) family life cycle. These models create norms and definitions of healthy functioning that marginalize or even make deviant many populations.

In her work on gender and social work education, Tice (1990) points out that the norms of theories that form the basis of social work knowledge often exclude women or other diverse groups. Tice suggests that when women are mentioned, they are often treated as a "monolithic category" which does not distinguish their experience by race, sexual orientation or class. Tice formulates "challenges to foundation knowledge that critically assess it to determine if the experiences of women and non-white, non-elite men are included; if women of different classes, color, cultures, and sexual preference are represented" (1990:138). She also calls for an examination of the politics of knowledge that would point out value and power issues in the knowledge base that students develop. These changes suggested by Tice could shape a curriculum that would not only include diversity but create an environment throughout the profession that would promote critical thinking about theories, research, and practice models, and enhance our knowledge base by embracing diversity in the paradigms taught and applied.

Although few, if any, schools at present engage in such a comprehensive approach, the 1992 Council on Social Work Education CPS strengthened educational standards that require content on diverse populations. The standards on populations-at-risk require that programs of social work education present "theoretical and practice content about patterns, dynamics and consequences of discrimination, economic deprivation, and oppression" (CSWE 1992, Standards B6.6, M6.8). These standards emphasize that all oppressed groups are a concern of social work. Content on minorities of color, women, disability, sexual orientation, class, and political oppression must be part of the social work knowledge base because these are sources of diversity and oppression for the majority of the populations of concern. The study of what creates oppression for all groups is essential to this understanding of conditions in clients' environments that set up barriers and limits to their choices and resources.

The 1992 CPS added "content on diversity, social and economic justice, and populations at risk" (CSWE 1992, Standards B6.1, M6.1) to the traditional professional foundation areas for social work practice of human behavior and the social environment, social welfare policy and services, social work practice, research, and the field practicum. In addition, the 1992 standard on populations-at-risk mandated content on the lesbian and gay population. These changes acknowledge diversity as part of the professional foundation and identify lesbian and gay issues as an essential part of the foundation curriculum. The quality of the inclusion of lesbian and gay content in schools of social work will vary somewhat depending on the initial motivation of each school, but even more so on the developing knowledge base of the faculty and students. The extent to which knowledge about the lesbian and gay population is included in schools will have some influence on the extent to which these issues are addressed in practice settings.

Formulating learning objectives that identify what social workers should know and the effects this knowledge base should have on practice will not be an easy process in any setting. Education that incorporates content on lesbian and gay persons would have multiple learning objectives. Critical knowledge about the lesbian and gay population consists of:

1. an understanding of the commonalities of oppression across populations;

2. an awareness and understanding of lesbian and gay issues for individuals, families and organizations and communities;

3. skills for practice with lesbian, gay and bisexual persons; and

4. skills for working to eliminate discriminatory policies and practices.

A variety of concepts, theories and approaches are necessary to address each of these topics.

Commonalities of Oppression Across Populations

Suzanne Pharr (1988) argues that in order to eliminate one oppression successfully, all oppression must be ended because all forms of oppression have common links to each other. Sexism, classism, racism, heterosexism, ableism, ageism are all forms of discrimination based upon the common elements of a defined norm backed up with institutional and economic power and institutional and individual violence. Social workers who believe that one group is more oppressed than another will be unable to see the destructiveness and distortion that are products of any form of oppression. Moreover, social workers who understand the commonalities of oppression across populations have greater potential to increase the power of all groups determined to end discrimination and oppression.

There appear to be several reasons that explain why forms of oppression against the gay and lesbian population are often ignored or excluded from schools of social work content on diversity and oppression. First and foremost is the high level of homophobia and heterosexism within the social work professional community (Humphreys 1983; Weiner 1989; Wisniewski and Toomey 1987). Second, rejection of homosexuality appears to be a dominant attitude among minority cultures (Chan 1989; Dahlheimer and Feigal 1991; Hidalgo and Christensen 1976–77; Icard 1986; Loiacano 1989). Third is the "zero sum game" in which the idea exists that if one group gets resources, it is at the expense of another; or if gays and lesbians are included in the social work curriculum, it will leave less room for minorities of color or women, or content on research methods.

Socialization in American society includes countless messages that homosexuality is unnatural and immoral. Whether gay or straight, no one is immune from socialization that rejects homosexuality. Surveys of

American public attitudes toward homosexuals suggest that negative attitudes persist. Levitt and Klassen's (1974) analysis of 1970 data from a nationwide probability sample reported that 70 percent believed that homosexual relations were always wrong. Alston (1974) used the 1973 data from the Annual General Social Survey of the American adult population and found that 68.5 percent believed that sexual relations between two persons of the same sex were always wrong. Nyberg and Alston's (1976–77) analysis of 1974 data reported that over 72 percent of the general population believed that homosexual relations were always wrong. The 1982 and 1984 General Social Surveys sponsored by the National Opinion Research Center indicated that 73 percent of a national cross-section of American adults (for both years) believed that sexual relations between same-sex adults were always wrong (Davis 1982; Davis and Smith 1984). Although it uses a less representative sample of the American public and results in a somewhat lower percentage objecting to homosexuality, a recent telephone survey illustrates what little change has occurred in the last twenty years. When asked in 1972, "Are homosexual relationships between consenting adults morally wrong?," 54 percent of the 1,250 American adults surveyed responded yes. The same question in 1992 resulted in 53 percent agreement among the 1,000 American adults sampled (reported in Castro 1992). Given the prevalence of these kinds of rejecting attitudes, it is likely that some percentage of social work educators, students, and practitioners will have negative attitudes about homosexuality.

Research studies of social work practitioners (Casas, Brady and Ponnterotto 1983; Wisniewski and Toomey 1987), social work students (Thompson 1992; Weiner 1989), and social work educators (Humphreys 1983) demonstrate the existence of homophobia. In one of the few studies of homophobia among practitioners, Wisniewski and Toomey (1987) reported that 31 percent of their sample of mostly direct service social workers were homophobic. Weiner (1989) found that her sample of undergraduate and graduate social work students was more homophobic than sexist or racist and that they reported receiving more content on blacks and women than on lesbians and gay men. Humphreys (1983) concluded that homophobia is a major obstacle in the inclusion of this content. He found that the greater the degree of social work educators' homophobia, the more likely that their course content on homosexuality would exclude gay and lesbian issues in their courses. Negative, rejecting, and judgmental attitudes about lesbian, gay, and bisexual people will surely interfere with the profession's education, research, and practice efforts.

Rejection of homosexuality by ethnic minority communities may be a barrier to treating lesbian and gay issues with equity when covering content on diversity and oppression. Few recent studies of the correlation between race and attitudes toward homosexuals exist. Previous studies suggest that race is either marginally or not related at all, but sample sizes of nonwhite populations have been small and mostly African American (Alston 1974; Levitt and Klassen 1974; Nyberg and Alston 1977; Simmons 1965). Both Icard (1986) and Chan (1989), however, suggest that homosexuality is commonly perceived by ethnic minority groups as a "white, Western phenomenon." This may contribute to the limited recognition of lesbian and gay issues as relevant to diversity and oppression. The idea that including gay and lesbian content will detract from content on minorities of color or other at-risk populations is not only divisive, but also distorts the experiences of lesbians and gay men who are of color, low socioeconomic status, older, or disabled. Invisibility of gay and lesbian persons in society has perpetuated the myths surrounding homophobia for centuries. For lesbians and gay men who are ethnic minorities, invisibility in both their own and the lesbian and gay community has been an even more destructive force (Chan 1989; Icard 1986; Loiacano 1989). Social work clients who are lesbian or gay may remain invisible unless social workers have some knowledge base.

Lesbian and gay content is not in competition with other curriculum content or with other diverse populations. How we conduct research on, do practice with, formulate theory about, and create policies for diverse groups is basic social work content. Social work practice, research and education must be understood in the context of diversity and oppression. Knowledge about any population is incomplete without considering special issues for members who are lesbian, gay, or bisexual. Similarly, learning about the lesbian and gay population must include differential experiences of gay individuals because of age, class, ethnicity, gender, and disability.

A continuing problem in formulating a knowledge base on lesbian and gay people is the virtual absence of research findings that are representative of the entire population. Predominantly middle-class, white, and young adult samples of lesbians and gays form the data pools for the existing research. Recently, Harry (1990) reported data from a national probability sample of American males that includes information on sexual orientation. A little over 3 percent responded that they were homosexual or bisexual. Of those, 42 percent were married and 52 percent were living in small towns. There was a significant difference between the heterosexual and homosexual groups in the percentage of minority persons; 38 percent of the homosexual/bisexual group were black or Hispanic compared to 18 percent in the heterosexual group. Harry's work reveals that the nonprobability samples of gay respondents that draw from openly gay settings do not represent those in the larger population who experience homosexual feelings and behaviors. Many social work clients do not self-identify as lesbian or gay. A social worker's approach might need to include a sensitivity about and recognition of when sexual orientation issues are relevant for individuals, families, and communities in all settings. This approach must also be sensitive to individuals who do not wish to identify as gay or lesbian, but are experiencing difficulties related to sexual orientation or internalized homophobia. Assessment and intervention strategies must include issues of sexual orientation.

Strategies of intervention, social action, policy and program planning, and administration must be based on knowledge and values that include the social and civil rights of all groups. Social change strategies based on an understanding of the commonalities of oppression may prove most effective. In addition to perceiving the common methods of oppression across all groups, the social work knowledge base needs to include an awareness and understanding of the unique experiences and issues for individuals, families and communities in each population.

Understanding Lesbian and Gay Issues for Individuals, Families, and Communities

Sexual orientation is an integral part of the human experience. The development of gender identity, gender roles and sexual orientation are conception-to-death issues that need to be studied to more fully explore human behavior in the social environment. The concept of gender is multidimensional and developmental with strong biological, psychological and social influences.

Developmental theorists often refer to gender identity, gender roles, and sexual orientation as representing major dimensions of gender (Matteson 1979; Money 1990). Condry (1984) presents a developmental perspective of gender from in utero through adolescence that provides specific biological, social, and psychological influences on the development of gender identity and gender roles. He suggests that gender begins to develop in utero when fetuses differ based on their chromosomal makeup, hormonal production, and physical development. He calls the period of birth to eighteen months preawareness, although the gender labeling by others is recognized as having a great impact. Condry argues that young children become aware of gender and then develop a gender orientation through imitation and modeling. He concludes that gender role choices (which he calls gender identity) begin at adolescence with a selection of traits based on the degree of perceived freedom of choice and other environmental influences. Condry does not address the development of sexual orientation.

The development of sexual orientation is considered by many theorists to be determined early in life (Money 1963 cited in Feldman 1989; Reiter 1989). This idea, however, is challenged by other theorists who observe that sexual behavior patterns and sexual self-labeling can change dramatically within an individual over the life span (Sanders, Reinisch, and McWhirter 1990). The extent to which sexual orientation is seen to be fixed or dynamic; predetermined or a matter of choice; biologically, socially, or cognitively derived remains a theoretical debate.

The concept of sexual orientation has been operationally defined and measured by a number of authors. The most common method for measuring sexual orientation continues to be the Kinsey Heterosexual-Homosexual Scale (Kinsey, Pomeroy, and Martin 1948) in which sexual orientation is measured on an interval scale of seven points based on the respondents' self-described rating. The two poles are exclusively heterosexual and exclusively homosexual. The midpoint is equally heterosexual and homosexual, with mixed but predominantly homosexual or mixed but predominantly heterosexual categories in between. Kinsey and colleagues' groundbreaking works (Kinsey, Pomeroy, and Martin 1948; Kinsey et al. 1953) established recognition for the presence of homosexuality in the American population and opened up the discussion about homosexuality in the scientific community. The Kinsey scale was the first to operationalize sexual orientation as a continuum with several points. Criticisms of the scale, however, are that it is a single-item indicator and it assumes that sexual orientation is based on one group of behaviors and feelings and does not change over time (Berkey, Perelman-Hall, and Kurdek 1990).

Moses and Hawkins (1982) were among the first theorists to suggest multiple sources of sexual orientation and a temporal component. They conceptualized past and present feelings, fantasy and behavior as contributing to a person's sexual orientation. Klein (1985, 1990) has developed a grid measure with seven boxes rating behaviors, emotions, attractions, and fantasies in the past, present, and ideal future. Storms (1980) presents a graphic representation based on high attraction and low attraction ratings for same sex and opposite sex. The resulting four cells are labeled heterosexual, homosexual, bisexual, and asexual.

A recent attempt to measure sexual orientation is the development of the Multidimensional Scale of Sexuality (Berkey, Perelman-Hall, and Kurdek 1990). This forty-one-item scale expands the definition of sexual orientation by including ratings of behavioral, cognitive and affective factors over time and proposes nine categories of sexual orientation with six categories of bisexuality, in addition to heterosexuality, homosexuality, and asexuality. This scale approaches sexual orientation as a dynamic phenomenon and reflects more variations than Kinsey's work suggested. In addition to those rated as exclusively heterosexual and exclusively homosexual, three categories of bisexuality were found among the sample: sequential bisexuality (behaviorally heterosexual with some homosexuality); concurrent bisexuality (behaviorally homosexual with some heterosexuality); and homosexuality with some past heterosexuality (behaviorally homosexual with previous heterosexuality). Respondents who fall into this last category might not see themselves as bisexual, but as exclusively gay or lesbian at present.

Bisexuality has seldom been addressed, particularly in the research, practice, or curriculum development efforts of social workers. In Harrison's (1987) review of contributions of social workers in relation to sexual orientation, bisexuality was not identified as a critical issue in any of the existing social work literature on sexuality. Social work literature has often treated sexual orientation as consisting of heterosexual and homosexual divisions (see Berger 1983). This may be a valid conceptualization because the experiences and needs of lesbian and gay persons are distinct and must be addressed apart from heterosexual or bisexual persons. Nevertheless, the issue of other expressions of sexual orientation or the idea that more variation than Kinsey's continuum suggests needs to be examined further. The feelings, experiences, emotions, affections, and commitments related to sexual orientation may be broader than were previously theorized.

In the past, research on sexual orientation was based on the assumption that homosexuality was pathological. This assumption resulted in a search for its etiology. Two major "causes" of homosexuality were hypothesized to be biological differences that were expected to exist in any physiological disease, or psychoanalytic explanations of environmental and familial determinants of what was seen as a fixated and regressed state. More recently, however, research data have disconfirmed these hypotheses, especially those suggesting familial dysfunction or personality disorders.

Bell, Weinberg, and Hammersmith's rigorous (1978) study of a large sample of heterosexual and gay men and women showed little support for the role of parents, poor peer relationships, or atypical heterosexual relationships as causal variables to the development of homosexuality. Dancey (1990a) points out that most studies investigating psychoanalytic interpretations have found little or no difference between heterosexual and homosexual groups on most variables studied. She also suggests that when differences have been found, the homosexual group is often different from the heterosexual group in other important ways (e.g., marital and employment status or age). In contrast, Dancey found no difference in any discriminant function analysis of the effects of multiple familial or personality variables between heterosexual and homosexual women matched on age, marital status, and occupation.

Biological studies have tended to focus on chromosomal aspects, genetics, and hormonal and endocrine levels. They also included sociobiological explanations such as evolutionary theories of natural selection that hypothesized that homosexuals were biologically unfit for reproduction (Ruse 1990); or reproductively altruistic, exerting lower reproductive rates to the reproductive benefit of kin such as brothers (Weinrich 1987).

In retrospect, past biological studies appear to impose erroneous assumptions and use unrepresentative samples. Despite any empirical evidence to support it, an equation was consistently made between male homosexuality and femaleness and lesbian sexuality and maleness. Studies used transsexual and "homosexual" subjects without any clear definitions of either group. The presumption that heterosexuality was the only normal sexual orientation guided the direction of this research and led to an assumption of deviance for any form of diversity and a blending of individuals who differed from this heterosexual norm. This created research questions and methods that continued the search for biological determinants despite little supporting evidence.

In 1980 Money reviewed attempts at empirical verification of chromosomal differences. At that time, these kinds of studies had been based on examination of sex ratio in the family (ratio of brothers to sisters); ordinal birth position; and twin concordance. Research in each of these areas comprised only a handful of studies. Surprisingly, studying the ratio of brothers to sisters as a predictor of male homosexuality had aroused the most interest, with six studies. These data, however, showed no pattern of more brothers among gay men, and so did not support the hypothesis that gay men were fulfilling a sister role as children because there was a shortage of sisters in those families. (This idea illustrates the extent to which male homosexuality was equated with femaleness.) Two studies, both by Slater (1958, 1962, cited in Money 1980), that examined ordinal birth position reported that "compared with exhibitionists," gay men are born later in the family with older mothers. The lack of a heterosexual comparison group was apparently not considered necessary perhaps because homosexual people were assumed to be so different that no comparison was possible. Money, who has been at the forefront of biomedical research on gender, concluded in his 1980 publication that "there is no basis on which to justify an hypothesis that homosexuals or bisexuals are chromosomally discrepant from heterosexuals" (66).

Kallman's (1952) study, which reported a high degree of concordance for homosexuality in each of thirty-seven pairs of identical monozygotic twins, has often been cited to support the idea of genetic differences. Money (1980) points out that the twins in this study were raised in the same environment and could be showing a unified response expected of identical twins in similar life experiences. However, Puterbaugh (1990) reports that data from monozygotic twin studies to date suggest a concordance rate of about 88 percent for homosexuality. These studies have been mostly limited to men with few studies of twins reared apart. Nevertheless, the high concordance rate suggests some genetic contribution to sexual orientation.

Some studies have used samples of individuals born with endocrine disorders to investigate the percentage of those who had a homosexual orientation. Gooren (1990) reviews research on samples of men and women with androgen syndrome and those who were prenatally exposed to hormones. He concludes that these studies "suggest that hormones may contribute to, but do not determine the course of sexual orientation in individuals with an abnormal sex-steroid history" (76). He also shows that findings are inconsistent for the effects of androgens and estrogen. In addition, the direction of the relationship between increased hormones and sexual orientation is suspect because of the possible effects of familial and social expectations following awareness of this condition. Another caveat is that these findings were intended to generalize to the homosexual population, not a population with androgen syndrome or exposure to estrogen. Samples of people who have a hormonal syndrome do not represent the general homosexual population. Nevertheless, the purpose of these studies was to draw conclusions about what "caused homosexuality" in general.

Other studies that have attempted to develop samples of heterosexual and homosexual men and women have produced mixed results. Starka, Sipova, and Hynie (1975) analyzed testosterone levels in 79 heterosexual men, 17 male transsexuals, 3 male transvestites, 18 homosexual men who they typed as feminine stereotyped, and 3 homosexual men typed as masculine stereotyped. They reported lower levels of testosterone in all groups as compared with the heterosexuals. Dancey (1990b) points out that studies comparing hormone levels in groups of lesbian women with those of heterosexual women have produced conflicting results. Two studies she cites found no differences between the two groups on hormones (testosterone, estrogen, cortisol, and andostenedione). Two other studies that Dancey reports on found that lesbian women as a group had significantly higher levels of testosterone. One of these latter two studies, however, included only two lesbian couples in the sample. Dancey (1990b) measured levels of estrogen in 10 heterosexual and 30 lesbian women and found no differences. She suggests that there is a lack of supporting evidence for difference in levels of sex hormones in lesbians or gay men.

The idea that homosexuality is solely caused by some discernible variable in the chemistry of men and women appears to be erroneous. Sanders, Reinisch, and McWhirter (1990) suggest that different factors may play varying roles in different individuals. They point out that both biological and socioenvironmental factors have been identified that may affect the development of sexual orientation, concluding that an interactionist perspective may be most productive. Whether heterosexual, homosexual, or bisexual, sexual orientation does not appear to have a single cause or developmental pathway. Sexual orientation can perhaps be better understood as complex behaviors and feeling states that consist of healthy group and individual variations.

The complexity and dimensions that surround sexual orientation are difficult to measure and to understand. However, information about these dimensions could be helpful to clients who have questions about their sexual orientation. It is important to know that behaviors alone do not contribute to sexual orientation. An exploration of cognitive thoughts and fantasies, emotional expressions of attachment, bonding and love, along with behavior is important. A recognition that these multiple dimensions of sexuality are not always consistent (Berkey, Perelman-Hall, and Kurdek 1990) may also be helpful. Although some people do experience exclusive homosexuality or exclusive heterosexuality, expressions of sexual orientation can be variable. It appears that for some persons, feelings, and behaviors around sexual orientation change during the life span (Berkey, Perelman-Hall, and Kurdek 1990; Schneider and Tremble 1985–86; Sophie 1986).

Longres (1990) has suggested an approach for understanding sexual orientation as part of the study of the life cycle. This approach examines the prenatal period for biological theories of homosexuality; and infancy and early childhood for cognitive and social learning theories of homosexuality. In Longres' model, adolescence and young adulthood are stages in which gender roles and sexual orientation identity are most relevant. The study of adulthood incorporates issues of relationship, separation, gay and lesbian parents, and gays and lesbians in the workplace.

Although understanding of developmental issues is important over the life cycle, the developmental and social needs of gay and lesbian adolescents may be one of the most critical bodies of knowledge about the lesbian and gay population. Gibson (1989) concludes that up to 30 percent of all youth suicides are gay-related. Hetrick and Martin (1987), Savin-Williams (1988, 1990), and Schneider and Tremble (1985–86) are among those who have documented many of the developmental tasks and needs of gay and lesbian adolescents. Schneider (1989) suggests that adolescent development is different for lesbian and gay adolescents because coming out adds a new dimension to other developmental tasks of adolescence. Her content analysis of personal interview data with twenty-five lesbian adolescents provides insight into needs and struggles of these young women. Social service and family support needs of lesbian and gay adolescents are reviewed in two additional studies (see Mercier and Berger 1989; Saperstein 1981).

The needs of adolescents trying to resolve sexual orientation issues are critical because this group appears to have the least support from their peers, their families, the educational system, the social service system, and even the gay community. They experience what Hetrick and Martin (1987) call informational, emotional, and social isolation. They are two to three times more likely to attempt suicide than their heterosexual counterparts (Gibson 1989).

Schneider and Tremble (1985–86) identify indicators that might represent an adolescent's struggle with sexual orientation. They also provide counseling approaches and strategies to assist adolescents to explore the confused feelings often experienced when questioning their sexual orientation. Cates (1987) reviews practice techniques with two case examples of adolescents struggling with lesbian and gay issues. Social workers must understand the experiences of adolescents who are struggling with sexual orientation issues. They must also feel comfortable enough to discuss these issues and to provide the informational, emotional, and social support needed to assist adolescent clients during the coming-out process.

Coming out can occur during adolescence or at any time during adulthood. A number of theoretical models of coming out are present in the literature (Cass 1979; Coleman 1982; Dank 1971; Lewis 1983; Troiden 1979). Levine (1992) reviews attempts to validate Cass's model with empirical support. Lewis's (1983) model can be helpful because it identifies effective social work strategies with lesbians at each stage of the coming-out process. Most models of coming out are stage theories that suggest a sequential development of a lesbian or gay identity. They usually begin with awareness and confusion and culminate in integration of a gay identity as a positive aspect of self.

Sophie (1986) provides a critique of six models of coming out using a qualitative analysis. She calls into question the linear model of the stage theories. Her study, based on personal interviews with fourteen women currently experiencing changes in their sexual orientation, suggests that variance exists in the order and timing of events hypothesized by stage theories, and that some anticipated events do not occur at all. It appears that theoretical models of coming out, like most theoretical models, can provide a beginning framework to understand identity development, but must be measured against the subjective reality and unique experience of each individual.

Being gay or lesbian in a homophobic society raises issues of differential experiences of development, relationship, work, civil rights, and community. A growing literature exists on developmental perspectives of the lesbian and gay population (Berger 1980, 1982b; Browning 1987; Cornett and Hudson 1987; D'Augelli 1991; Grace 1992; Hetrick and Martin 1987; Friend 1987; Gibson 1989; Kimmel 1978; Lee 1992; Rosser, Simon, and Michael 1989; Tully 1989). These studies identify how lesbian and gay individuals who are in the life stages of adolescence, early, middle, and later adulthood negotiate the necessary developmental tasks along with additional developmental tasks associated with being gay or lesbian in a homophobic society.

Although often limited to white lesbian and gay couples, research and clinical studies of relationship issues have also flourished (Baptiste 1987; Colgan 1987; Decker 1983–84; George and Behrendt 1987; Krestan and Bepko 1980; McCandlish 1982; McWhirter and Mattison 1984; Peplau et al. 1978; Smalley 1987; Terry 1992). A social worker's knowledge base for helping lesbian and gay couples to resolve relationship issues is, in part, dependent upon knowledge of relationship issues for gay or lesbian couples and an overall knowledge of relationship dynamics and processes for any couple.

Some studies demonstrate the similarities of relationship issues for both opposite sex and same sex couples. Duffy and Rusbult (1986) found that the predictors of satisfaction and commitment were the same for heterosexual and homosexual couples. In their study, heterosexuals reported greater costs and slightly greater investments in their relationships. However, they found that close couples were very similar, regardless of whether they were homosexual or heterosexual. Certain relationship issues, such as communication and mutual respect, feelings of attraction and love, dyadic attachment, and relationship quality appear to be the same regardless of sexual orientation (Duffy and Rusbult 1986; Kurdek and Schmitt 1986a, b; Woodman and Lenna 1980).

On the other hand, there may be some cause for differences in lesbian and gay couples. Relationships in a lesbian or gay marriage may differ because of the absence of legal sanctions for same-sex couples. Gunter (1992) points out that society does not recognize lesbian or gay marriages and continues to treat each individual in the relationship as single. Social expectations around work, leisure, social interactions, and family relations may create conflicts that are not present in heterosexual marriages. Duffy and Rusbult (1986) discuss a variety of other social factors that might differentiate lesbian and gay relationships. They point out that negative social sanctions may make it more difficult to establish and maintain long-term relationships, and that communal property laws only apply to heterosexual marriages. In addition, homophobia creates a social context in which lesbian and gay relationships exist. Issues of passing, negotiating in the couple relationship the amount and types of self-disclosure and couple experiences of gay-related discrimination or violence are common in this context (Berger 1990b; Krestan and Bepko 1980).

Another difference, that of the same sex dyad, may result in different dynamics that social workers might need to consider. Kurdek and Schmitt (1986b) found that gender differences were a more important predictor of relationship behaviors than sexual orientation. It has been suggested in a number of studies that dynamics between partners vary as a result of the same sex nature of the relationship. Sex-role stereotypes may have a different influence when both marriage partners are male or female (Maracek, Finn, and Cardell 1982). Blumstein and Schwartz (1983 cited in Berger 1990a) found that gay men in couples sometimes competed with each other more than lesbian or heterosexual couples for symbols of power such as achievements and income.

Role and power in lesbian relationships may differ from those in heterosexual or male couple relationships. Status variables, which Lynch and Reilly (1986) point out are traditional correlates of power in heterosexual relationships, did not predict a power imbalance in lesbian relationships in their sample. Their study of seventy lesbian couples found household roles, who usually initiated sexual intimacy, and the frequency of and satisfaction with sex unrelated to status variables, such as income, assets, age, or occupation. Nevertheless, 42 percent of their sample reported that they or their partner had more power in the relationship. Lynch and Reilly report conflicting results compared to an earlier study when both measured balance of power by responses to the question, "Who do you think has more of a say about what you and your partner do together?" Lynch and Reilly (1986) found no significant relationships between who had more say and any of their status variables. Caldwell and Peplau (1984) reported significant correlations between partners' income and their power, and education and power.

Differentiation, dependency, and autonomy issues in lesbian and gay male relationships have also been addressed (see, for example, Colgan 1987; Krestan and Bepko 1980; Smalley 1987). Krestan and Bepko

(1980) suggest that lesbians demonstrate a tendency to experience fusion within a relationship, while gay men tend to distance from each other. They attribute these differences to differential socialization of men and women, and the dynamics that result when both persons in the couple are of the same sex. They also suggest that fusion in lesbian relationships results, in part, from lack of recognition of the relationship within the society. Recently, gay and lesbian couples have begun creating their own ceremonies of commitment that may counteract these larger societal forces (Berger 1990a; Butler 1990).

Violence in lesbian and gay relationships has just recently begun to be studied. Causal factors and implications for services are among the topics discussed (for examples, see Humphrey, Sowers-Hoag, and Harrison 1992; Humphrey, Harrison, and Sowers-Hoag 1991; Island and Letellie 1991; Renzetti 1988; Schilit, Lie, and Montagne 1990; Waterman, Dawson, and Bologna 1989).

Practitioners who work with lesbian and gay couples must be aware of special issues that may arise in gay or lesbian relationships because of societal homophobia and a potential for differential dynamics because of gender differences. Peplau and Cochran (1990) provide a thorough review of research studies on dynamics of lesbian and gay relationships. In addition to an understanding of these kinds of dynamics, social workers must also be familiar with research that shows the similarities of predictors to relationship quality and sources of satisfaction, whether the couple is heterosexual, gay or lesbian (see Duffy and Rusbult, 1986; Kurdek and Schmitt 1986b). Therefore, assessment and intervention strategies with lesbian and gay couples must include an understanding of special internal and external stresses for these couples as well as dynamics that are universal to any form of intimacy.

Awareness of family issues relevant to lesbians, gay men or other sexual minorities should also be part of a social worker's practice knowledge. Dahlheimer and Feigal (1991) calculate that one in every five families has a gay or lesbian member. They suggest that "families grappling with confusion and homophobia" exist in all caseloads. Strommen (1989) provides an excellent literature review of parental, sibling, children, and spouse reactions to disclosure of a homosexual identity.

Gunter (1992) identifies a number of principles of practice that are helpful. She states that the first factor important to practice with lesbian and gay clients is to recognize the diversity of family configurations.

An ability to accept various family forms is critical for anyone working with families. In working with lesbian and gay clients, it is also essential. Many of the issues that gay or lesbian families struggle with are concerned with the ability to accept the gay person and her or his family of creation. For example, gay or lesbian individuals often struggle with decisions about disclosure to family members. Adolescents or young adults coming out to their parents is a common phenomenon. For the individual coming out, friendship networks perform many family functions, especially emotional and social support. The family of friends needs to be acknowledged and included in the social worker's efforts to help clients meet their needs during this potential crisis (Dahlheimer and Feigal 1991).

However, structure and function vary regarding disclosure issues depending upon which family member is coming out and when in the family's life cycle. As in any family, the developmental and other needs of the individuals and family system will vary. A middle age parent coming out to her adolescent or young adult daughter, a gay father coming out to his wife and child, a lesbian couple coming out to their three year old son represent only a few configurations and roles that shape this issue. The practitioner's ability to join with any family in its struggle for health and well-being is partially a product of her ability to accept this configuration as a family. It is also a product of her clinical and research based knowledge of diverse family structures and family needs (see, for example, Anderson 1987; Berzon 1978; Borhek 1983; Erlichman 1988; Gollman 1989; Hall 1978; Harris and Turner 1985–86; Huggins 1989; Pagelow 1980; Pies 1987, 1989; Polikoff 1986; Saperstein 1981; Savin-Williams 1989; Ricketts and Achtenberg 1989; Robinson, Walters, and Skeen 1989; Strommen 1989; Turner, Scadden, and Harris 1990; Voeller and Walters 1978; Wirth 1978).

Although the struggle for acceptance is necessary for both young children of lesbian or gay parents, and adult children of middle or later adulthood lesbian or gay parents, each is attempting to resolve different developmental tasks and will experience coming out accordingly. The context and reasons for coming out will vary widely and raise different issues. Parents coming out to their children could also be introducing their partner as a family member. Gay or bisexual men or women who are diagnosed with HIV/AIDS might be coming out for the first time with their family. The openness of communication and ability for all family members to continue to accept each other and express their feelings are all critical to acceptance in any context.

Families, of course, range in their reactions to learning that a family member is lesbian or gay. Many families experience this disclosure as a crisis event. Some families can benefit from the support of organizations such as Parents and Friends of Lesbians and Gays (PFLAG), if this group is present in the community and if the parents are motivated to seek them out. For others, family rejection and violence are a response to learning this information about their child (Herek 1989; Hetrick and Martin 1987).

There has been little research on the adjustment of adult children whose parent comes out at a later life stage. Recently, some research has developed on children growing up with lesbian or gay parents. In one of the first studies on children of lesbians, Lewis (1980) reported that the children of lesbian mothers whom she interviewed showed the best adjustment when they were encouraged to express their feelings and were able to find social and emotional support in the process of resolving negative feelings. A number of studies have described coping styles and strengths of lesbian mothers (Miller, Jacobsen, and Bigner 1981; Oberstone and Sukoneck 1976; Pagelow 1980; Polikoff 1986). Harris and Turner (1985–86) and Turner, Scadden, and Harris (1990) report that homosexuality had not caused long-term problems for the children in their samples of lesbian and gay parents. They also found that most of the fathers and mothers in their study reported overall positive relationships with their children and strong parent-child bonds.

These findings also support lesbian and gay individuals who make efforts to become foster or adoptive parents. Uhl (1986) reviews court decisions in Massachusetts regarding the rights of lesbian and gay parents and reports on a survey of states' policies regarding foster care placement with lesbian and gay parents. Ricketts and Achtenberg (1989) review the history of lesbian and gay foster and adoptive parenting and recent case studies and legal decisions regarding this issue. Although literature on this topic is limited, these two articles can be resources for policy setting and practices of foster and adoption agencies.

Lesbian and gay individuals, families and communities all function within the context of the society power structure. The effects of this structure often provide examples of values, practices and laws that result in discrimination and violence against this group. Unfortunately, the stigmatization of lesbian and gay individuals is upheld in many state laws and court decisions that fail to protect lesbian and gay constitutional rights to privacy and equal protection under the law (Bersoff and Ogden 1991). For example, the United States Supreme Court in 1986 upheld the constitutionality of a law that makes it illegal to have a sexually intimate relationship with someone of the same sex (*Bowers v. Hardwick* 1986, reported in Herek 1989). Only a few states have laws that explicitly make it illegal to discriminate in housing and employment because of homosexuality. Previous court decisions on child custody issues have blatantly ignored constitutional rights of lesbian mothers and gay fathers, denying custody or threatening removal of children if any expression of attachment was visible with a same sex partner (Rand, Graham, and Rawlings 1982).

Since prejudicial treatment of lesbian or gay workers remains a form of de facto discrimination for which there exists no federal protection, unfair practices often go unreported or undocumented in any way. Present federal civil rights statutes do not protect people on the basis of sexual orientation. City ordinances, agency and university policies that explicitly prohibit discrimination on the basis of sexual orientation have developed recently. However, courts continue to refuse requests to apply Title VII antidiscrimination policies to sexual orientation (Poverny and Finch 1988b).

Surveys conducted by lesbian and gay organizations document the widespread incidence of discrimination, verbal abuse and physical violence against the gay population (Gross, Aurand, and Adessa 1988; Herek 1989; Seattle Commission for Lesbians and Gays 1991). Herek (1989) calls for in-service training for all social service and mental health professionals that addresses hate crime survivors' needs and making outreach efforts to the gay and lesbian community. Herek also recommends policy work that results in explicit laws protecting lesbian and gay persons from victimization and discrimination and education for criminal justice personnel that sensitizes them to antigay bias crimes.

The strengths of the gay community to organize for social change and service delivery can be seen in its response to AIDS, violence, and discrimination. Countless lesbian and gay organizations have developed nationally and locally to work for education, service, and advocacy. Social workers need to be aware of these community resources as well as the needs and strengths of gay and lesbian individuals and families as they begin to develop the practice skills to work with lesbian and gay clients.

Skills for Practice with Lesbian, Gay, and Bisexual Persons

A first step in developing skills to effectively work with lesbian and gay clients is a self-examination of personal feelings, attitudes, ideas and beliefs about sexuality, sex roles and sexual orientation (Dulaney and Kelly 1982; Tully and Albro 1979; Woodman and Lenna 1980). This kind of introspection is critical to preparing for work with any diverse group, but particularly lesbian and gay clients because of the acceptance of homophobia in our society. Forrister (1992) suggests that this self-examination should be done in the context of social work values which can provide a framework for students to understand their responsibility to lesbian and gay clients.

The practice skills necessary for work with lesbian and gay clients begin with the same skills necessary for practice with any population. Dulaney and Kelly (1982) point out as guiding principles acceptance of the client as a total human being and acceptance of the client's sexual orientation. Discarding the assumption that all clients are heterosexual is another initial task for acquiring the necessary practice skills to effectively work with lesbian and gay clients.

In addition to foundation practice skills, the necessity of a sensitivity to and awareness of the diverse life experiences of gay and lesbian persons and familiarity with the needs and treatment issues of gay and lesbian clients because of both internalized and external sources of homophobia require some specific key practice skills. Garnets et al.'s (1991) survey of practicing psychologists identifies themes and examples of exemplary practice, and themes and examples of inappropriate practice with lesbian and gay clients. Their discussion illustrates some key clinical skills when working with lesbian, gay, or bisexual clients. Examples of requirements for appropriate practice include an understanding of homosexuality as one healthy part of a client, recognizing the importance of this attribute, but not seeing it as the only central characteristic of the client nor assuming that it is necessarily relevant to the client's problem. Recognition and assessment of multiple sources of discrimination and harassment as external barriers in the lives of lesbian and gay clients are other essential skills. An ability to recognize and help clients reduce their own internalized homophobia is also critical.

A high level of acceptance of lesbian, gay, and bisexual clients on the worker's part can often counteract a tendency for clients to feel guilty because of internalized homophobia. Taking into account the extent to which lesbian or gay male identity development is complicated by the client's own negative attitudes toward homosexuality is necessary for effective practice with lesbian and gay clients (Garnets et al. 1991). A recognition of the interactive effects of race, class, and ethnicity along with sexual orientation for gay men and lesbians of color is another crucial practice skill. Garnets and colleagues (1991) argue that all practitioners need a knowledge base of lesbian and gay identity development and the ability to understand the diverse nature of lesbian and gay relationships and family issues. Strategies are needed to effectively confront denial and resistance of self for clients struggling with their sexual orientation, and to confront, help clients cope with, and actively counter homophobia in their lives.

Sophie (1987) develops therapeutic strategies to help women who are having difficulty accepting their attractions to other women to reduce internalized homophobia. The strategies she outlines include cognitive restructuring that will challenge the meanings of concepts such as woman, lesbian; and of values and religious beliefs concerning homosexuality. Sophie stresses the need for an affirming group of lesbian friends in the process of developing a positive lesbian identity. She recommends that both worker and client keep an openness to the client's definitions of self over time and an awareness of the great amount of variation that exists in the way persons negotiate issues around sexual orientation (Sophie 1987).

One issue that all lesbian and gay people consistently negotiate is the decision to self-disclose to significant others in their lives. The most recognized time for decisions about this is when a person first realizes that he or she is gay. However, coming-out decisions continue whenever a new relationship is established or a new situation is encountered. Social workers must be prepared to work with clients struggling with self-disclosure decisions. Cain (1991) provides research findings on reasons why gay men self-disclose and reasons why gay men conceal their identity that can be helpful when working with clients making self-disclosure decisions. Reasons he found for disclosure include:

to further build a relationship; to resolve a specific problem such as always being questioned about dating the opposite sex; to prevent problems from hiding sexual orientation; or to make a political statement. Reasons for concealing being gay included: deference to another person; a perception that the disclosure would create problems; or a feeling of lacking courage or security to disclose. Cain suggests that with information about how gay men manage their identity, social workers can better understand clients' feelings and fears and help them to evaluate the potential consequences of self-disclosure.

Social work practitioners must also be aware of the often difficult challenges facing African Americans, Asian Americans, and Hispanic individuals who are struggling with a lesbian or gay identity (Chan 1989; Hidalgo and Christensen 1976–77; Icard 1986; Loiacano 1989). Loiacano (1989) identifies part of the challenge as a struggle for African-American individuals to gain acceptance of self as "blacks in the predominantly white gay and lesbian community and as gay men and lesbian women in the predominantly heterosexual black community" (21). Chan (1989) suggests that Asian-American lesbians and gay men often experience strong conflicts between traditional Asian cultural values and the development of a lesbian or gay identity. Hidalgo and Christenson (1976–77) found in their sample of Puerto Rican lesbians that although some families supported their daughters, the majority rejected them or denied knowing that they were lesbians.

Lesbian and gay people of color have neither been fully included in the lesbian and gay communities nor in their own ethnic minority populations. Homosexuality may be seen to violate traditional gender role expectations and other cultural values of Asian, black and Hispanic communities (Chan 1989; Hetrick and Martin 1986; Hidalgo and Christensen 1976–77; Loiacano 1989). Newman and Muzzonigro (1993) found that families of gay male adolescents were perceived by the adolescents as least accepting of homosexuality when they had traditional ethnic values. These conflicts create difficulties for individuals who may fear rejection from their families and ethnic communities. Social workers need to be aware of these and other special issues for lesbians and gays who are also members of an ethnic minority community.

Some of these special gay minority issues were illustrated in an exploratory study drawing from personal interview data with a small sample of black gay men and lesbian women. Loiacano (1989) found that many of the individuals interviewed discussed feeling a lack of support from the predominantly heterosexual black community for their gay or lesbian identity. They reported pressure from the black community to be secretive about their homosexuality, and a lack of role models for black American gay couples from their own ethnic community. Lack of support and inclusion were also experienced in the mainly white lesbian and gay community. These kinds of feelings of managing a dual identity and struggling with feelings of rejection from both communities have been expressed by lesbian and gay men who are Puerto Rican and Asian-American in two other studies (Chan 1989; Hidalgo and Christensen 1976–77).

Although HIV/AIDS is a public health issue that affects all populations, there are some special practice issues in relation to HIV/AIDS, lesbian and gay individuals and the gay community. In some large urban areas, entire friendship networks of gay men are literally dying. A study by the AIDS Health Project of the University of California (1990, reported in ActionAIDS 1992) found that many HIV-negative San Francisco gay men may be suffering from serious mental health problems as the result of AIDS-related experiences of anxiety, guilt, and loss. Biller and Rice (1990) address bereavement issues that may arise as a result of multiple losses of persons with AIDS.

Social workers must have a knowledge base for working with gay, straight, and bisexual individuals who test HIV-positive or who are experiencing full-blown AIDS. Reamer (1991) provides a review of relevant literature and a discussion that clarifies the need to protect client confidentiality and potential conflicts with the worker's duty to protect third parties when clients remain sexually active without revealing their HIV status. Huggins et al. (1991) surveyed emotional and behavioral responses of gay and bisexual men to HIV antibody testing. Their results demonstrated that those who test positive often experience increased anxiety and a change in sexual behavior. Not surprisingly, higher levels of depression and anxiety about AIDS were found among those who tested positive compared to those with negative test results. The percentages of HIV positive men who intended to tell their partners and those who changed their sexual behavior following the positive test result were also reported. Clinical implications for pretest and post-test counseling are identified, including the need to assess level of risk for infection, persons's knowledge about AIDS and HIV testing; the individual's psychological strengths and weaknesses and the quality of his support systems; and ethical dilemmas of working with a client who is HIV-positive, but who has not told his partner (Huggins et al. 1991). These issues would appear to apply to HIV/AIDS work with any individual, regardless of his or her sexual orientation.

To provide effective counseling, information and education, social, emotional and financial support, access to health care, and advocacy for persons with HIV/AIDS, social workers obviously need to have knowledge about the disease. When working with lesbian and gay individuals on this issue, however, acceptance and knowledge of the gay and lesbian community are also critical. Models of services for this population are often described in the HIV/AIDS literature. For example, Coleman and Harris (1989) describe the structure and services provided by a support group for persons testing HIV-positive offered by the Gay and Lesbian Community Services Center. Feldman (1989) discusses special issues for gay youth and HIV/AIDS, such as a tendency for gay adolescents to believe that only older gay men are at risk for AIDS, a form of denial that the AIDS crisis is relevant to them.

There is some evidence that stigma and prejudice about AIDS have often been directed toward the gay population. Herek (1989) reports that many incidents of violence toward gay men have been accompanied by verbal abuse in relation to AIDS. In a recent experimental study, college students evaluated homosexual AIDS patients more negatively, considering them more deserving of their illness than any other group when rating vignettes that varied by sexual orientation (heterosexual or homosexual man) and disease (leukemia or HIV/AIDS) (St. Lawrence et al. 1990). Social workers who work in the area of HIV/AIDS will be confronted with these fears and prejudices and need to be prepared to educate others and to work toward reducing stigma associated with the disease. As content on HIV/AIDS is introduced more frequently into social work education and in-service training, it is essential that homosexuality be covered in an affirmative way.

"We are everywhere" is a popular gay and lesbian rights slogan that captures the idea that not only are lesbian and gay social work practitioners, educators, and students in virtually every social work agency and school of social work, but that lesbian and gay clients are also a part of every social work client group. Considering sexuality an important and valued aspect of the client's life and being able to accurately and comfortably communicate about it are necessary in working with any population (Dulaney and Kelly 1982). The abilities to establish a relationship and provide positive regard for clients are quintessential practice skills that require the worker's comfort with homosexuality, and a specific knowledge base regarding challenges and struggles that lesbian and gay clients face in a homophobic society.

Skills for Working to Eliminate Discriminatory Practices and Policies

Pierce (1992) recommends that the history of social welfare policies and services needs to include historical and contemporary policies regarding lesbian and gay people. One area might be an examination of social work as a profession in relation to all devalued groups, including the lesbian and gay population, the poor, people of color, women, and refugees. Study of our own profession's history will reveal actions that show leadership and effective strategies at times; however, our inaction and failure to organize and take risks will also be discovered. This historical analysis might provide social work professionals with a useful perspective to work toward social change in the future.

Examples of historical mistreatment of stigmatized and devalued populations are weaved throughout employment, military, child custody, and public access policies that affect populations because of race, gender, sexual orientation, age, disability, class, and religion. Study of these historical practices reveals varied sources of discrimination and prejudice. Social welfare legislation, court decisions, administrative policies, and program practices that affect the lesbian and gay population have often been discriminatory in both subtle and blatant forms. Many of these policies and practices continue to discriminate and treat unfairly lesbian and gay people. A number of publications are available that illustrate recent past and present discriminatory practices in employment, family and marriage laws, child custody, foster care and adoption decisions, immigration and naturalization policies, military, social services, and mental health systems (Bernstein 1977; Casas, Brady and Ponterotto 1983; Hedgpath 1980; Hitchens 1980; Knutson 1977; McCrary and Guttierez 1980; Polikoff 1986; Poverny and Finch 1985, 1988a; Reynolds 1980; Richards 1980; Ricketts and Achtenberg 1989; Tievsky 1988; Uhl 1986; Vetri 1980).

Social workers must recognize the homophobic nature of society which results in differential treatment, discrimination, violence and other forms of homophobia for lesbian and gay clients. Counseling, information and referral, advocacy and community work regarding these issues are often necessary. Skills needed to help individuals who are discriminated against or are victims of violence as a result of their sexual orientation must be based upon knowledge of the extent and types of discrimination and violence that lesbian and gay clients are subject to. Social action and advocacy that address discrimination and oppression must include awareness of relevant policies and skills to advocate for clients; skills to work with clients and communities to advocate for themselves by challenging specific cases of discrimination; and skills to engage in larger scale reforms such as lobbying for legislative and administrative changes.

Social workers must also be prepared to develop further the existing knowledge base about the lesbian and gay population and to be critical consumers of past and current research findings. The majority of historical studies provide a pathological view of homosexuality based on prejudicial values, assumptions, and theories. Brooks (1992) points out that in most past studies heterosexist bias has been exhibited throughout the entire research process starting with problem selection and formulation, selection of population and sample, and continuing through interpretation of research results.

Pierce (1992) asserts that too little research has been done regarding lesbian and gay persons. Further, when research has been conducted, it has too often relied on clinical samples for the purposes of establishing the "etiology of homosexuality." Herek et al. (1991) provide guidelines for avoiding the kinds of heterosexist bias that has existed in research efforts. The past focus of research studies on homosexuality demonstrates how prejudice can contribute to poorly conceived and biased research questions and overgeneralized misleading results.

Morin's (1977) early work and Waters's updated (1986) study of the categories of research conducted on lesbian and gay issues validate these assertions. Morin (1977) demonstrated that between 1967 and 1974, research about gay men and lesbian women was primarily concerned with diagnosis, cause, and cure. He recommended that research should give priority to the dynamics of gay relationships, the development of a positive gay identity, and specific problems of gay children, adolescents, and older gay men and lesbian women. Waters (1986) reviewed the research on lesbian and gay issues between 1979 and 1983 and discovered that the overall volume of research had almost doubled; that studies of diagnosis had dropped in number from 16 percent to 1 percent; and that relationship and identity issues had become the focus of many of the research studies.

Although research methods used on lesbian and gay issues have become less heterosexist in recent years, studies continue to search for differences that "cause" homosexuality. Causes of homosexuality will remain an issue as long as homosexuality is looked at as deviant from the norm. In contrast, causes of heterosexuality are neither questioned nor researched. This search for differences continues to result in research designed to test for the effects of hormonal and personality variables or traumatic experiences on the development of homosexuality (examples are Brannock and Chapman 1990; Dancey 1990a, b; Gilgun and Reiser 1990; Kallman 1952; Starka, Sipova, and Hynie 1975). For the most part, these studies disconfirm between-group differences and support the idea that there is no basis for seeing homosexuality as deviant or pathological. For instance, Dancey (1990a, b) found no differences between lesbian and heterosexual women on hormonal, personality, or family background variables. Storms (1980) examined the association of sexual orientation with sex roles and found no statistically significant difference between self-identified gay and straight men. Brannock and Chapman (1990) demonstrated an equivalent number of traumatic experiences with men existed in her sample of heterosexual and lesbian women, thus disconfirming the hypothesis that lesbian women have had a greater number of traumatic experiences with men than heterosexual women.

Being gay or lesbian is no longer grounds for a diagnosis of mental illness, although until 1973 homosexuality was included as a mental disorder in the American Psychiatric Association *Diagnostic and Statistical Manual* (DSM). The disorder "ego dystonic homosexuality" was removed from the DSM-IIIR (1987). Although listed in the index of the DSM-IIIR, ego dystonic homosexuality was no longer a specific diagnosis. The index refers the clinician to "Sexual Disorders, Not Otherwise Specified (302.90)", which includes an example of "persistent and marked distress about one's sexual orientation" (296). These changes were partly a result of consistent findings from studies which demonstrate that the mental health of lesbian and gay persons is no different from their heterosexual counterparts; findings which have been replicated and confirmed repeatedly (see Armon 1960; Berger 1980; Christie and Young 1986; Hart et al. 1978; Hopkins 1969; Larsen 1981; Oberstone and Sukoneck 1976; Saghir et al. 1970; Siegelman 1972).

A recent study provides data that could decrease discrimination and stereotypes about gay and lesbian people working with children or in other socially responsible positions. This study by Whitehead and Nokes (1990) found that there were no differences in nurturance or empathy between homosexual and heterosexual Big Brother/Big Sister volunteers. In fact, some studies demonstrate certain personality strengths present in lesbian or gay people which are not found as readily in the straight population (Larsen 1981; Polikoff 1986).

Despite the promising nature of some of these changes, certain research practices continue to distort our knowledge base in this area. One distorting practice is the disregard of whole segments of the lesbian and gay population. For example, there exist few, if any, representative studies of lesbian and gay elderly; of those who are of low socioeconomic status; of lesbian and gay people of color; or of the presence of and special issues for lesbian and gay people in diverse service populations, such as those who are physically disabled, welfare recipients or the elderly. Small sample size is often a problem due to a reluctance to disclose, especially in the least visible parts of this population. Tully (1992) points out that all that is known about older lesbian women is based on data from a total of 183 women. Similarly, representative samples are absent for lesbian and gay people who are disabled and those who express homosexual feelings and behaviors, but do not identify as lesbian or gay. Information about these groups is critical to further develop an accurate knowledge base and effective strategies.

There are some promising studies with small sample sizes that create a beginning knowledge base for understanding lesbian, gay and bisexual issues in all populations. For example, Mapou (1990) reports on a research study of head injury trauma among gay and lesbian individuals. Epstein and Zak (1992) review recent articles about working with lesbian and gay substance abuse clients, gay persons with AIDS, and lesbian and gay people of color. In a clinical case study, Rubin (1981) reports on an interview with Ricki Boden, a therapist who cofacilitated a consciousness-raising group of disabled lesbian women. Boden, who identifies herself as a disabled lesbian, provides critical information about the need for such groups and their potential effectiveness. Icard and Traunstein (1987) break some new ground with their synthesis of previous research relevant to the experiences of black, gay, alcoholic men. Awareness of information about lesbian and gay individuals within all communities must be developed through our practice and research efforts.

To support a more inclusive knowledge base as a profession, however, requires continued efforts to be open to our many sources of diversity. Emotions, fears, and negative attitudes about our differences have evolved as a product of the deeply entrenched prejudices of our society. Neither social work students, faculty, nor practitioners are immune from the socialization process that instills rejection of homosexuality (Humphreys 1983; Newman 1989; Weiner 1989; Wisniewski and Toomey 1987). Schools of social work and social work practice settings may need to work on creating an environment to examine and critique our fears, attitudes and emotions about lesbian and gay people, in addition to our attitudes and emotions about other sources of diversity. This environment may need to be developed as part of the process of making content on lesbian, gay and bisexual issues part of the social work knowledge base. School or agency in-services can facilitate the profession's ability to effectively teach about and practice with lesbian, gay, and bisexual individuals in any population.

Part of inclusion of lesbian and gay content in a class or in-service workshop requires an atmosphere that makes an open exchange of information, feelings, and attitudes on this subject result in all participants gaining greater understanding about and sensitivity to lesbian, gay, and bisexual issues. Silver-Jones (1990) suggests that each person (including the instructor) begin classes and in-service training workshops that include the topic of homosexuality by "naming the fears" that they are experiencing about this inclusion. Silver-Jones stresses that time spent on creating a safe climate where feelings can be expressed and where challenges to misconceptions are possible is part of the learning process, not a tangent.

It is important for practitioners, students, and educators to consider possible barriers or facilitators, such as their motivation for addressing this content; knowledge about lesbian and gay issues; fears and feelings; and overall comfort level with the general topic. Effectively including this content in a school of social work requires that the faculty become knowledgeable about and comfortable with this population. Ensuring that the needs of lesbian and gay clients are addressed also requires comfort with and knowledge about this population by all agency staff.

The subject of sexual orientation raises some difficult issues because of its association with sexuality; because it is not obvious who is gay, lesbian, or bisexual; and because of the widespread homophobia that affects us all. Social workers must create an atmosphere in which an openness can develop for differing attitudes on a sensitive subject. Because this subject often evokes strong feelings, a process which feels relatively safe to everyone, but that challenges misconceptions and myths, needs to be established.

Facilitation of this process can occur in an interactive atmosphere with discussion of feelings about and reactions to the topic of social work with the lesbian and gay population. Strong beliefs and attitudes about homosexuality will usually be expressed verbally and nonverbally. Promoting an exchange of experiences and ideas among participants can provide the kind of personal exchange that this topic requires. All participants, but particularly lesbian and gay students or workers, must feel that they have a choice about self-disclosure. However, when self-disclosure is chosen, the expression of personal feelings and experiences in relation to sexual orientation often facilitate learning and attitude change. If homophobic attitudes are expressed, gentle confrontation without promoting hostility, defensiveness, or withdrawal of some participants is necessary. The process through which information about gay and lesbian issues gets communicated can establish the kind of environment needed for negative attitudes to change and genuine acceptance to occur.

The profession of social work has struggled to fully include issues of sexual orientation, race, class, culture, physical ability differences, and other aspects of diversity for many decades. This struggle has often been led by individuals and groups of social workers, but has sometimes been met with resistance within the profession. In most cases, the struggle has moved from exclusion to tolerance to inclusiveness to acceptance, respect, and appreciation. The recently passed CSWE curriculum requirement that lesbian and gay issues be included in social work education demonstrates a new level of commitment to ensuring that lesbian and gay issues are part of the social work knowledge base.

Populations who are diverse continue to be the populations most at risk for social conditions of discrimination and oppression. Including diversity into the professional knowledge base can result in better social work theory, practice skills, research studies, and policy recommendations. To this end, social workers need accurate perceptions, information, and skills in relation to diverse populations. To provide responsible and effective services to lesbian, gay, and bisexual people, an awareness and understanding of lesbian and gay issues for individuals, families, organizations, and communities, and the development of skills for practice with lesbian, gay, and bisexual persons should be part of basic social work knowledge. Social workers who learn about gay and lesbian issues will be better prepared to work with lesbian, gay, and bisexual clients and to perform social action around the issue of sexual orientation. Social workers who perceive and understand the commonalities of oppression across populations will develop more effective social action skills. Social workers who can create coalitions among diverse communities, develop and advocate for effective antidiscriminatory policies, provide social work intervention based on sensitivity and full acceptance will contribute to a society more responsive to the well-being of its people.

An existing body of knowledge about lesbian and gay issues based on theoretical frameworks, empirical, clinical, and qualitative research studies, and practice wisdom is available. Much of this knowledge is published in professional journals; much has been developed in practice settings and schools of social work. All social workers can take advantage of what is known about social work with lesbian, gay, and bisexual individuals and communities.

However, there is still much that is not understood about the concept of sexual orientation and other aspects of lesbian, gay, and bisexual issues. Theoretical arguments have historically consisted of debates about causation of one variable, homosexuality. Is homosexuality an inversion or perversion; a biological variation; a fixated and regressed state; a social construction; a deviant social role? Recently, social work and several other disciplines conceptualized homosexuality and bisexuality as natural, healthy expressions of sexual orientation.

Nevertheless, the continued search for the cause of homosexuality reflects a need to see homosexuality as unnatural, caused by some deviation in the person or environment. Research that follows this question of causation needs to investigate the nature of sexual orientation itself. A fuller understanding of how all humans develop their sexual orientation is critical to an understanding of this central part of human behavior. Existing research and literature about sexual orientation are only beginning to reveal the complexity and diversity of this human attribute.

The concept of bisexuality as one variation of sexual orientation is not well understood. The extent to which individuals express bisexual feelings and develop intimate bisexual relationships over the life cycle is not known. The place of bisexuality in relation to lesbian and gay issues needs to be explored. The tendency to exclude bisexuality as part of lesbian and gay studies should be examined further.

Including gay, lesbian, and bisexual issues for health and mental health, child welfare, physical disabilities, drug and alcohol, and all other fields of service is a necessity. It is essential that social workers be aware of special issues for lesbians and gays who are disabled, drug and alcohol abusers, mental health consumers, battered women, in foster care, elderly, or unemployed. Because the literature and research are undeveloped in this area (with a few notable exceptions such as, Anderson and Henderson 1985; Berger 1982b; Humphrey, et al. 1992; Icard and Traunstein 1987; Ricketts and Achtenberg 1989; Rubin 1981), research, education, and practice knowledge about these clients need to be pursued more aggressively.

Practice and policy decisions based on sound, unbiased research, an accurate knowledge of human development and behavior, and use of effective practice skills are needed to provide an environment that fights the distorting effects of homophobia in any practice or education setting. Toward these ends, schools of social work and social work agencies must work toward changes in practice, policies, and research endeavors. These changes must be preceded by the full inclusion of the lesbian and gay population as part of the foundations of social work knowledge.

Pierce (1991) has stated that "we are a part of every group and apart from every group." This idea clarifies the importance of including knowledge about the lesbian and gay population. Although we are part of every race and ethnic group, each gender, class, religion, socioeconomic status, and problem or service group, we are also set apart. Gay and lesbian people are often not accepted into educational, religious, social work, and political systems; not accepted by the military, the family, or the labor market (Pierce 1992). Gay and lesbian minorities of color may face even more difficult separations from both their own ethnic community, which might reject them, as well as from the gay and lesbian community. Social work education must include content that provides students with the knowledge and value base to work effectively with individual clients, groups, and communities who are lesbian, gay, or bisexual; people who may also be of color, physically disabled, elderly, or poor. The centrality of these issues to social work emerges from the profession's long-standing commitment to knowledge about diversity.

REFERENCES

ActionAIDS. 1992. *Fast Facts about AIDS*. Philadelphia: ActionAIDS.

Alston, J. 1974. "Attitudes Toward Extramarital and Homosexual Relations." *Journal for the Scientific Study of Religion* 13:479–81.

American Psychiatric Association. 1987. *Diagnostic and Statistical Manual of Mental Disorders*. 3d ed. Washington, D.C.: American Psychiatric Association.

Anderson, D. 1987. "Family and Peer Relations of Gay Adolescents." *Adolescent Psychiatry* 14:162–178.

Anderson, S. C. and D.C. Henderson. 1985. "Working with Lesbian Alcoholics." *Social Work* 30:518–528.

Armon, V. 1960. "Some Personality Variability in Overt Female Homosexuality." *Journal of Projective Techniques* 24:292–309.

Baptiste, D. A. 1987. "Psychotherapy with Gay/Lesbian Couples and their Children in `Stepfamilies': A Challenge for Marriage and Family Therapists." *Journal of Homosexuality* 14(1/2):223–237.

Bell, A. P., M. S. Weinberg, and S. K. Hammersmith. 1981. *Sexual Preference: Its Development in Men and Women*. Bloomington: Indiana University Press.

Berger, R. M. 1977. "An Advocate Model for Intervention with Homosexuals." *Social Work* 2:280–283.

——. 1980. "Psychological Adaptation of the Older Homosexual." *Journal of Homosexuality* 5(3):161–175.

——. 1982a. *Gay and Gray: The Older Homosexual Man*. Champaign: University of Illinois Press.

——. 1982b. "The Unseen Minority: Older Gay and Lesbians." *Social Work* 27(3):236–249.

——. 1983. "What is a Homosexual: A Definition Model." *Social Work* 28(2):132–135.

——. 1990a. "Men Together: Understanding the Gay Couple." *Journal of Homosexuality* 19(3):31–49.

——. 1990b. "Passing: Impact on the Quality of Same-Sex Couple Relationships." *Social Work* 35:328–332.

Berkey, B. R., T. Perelman-Hall, and L. A. Kurdek. 1990. "The Multidimensional Scale of Sexuality." *Journal of Homosexuality* 19(4):67–87.

Bernstein, B. 1977. "Legal and Social Interface in Counseling Homosexual Clients." *Social Casework* 50(1):36–40.

Bersoff, D. N. and D. W. Ogden 1991. "APA Amicus Curiae Briefs: Furthering Lesbian and Gay Male Civil Rights." *American Psychologist* 9:950–956.

Berzon, B. 1978. "Sharing Your Lesbian Identity with Your Children." In G. Vida, ed., *Our Right to Love: A Lesbian Resource Book*. Englewood Cliffs, N.J.: Prentice-Hall.

Biller, R. and S. Rice 1990. "Experiencing Multiple Loss of Persons with AIDS: Grief and Bereavement Issues." *Health and Social Work* 15:283–290.

Billingsley, A. 1970. "Black Families and White Social Science." *Journal of Social Issues* 26(3):127–142.

Borhek, M. V. 1983. *Coming Out to Parents: A Two-Way Survival Guide for Lesbians and Gay Men and Their Parents*. New York: Pilgrim Press.

Bozett, F. W. 1989. "Gay Fathers: Review of the Literature." *Journal of Homosexuality* 18(1/2):137–162.

Brannock, J. C. and B. E. Chapman. 1990. "Negative Sexual Experiences with Men among Heterosexual Women and Lesbians." *Journal of Homosexuality* 19(1):105–110.

Brooks, W. K. 1992. "Research and the Gay Minority: Problems and Possibilities." In N. Woodman, ed., *Lesbian and Gay Lifestyles: A Guide for Counseling and Education*. New York: Irvington.

Browning, C. 1987. "Therapeutic Issues and Intervention Strategies with Young Adult Lesbian Clients: A Developmental Approach." *Journal of Homosexuality* 14(1/2):45–52.

Butler, B. 1990. *Ceremonies of the Heart: Celebrating Lesbian Unions*. Seattle: Seal Press.

Cain, R. 1991. "Stigma Management and Gay Identity Development." *Social Work* 36(1):67–73.

Caldwell, M. A. and L. A. Peplau. 1984. "The Balance of Power in Lesbian Relationships." *Sex Roles* 10(7/8):587–599.

Carter, B. and M. McGoldrick. 1989. *The Changing Family Life Cycle*. Boston: Allyn and Bacon.

Casas, J. M., S. Brady, and H. G. Ponterotto. 1983. "Sexual Preference Biases in Counseling: An Information Processing Approach." *Journal of Counseling Psychology* 30(2):139–145.

Cass, V. C. 1979. "Homosexual Identity Formation: A Theoretical Model." *Journal of Homosexuality* 4:219–235.

Castro, J. 1992. "Grapevine." *Time* (June 22):21.

Cates, J. A. 1987. "Adolescent Sexuality: Gay and Lesbian issues." *Child Welfare* 66(4):353–364.

Chan, C. S. 1989. "Issues of Identity Development among Asian- American Lesbians and Gay Men." *Journal of Counseling and Development* 68:16–20.

Chapman, B. E. and J. C. Brannock. 1987. "Proposed Model of Lesbian Identity

Development: An Empirical Examination." *Journal of Homosexuality* 14(3/4): 69–80.

Chestang, L. 1972. "Character Development in a Hostile Environment." Occasional paper No. 3. Chicago: University of Chicago School of Social Service Administration.

Christie, D. and M. Young. 1986. "Self-Concept of Lesbian and Heterosexual Women." *Psychological Reports* 59(3):1279–1282.

Coleman, E. 1982. "Developmental Stages of the Coming Out Process." *Journal of Homosexuality* 7(2/3):31–43.

Coleman, V. E. and G. N. Harris. 1989. "A Support Group for Individuals Recently Testing HIV Positive: A Psychoeducational Group Model." *Journal of Sex Research* 26(4):539–548.

Colgan, P. 1987. "Treatment of Identity and Intimacy Issues in Gay Males." *Journal of Homosexuality* 14(1/2):101–123.

Compton, D. 1974. "Minority Content in Social Work Education: Promise or Pitfall?" *Journal of Education for Social Work* 10:9–18.

Condry, J. 1984. "Gender Identity and Social Competence." *Sex Roles* 11:485–511.

Cornett, C. W., and R. A. Hudson. 1987. "Middle Adulthood and the Theories of Erikson, Gould, and Vaillant: Where Does the Gay Man Fit?" *Journal of Gerontological Social Work* 20(3/4):61–73.

Council on Social Work Education. 1982. *Curriculum Policy Statement for the Masters Degree and Baccalaureate Degree Programs in Social Work Education.* New York: CSWE.

——. 1992. *Curriculum Policy Statement for the Masters Degree and Baccalaureate Degree Programs in Social Work Education.* Alexandria, Va.: CSWE.

Dahlheimer, D. and J. Feigal. 1991. "Bridging the Gap." *Networker* (January-February):44–53.

Dancey, C. P. 1990a. "The Influence of Familial and Personality Variables on Sexual Orientation in Women." *The Psychological Record* 40:437–449.

——. 1990b. "Sexual Orientation in Women: An Investigation of Hormonal and Personality Variables." *Biological Psychology* 30(3):251–264.

Dank, B. M. 1971. "Coming Out in the Gay World." *Psychiatry* 34:180–197.

D'Augelli, A. R. 1991. "Gay Men in College: Identity Processes and Adaptations." *Journal of College Student Development* 32(2):140–146.

Davis, J. A. 1982. *General Social Survey:1972–1982: Cumulative Codebook.* Chicago: National Opinion Research Center.

—— and T. W. Smith. 1984. *General Social Survey: 1972–1984: Cumulative Codebook.* Chicago: National Opinion Research Center.

Davis, L. 1986. "A Feminist Approach to Social Work Research." *Affilia: Journal of Women and Social Work* 1(1):32–47.

Decker, B. 1983–84. "Counseling Gay and Lesbian Couples." *Journal of Social Work and Human Sexuality* 2(2/3):39–52.

Duffy, S. M. and C. E. Rusbult. 1986. "Satisfaction and Commitment in Homosexual and Heterosexual Relationships." *Journal of Homosexuality* 12(2):1–23.

Dulaney, D. and J. Kelly. 1982. "Improving Services to Gay and Lesbian Clients." *Social Work* 27(2):178–183.

Epstein, A. L. and P. Zak. 1992. *The Master of Social Work Core Curriculum: Inculusion of Gay, Lesbian, and Bisexual Content.* Professional Practice Project. San Francisco: San Francisco State University.

Erikson, E. 1963. *Childhood and Society.* New York: W. W. Norton.

Erlichman, K. L. 1988. "Lesbian Mothers: Ethical Issues in Social Work Practice." *Women and Therapy* 8(1/2):207–224.

Feldman, D. A. 1989. "Gay Youth and AIDS." *Journal of Homosexuality* 17(1/2):185–193.

Forrister, D. K. 1992. "The Integration of Lesbian and Gay Content in Direct Practice Courses." In N. Woodman, ed., *Lesbian and Gay Lifestyles: A Guide for Counseling and Education.* New York: Irvington.

Friend, R. A. 1987. "The Individual and Social Psychology of Aging: Clinical Implications for Lesbian and Gay Men." *Journal of Homosexuality* 14(1/2):347–350.

Garnets, L., K. A. Hancock, S. D. Cochran, J. Goodchilds, and L. A. Peplau. 1991. "Issues in Psychotherapy with Lesbians and Gay Men: A Survey of Psychologists." *American Psychologist* 46(9):964–972.

George, K. D. and A. E. Behrendt. 1987. "Therapy for Male Couples Experiencing Relationship Problems." *Journal of Homosexuality* 14(1/2):77–87.

Gibson, P. 1989. "Gay Male and Lesbian Youth Suicide." *Report of the Secretary's Task Force on Youth Suicide.* Washington, D.C.: Department of Health and Human Services.

Gilgun, J. F. and E. Reiser. 1990. "The Development of Sexual Identity Among Men Sexually Abused as Children." *Families in Society* 71(9):515–523.

Gollman, J. S. 1989. "Children of Gay and Lesbian Parents." *Marriage and Family Review* 14(3/4):177–196.

Gooren, L. 1990. "Biomedical Theories of Sexual Orientation: A Critical Examination." In D. P. McWhirter, S. A. Sanders, and J. M. Reinisch, eds., *Homosexuality/Heterosexuality: Concepts of Sexual Orientation.* New York: Oxford University Press.

Grace, J. 1992. "Affirming Lesbian and Gay Adulthood." In N. Woodman, ed., *Lesbian and Gay Lifestyles: A Guide for Counseling and Education.* New York: Irvington.

Gramick, J. 1983. "Homophobia: A New Challenge." *Social Work* 28(2):137–141.

Gross, L., S. K. Aurand, and R. Adessa. 1988. *Violence and Discrimination Against Lesbian and Gay People in Philadelphia and the Commonwealth of Pennsylvania.* Philadelphia: Philadelphia Lesbian and Gay Task Force.

Gunter, P. L. 1987. "Status of Lesbian and Gay Issues in Accredited Schools of Social Work." Paper presented at the 33rd Council on Social Work Education Annual Program Meeting, St. Louis.

———. 1992. "Social Work with Non-traditional Families." In N. Woodman, ed., *Lesbian and Gay Lifestyles: A Guide for Counseling and Education*. New York: Irvington.

Hall, M. 1978. "Lesbian Families: Cultural and Clinical Issues." *Social Work* 23:380–385.

Harris, M. B. and P. H. Turner. 1985–86. "Gay and Lesbian Parents." *Journal of Homosexuality* 12(2):101–113.

Harrison, D. 1987. "Behavioral Social Work and Sexuality." *The Behavior Therapist* 10(8):177–181.

Harry, J. 1990. "A Probability Sample of Gay Males." *Journal of Homosexuality* 19(1):89–103.

Hart, M., H. Robach, B. Tittler, L. Weitz, B. A. Walston, and E. McKee. 1978. "Psychological Adjustment of Nonpatient Homosexuals: Critical Review of the Research Literature." *Journal of Clinical Psychiatry* 39(7):604–608.

Hedgpath, J. M. 1980. "Employment Discrimination Law and the Rights of Gay Persons." *Journal of Homosexuality* 14(1/2):25–44.

Herek, G. 1989. "Hate Crimes against Lesbians and Gay Men: Issues for Research and Policy." *American Psychologist* 44(6):948–955.

Herek, G. M., D. C. Kimmel, H. Amaro, and G. B. Melton. 1991. "Avoiding Heterosexist Bias in Psychological Research." *American Psychologist* 46(9):957–963.

Hetrick, E. S. and A. D. Martin. 1987. "Developmental Issues and their Resolution for Gay and Lesbian Adolescents." *Journal of Homosexuality* 14(1/2):25–43.

Hidalgo, H. and E. H. Christensen. 1976–77. "The Puerto Rican Lesbian and the Puerto Rican Community." *Journal of Homosexuality* 2(2):109–120.

Hidalgo, H., T. Peterson, and N. Woodman. eds. 1985. *Lesbian and Gay Issues: A Resource Manual for Social Workers*. Silver Spring, Md.: National Association of Social Workers.

Hitchens, D. 1980. "Social Attitudes, Legal Standards, and Personal Trauma in Child Custody Cases." *Journal of Homosexuality* 5(1/2):89–95.

Hopkins, H. H. 1969. "The Lesbian Personality." *British Journal of Psychiatry* 115:1433–1436.

Huggins, J., N. Elman, C. Baker, R. G. Forrester, and D. Lyter. 1991. "Affective and Behavioral Responses of Gay and Bisexual Men to HIV Antibody Testing." *Social Work* 36(1):61–66.

Huggins, S. 1989. "A Comparative Study of Self-esteem of Adolescent Children of Divorced Lesbian Mothers and Heterosexual Mothers." *Journal of Homosexuality* 18:123–135.

Humphrey, F. A., D. F. Harrison, and K. M. Sowers-Hoag. 1991. "A Behavioral Framework for Understanding Lesbian Battering." Paper presented at the 37th Council on Social Work Education Annual Program Meeting, New Orleans.

Humphrey, F. A., K. M. Sowers-Hoag, and D. M. Harrison. 1992. "The Prevention and Intervention of Lesbian Batterings: A National Survey." Paper presented at the 38th Council on Social Work Education Annual Program Meeting, Kansas City.

Humphreys, G. E. 1983. "Inclusion of Content on Homosexuality in the Social Work Curriculum." *Journal of Education for Social Work* 19(1):55–60.

Icard, L. 1986. "Black Gay Men and Conflicting Social Identities: Sexual Orientation Vs. Racial Identity." *Journal of Social Work and Human Sexuality* 4(1/2):83–93.

—— and D. M. Traunstein. 1987. "Black, Gay, Alcoholic Men: Their Character and Treatment." *Social Casework* 68:267–272.

Island, D. and P. Letellie. 1991. *Men Who Beat the Men Who Love Them: Battered Gay Men and Domestic Violence*. New York: Harrington Park Press.

Kallman, F. J. 1952. "Comparative Twin Study on the Genetic Aspects of Male Homosexuality." In G. Puterbaugh, ed., 1992. *Twins and Homosexuality: A Casebook*. New York: Garland.

Kimmel, D. C. 1978. "Adult Development and Aging: A Gay Perspective." *Journal of Social Issues* 34(3):113–130.

Kinsey, A. C., W. B. Pomeroy, and C. E. Martin. 1948. *Sexual Behavior in the Human Male*. Philadelphia: W. B. Saunders.

—— and P. H. Gebhard. 1953. *Sexual Behavior in the Human Female*. Philadelphia: W. B. Saunders.

Klein, F. 1985. *Bisexualities: Theory and Research*. New York: Haworth Press.

——. 1990. "The Need to View Sexual Orientation as a Multivariable Dynamic Process: A Theoretical Perspective." In D. P. McWhirter, S. A. Sanders, and J. M. Reinisch, eds., *Homosexuality/Heterosexuality: Concepts of Sexual Orientation*. New York: Oxford University Press.

Knight, C. 1991. "Gender-Sensitive Curricula in Social Work Education: A National Study." *Journal of Social Work Education* 27(2):145–55.

Knutson, D. 1977. "The Civil Liberties of Gay Persons: Present Status." *Journal of Homosexuality* 2(4):337–342.

Krestan, J. and C. Bepko. 1980. "The Problem of Fusion in the Lesbian Relationship." *Family Process* 19:277–289.

Kurdek, L. A. and J. P. Schmitt. 1986a. "Relationship Quality of Gay Men in Closed or Open Relationships." *Journal of Homosexuality* 12(2):85–99.

——. 1986b. "Relationship Quality of Partners in Heterosexual Married, Heterosexual Cohabiting, and Gay and Lesbian Relationships." *Journal of Personality and Social Psychology* 51(4):711–720.

Larsen, K. S., R. Cate, and M. Reed. 1983. "Anti-Black Attitudes, Religious Orthodoxy, Permissiveness, and Sexual Information: A Study of the Attitudes of Heterosexuals toward Homosexuals." *Journal of Sex Research* 19(2):105–118.

Larsen, P. 1981. "Sexual Identity and Self-Concept." *Journal of Homosexuality* 7(1):15–32.

Lee, J. A. B. 1992. "Teaching Content Related to Lesbian and Gay Identity Formation." In N. Woodman, ed., *Lesbian and Gay Lifestyles: A Guide for Counseling and Education*. New York: Irvington.

Levine, H. 1992. "An Exploration of the Utilization of a Sexual Identity Formation Questionnaire with a Sample of Lesbian Women." Dissertation proposal at Temple University, Philadelphia.

Levitt, E. and A. Klassen. 1974. "Public Attitudes toward Homosexuality: Part of the National Survey by the Institute for Sex Research." *Journal of Homosexuality* 1:29–43.

Lewis, K. G. 1980. "Children of Lesbians: Their Point of View." *Social Work* 25:198–203.

Lewis, L. A. 1983. "The Coming Out Process for Lesbians: Integrating a Stable Identity." *Social Work* 29(4):464–469.

Loiacano, D. K. 1989. "Gay Identity Issues Among Black Americans: Racism, Homophobia, and the Need for Validation." *Journal of Counseling and Development* 68:21–25.

Longres, J. 1990. *Human Behavior in the Social Environment*. Itasca, Ill.: F. E. Peacock.

———. "Integrating Content on Lesbians and Gays in the Human Behavior in the Social Environment Curriculum." Paper presented at the 38th Council on Social Work Education Annual Program Meeting, Kansas City.

Lynch, J. M. and M. E. Reilly. 1986. "Role Relationships: Lesbian Perspectives." *Journal of Homosexuality* 12(2):53–69.

McCandlish, B. N. 1982. "Therapeutic Issues with Lesbian Couples." *Journal of Homosexuality* 5(1/2):115–124.

McCrary, J. and L. Gutierez. 1980. "The Homosexual Person in Military and in National Security Employment." *Journal of Homosexuality* 5:115–146.

McWhirter, D. P., and A. M. Mattison. 1982. "Psychotherapy for Gay Male Couples." *Journal of Homosexuality* 7(2/3):79–91.

McWhirter, D. P. and A. M. Mattison. 1984. *The Male Couple*. Englewood Cliffs, New Jersey: Prentice-Hall.

Mapou, R. L. 1990. "Traumatic Brain Injury Rehabilitation with Gay and Lesbian Individuals." *Journal of Head Trauma Rehabilitation* 5(2):67–72.

Maracek, J., S. E. Finn, and M. Cardell. 1982. "Gender Roles in the Relationships of Lesbian and Gay Men." *Journal of Homosexuality* 8(2):45–49.

Marmor, J. 1980. "Epilogue: Homosexuality and the Issue of Mental Illness." In J. Marmor, ed., *Homosexual Behavior*. New York: Basic Books.

Matteson, D. R. 1979. "Gender isn't Everything." *American Psychologist* 35(10):940–941.

Maylon, A. K. 1982. "Psychotherapeutic Implications of Internalized Homophobia in Gay Men." *Journal of Homosexuality* 7(2/3):59–69.

Mercier, L. R. and R. M. Berger. 1989. "Social Service Needs of Lesbian and Gay Adolescents: Telling It Their Way." *Journal of Social Work and Human Sexuality* 8(1):75–95.

Miller, J. A., R. B. Jacobsen, and J. J. Bigner. "The Child's Home Environment for Lesbian vs. Heterosexual Mothers: A Neglected Area of Research." *Journal of Homosexuality* 7:49–56.

Money, J. 1980. "Genetic and Chromosomal Aspects of Homosexual Etiology." In J. Marmor, ed., *Homosexual Behavior*. New York: Basic Books.

——. 1990. "Agenda and Credenda of the Kinsey Scale." In D. P. McWhirter, S. A. Sanders, and J. M. Reinisch, eds., *Homosexuality/Heterosexuality: Concepts of Sexual Orientation*. New York: Oxford University Press.

Morin, S. 1977. "Heterosexual Bias in Psychological Research." *American Psychologist* 32(8):629–637.

Moses, A. and R. Hawkins. 1982. *Counseling Lesbian Women and Gay Men: A Life Styles Approach*. St Louis: C. V. Mosby.

National Association of Social Workers. 1979. *Code of Ethics of the National Association of Social Workers*. Silver Spring, Md.: NASW.

Newman, B. 1989. "Including Curriculum Content on Lesbian and Gay Issues." *Journal of Social Work Education* 25(3):202–211.

—— and P. Muzzonigro. 1993. "The Effects of Traditional Family Values on the Coming Out Process for Gay Male Adolescents." *Adolescence* 28(109):213–226.

Norton, D. G. 1978. *The Dual Perspective: Inclusion of Ethnic Minority Content into the Social Work Perspective*. New York: Council on Social Work Education.

Nyberg, K. and J. P. Alston. 1976—77. "Analysis of Public Attitudes Toward Homosexual Behavior." *Journal of Homosexuality* 2(2):99–107.

Oberstone, A. K. and H. Sukoneck. 1976. "Psychological Adjustment and Lifestyle of Lesbian and Single Heterosexual Women." *Psychology of Women Quarterly* 1(2):172–188.

Pagelow, M. 1980. "Heterosexual and Lesbian Single Mothers: A Comparison of Problems, Coping, and Solutions." *Journal of Homosexuality* 5(3):180–204.

Peplau, L. and S. Cochran. 1990. "Relational Perspective on Homosexuality" In D. P. McWhirter, S. A. Sanders, and J. M. Reinisch, eds., *Homosexuality/Heterosexuality: Concepts of Sexual Orientation*. New York: Oxford University Press.

——, K. Rook, and C. Padesky. 1978. Loving Women: Attachment and Autonomy in Lesbian Relationships. *Journal of Social Issues* 34(3):7–27.

Peplau, L. A. and S. L. Gordon. 1983. "The Intimate Relationships of Lesbian and Gay Men." In E. R. Allgeier and N.B. McCormick, eds.,*Changing Boundaries: Gender Roles and Sexual Behavior*. Palo Alto, California: Mayfield.

Pharr, S. 1988. *Homophobia: A Weapon of Sexism*. Inverness, Ca: Chardon Press.

Pierce, D. 1989. *Social Work and Society*. New York: Longman.

——. 1991. Keynote address. University of Maryland School of Social Work. Building Bridges: Lesbian and Gay Education and Practice Conference. April 6, 1991.

——. 1992. "Lesbian/Gay Curriculum Content: Implications from the Curriculum Policy Statement." Paper presented at 38th Council on Social Work Education Annual Program Meeting, March, 1992, Kansas City, Missouri.

Pies, C. 1987. "Lesbians Choosing Children: The Use of Social Group Work in Maintaining and Strengthening the Primary Relationship." *Journal of Social Work and Human Sexuality* 5(2): 79–88.

———. 1989. "Lesbians and the Choice to Parent." *Marriage and Family Review* 14(3–4):137–154.

Polikoff, N. 1986. "Lesbian Mothers, Lesbian Families: Legal Obstacles, Legal Challenges." *Review of Law and Social Change* 14(4):907–914.

Potter, S. and T. Darty. 1981. "Social Work and the Invisible Minority: An Exploration of Lesbianism." *Social Work* 26:187–92.

Poverny, L. M. and W. A. Finch. 1985. "Job Discrimination against Gay and Lesbian Workers." *Social Work Papers* 19:35–45.

———. 1988a. "Gay and Lesbian Domestic Partnerships: Expanding the Definition of Family." *Social Casework* 69(2):116–121.

———. 1988b. "Integrating Work-Related Issues on Gay and Lesbian Employees into Occupational Social Work Practice." *Employee Assistance Quarterly.* 4(2):15–29.

Proctor, E., and L. W. Davis. 1983. "Minority Content in Social Work Education: A Question of Objectives." *Journal of Education for Social Work* 19(2): 85–93.

Puterbaugh, G. 1990. *Twins and Homosexuality: A Casebook.* New York: Garland.

Rand, C., D. Graham, and E. Rawlings. 1982. "Psychological Health and Factors the Court Seeks to Control in Lesbian Mother Custody Trials." *Journal of Homosexuality* 8(1):27–39.

Reamer, F. 1991. "AIDS, Social Work, and the Duty to Protect." *Social Work* 36(1):56–60.

Reiter, L. 1989. "Sexual Orientation, Sexual Identity, and the Question of Choice." *Clinical Social Work Journal* 17(2):138–50.

Renzetti, C. M. 1988. "Violence in Lesbian Relationships: A Preliminary Analysis of Causal Factors." *Journal of Interpersonal Violence* 3(4):381–399.

Reynolds, W. T. 1980. "The Immigration and Nationality Act and the Right of Homosexual Aliens." *Journal of Homosexuality* 5(1/2):79–88.

Richards, D. A. J. 1980. "Homosexual Acts and the Constitutional Right to Privacy." *Journal of Homosexuality* 5(1/2):43–65.

Ricketts, W. and R. Achtenberg. 1989. "Adoption and Foster Parenting for Lesbians and Gay Men: Creating New Traditions in Family." *Marriage and Family Review* 14(3–4):83–118.

Robinson, B. E., L. H. Walters, and P. Skeen. 1989. "Response of Parents to Learning that their Child is Homosexual and Concern over AIDS: A National Study. *Journal of Homosexuality* 18(1/2): 59–81.

Rosser, B., R. Simon, and W. Michael. 1989. "A Gay Life Events Scale for Homosexual Men." *Journal of Gay and Lesbian Psychotherapy* 1(2):87–101.

Rubin, N. 1981. "Clinical Issues with Disabled Lesbians: An Interview with Ricki Boden." *Catalyst* 3(4):31–46.

Ruse, M. 1990. "Are There Gay Genes? Sociobiology and Homosexuality." In G. Puterbaugh, ed., *Twins and Homosexuality: A Casebook.* New York: Garland.

Saghir, M., E. Robins, B. Walbran, and K. Gentry. 1970. "Homosexuality: Psychological Disorders and Disabilities in the Female Homosexual." *American Journal of Psychiatry* 127:147–154.

Sanders, S. A., J. M. Reinisch, and D. P. McWhirter. 1990. An Overview. In D. P. McWhirter, S. A. Sanders, and J. M. Reinisch. eds., *Homosexuality/Heterosexuality: Concepts of Sexual Orientation*. New York: Oxford University Press.

Sands, R. G. and V. Richardson. 1985. "Clinical Practice with Women in their Middle Years." *Social Work* 31(1):36–43.

Saperstein, S. 1981. "Lesbian and Gay Adolescents: The Need for Family Support." *Catalyst* 12:61–69.

Savin-Williams, R. C. 1988. "Theoretical Perspectives Accounting for Adolescent Homosexuality." *Journal of Adolescent Health Care* 9(2):95–104.

——. 1989. "Parental Influences of the Self-Esteem of Gay and Lesbian Youths: A Reflected Appraisals Model." *Journal of Homosexuality* 17:3–109.

——. 1990. *Gay and Lesbian Youth: Expressions of Identity*. New York: Hemisphere.

Schilit, R., L. Gwat-Yong, and M. Montagne. 1990. "Substance Use as a Correlate of Violence in Intimate Lesbian Relationships." *Journal of Homosexuality* 19(3):51–65.

Schneider, M. 1989. "Sappho was a Right-On Adolescent: Growing Up Lesbian." *Journal of Homosexuality* 17(1/2):111–130.

—— and B. Tremble. 1985–86. "Gay or Straight: Working with the Confused Adolescent." *Journal of Social Work and Human Sexuality* 4(1/2):71–83.

——. 1986. "Training Service Providers to Work with Gay or Lesbian Adolescents: A Workshop."*Journal of Counseling and Development* 65:98–99.

Seattle Commission for Lesbians and Gays. 1991. *A Survey of the Seattle Area Lesbian and Gay Community:Identity and Issues*. Seattle: Seattle Commission for Lesbians and Gays.

Serdahely, W. J. and G. J. Ziemba. 1984. "Changing of Homophobic Attitudes through College Sexuality Education." *Journal of Homosexuality* 10(1/2): 109–116.

Siegelman, M. 1972. "Adjustment of Homosexual and Heterosexual Women." *British Journal of Psychiatry* 120:477–481.

Silver-Jones, J. 1990. "Teaching about Homophobia: A Cautionary Tale." Paper presented at the CSWE Annual Program Meeting, New Orleans.

Simmons, J. L. 1965. "Public Stereotypes of Deviants." *Social Problems* 12:223–232.

Smalley, S. 1987. "Dependency Issues in Lesbian Relationships." *Journal of Homosexuality* 14:125–135.

Sophie, J. 1986. "A Critical Examination of Stage Theories of Lesbian Identity Development." *Journal of Homosexuality* 12(2):39–51.

——. 1987. "Internalized Homophobia and Lesbian Identity." *Journal of Homosexuality* 14:53–69.

Starka, L., I. Sipova, and J. Hynie. 1975. "Plasma Testosterone in Male Transsexuals and Homosexuals." *The Journal of Sex Research* 11(2):134–138.

St. Lawrence, J. S., B. A. Husfeldt, J. A. Kelly, H. V. Hood, and S. Smith. 1990.

"The Stigma of AIDS: Fear of Disease and Prejudice Toward Gay Men." *Journal of Homosexuality* 19(3):85–101.

Storms, M. 1980. "Theories of Sexual Orientation." *Journal of Personality and Social Psychology* 38(5):783–792.

Strommen, E. F. 1989 " `You're a What?': Family Member Reactions to the Disclosure of Homosexuality." *Journal of Homosexuality* (18):37–57.

Terry, P. 1992. "Relationship Termination for Lesbians and Gays." In Woodman, N.. ed., *Lesbian and Gay Lifestyles: A Guide for Counseling and Education.* New York: Irvington.

Thompson, C. P. 1992. "Homophobia: A Comparison Study: MSW Students and Lesbians." *Masters Abstracts International* 29(4):593.

Tice, K. 1990. "Gender and Social Work Education: Directions for the 1990s." *Journal of Social Work Education* 26(2):134–144.

Tievsky, D. L. 1988. "Homosexual Clients and Homophobic Workers." *Independent Social Worker* 20(3):51–62.

Troiden, R. R. 1979. "Becoming Homosexual: A Model of Gay Identity Acquisition." *Psychiatry* 42(4):362–373.

Tully, C. 1989. "Caregiving: What do Midlife Lesbians View as Important?" *Journal of Gay and Lesbian Psychotherapy* 1(1):41–51.

——. 1992. "Research on Older Lesbian Women: What is Known, What is Not Known, and How to Learn More." In N. Woodman, ed., *Lesbian and Gay Llifestyles: A Guide for Counseling and Education.* New York: Irvington.

—— and J. C. Albro. 1979. "Homosexuality: A Social Worker's Imbroglio." *Journal of Sociology and Social Welfare* 6(2):154–165.

Turner, P., L. Scadden, and M. B. Harris. 1990. "Parenting in Gay and Lesbian Families." *Journal of Gay and Lesbian Psychotherapy* 1(3):55–66.

Uhl, B. A. 1986. "A New Issue in Foster Parenting: Gays." *Journal of Family Law* 25:577–597.

Vetri, D. 1980. "The Legal Arena: Progress for Gay Civil Rights." *Journal of Homosexuality* 5(1/2):25–34.

Voeller, B. and J. Walters. 1978. "Gay Fathers." *The Family Coordinator* (April):149–157.

Waterman, C. K., L. J. Dawson, and M. J. Bologna. 1989. "Sexual Coercion in Gay Male and Lesbian Relationships: Predictors and Implications for Support Services." *Journal of Sex Research* 26(1):118–124.

Waters, A. 1986. "Heterosexual Bias in Research on Lesbianism and Male Homosexuality (1979–1983), Utilizing the Bibliographic and Taxonomic System of Morin (1979)." *Journal of Homosexuality* 13(1):35–58.

Weiner, A. 1989. "Racist, Sexist, and Homophobic Attitudes among Social Work Students and the Effects on Assessments of Client Vignettes." *Dissertation Abstracts International* 50(11A):3741.

Weinrich, J. D. 1987. "A New Sociobiological Theory of Homosexuality Applicable to Societies with Universal Marriage." *Ethology and Sociobiology* 8:37–47.

Whitehead, M. M. and K. M. Nokes. 1990. "An Examination of Demographic

Variables, Nurturance, and Empathy among Homosexual and Heterosexual Big Brother/Big Sister Volunteers." *Journal of Homosexuality* 19(4):89–101.

Wirth, S. 1978. "Coming Out Close to Home: Principles for Psychotherapy with Families of Lesbians and Gay Men." *Catalyst* 1(3):6–22.

Wisniewski, J. and B. Toomey. 1987. "Are Social Workers Homophobic?" *Social Work* 32(5):454–455.

Woodman, N. 1985. "Parents of Lesbians and Gays: Concerns and Interventions." In H. Hidalgo, T. Peterson, and N. Woodman., eds., *Lesbian and Gay Issues: A Resource Manual for Social Workers*. Silver Spring, MD.: NASW.

——, ed. 1992. *Lesbian and Gay Lifestyles: A Guide for Counseling and Education*. New York: Irvington.

—— and H. Lenna. 1980. *Counseling with Gay Men and Women: A Guide for Facilitating Positive Life-Styles*. San Francisco: Jossey-Bass.

12

Diversity and Populations at Risk: People with Disabilities

RITA BECK BLACK

Whether one looks at the current scene or turns back to the early days of social work, programs and services for people with disabilities stand at the center of the profession's concerns. Since the early part of this century, social workers have been employed as professionals in the health care system, in institutional and community-based programs for people with physical and mental disabilities, and in public health programs designed to prevent disabling conditions in children (Adams 1971; Bartlett 1961, 1975; Browne, Kirlin, and Watt 1981; Callicut and Lecca 1983; Germain 1984; Gitterman, Black, and Stein 1985; Kerson 1982). Although specializations now exist for social work practice in mental retardation and developmental disabilities, mental health, chronic illness, and rehabilitation, foundation-level knowledge about disabilities remains an essential element of the education of all social workers.

Thus it seems straightforward to include in this volume a chapter on people with disabilities. However, despite social work's intense involvement with services for people with many types of disabilities, neither the profession nor its educational curricula has articulated a clear understanding that people with disabilities are members of a common population. This vision requires a significant shift in not only social work's but our society's ways of thinking about people with disabilities. People with different disabling conditions sometimes do have differing service needs, and social work appropriately has developed advanced level knowledge and career paths for specialized work with certain subpopulations. However, people with different physical and mental difficulties also share the powerful bond of disability. This chapter will consider what all social workers should know about the common experience of being disabled in our society, about the power of our society's laws and policies to both support and at times impede the empowerment of people with disabilities, and about the application of generalist practice principles in enhancing the lives of people from this largest of all minority groups.

Defining the Population

A first step in articulating foundation-level knowledge about people with disabilities is to define disability; i.e., what are the criteria for membership in this population. But the complicated nature of this first step is illustrated by noting just a few of the additional questions it generates. For example, how does the definition of physical and mental abilities influence the development of one's self-concept and self-esteem; what is the role of personal definitions of disabilities in shaping the lives of individuals and families who experience disabilities; how do the ways in which society defines disability shape access to resources and services? The very process of attempting to answer the question of what is disability illustrates the centrality to social work of considerations about the personal, social, and political experience of disability.

Forty-three million Americans have one or more physical or mental disabilities, a number that marks persons with disabilities as the single, largest minority group, larger even than the populations of elderly and black people (26 and 28 million respectively) (Jones 1991; LaPlante 1991). People with disabilities are more likely to be poor, women, black, elderly, live alone, to have lower education, and to have poorer general health (Mathematical Policy Research 1989, cited in Albrecht 1992:15). Chronic illnesses have emerged as the main cause of activity limitations and broadened society's conceptualization of disability (LaPlante 1991).

The recently enacted Americans with Disabilities Act (ADA) (which will be discussed in a later section) currently provides the most powerful definition of disability, one that addresses the functional as well as social dimensions of disability. The ADA defines a person with a disability as meeting one or more of the following criteria:

1. a physical or mental impairment that substantially limits one or more of the major life activities of such individual;

2. a record of such an impairment;

3. being regarded as having such an impairment.

Examples provided of "major life activities" are "functions such as caring for one's self, performing manual activities, walking, seeing, hearing, speaking, breathing, learning, working, and participating in community activities." "Substantial limitation" is described as occurring when the person's major "life activities are restricted as to the conditions, manner, or duration under which they can be performed in comparison to most people" (U.S. House of Representatives 1990:51–52; as cited in LaPlante 1991:57–58). This definition thus emphasizes the common ground of functional limitations as the hallmark of disability.

By linking disability to functional limitations the ADA's definition addresses a longstanding debate about whether specific physical or mental impairments or limitations constitute a disability. The basic question is whether "disability refers to actions [or] activities" (LaPlante 1991:59). Talking, thinking, seeing, or walking are examples of actions. Playing, working, or reading a book are examples of activities. Since a given activity might be accomplished in different ways, specific limitations of actions need not necessarily limit the activity. The person with a motorized wheelchair can walk to work with a colleague; the person with a visual impairment might choose to read a book with the assistance of a computer's voice synthesizer. The impact of a specific impairment "depends on the nature of the activities, the human and physical capital of the individual (e.g., intelligence, education) and characteristics of the individual's environment (e.g., family and community support)" (LaPlante 1991:59–60). The ADA's definition thus can be seen as an official recognition that disabilities are social constructions that result from an interaction between people and both their physical and social environments, a view congruent with the ecosystems perspective of social work practice (Meyer 1976, 1983; Germain and Gitterman 1980).

The ADA's definition of disability also recognizes that being *regarded* as having a substantial impairment can indeed define one as disabled and provoke discrimination. Recognition that people with disabilities share with others from oppressed minorities the experience of discrimination represents a major victory for disability activists (Bowe 1980; DeJong 1979; Fine and Asch 1988b; Gliedman and Roth 1980; Shapiro 1993) and places content about people with disabilities squarely within social work education's mandate to address the concerns of oppressed groups. As social workers learn about the experiences of people with disabilities, they deepen their understanding of the impact of discrimination throughout our society. In turn, foundation level study of other oppressed groups similarly will reinforce and elaborate understanding of the position of people with disabilities.

The view of disability as social construction leads also to questions about how language reflects and in turn shapes our personal and social views of impairment (Black and Weiss 1991), questions that reinforce and deepen similar inquiries into the place of language in oppression of other groups. For example, Fine and Asch (1988b), noting the parallels with feminist researchers' differentiation between gender and sex, have described disability rights activists' similar calls for decoupling disability (the biological condition) from handicap (the social ramifications of the disability). Much as women have been assumed to have certain limitations because of their biological status as females, so too has the fact of having a serious physical or mental impairment been overgeneralized to characterize the person (Hobbs, Perrin, and Ireys 1985). All too often the person who has epilepsy becomes an "epileptic" or the person with a limb loss becomes an "amputee." Official recognition of the negative connotations of "handicap" has led to an increasing preference for the terms "disabled" and "disability" rather than "handicap" or "handicapped." As a result, the names of a number of major groups and organizations have been changed in recent years. For example, the U.S. Senate Subcommittee on the Handicapped is now the Subcommittee on Disability Policy; the National Council on the Handicapped is now the National Council on Disability; and the President's Committee on Employment of the Handicapped has become the President's Committee for the Employment of People with Disabilities (West 1991).

By defining disability socially and functionally we turn our attention away from questions of what is physically or mentally "wrong" with people and toward questions of what limits people's abilities to carry out important life activities. The latter are social work questions because they point to ecological assessment of personal, familial, social, environmental, and policy factors that influence the functioning of individuals with disabilities and of people with disabilities as a group.

Practice for Empowerment

The generalist perspective that informs foundation-level preparation of social workers (CSWE 1992) calls for education that equips professionals to enhance people's personal well-being and to ameliorate adverse environmental conditions. Social work has found the concept of empowerment useful for deepening the concerns of the generalist by specifying practice objectives that combine personal control, ability to affect the behavior of others, enhancement of personal and community strengths, increased equity in distribution of resources, ecological assessment, and the generation of power through the empowerment process. The helping relationship is based on collaboration and mutual respect and emphasizes building on existing strengths (Gutierrez 1990:150–151). The empowerment perspective of generalist practice supports social work's commitment to serving people of diverse physical and mental abilities (CSWE 1992).

The importance of the empowerment perspective for framing practice grows out of recognition that people with disabilities belong to a population-at-risk not only because of biologically influenced impairments but also because of stigma and discrimination. People with disabilities and their families have much to teach social work. Many of our social welfare policies and services concern how our society defines and addresses the needs of people with functional limitations that interfere with major life activities. Considerations of physical and mental impairment are integral parts of any foundation-level study of human behavior and the social environment, which asks students to look at human growth and development in a biopsychosocial context. Exposure to the research that has informed and shaped the evolution of professional thinking about people with disabilities highlights the powerful potentials of research for social work practitioners.

Themes of empowerment are evident across the diverse literatures that concern people with disabilities. In the latter half of this century we have seen profound changes in how professionals think about and work with people with disabilities and their families. While still acknowledging and attending to the tremendous emotional, social, and financial upheavals that disabilities can precipitate in individuals and families, we have begun to look beyond individuals both for explanations of distress and for solutions. The limited usefulness of the medical/disease model in assessment and treatment planning has become evident as people with disabilities have called attention to themselves as people first, rather than just patients with illnesses. Our society has moved slowly but nevertheless has embraced a shift away from viewing people with disabilities as targets of charity and instead toward recognizing them as citizens with equal rights to education, employment, and full participation in the mainstream culture.

Because we are entering a new era in emphasizing the common experiences and rights of people with disabilities, many different knowledge bases must inform this inquiry. Social work educators will draw from the domains of policy and practice, from lay and professional writers, and from specialists in such fields as mental retardation and developmental disabilities, chronic mental illness, and chronic physical illness and disabilities. I have organized the remainder of this chapter to illustrate specific content that deepens the definitional material already presented and that is appropriate for incorporation into the foundation areas of policy, practice, and human behavior. Research evidence also is cited. I assume throughout that, depending on curricular priorities and resources, content on disabilities will at times stand in the foreground of a curriculum, providing powerful illustrations of principles that apply across population groups; at other times, content on disabilities will move to the background, as attention focuses on other groups. Some teaching examples will be drawn from specific subspecializations (e.g., mental retardation, mental illness), while other examples can be developed to illustrate the commonality of themes across subgroups. But pedagogical decisions aside, an important premise remains: people with disabilities and the empowerment perspective occupy a central position in the thinking and education of social workers.

Policies and Programs

Content on policies and programs that address the needs of people with disabilities provides a rich resource for highlighting the foundation-level priority of showing the "role of social policy in helping or deterring people in the maintenance or attainment of optimal health and well-being" (CSWE 1992:9). A closer look at the topics of civil rights, income maintenance, and health policy serves to illustrate the integral place of disability-related content in the study of social welfare policies and services.

Civil Rights

An important backdrop to any discussion of social work services for people with disabilities is the landmark legislation called the Americans with Disabilities Act (ADA). Passed in 1990, with its major provisions becoming operational in 1992, the ADA uses disability as its organizing concept and provides legal confirmation of the common experiences of people with many different specific impairments. As noted earlier, the ADA's definition of disability is functional and social, thereby including under its umbrella people who experience substantial limitations in functioning as a direct result of physical or mental impairments or the social perceptions of such impairments. The ADA mandates the elimination of discrimination against people with disabilities in all settings, whether or not federal funds are involved. The ADA provides our nation for the first time with the fundamentals of a disability policy and affords individuals with disabilities a "degree of antidiscrimination protection comparable to that of women and members of other minority groups" (West 1991: 21). As such, content on the ADA and tracking of its impact is likely to become a core element of social work studies in the future.

Study of the antecedents of the ADA demonstrates how historical analyses of legislation can illuminate the evolution of social perspectives, policies and laws and how implementation of a basic principle, such as civil rights, can reverberate across our society to the benefit of many oppressed groups. The ADA legislation came about as the culmination of a series of laws and policies that were shaped by the larger civil rights movement and, in turn, have reshaped in fundamental ways the position of people with disabilities in the United States (West 1991). Evident in this evolution is the growing convergence of the concerns and rights of people with mental retardation or other developmental disabilities, serious mental illness, and physical disabilities.

Working from the assumption that people with physical and mental disabilities should not be deprived of their fundamental civil rights, advocates have successfully forged a package of judicial and legislative protections of those rights. A fundamental premise emerging from these debates is the right of all persons with disabilities to live and learn in the least restrictive environment (Callicut 1987; McDonald-Wikler 1987). Acceptance of this premise has been a major force in the deinstitutionalization movement for both mentally ill and mentally retarded citizens. Rights also have been defined regarding a person's right to treatment, conditions for confinement, required preparation of individualized treatment or educational plans, and adequacy of staffing ratios in institutional settings (Callicut 1987; McDonald-Wikler 1987).

Highlights from a few of the landmark court decisions illustrate the role played by the judicial branch. The decision in *Wyatt v. Stickney* (1971) established a constitutional right to treatment in the least restrictive environment and ordered standards for habilitation. The Willowbrook Developmental Center case, or *ARC and Parisis v. Carey* (1972) exposed poor conditions in an institution as the result of a campaign by physicians and social workers (McDonald-Wikler 1987). A result of both the Willowbrook case and *Halderman v. Pennhurst* (1977) was the shifting of residents from institutional to community-based settings. The 1981 case of *RAJ v. Miller* required Texas to provide specific staff-patient ratios in its state hospitals, to develop exacting procedures to insure proper administration of medication, and established a panel to monitor state compliance with the settlement (Callicut 1987).

A series of important legislative building blocks (I draw the following highlights from West's [1990:15–19] review of these "legislative building blocks" of the ADA) of the civil rights protections for people with disabilities also can be identified.

The Architectural Barriers Act of 1968 required that all buildings constructed, altered, or financed by the federal government after 1969 be accessible and usable by persons with physical disabilities. The Architectural and Transportation Barriers Compliance Board established standards and enforcement guidelines that went into effect in 1982.

Section 504 of the Rehabilitation Act of 1973. Section 504 provides the most significant legislative cornerstone for the ADA. It prohibits discrimination against otherwise qualified people with disabilities in any program receiving federal funds. The implementation of Section 504 helped define such crucial concepts as "reasonable accommodation" and "undue burden." Refinement of these and other details of implementation provided a solid base for considering the ADA's broadening of Section 504's principles to the entire society.

The Developmental Disabilities Services and Facilities Construction Act (P.L. 91–517) of 1970. This act and its later amendments provided an early model for the functional definition of disability. Previously separate categories of disorders (e.g., mental retardation, autism, severe cerebral palsy, epilepsy) were brought together as a population with similar service needs resulting from persistent and significant impairments that are manifest during the developmental period. This act also included a section called "Rights of the Developmentally Disabled." (McDonald-Wikler 1987)

The Developmental Disabilities Assistance and Bill of Rights Act, enacted in 1975, built on early legislation and provided a strong statement from Congress that people with developmental disabilities have rights to appropriate treatment, services, and habilitation provided in a setting least restrictive to personal liberty. The Developmental Disabilities Act of 1975 also provided funds for states to establish a system of protection and advocacy organizations independent of other service organizations.

The Education for All Handicapped Children Act of 1975 (Public Law 94–142), now called the *Individuals with Disabilities Education Act.* This law mandates that all children with disabilities have access to a free, appropriate public education provided in the "least restrictive environment." This simple yet profound statement of children's rights has supported an increasingly powerful movement to develop educational plans and techniques based on the premise that it is in the best interests of *all* children to learn together in environments that include children with a wide diversity of varying abilities.

The Civil Rights of Institutionalized Persons Act of 1980 says that the U. S. Department of Justice can sue states for violating the rights of people in institutions serving the mentally ill and the mentally retarded.

Income Maintenance

Income supports in the United States are a patchwork of programs approved for particular needs and constituencies (Mudrick 1988). The implications of this basic principle become evident when we consider the situation of people with disabilities. Specifically, income assistance is not available solely on the basis of physical impairment (Mudrick

1988). In addition to meeting medical criteria, individuals also must have been in the military, worked for an extended period in employment covered by social security or a public employee benefit program, been injured on the job, or have a poverty-level income.

Payments under programs such as Workers Compensation, Social Security, and Federal Employees Retirement System are associated with the amount of wages lost (Mudrick 1988). If the amount of the disabled person's income is not associated with disability-related costs, this can create major problems for the person who faces high costs for physical equipment or personal assistance needed to return to work. In such a situation, the inadequate income support in effect will be a more significant cause of disablement than the biological injury.

The two major cash transfer programs that serve people with disabilities are Disability Insurance (DI) and Supplemental Security Income (SSI). These programs mirror the general policy in this country which sharply separates the insurance-based system of Social Security from the welfare system. DI covers disabled workers who had Social Security coverage. SSI covers low-income disabled children and adults who have no work experience or too little to qualify for DI. After two years, recipients of DI qualify for medical insurance through Medicare. SSI recipients qualify for Medicaid coverage. Smaller numbers of disabled people receive assistance under Aid for Families with Dependent Children (AFDC; for low-income families in which there is a disabled parent), veterans' pensions, and Workers Compensation (for workers injured on the job) (Mudrick 1988).

Health Policy

Study of the health care system and the lack of coordinated health care policy is an important element of foundation-level inquiry for all social workers. By looking at the experiences of people with chronic, disabling conditions, many of the problems with current health care policy can be seen in bold relief.

While all people are vulnerable to the threat of exorbitant health care costs and unreimbursed medical expenses, people with disabilities continue to pay an especially high price for the United States' failure to develop a comprehensive system of health care services and financing. In particular, the narrow, disease-specific focus of health services results in inattention to the management of chronic illnesses in every-

concepts and theories of power and social conflict into practice and eventually into some HBSE courses. The 1962 CPS renamed the sequence HBSE, which was now to include social and cultural influences on behavior. Later, the 1969 CPS called for 1) a shift from the psychiatric model of HBSE to an interdisciplinary approach that would present human development and behavior in families, groups, and communities instead of the heretofore single emphasis on the individual alone; and 2) a shift from providing foundation knowledge for "micro" practice alone to foundation knowledge for "macro" practice as well.

As a consequence of these factors, some HBSE instructors (by then nearly all were social workers) followed the lead of practice and seized upon social systems theory (Parsons 1951) as a potential avenue to the desired integration of the person-in-environment. Others were drawn to general systems theory. Throughout the 1970s and 1980s, it was clear that the chief competitive perspectives in the selection and organization of HBSE content were the psychoanalytic and systems approaches. Several other perspectives took minor roles in the contest, such as behavioral and cognitive approaches.

Before taking up the competing theory bases and 1992 curriculum policy, HB courses at the undergraduate level in the decades prior to 1980 are examined.

HBSE in Undergraduate Programs

At the undergraduate level, growing numbers of early social work programs that prepared students for the public services either required or merely advised students to take courses in sociology, psychology, and sometimes biology during the first two years of their liberal arts education, whatever the actual content of such courses and however they were taught. Undergraduate psychology courses, for example, often consisted of experimental studies of animal behavior.

By the 1950s and beyond, many undergraduate programs still relied mainly on biological/maturational and non-Freudian psychological theories of human development to supplement their traditional sociological emphasis. In most instances these courses continued to be taught by faculty in the biology, psychology, and sociology departments of the college or university. Their application to social work, however, was left to social work faculty, who also were responsible for connecting social work content to the liberal arts base of the students.

In 1969 the National Association of Social Workers (NASW) reversed an earlier stand and granted professional status and full membership to graduates of BSW programs that are approved by CSWE. By 1971, CSWE standards for approval were in place, and in 1974 approval became accreditation. A continuum of professional education for social work was now a reality, and the number of BSW programs grew rapidly. The 1984 CSWE Accreditation Standard on HBSE content referred to both BSW and MSW programs, but decisions on content and focus of HBSE were left to the individual BSW program.

Interested in securing data on the current state of HBSE in the baccalaureate curriculum, Gibbs (1986) conducted a survey by mail (date not given) of all 303 BSW programs accredited as of 1981, and received 191 responses (63 percent). Of the programs responding, 171 (89.5 percent) reported that the HBSE course(s) were taught within the social work department. This is a strong trend (in contrast, only 21.8 percent of the programs in a 1971 study taught a required HBSE course). Conceptual frameworks used by the 171 programs included the following: ecosystems, 46 programs (26.9 percent); systems, 38 (22.2 percent). However, 53 additional programs (31 percent) used systems combined with other approaches (developmental, psychosocial). The remaining 24 of the 171 programs taught varied approaches or their combinations. Alone or in combination, systems clearly was the dominant approach in 90 percent of the reporting programs. Prerequisites to social-work-taught HBSE courses that were most frequently mentioned included psychology (83 times) and sociology (77 times). Notably, biology was mentioned only 33 times. Hence, a serious gap in required content exists, and this is probably the case in MSW programs as well.

Competing Theoretical Perspectives

This section summarizes psychoanalytic and systems theories as the dominant approaches to the selection and organization of HBSE foundation content. Psychoanalytic theory is the oldest continuing approach to HBSE at the graduate level, while systems theory entered HBSE courses at both levels more recently. Both perspectives are given primary attention in this section because they have influenced the substance and direction of the profession's development more than any other systems

day life (Black, Dornan, and Allegrante 1986) and poor coordination of care (Hobbs, Perrin, and Ireys 1985). Since many of the costs associated with living with a disability, (e.g., home modifications, special clothing, adaptive equipment) fall outside medically defined treatment costs, people with disabilities often assume large out-of-pocket expenses or fall into poverty.

As noted previously, current, fragmented income maintenance policies separate people with disabilities by work history. This separation continues in health care coverage, where people with disabilities who have not worked often find themselves forced into the Medicaid system, with its associated stigma of poverty. Here they are likely to experience the poorer services and indignities faced by other oppressed groups when they use this country's two-class system of care.

The lack of universal health insurance coverage in the United States means that people with disabilities often fall into that group of consumers least desired by insurers, those with preexisting and costly medical conditions. As a result, people with disabilities frequently face battles with insurance companies about maintaining eligibility for coverage. As long as insurance coverage remains linked to employment, they and their families may be limited in job opportunities or job mobility because of fears about obtaining new insurance coverage on their own or with a new employer.

Changing Clinical and Psychosocial Perspectives

Although recognizing that policy and programmatic concerns shape practice and directly influence human behavior, it is useful also to consider the clinical and psychosocial literatures that are essential to informed application of the empowerment perspective of generalist practice. The bases for empowerment practice and the historical threads that link the specializations within the field of disabilities become visible as one looks across the seemingly separate yet overlapping fields of mental retardation and developmental disabilities, chronic mental illness, and chronic physical illness and disabilities.

Mental Retardation and Developmental Disabilities

Social work has a strong tradition of focusing on the ramifications of disabilities for the affected person, his or her parents, and other family members. The literature on social work and mental retardation illustrates the ongoing refinement of clinical practice wisdom about the psychosocial impact of disabilities and about clients' and families' needs for both support and information (Adams 1971; Brantley 1988; Dickerson 1981; Wikler and Keenan 1983). In the field of mental retardation, as in other disability areas, psychoanalytic perspectives were influential in shaping early thinking about the impact on parents of having a child with mental retardation. Solnit and Stark (1961) conceptualized the challenge for the mother as one of withdrawing libido from the "lost" normal child that she had expected. This process was seen as disrupted by concurrent demands to accept the "living, blighted child." Solnit and Stark emphasized the importance of realistic interpretations and opportunities to review thoughts and feelings in order to help parents through this process.

Unfortunately, psychoanalytic interpretations also tended to emphasize the role of guilt in the parents, with certain parental difficulties sometimes taken as evidence of "rejection" or "nonacceptance" of the affected child (Wolfensberger and Menolascino 1970). The services for parents that developed from this perspective had the unfortunate consequence of suggesting that parents of children with disabilities were akin to "patients," with psychotherapy the logical model of treatment.

Vigorous disagreement with certain psychoanalytic emphases was evident even at the time of their ascendancy. For example, Olshansky (1962) suggested that the parents of a child with mental retardation suffer from a "chronic sorrow" which is a natural response to a tragic fact. The professional worker should not see the parents' reactions as neurotic. Olshansky strongly criticized the psychoanalytic emphasis on "acceptance" of the affected child and pointed out that parents may perceive that they are expected to accomplish the impossible task of viewing the child from the professional's perspective. Olshansky offered instead a goal for parents of "increased comfortableness" in living with and helping their child with daily life.

Movement away from a predominate focus on a psychotherapeutic model became stronger as writers began to consider families' changing needs after the initial diagnostic period. Birenbaum (1970), drawing on Goffman's (1963) work on stigma, described parents of children with mental retardation as having a "courtesy stigma" by virtue of their association with their stigmatized child. He described how families worked to maintain conventional family norms, even as the affected child's deviations from normal development tended to "arrest" the family's development, e.g., when the affected offspring reached adulthood but did not become independent from the family. Birenbaum's work provides a sociological grounding for professional assistance to families over the lifetime of the family member with a disability.

Schild (1964) helped articulate the social work implications of the life-span perspective as she wrote about providing services to families over "spaced intervals" (91). Matheny and Vernick (1969), also social workers, coined the phrase "informationally deprived" to dramatize how much parents can benefit from information and clear communication from professionals.

Empirical support for Olshansky's (1962) concept of "chronic sorrow" was provided by Wikler's (1981; Wikler and Keenan 1983) research findings on the predictable developmental crises experienced by families who have children with mental retardation. Wikler (1981) reframed the periodic grieving that parents often experience as a "strength in coping" (69) and emphasized parents' major needs for support and information during these predictable periods of rekindled confusion and disappointment.

The field of mental retardation also provides an excellent example of the origins of the emerging principle of equal partnership between clients or family members and social workers. Parents of children with mental retardation were the catalysts over 40 years ago of a still active movement to lobby for services and programs for citizens with mental retardation and other disabilities. The early 1950s have been described as the "Parents' Years" (Boggs 1971), for 1950 saw the establishment of the National Association for Retarded Children (later renamed the National Association for Retarded Citizens [NARC]).

In subsequent decades NARC grew in lobbying sophistication and joined with other voluntary and professional organizations in advocating for a major shift away from narrow diagnostic categorizations and toward a functional approach in which eligibility for services was based on service needs rather than diagnostic categories. Thus the concept of "developmental disabilities" was born (see previous section on "Policies and Programs" for a more detailed discussion of Developmental Disabilities legislation).

Chronic Mental Illness

Social workers, along with other mental health professionals, have been central players in the unfolding saga of defining chronic mental illness and in shaping society's thinking about its remediation or cure. We look back at what now appears naive optimism about the dramatic impacts many of us thought we could make using community mental health centers to provide early detection and treatment. Many social workers feel frustrated and perplexed at the failure of community-based services to adequately serve the needs of this population. (Sullivan 1992) A fundamental shift in thinking has come about in recent years with increased understanding of the contribution of genetic and biological factors in producing severe mental illness (Kales, Stefanis, and Talbott 1990). Yet we remain uneasy about how to integrate notions of biological etiology with observations about the sometimes powerful influences of family on the development and expression of mental illness (Lefley 1992). Sometimes it seems easiest to "blame the victims" themselves (i.e., their biology) for the burdens that the chronically mentally ill seem to place on families and society; to say that these individuals are too impaired (i.e., too ill or disabled) to function in our communities (Sullivan 1992).

The powerful role of social construction, translated into practice through professional paradigms, is illustrated by looking at previous thinking about the etiology of severe mental illness. Early psychoanalytic thinking about families of people with serious mental illnesses tended to attribute the illness to "craziness-making families" (Hatfield 1990:7). This unfortunate perspective, although unsupported by research evidence, continued to inform much of the work of the family theorists who emerged later with new emphases on families as systems (Hatfield 1990; Howells and Guirguis 1985). Therapy to change the supposedly dysfunctional family system was for many years part of the standard treatment model used by social workers.

Changes in mental health professionals' views about families and about intervention parallel changes seen in the field of mental retardation. Current treatment models are less likely to describe families as in need of therapy and instead emphasize families' needs for information about mental illness. These changes are evident in the growing endorsement of models for working with families that emphasize support, collaboration, and education (Hatfield 1990; Hatfield and Lefley

1987). However, this is not to say that the views of professionals and families are always congruent. Family behavior patterns showing a high level of "expressed emotions" ("high EE," defined as criticism, hostility, or emotional overinvolvement by at least one family member) have been implicated as contributing to relapse in some patients with schizophrenia (Lefley 1992). Psychoeducational programs for family members have become a common treatment approach for helping families who show "high EE" to change their behavior. However, as Lefley (1992) points out, although current researchers have not claimed that high EE causes schizophrenia or even relapse, there is growing concern that some clinicians are viewing the EE construct as a confirmation of the old theories about family pathogenesis. The phrase "high-EE mother," which is heard in some settings, has the ring of just a more acceptable, contemporary analogue of the now outdated "schizophrenogenic mother" (Lefley 1992). Families are protesting that this framework perpetuates a professional view of families as responsible for patients' relapses and therefore in need of therapy. Moreover, it ignores the powerful influences on relapse of environmental stresses and medication compliance (Hatfield 1987, 1990; Lefley 1992).

Families and former patients have organized to become powerful forces in the field of mental health (Grosser and Vine 1991). The National Alliance of the Mentally Ill (NAMI), although founded as recently as 1979, quickly has become a major player in mental health services delivery. Before NAMI there was little or no involvement of consumers in the planning of mental health services (Hatfield 1990). NAMI now is a major leader in educating families and professionals about mental illness, in critically examining professional assumptions and models about practice with clients and their families, and in influencing mental health policy. There has been a similar growth in self-help groups, which are now available to address former patients' various interests in obtaining personal support, learning more about mental illnesses, and/or becoming involved in advocacy efforts (Emerick 1990; Kurtz and Chambon 1987). Social workers now are challenged to become not only knowledgeable about the potential power of consumer-professional collaborations but also to become skilled in maximizing the effectiveness of those collaborations (Black and Weiss 1990; Mayer et al. 1990; Powell 1987, 1990). Indeed, advocacy opportunities provided by organizations such as NAMI may offer families a very "real therapy" arising out of families' "political potential for attaining mastery over the conditions that have diminished their lives and those of their loved ones" (Lefley 1992:597).

Shifting from families to the issue of service models for patients themselves, we find the emerging theme of empowerment. Although presented with various names, e.g., "strengths perspective" (Sullivan 1992) or "habilitation" rather than "rehabilitation" (Parsons, Hernandez, and Jorgensen 1988), there is a common emphasis on enhancing competencies of people with even very serious mental illnesses. Work with individual clients emphasizes education and skill building (Parsons, Hernandez, and Jorgensen 1988), based on a mutual assessment by social worker and client of the individual's strengths (Sullivan 1992). "An evaluation of empowerment asks the question `Did the client system retain increased capacity for solving problems when the social worker was no longer present?' `Was expertise given to the client?' " (Parsons, Hernandez, and Jorgensen 1988:420). Empowerment also includes understanding that clients' problems are fundamentally social problems. The target of intervention includes the social problems themselves, rather than just rehabilitating the victims of those social problems (Parsons, Hernandez, and Jorgensen 1988).

Chronic Physical Illness and Disability*

For those disorders in which mental impairment is the central feature, parents and other family members have been the major forces for change. Recognition has come slowly of the rights and often underestimated abilities of people with mental retardation and severe mental

---

*This section on chronic physical illnesses and disabilities highlights the awkwardness involved in discussing people with disabilities as members of one group, while also drawing from the specialized literatures that have developed concerning different types of disabilities. While overlaps are evident across all the groups covered in this chapter, the question of separate versus combined coverage becomes most difficult when addressing chronic illnesses and disabilities. Even though the phrase *physical disability* is likely to evoke images of a blind person or someone in a wheelchair, any chronic illness that substantially interferes with major life activities indeed is a physical disability. Although the literature cited in this section may use the seemingly separate language of "chronic illness" or "physical disability," the reader should understand these as largely overlapping and often interchangeable terms. Where it becomes awkward to repeat the phrase "chronic physical illness and disability," I will substitute "physical disability" or just "disability."

illness to speak for themselves. However, people with chronic physical illnesses and disabilities have forged their own changes, and the literature in this area has been shaped increasingly in recent years by their eloquent and strong voices.

I have noted in the previous sections how parents and professionals came to challenge certain professional paradigms that presumed to describe the impact and/or etiology of mental disorders. Similarly, people with chronic illnesses and physical disabilities have examined critically the assumptions about the psychosocial impact of disability that have pervaded the professional literature. While in-depth study of the social psychology literature on disabilities is beyond the boundaries of foundation-level social work education, content on human growth and development should include consideration of certain basic assumptions that are now being challenged. As described by Fine and Asch (1988a:8–15), these major assumptions are:

1. *That disability is located solely in biology, and thus accepted uncritically as an independent variable.* All too often, researchers and clinicians have assumed that the reactions of others to a person with a disability are based solely on the disability. Disability has been viewed as a characteristic equivalent to race or gender, without full consideration of how social context shapes the meaning of a disability to the affected person or others.

2. *That when a disabled person faces problems, the impairment causes them.* The concept of stigma has done much to illuminate the experience of disabled persons in our society. However, noted scholars' analyses of stigma and physical disability (Barker 1948; Jones et al. 1984) have tended to assume a fixed limit of possible change in a world constructed primarily for those without physical disabilities. When a "disabling environment" (Hahn 1983) is taken as natural, then any obstacles must be due to biological limitations rather than human creations such as architectural barriers or social discrimination.

3. *That the disabled person is a "victim."* This assumption presumes that disability is a "tragedy" with which one copes by denial, self-blame, or reinterpreting the suffering to find positive meaning. The critique of this assumption asks us to consider, first, that disability (although never wished for) may not always be so disastrous for the person affected, and, second, that disability itself is not the victimizing experience. In other words, reactions or deprivations experienced because of others' reactions to a disability have not been given equal

weight. Disability incorrectly has been seen primarily as an experience of biological rather than social injustice.

4. *That disability is central to the disabled person's self-concept, self-definition, social comparisons, and reference groups.* While recognizing that disability often is salient for the nondisabled, people with disabilities are challenging the assumption that they primarily think of themselves in terms of their disabilities. The reference groups of people with disabilities may be just as likely to include other people of their own age, occupation, race, class, gender, etc. Mest (1988) links this observation to the experiences of people with mental retardation in her description of how irrelevant the stigma of mental retardation can be for individuals living and working together in supportive contexts.

5. *That having a disability is synonymous with needing help and social support.* This assumption may be the one social workers initially find the most difficult to question. It is not a surprising assumption since the "handicapped role" in our society has been one of helplessness, dependence, and passivity—an extended sick role (Brickman et al. 1982; Gliedman and Roth 1980; Goffman 1963). If disability rather than environment is the focus of blame, then we are unlikely to question whether the "help" needed by a person with a disability would indeed be needed if the environment were structured differently. Moreover, the limited attention usually given to disabled people as providers of support sustains a view of them as always the recipients.

In effect, people with disabilities have defined themselves as a minority group in our society, a group that shares similar experiences of stigma, paternalism, and segregation (Bowe 1980; Gliedman and Roth 1980). They have asked professionals and society at large to recognize the social construction of disability; to consider what it means to look at physical differences as a challenge rather than a tragedy; and to examine how environmental and social factors disable people who are physically challenged.

People with physical disabilities have moved to action with the disability rights movement. This movement has grown in size and power since its early roots in the independent-living movement. The philosophy of independent living for people with disabilities was influenced and in turn has influenced other powerful social movements that blossomed in the 1960s. The civil rights movements for people of color and women increased recognition of people's rights to certain procedures and benefits. The consumer movement increased the legitimacy of questioning professional dominance. For people with disabilities this has meant challenging the appropriateness of using a medical model that speaks of palliation or cure rather than of strategies to maximize independent living in the general community. The self-help movement similarly has supported the independent living movement's philosophy of maximizing people's personal control over their own lives (DeJong 1979; Lachat 1988; West 1991).

Returning to the more personal level of experience with disability, we find a positive frame of reference in literature that seeks to understand the many factors that support, shape, or impede coping and adaptation over time. The building blocks of coping and adaptation are adequate information, satisfactory internal conditions, and the autonomy and skills sufficient for choosing and altering coping strategies (Coelho, Hamburg, and Adams 1974). These are basic to social work teaching about human behavior and useful in conceptualizing social work services that address the range of personal and societal challenges faced by people with chronic illnesses or other disabilities (Black, Dornan, and Allegrante 1986; Black and Weiss 1991). Within this triadic model of coping, empowerment for the person with a disability can be characterized as the continuous development of new competence simultaneous with the ongoing or advancing course of the biological condition (Coelho, Hamburg, and Adams 1974). People with disabilities, in addition to pursuing the development of disability-related competencies, also face such disability-related challenges as learning to accept help without feeling devalued and learning to integrate disability into the broader texture of their lives. Positive integration becomes evident as people come to see their disability as a part of self that is accepted and dealt with, as needed, but not always the central focus of attention or energies (Matson and Brooks 1977).

From Corbin and Strauss's (1985) study of the experiences of couples' coping with chronic illness has come the compelling concept of the trajectory of a chronic illness. This trajectory describes not only the physical unfolding of the illness but also the nature of the "work" generated by the illness over time. Illness trajectories vary in "shape" depending on biological, social, and environmental factors. Trajectories may be stable or unstable, show upward or downward progressions, or acute or comeback periods. Consideration of the past and projected shape of a client's illness trajectory thus becomes an essential element in a social worker's thinking about a client's experiences and service needs (Black and Weiss 1991).

A Foundation for Social Work Practice

This review suggests that foundation-level study about people with disabilities should equip practitioners with a basic understanding of: 1) the policies and programs that define the fundamental rights of people with disabilities and their families to full inclusion in the mainstream of society; in education, housing, employment, health care, and social activities; 2) the ways that the social construction of disability has shaped not only the often negative psychological and social impact of disability on affected individuals and their families but our society's views of people with disabilities as less than equal citizens; 3) the powerful personal impact of disabilities on affected persons and their families, with particular attention to the many ways that illness trajectories are shaped by biological, intrapersonal, social, and societal influences; 4) the rights of clients and family members to work independently as well as in partnership with social workers and other professionals in identifying, planning, providing, and advocating for needed services; and 5) how to use generalist practice, premised on an empowerment perspective, on behalf of clients with disabilities and their families.

These five dimensions reflect content that is congruent with social work's foundation-level commitment to prepare professionals who are committed to practice with diverse peoples and populations and to the promotion of social and economic justice (CSWE 1992). Indeed, these learning objectives are fundamental to social work practice with all client groups who share with the disabled population not only personal anguish but also social policies based on pity, patronization, and exclusion (West 1991:4). The key professional challenge in serving all such groups comes in moving beyond mere recognition of the importance of these five dimensions and bringing them to life in practice. Empowerment practice, with its dual commitment to increasing both personal and political power, provides an overarching perspective for integrating the other four dimensions and using them in practice. Admittedly, this is a difficult task because it calls for creative, flexible thinking and practice skills that combine the clinician's acumen with the organizer's energy and zeal. However, to the extent that all social workers combine foundation knowledge about people with disabilities with solid skills in empowerment practice, all clients will profit.

REFERENCES

Adams, M. 1971. *Mental Retardation and Its Social Dimensions*. New York: Columbia University Press.

Albrecht, G. L. 1992. *The Disability Business: Rehabilitation in America*. Newbury Park, Calif.: Sage.

Barker, R. G. 1948. "The Social Psychology of Physical Disability." *Journal of Social Issues* 4:28–37.

Bartlett, H. 1961. *Social Work Practice in the Health Field*. Washington, D.C.: National Association of Social Workers.

——. 1975. "Ida M. Cannon: Pioneer in Medical Social Work." *Social Service Review* 49:208–229.

Berkowitz, E. D. 1987. *Disabled Policy America's Programs for the Handicapped*. New York: Cambridge University Press.

Birenbaum, A. 1970. "On Managing a Courtesy Stigma." *Journal of Health and Social Behavior* 11:196–206.

Black, R. B., D. Dornan, and J. Allegrante. 1986. "Challenges in Developing Health Promotion Services for the Chronically Ill." *Social Work* 31:287–293.

Black, R. B., and J. O. Weiss. 1990. "Genetic Support Groups and Social Workers as Partners." *Health and Social Work* 15:91–99.

——. 1991. "Chronic Physical Illness and Disability." In A. Gitterman, ed., *Handbook of Social Work Practice with Vulnerable Populations*, pp. 137–164. New York: Columbia University Press.

Boggs, E. M. 1971. "Federal Legislation." In J. Wortis, ed., *Mental Retardation*, vol. III, pp. 103–127. New York: Grune and Stratton.

Bowe, F. 1980. *Rehabilitating America: Toward Independence for Disabled and Elderly People*. New York: Harper and Row.

Brantley, D. 1988. *Understanding Mental Retardation*. Springfield, Ill.: Charles C. Thomas.

Brickman, P., V. C. Rabinowitz, J. Karuza, D. Coates, E. Cohn, and L. Kidder. 1982. "Models of Helping and Coping." *American Psychologist* 37:368–364.

Browne, J. A., B. A. Kirlin, and S. Watt, eds. 1981. *Rehabilitation Services and the Social Work Role: Challenge for Change*. Baltimore, Md.: Williams and Wilkins.

Callicut, J. W. 1987. "Mental Health Services." In A. Minahan, ed., *Encyclopedia of Social Work*. 18th ed. Silver Spring, Md.: National Association of Social Workers.

—— and P.J. Lecca, eds. 1983. *Social Work and Mental Health*. New York: Free Press.

Coelho, G. V., D. A. Hamburg, and J. E. Adams, eds. 1974. *Coping and Adaptation*. New York: Basic Books.

Corbin, J. M. and A. Strauss. 1988. *Unending Work and Care: Managing Chronic Illness at Home*. San Francisco: Jossey-Bass.

Council on Social Work Education. 1992. Curriculum Policy Statement for Master's Degree Programs in Social Work Education, Alexandria, Va.

DeJong, G. 1979. "Independent Living: From Social Movement to Analytic Paradigm." *Archives of Physical Medicine and Rehabilitation* 60:435–446.

Dickerson, M. U. 1981. *Social Work Practice with the Mentally Retarded*. New York: Free Press.

Emerick, R. E. 1990. "Self-help Groups for Former Patients: Relations with Mental Health Professionals." *Hospital and Community Psychiatry* 41:401–407.

Fine, M. and A. Asch. 1988a. "Disability Beyond Stigma: Social Interaction, Discrimination, and Activism." *Journal of Social Issues* 44:3–21.

——, eds. 1988b. *Women with Disabilities: Essays in Psychology, Culture, and Politics*. Philadelphia: Temple University Press.

Germain, C. 1984. *Social Work Practice in Health Care*. New York: Free Press.

—— and A. Gitterman. 1980. *The Life Model of Social Work Practice*. New York: Columbia University Press.

Gitterman, A., R. B. Black, and F. Stein, eds. 1985. *Public Health Social Work in Maternal and Child Health: A Forward Plan*. New York: Columbia University.

Gliedman, J., and W. Roth. 1980. *The Unexpected Minority*. New York: Harcourt Brace Jovanovich.

Goffman, D. 1963. *Stigma: Notes on the Management of Spoiled Identity*. Englewood Cliffs, N.J.: Prentice-Hall.

Grosser, R. C. and P. Vine. 1991. "Families as Advocates for the Mentally Ill: A Survey of Characteristics and Service Needs." *American Journal of Orthopsychiatry* 61:282–290.

Gutierrez, L. M. 1990. "Working with Women of Color: An Empowerment Perspective." *Social Work* 35:149–154.

Hahn, H. 1983. "Paternalism and Public Policy." *Society* March/April:36–46.

Hatfield, A. B. 1987. "The Expressed Emotion Theory: Why Families Object." *Hospital and Community Psychiatry* 38:341.

——. 1990. *Family Education in Mental Illness*. New York: Guilford Press.

—— and H. P. Lefley, eds. 1987. *Families of the Mentally Ill: Coping and Adaptation*. New York: Guilford.

Hobbs, N., J. M. Perrin, and H. T. Ireys. 1985. *Chronically Ill Children and Their Families*. San Francisco: Jossey-Bass.

Howells, J. G., and W. R. Guirguis. 1985. *The Family and Schizophrenia*. New York: International Universities Press.

Jones, E. E., A. Farina, A. H. Hastorf, H. Markus, D. T. Miller, R. A. Scott, and R. deS. French. 1984. *Social Stigma: The Psychology of Marked Relationships*. New York: Freeman.

Jones, N. L. 1991. "Essential Requirements of the Act: A Short History and Overview." In J. West, ed. *The Americans with Disabilities Act: From Policy to Practice. The Milbank Quarterly* 69 (Supplements 1/2):25–54. Port Chester, N.Y.: Cambridge University Press.

Kales, A., C. Stefanis, and J. Talbott, eds. 1990. *Recent Advances in Schizophrenia.* New York: Springer-Verlag.

Kerson, T. S. 1982. *Social Work in Health Settings: Practice in Context.* New York: Longman.

Kurtz, L. F., and A. Chambon. 1987. "Comparison of Self-Help Groups for Mental Health." *Health and Social Work* 12:275–283.

Lachat, M. A. 1988. *The Independent Living Service Model: Historical Roots, Core Elements and Current Practice.* Hampton, N.H.: Center for Resource Management.

LaPlante, M. P. 1991. "The Demographics of Disability." In J. West, ed., *The Americans with Disabilities Act: From Policy to Practice. The Milbank Quarterly* 69 (Supplements 1/2):55–77. Port Chester, N.Y.: Cambridge University Press.

Lefley, H. P. 1992. "Expressed Emotion: Conceptual, Clinical, and Social Policy Issues." *Hospital and Community Psychiatry* 43:591–598.

Mathematical Policy Research. 1989. *Task I. Population Profile of Disability.* Washington, D.C.: Department of Health and Human Services, Assistant Secretary for Planning and Evaluation.

Matheny, A. P. and J. Vernick. 1969. "Parents of the Mentally Retarded Child: Emotionally Overwhelmed or Informationlly Deprived?" *Journal of Pediatrics* 74:953.

Matson, R. R. and N. A. Brooks. 1977. "Adjusting to Multiple Sclerosis: An Exploratory Study." *Social Science and Medicine* 11:245–250.

Mayer, J. B., L. R. Kapust, A. L. Mulcahey, L. Helfand, A. N. Heinlein, M. M. Seltzer, L. C. Litchfield, and R. J. Levin. 1990. "Empowering Families of the Chronically Ill: A Partnership Experience in a Hospital Setting." *Social Work in Health Care* 14:73–90.

McDonald-Wikler, L. 1987. "Disabilities: Developmental." In A. Minahan, ed. *Encyclopedia of Social Work.* 18th ed. Silver Spring, Md.: National Association of Social Workers.

Mest, G. M. 1988. "With a Little Help from Their Friends: Use of Social Support Systems by Persons with Retardation." *Journal of Social Issues* 44:117–125.

Meyer, C. 1976. *Social Work Practice: The Changing Landscape.* 2d ed. New York: Free Press.

——. 1983. *Clinical Social Work in the Eco-Systems Perspective.* New York: Columbia University Press.

Muddrick, N. R. 1988. "Disabled Women and Public Policies for Income Support." In M. Fine and A. Asch, eds., *Women with Disabilities,* pp. 245–268. Philadelphia: Temple University Press.

Olshansky, S. 1962. "Chronic Sorrow: A Response to Having a Mentally Defective Child." *Social Casework* 43:190–193.

———. 1966. "Parent Responses to a Mentally Defective Child." *Mental Retardation* (August):21–23.

Parsons, R. J., S. H. Hernandez, and J. D. Jorgensen. 1988. "Integrated Practice: A Framework for Problem Solving." *Social Work* 33:417–421.

Powell, T. J. 1987. *Self-Help Organizations and Professional Practice.* Washington, D.C.: National Association of Social Workers.

———. 1990. *Working with Self-Help.* Washington, D.C.: National Association of Social Workers.

Roth, W. 1987. "Disabilities: Physical." In A. Minahan, ed., *Encyclopedia of Social Work.* 18th ed. Silver Spring, Md.: National Association of Social Workers.

Schild, S. 1964. "Counseling with Parents of Retarded Children Living at Home." *Social Work* (January):86–91.

Shapiro, J. P. 1993. *No Pity: People with Disabilities Forging a New Civil Rights Movement.* New York: Times Books.

Simonson, S. K. 1987. "Peer Counseling in Health Care: A Collaboration of Social Work and Voluntarism." *Social Work in Health Care* 12:1–19.

Solnit, A. J. and M. H. Stark. 1961. "Mourning and the Birth of Defective Child." *Psychoanalytic Study of the Child* 16:523–537.

Sullivan, W. P. 1992. "Reclaiming the Community: The Strengths Perspective and Deinstitutionalization." *Social Work* 37:204–209.

United States House of Representatives. 1990. *Americans with Disabilities Act of 1990: Report together with Minority Views,* report no. 101–485, part 2. Washington, D.C.

West, J. 1991. "The Social and Policy Context of the Act." In J. West, ed. *The Americans with Disabilities Act: From Policy to Practice. The Milbank Quarterly* 69 (Supplements 1/2):3–24. Port Chester, N.Y.: Cambridge University Press.

Wikler, L. 1981. "Chronic Sorrow Revisited: Parent vs. Professional Depiction of the Adjustment of Parents of Mentally Retarded Children." *American Journal of Orthopsychiatry* 51:63–70.

——— and M. Keenan, eds. 1983. *Developmental Disabilities: No Longer a Private Tragedy.* Washington, D.C.: National Association of Social Workers.

Wolfensberger, W., and F. J. Menolascino. 1970. "A Theoretical Framework for the Management of Parents of the Mentally Retarded." In F. J. Menolascino, ed., *Psychiatric Approaches to Mental Retardation,* pp. 475–493. New York: Basic Books.

About the Contributors

RITA BECK BLACK is Associate Professor of the Columbia University School of Social Work.

ANNE E. FORTUNE is Associate Dean and Associate Professor of the School of Social Welfare, State University of New York at Albany.

CAREL B. GERMAIN is Professor Emerita of the University of Connecticut School of Social Work.

DAVID G. GIL is Professor of the Florence Heller Graduate School for Advanced Studies in Social Welfare, Brandeis University.

ANN HARTMAN is Dean of the Smith College School for Social Work.

NANCY R. HOOYMAN is Dean of the University of Washington School of Social Work.

BRUCE S. JANSSON is Professor of the School of Social Work, University of Southern California.

BERNIE SUE NEWMAN is Associate Professor of the Temple University School of Social Administration.

ELAINE PINDERHUGHES is Professor of the Boston College Graduate School of Social Work.

FREDERIC G. REAMER is Professor of the Rhode Island College School of Social Work.

WILLIAM J. REID is Professor of the School of Social Work, State University of New York at Albany.

Index

Text: 10/12.5 Palatino
Compositor: Columbia University Press
Printer: BookCrafters
Binder: BookCrafters